Louisa

THE M)

THE MYTH OF AUTISM

MEDICALISING MEN'S AND BOYS' SOCIAL AND EMOTIONAL COMPETENCE

Sami Timimi
Neil Gardner
and
Brian McCabe

palgrave
macmillan

© Sami Timimi, Neil Gardner and Brian McCabe 2011

All rights reserved. No reproduction, copy or transmission of this publication may be made without written permission.

No portion of this publication may be reproduced, copied or transmitted save with written permission or in accordance with the provisions of the Copyright, Designs and Patents Act 1988, or under the terms of any licence permitting limited copying issued by the Copyright Licensing Agency, Saffron House, 6-10 Kirby Street, London EC1N 8TS.

Any person who does any unauthorised act in relation to this publication may be liable to criminal prosecution and civil claims for damages.

The authors have asserted their rights to be identified as the authors of this work in accordance with the Copyright, Designs and Patents Act 1988.

First published 2011 by
PALGRAVE MACMILLAN

Palgrave Macmillan in the UK is an imprint of Macmillan Publishers Limited, registered in England, company number 785998, of Houndmills, Basingstoke, Hampshire RG21 6XS.

Palgrave Macmillan in the US is a division of St Martin's Press LLC, 175 Fifth Avenue, New York, NY 10010.

Palgrave Macmillan is the global academic imprint of the above companies and has companies and representatives throughout the world.

Palgrave® and Macmillan® are registered trademarks in the United States, the United Kingdom, Europe and other countries.

ISBN: 978–0–230–54526–7

This book is printed on paper suitable for recycling and made from fully managed and sustained forest sources. Logging, pulping and manufacturing processes are expected to conform to the environmental regulations of the country of origin.

A catalogue record for this book is available from the British Library.

A catalog record for this book is available from the Library of Congress.

10 9 8 7 6 5 4 3 2 1
20 19 18 17 16 15 14 13 12 11

Printed and bound in Great Britain by
CPI Antony Rowe, Chippenham and Eastbourne

Contents

Preface vii
Acknowledgements xi

1 Introduction 1
2 The Missing Voices: Our Case Histories 15

I Autism: The Historical and Cultural Context

3 History of Autism 45
4 The Cult of Child Development 79

II Autism: The Science

5 Biological Evidence 105
6 Classification 141
7 The Problem of Heterogeneity 173
8 Treatment 189

III Autism: Politics and Society

9 Gender 211
10 Culture and Socialisation 235
11 The New Eugenics 269
12 Conclusion 285

References 301
Index 323

Preface

A few years ago I got to hear about Neil Gardner's work and website (http://www.outsider-insight.org.uk) after one of the circular e-mails I receive through being a member of the Critical Psychiatry Network carried an article about Asperger's Syndrome written by him. I contacted Neil to congratulate him on his article and we began a correspondence. A few months later Brian McCabe wrote to me separately about one of my books. In my resulting correspondence with him I discovered that he was working on a thesis about autism. Having already done a considerable amount of work researching and writing about ADHD, together with noting that autism and autism spectrum diagnoses were being given ever more frequently, I had for a while wanted to turn my attention to this other 'boy' disorder. Having now established contact with Neil and Brian, who had both already written about and researched this subject, I contacted them and suggested we write a book on autism. To my delight, they agreed.

After exchanging ideas by e-mail and developing an outline book proposal, we met in York in November 2006 and from here started work on this book in earnest. We had some differing perspectives and differing areas of interest but we shared scepticism about the science and a concern about both the reasons for the rapid increase in the numbers of those being diagnosed with autism and the personal and cultural impact of this. We also discovered that we shared an interest in left of centre politics.

Over the coming months and years our project proceeded in a stuttering fashion due to a mixture of work demands and personal difficulties. We finally came to the finishing straight just as the economy went into a steep decline and the extent of the financial crises in the banking sector, resulting from a politics that encouraged unregulated greed, became apparent. It seems that at the psychological level we had, as a government, economy and society, been in 'denial' about the unsustainable nature of the economic and financial system, believing that everlasting growth was possible. When the collapse came, it was dramatic. We had been building elaborate palaces on sand – while the palace appeared modern, dynamic, well managed and well run, its foundations were rotten. As the building started to creak, people finally noticed the poor foundations and ran.

We have discovered that autism and its associated 'industry' of research, services (private and public), advocacy organisations etc. are similarly built on shaky foundations. Its existence depends on an act of faith in the so-called 'experts' who promote it and proselytise about it. One day, enough people will have done what we have done and cast a critical eye on the evidence base supporting the construct and the types of practice and interventions attached to it. If we are to be truly 'evidence based' in our approach, then this day can't be long as autism promoters have promised so much for so long (like discovering genes, neurological markers or specific treatments) and delivered so little, that the witting and unwitting deceit of the banks seems like a Sunday stroll compared to the lack of decent returns from the autism sector. Once we have embraced a thorough and robust evidence-based approach to mental health, then the palace called 'autism' will be destroyed due to having unsafe foundations and the autism industry will join other well-meaning but ultimately dangerous pseudoscientific fads (like phrenology and eugenics) in the pages of history.

SUMMARY OF THE CHAPTERS

The book is essentially divided into three broad areas of enquiry. First, we set the broad context that shows that the beliefs and practices that we have in any society, in relation to childhood and the types of people we are expected to become as adults, is culturally constructed. This study of what it means to be considered 'normal' is a crucial backdrop to subsequently understanding what a society considers to be deviant or abnormal. Second, we examine the scientific literature on autism, looking with a critical eye at the evidence base that supports (or not) the claims made in much of the mainstream autism literature. Third, we examine the recent past and contemporary politics and cultural dynamics associated with the types of Western societies within which the current expanded notion of the autism spectrum has become popular.

Before starting to review the literature, Chapter 2 provides a more personal perspective. All three authors write about their own personal history. These experiential narratives give voice to a perspective that is missing from the mainstream literature – encounters by service users and a clinician with the negative impact on peoples' lives of the diagnosis. Two of the authors (NG and BM) received an ASD diagnosis as adults. They recount the circumstances that led up to this and the impact this had on them and their personal understanding of these labels now. The third author (ST), a child psychiatrist, discusses his own history and professional encounters with this diagnosis.

In Chapter 3 we examine the history of childhood and then of autism in Western culture. By first setting the broad context in which our ideas about what makes up a normal or deviant childhood has changed over time, we are then able to refer to our concurrently changing ideas about what is considered as 'autism'. In Chapter 4 we examine the area of child development and personality development (i.e., what sort of person our society wants children to grow into). These two chapters draw on writing and evidence from a variety of disciplines, in particular sociology, cultural studies and philosophy, and put forward arguments to suggest that our ideas about what should be considered a 'normal' or 'disordered' child and adult personality is dependent on the dominant beliefs in a given culture and that certain forces, in particular economic and political, have a big hand in shaping the nature of these beliefs and associated practices.

In Chapter 5 we start examining the empirical evidence available from the 'scientific' autism literature. In this and the following three chapters we use a scientific empirical paradigm to analyse the claims made in the 'scientific' literature. While an apparently reasonable criticism may be that we have not carried out a comprehensive search of the literature, we would refute that on the grounds that this is not necessary. We have examined some of the most widely quoted papers, authoritative reviews and the work of those believed to be the leading 'scholars' in this area. Perhaps there are hidden gems that lie undiscovered somewhere in the voluminous literature on the subject; however, this seems unlikely, as whichever area of enquiry we entered into we were eventually led to a scientific dead end. In Chapter 5 we examine the evidence with reference to the two main areas of investigation and upon which claims concerning the biological nature of the disorder are dependent: genetics and neuroimaging.

In Chapter 6 we look at the development of systems of classification and find a mish-mash of competing concepts, name changes and boundary shifting. We also examine how classification in clinical practice has developed, looking at common diagnostic questionnaires and population screening tools. In Chapter 7 we examine the problem of heterogeneity, noting how, as the boundaries of what is considered part of the spectrum of autistic disorders expanded, it crossed into the criteria for many other disorders and into behaviours previously considered by most to be within the 'spectrum' for normality.

In Chapter 8 we examine treatments for autism focusing in particular on the evidence base for pharmacological and behavioural interventions. We conclude (like most mainstream reviews) that there are no specific treatments for autism and (unlike most mainstream reviews) that a diagnosis of autism does not assist in choosing an appropriate intervention.

Chapter 9 is the first of three chapters looking at the relationship between autism and society. Having set the context of the cultural construction of deviance and shown how the development of the concept of autism and the beliefs around it are not supported by the science, we asked the question: 'Why then have the rates of diagnosis increased so rapidly in recent years in some Western societies?' We look at gender dynamics in neo-liberal societies in order to begin to shed light on why we have come to be increasingly troubled by boys' and men's personality development. In Chapter 10 we look at the broader social dynamic examining the political and social processes that have led to the emergence of the autism epidemic, the relationship between human variation and patterns of social behaviour, and we finish with a critical look at the emergence of a counter discourse – that of the 'autistic rights' movement. In Chapter 11 we discuss the eugenic movement, a movement that was welcomed and highly influential in Western societies of the first half of the last century. Drawing parallels with the increasing tendency towards genetic determinism that we are witnessing today, of which autism is a prime example, we note how broad societal acceptance of the ideals of the eugenic movement was made possible through the process of medicalisation.

Chapter 12 concludes the book by bringing together the arguments and coming to a more radical conclusion than we had envisaged when we first started working on this project together: *there is no such thing as autism and the label should be abolished.*

SAMI TIMIMI

Acknowledgements

Sami Timimi would like to thank his wonderful wife, Kitty, and three children, Michelle, Lewis and Zoe, for their love, patience, support and for teaching him so much. Thanks to all the rest of his family and friends who 'have been there' when he has gone through difficult times. Thanks to all the colleagues he corresponds and carries out academic endeavours with, who have helped him learn so much, in particular (and in no particular order): everyone in the Critical Psychiatry Network, Begum Maitra, Jonathan Leo, Carl Cohen, David Cohen, Barry Duncan, Brad Lewis, Kenneth Thompson, Ann Miller, Joanna Moncrieff, Phil Thomas, Pat Bracken, Duncan Double, Eia Asen, Bob Johnston and Jacky Scott-Coombes. Thanks also to Mostafa Mohanna and Brian Ferguson for their personal understanding and support during some difficult times at work in recent years. In particular, I would of course like to thank Neil Gardner and Brian McCabe, two courageous individuals, who never stop asking questions and don't necessarily accept the answers they get. Despite not being professionals in the medical or psychological arena this capacity they have has, in my opinion, made them more insightful about the subject of this book than anyone else I know and certainly more insightful than the current crop of researchers and academics who believe they are 'experts' in autism.

Neil Gardner would like to thank his partner, Stefania, for her many years of love, devotion and broadening of his cultural horizons and social connections. He would also like to thank Maurice Frank for his many insights on the power of psychiatry and thank his many friends and acquaintances who have helped guide his critical analysis of humanity's darker sides.

Brian McCabe would like to thank his mother for her patience and love. He would also like to thank Stacey Meier and Ceri Tobin for showing him more about the human heart and mind than any professionals in the field. His heart goes out to all the 'burnt ones' who have struggled and are struggling to make sense of their lives.

1
INTRODUCTION

Our book does not merely seek to analyse critically current thinking on autism – it challenges the very idea that a wide range of behavioural patterns and hypersensitivities share the same aetiology, course, treatment and outcome. Indeed we question whether *today's* definition of autism reflects a disorder at all, let alone a genetic, neurobiological one.

Readers should be aware that we are not about to ask you to digest the umpteenth rehashing of the autistic spectrum theme, but are inviting you to dissect it, apply critical appraisal to the current literature and think through the implications of whatever model we choose as an 'explanation' for the diverse set of behavioural presentations currently being categorised as 'autism'. We are aware that the kind of regression that thousands of parents of severely withdrawn children have witnessed is highly unlikely to be explained by social or psychological factors alone. In such cases another agent, whether congenital, peri-natal, or a biological reaction to environmental pathogens, would seem to be at play, resulting in significant impairments across a range of areas of functioning for the individual concerned. However, we question whether the label of autism adds anything to understanding or helping even this group of individuals.

The meaning of, definitions and associations with autism have, of course, changed over time. There has been a rapid increase in the numbers of children receiving diagnoses under the recently invented rubric of 'autistic spectrum disorders' (ASD). The creation of ASDs, we believe, has led to a rapid deterioration in the scientific validity and practical utility of the concept of autism, particularly as those given one ASD diagnosis or another are often, these days, referred to simply as 'autistic'. That 'autism' as a concept is so vulnerable to such a radical recasting of its boundaries, illustrates a fundamental weakness inherent in the construct.

As we grappled with this subject our views developed from a starting point of critiquing the broad idea of ASD to the finishing point of casting doubt over the whole concept. We realise this is contentious and we may be cast as 'villains of the piece' at a time when those fighting for greater recognition of this 'disorder' and more help for those afflicted with it, have (in their view) succeeded in bringing much-needed public and indeed government attention to this problem. We may even be castigated for causing more stigma by questioning the biological basis of the problems of those diagnosed. Parents and those with the diagnosis, having got used to living with the label and who may have experienced some relief at getting the diagnosis, may feel hurt and let down. We are aware of all these and other real dangers that may become associated with our conviction that autism as a label should be abolished. We can only apologise to anyone who feels this way about our book and assure readers that it is not our *intention* to reduce services or increase stigma, quite the opposite. We want to see less stigma and better services for those who find themselves on the margins of society. We have come to believe that autism as a label *adds* to stigma and doesn't help improve services.

If we believed that our position would have only negative effects on those with the label we would not have written this book. We did so because we could not find good enough evidence to support a number of assumptions, such as the supposedly genetic/biological inheritance, the supposedly lifelong persistence of the condition, the ability of clinicians to differentiate this condition from others or 'normality' and, most importantly, that services and interventions currently offered to this group improved their lives in the long term. What we did find evidence for is that the numbers receiving the diagnosis has risen rapidly in the last few decades, led by practice in the industrialised English speaking world; that the diagnosis has a strong gender bias (being dominated by males); and that an 'industry' dealing with research, screening, diagnosis, education and treatment of this group has grown – despite the lack of a solid scientific evidence base to support such activity. We could not find the voices of protest that go beyond the 'autistic rights' movement and that question the fundamental biological and political assumptions about autism that have become mainstream.

In this book we will explain, using a variety of sources of 'evidence' and thinking, why we have come to believe that in order to better help those who could and do receive the diagnosis we may first need to dispense with it. The diagnosis has become a set of dogmas that writes a potentially dysfunctional and lifelong 'script' for people. Once an individual is diagnosed, their life story, relationship history and so on can be moulded into a narrow framework of interpretation, as in 'he behaves in that way *because* he is autistic'. This renders invisible other potential frameworks of meaning, from the more concretely socio-biological (e.g., epilepsy interfering with ability to concentrate, making it hard to follow games, making it hard to mix with a group of friends, making the sufferer more likely to find solitary pursuits to entertain themselves while keeping some sense of self/self-esteem in tact, etc.), to the completely social (e.g., the pressure on institutions to focus on social and emotional 'competence').

We have come to believe that if we are to genuinely open up a constructive approach to the group who attract the 'autism' label, then first we must remove the artificial distraction created by such a limiting, imagination-less (dare we say autistic?) approach to these people's lives. An array of potentialities interacts with a variety of bodily experiences (biology) and social contexts. The task of good clinical services is to take each individual and their family's narratives into account and find creative possibilities for change and for more hopeful potential stories that can emerge. While many clinicians find this an anxiety-provoking situation and are reassured when they can retreat to the certainties of an old-fashioned 'expert–patient' script, it is, as one of the authors (ST) has found in his professional life, entirely possible to move at least some from the hopelessness of believing they had a life of trouble, disorder and disability ahead, to the hopefulness of a future based on strengths, without the diagnosis hanging, like a millstone, around their neck.

SCIENCE

One of the first accusations that we may face is that we have been selective with the evidence, so our arguments are not balanced. As regards the 'balance' of our arguments, there are hundreds of books for readers to choose from if they want a view and a reading of the (so-called) science that is non-critical. This book will (at time of writing) be the only one casting a seriously critical eye. We therefore counter the 'balance' argument by insisting that we are thus trying to bring a little bit of balance to a seriously unbalanced field. On the actual science, we are very confident of our position. The potential numbers of papers we could have used and critically analysed is huge. One of us alone (BM) has a database of over 5,000 articles on autism that he has reviewed and collected. We have carefully chosen a mixture of reviews of certain areas and detailed analysis of particular papers in order to make our points about the mixture of poor methodology, inflated claims, lack of replication of key findings and the minimising of the scientific and ethical problems that bedevils the field. What this will illustrate is that the field of autism rests on ideological assumptions, *not* scientific evidence. We expect that those more sympathetic to the mainstream position (even if they criticise some aspects of it) may well have an emotive reaction, however carefully we phrase the text, as it is unlikely that they will have encountered the views we are putting forward. Our views may then feel like a threat to their 'cosmology' (we are saying the world of autism as they have conceived it doesn't exist – like atheists arguing with devout followers of a religion). For believers it won't matter how many references or papers we cite, we will still be criticised for being 'selective'.

We are aware that there is a potential problem with our interpretation of the evidence for those with more severe symptoms, who often have a clinical picture that is highly suggestive of neurological dysfunction (e.g., moderate to severe learning difficulties, epilepsy, failure to achieve a large number of developmental milestones, etc.). While for this group it would be unreasonable to ascribe their difficulties to non-biological factors, what is not clear is how far a diagnosis of autism adds to our knowledge about what has gone wrong in general and what we can do to help them in particular. At present we are not convinced that we have sufficient biological evidence to conclude that even this group of sufferers demonstrate a specific type of neurological dysfunction that can be separated from more generalised neurological dysfunction (see Chapter 5). While most neurological conditions that cause generalised intellectual delay are usually of unknown aetiology, some have recognised physical correlates. For example, a lesion or injury to an area in the brain located in the posterior inferior frontal gyrus, and known as Broca's area of the brain, leads to a specific deficit in language production leading to the loss of ability to speak. Autism definitely doesn't fall into this latter group (of having a recognised specific brain pathology), and in those with moderate to severe learning difficulties is usually part of the former (generalised intellectual delay of unknown aetiology).

With regard to how to help this group, we know of no convincing replicated research that demonstrates that particular interventions (whether educational, psychological, social, or physical) specifically and differentially help those who have these more severe forms of autism (when compared to a similarly impaired group who don't qualify for a diagnosis of autism) (see Chapter 8). This may well be an area in which it is worth investing properly designed research, to see if autism as a diagnosis has any practical, clinical utility that may help us choose such interventions. Until this is adequately demonstrated, however, we cannot and should not assume that the diagnosis has any clinical value, even for those with the more severe presentations.

We subscribe to the idea that good science should follow the criteria of refutability as laid down by Popper (1959, 1963). Most theorists will not find it too troublesome to verify a theory; it is more difficult to try to refute one. The presence of a black swan should be enough to refute the theory that *all* swans are white; a search for a better definition should be undertaken. We contend that autism and the autistic spectrum should be subject to the same refutability criterion and approached with the scepticism that should be the hallmark of a true scientist. Definitions of autism have become so 'elastic' and subjective that almost any behaviour that marks one out as non-conformist in any context (family, school, work) can now be squeezed into one of the definitions we have, making refutability as circular as the diagnosis. Without proper, consistent, definitions of 'caseness', which have some clear 'markers', we are unable to 'refute' the theory and search for a better definition (see Chapter 7).

In order to achieve a solid scientific footing, a syndrome such as autism would have to be rigorously defined as a concept, before the quest for its cause, course and prognosis could be achieved. This is the sort of criticism laid down by Michael Rutter (1998) against the diagnosis of 'dyslexia'. Unfortunately, he does not appear to apply the same standards to a similar critique of autism. When he explores conduct disorders and the rise in their prevalence, he is of the opinion that such a rise cannot be attributable to genetic causes. However, when it comes to the autistic spectrum, Rutter attributes the rise in their prevalence to better case ascertainment and a widening of the diagnostic criteria. In our opinion it is this type of double standard, which arises from ideological not scientific concerns, that is typical of the nature of the 'autistic discourse' that has become characteristic of the field.

POLITICS

In this book, after first setting the broad context in which our ideas about childhood and development evolve, we concentrate on the science of autism and find it a poor basis on which to develop a concept with such profound ramifications for the individuals who get this diagnosis. We try to understand why certain societies have become so preoccupied with labelling individuals with such a non-scientific construct that has so little clinical utility (see Chapters 9, 10 and 11). Expanding autism into a spectrum that includes many who would not have previously been considered 'disordered' and deciding that their behaviour is caused by unseen medical, neurological reasons has many implications that have not been thought through by zealous promoters of the autism industry.

In going about the task of making sense of the evidence, we have found Habermas's (1972) suggestion that there are three knowledge-constitutive interests, each tied to a particular idea of science and social science – technical, practical and emancipatory perspectives – useful. These categories determine how we decide what is to be interpreted as 'knowledge'. The technical or positivistic approach leads to 'work knowledge', which broadly refers to the way one controls and manipulates one's environment through working out the rules by which to understand the world. Positivism sees only 'naturalistic' accounts of human possibilities, including human subjectivity, culture and history, from this point of view. This knowledge is usually based upon empirical investigation and is governed by technical rules. Second, there is the equally deep-seated 'practical' interest in securing and expanding possibilities of mutual understanding in the conduct of life. This hermeneutic or interpretive approach leads to 'practical knowledge' and identifies the domain of human social interaction, which is grounded in interpersonal life where people develop an understanding of each other's intentions and subjectivity. The emancipatory domain identifies self-knowledge or self-reflection. Knowledge here is gained through internal reflection leading to a transformed consciousness that can help in overcoming dogmatism, compulsion and domination.

In his critique of 'technocracy' – governance by scientific experts and bureaucracy – Habermas originally distinguished between two modes of action, 'work' and 'interaction'. The former includes modes of action based on rational choices, whereas the latter refers to forms of 'communicative action' in which actors coordinate their behaviours on the basis of 'consensual norms': what may start out being governed by scientific enquiry into discovering 'natural laws' ends up becoming part of a human process of these turning into beliefs and 'ways of doing things' based on 'consensus' of a group of people, rather than (necessarily) solid evidence. This critique of science and technology suggests that for areas where solid empirical enquiry is hard to come by, the 'science' can easily become ideology. By reducing practical questions about the 'good life' to technical problems for 'experts' to solve, the need for public, democratic discussion of values is eliminated, thereby depoliticising the population. The legitimate human interest in technical control of nature thus functions as an ideology – a screen that masks the value-laden character of government decision-making in the service of the capitalist status quo.

Although we do not want to simplify science as 'positivist/empirical' only or suggest that a hermeneutic approach means we get stuck in seeing everything as 'relative', understanding the three categories helps us interrogate the nature of the production of knowledge including that in 'autism'. Perhaps more than any other child and adolescent psychiatric category, autism is viewed as the product of sound science, with knowledge about it arising from Habermas's first category – the 'positivistic' or technical approach. Our concern is that much of the literature on autism (like that on psychiatry more generally) is actually based on interpretation (hermeneutic knowledge), shot through with cultural, social and historical 'baggage'. This hermeneutic knowledge (produced by 'consensual norms') masquerading as positivistic knowledge, as we hope to convince the reader, is hugely problematic. It is our contention that the autism spectrum has become a catch-all metaphor for focusing on a disparate range of behaviours that suggest a lack of the type of social and emotional competences thought to be necessary for the functioning of societies dominated by neo-liberal economic and political foundations. This perceived lack has, we believe, meant a growing marriage between government and psychiatry (of the type Habermas was suggesting) rarely seen outside totalitarian regimes (see Chapter 10).

Interventions, regardless of whether they are behavioural or pharmacological, do not appear to have resulted in any visible improvement in those diagnosed (see Chapter 7). The new world of early screening, followed by a range of psychosocial and pharmacological interventions, has never been subject to proper scrutiny, evidence base to back such practice, or ethical discussion. This ethical blindness should give us cause for concern, as history teaches us again and again that one generation's most cherished therapeutic ideas and practices, especially when applied to the powerless, are repudiated by the next, but not without leaving countless victims in their wake. Lack of acknowledgement of the subjective nature of psychiatric practice leaves it wide open to abuse (Kopelman, 1990). The desire to control, amend or even extinguish human behaviours that depart from an increasingly narrow stereotype of normality has bedevilled the history of psychiatry. At extreme levels, it has resulted in genocidal murder under the Nazis and mass sterilisations in the USA, Sweden and Japan, in the last two well in to the 1970s (see Chapter 11). This desire to control human nature is why Habermas (1972) suggested a link between science and domination. Human beings have attempted to master nature (often with dire consequences) and to master and control human nature using similar principles. The desire to include 'loners' at the moderate end of the autism spectrum should make us wonder whether being alone, awkward, or just plain shy is well on the road to becoming a disease for doctors to 'manage' and something that helps governments obscure some of the human costs of creating an aggressive marketing/consumerist culture.

Many of the leading figures of modern-day child psychiatry (see Chapter 3) view autism as the child psychiatric condition that most completely fits into the 'medical model' of a genetic, neurodevelopmental (problem with the development of the nervous system) condition. Even academics like professor David Skuse, who has professed doubts about the neurological basis of conditions such as ADHD, regards autism as a 'quintessentially highly heritable condition' (Skuse, 2001: 395). Like schizophrenia is to adult psychiatry, so autism is to child psychiatry – if autism cannot belong in this type of medical model then how can other child psychiatric diagnoses? No wonder the thought that maybe there is no such 'thing' as autism cannot be entertained. However, there is now a movement calling for the abolition of the label of 'schizophrenia'. We are calling for a similar movement against the label of autism.

As we shall discuss, the claims of professionals involved often appear self-serving, though we certainly accept that the intention of these professionals is to help people who have found themselves in difficulty. It is not the intention of such professionals that we are questioning, it is the basis and subsequent results of propagating and institutionalising views that are at odds with the evidence. In researching and then writing this book we have come to wonder about the extent to which the explosion in the use of the label 'autism' was engineered by a handful of professionals. Interest in their ideas has coincided with the development of highly competitive neo-liberal economic policies, the emergence of a service economy (which depends upon face-to face-skills), increasing population surveillance coupled with a push towards removing boundaries between the 'public' and the 'private', and a populist agenda which focuses on threats from outside and in particular inside the 'body politic'. It is unlikely that the ideas embodied by this particular professionally developed 'autism movement' would have taken hold to the degree they have if they had little resonance with the demands of the socio-political environment.

We are not only concerned with how the external political environment facilitates the 'uptake' of a concept like autism and the implications of popularising it; we are also concerned about the politics within the autism 'industry'. Not only has 'autism' succeeded in becoming high profile for the media attention it receives (such as the MMR story), within services, autism charities and the autism academic community certain types of critique also have become taboo. Perhaps we can illustrate this by reference to a 'scandal' that embroiled one prominent academic, considered a world authority on autism (see Edwards, 2006, for further details on this story). The story of the unassailable rise of Christopher Gillberg, professor of child and adolescent psychiatry at Gothenburg, reveals the extent to which politics, power hierarchies and human fallibility enter into the discourse and shape which voices will be heard and which dismissed.

Gillberg is known internationally for his research projects into the genetics of autism and for his contribution to the widening of the concept of autistic spectrum disorders. He has proposed that ASD represents a variety of predetermined conditions with diverse causes leading to similar outcomes, which he groups under 'empathy disorders' (Gillberg, 1991). He is also credited with developing the concept of deficits in attention, motor control and perception (DAMP), which has become a generally accepted diagnostic category in many Nordic countries and which is based on attempts to define diagnostic criteria for minimal brain dysfunction, independent of hypotheses about aetiology.

The work of Christopher Gillberg's group has been, and continues to be, enormously influential, not only within 'mainstream' academic groups but also with policy-makers in Sweden, where he headed Sweden's most influential group of child neuropsychiatrists and was chief advisor to the national board of health and welfare. Gillberg's influence in Sweden reached its zenith in the late 1990s, with Gillberg being widely publicised through the national media (in Sweden) as claiming that about 10 per cent of Swedish children had lifelong neuropsychiatric dysfunction, needing a doctor's diagnosis. With approximately 1,200,000 Swedish school children and 100 community school doctors, Gillberg claimed that each school doctor could therefore be expected to have around 1,200 children with a neuropsychiatric diagnosis (made up mainly of ADHD and ASD or DAMP, depending on which diagnostic system was used).

In 1995, Dr Leif Ellinder, a paediatrician, returned to work in his native Sweden. Having been away for several years he was concerned to find the degree to which practice in paediatrics had changed and the numbers of children who were now attracting neuropsychiatric 'labels' and receiving psychiatric medication for this. He did not consider asking parents and teachers to fill in questionnaires about children's behaviour to be a valid procedure for diagnosing a, supposedly, hereditary brain dysfunction. He also noted that numbers of children attending special schooling had almost doubled in the previous two decades. He felt troubled by these new trends and equally troubled by the media coverage and claims of prominent doctors, such as Gillberg, that the rates of neuropsychiatric disorders in children were as high as 10 per cent and that the use of amphetamine-like drugs, such as methylphenidate (Ritalin), was both safe and effective. In 1998, Ellinder presented a critical review at a national doctors' conference in Gothenburg. His presentation did not go unnoticed and a television programme, titled *The Labelled Children*, followed on national television. However, Ellinder paid the price on a personal level for speaking out in this manner; he and his family, including his elderly parents, were subject to a variety of allegations and received abusive letters.

Ellinder then met with the University of Lund sociologist, Professor Eva Karfve, who had also criticised the neuropsychiatric labelling of children in various articles and a book. Things soon began to get nasty. The Gillberg group avoided attempts to enter into a debate on the issues. Instead Karfve and Ellinder were accused of being used by the Church of Scientology, despite neither of them having been members of that organisation (although Karfve had attended and spoken at a meeting organised by them).

In 2002, Ellinder and Karfve found some inconsistencies in the Gillberg group's research. For example, in 1978, Gillberg had diagnosed 42 seven-year-old children with minimal brain dysfunction (MBD). This same group of children was then followed up by his wife, Carina Gillberg, for her doctorate thesis and the diagnosis was changed from MBD to DAMP – the new concept that Gillberg was at that time pioneering. Colleagues, such as Lars Hellgrem, also used the same group of children when they were older (aged 16) for his doctorate thesis and the Gillberg group also followed these children up again when they were 22 years old. By this time Gillberg was saying that DAMP was similar to ADHD. Although the various studies cover 15 years, none of the children in this research were actually treated. However, Gillberg used this research to support his claim that DAMP/ADHD was the most prominent disorder among his grouping of neuropsychiatric disorders in childhood and that it affected about 10 per cent of children, making them candidates for potentially lifelong stimulant treatment.

Ellinder and Karfve decided to challenge the Gillberg group and requested access to the raw data from their studies. When the Gillberg group refused this, Ellinder and Karfve took legal action and, under Swedish law, a civil court ruled that they had the right to inspect the research material. However, Gillberg's group continued to refuse access despite this court ruling. As a compromise, Ellinder and Karfve suggested that an outside, independent investigation by the scientific council could review the matter. However, the Gillberg group turned this down and instead asked an ethics committee chairman, a Mr O. Lundgren, to look at the material. Lundgren was apparently given four hours to scrutinise the over 100,000 pages of research. Lundgren told Gillberg that he could find nothing obviously wrong but also pointed out that it was impossible to examine the information properly in such a short time. However, the Gillberg group and the chief of Sahlgrenska University Hospital at Gothenberg then made media announcements stating that the Gillberg group had been cleared by the ethics committee. Lundgren wrote to the editor of *Dagens Medicin* (Medicine of Today) stating that, never in his professional life, had he felt so exploited.

In the meantime Gillberg still had to face accusations of scientific misconduct in court due to his continued refusal to allow Ellinder and Karfve access to the research data. Despite facing this court appearance and a potential criminal record, Gillberg's wife and colleagues decided to shred the group's research material rather than hand it over as requested by the court, citing the reason of needing to protect the research participants' confidentiality.

In May 2005, Professor Gillberg, Gunnar Svedberg (University Dean) and Arne Wittlov (University Board Chairman) were put on trial at Gothenberg District Court. In June 2005, Gillberg was given a suspended sentence and fine, plus court costs. Svedberg, the University Dean, received a fine and costs, while Wittlov was found not guilty. In March 2006, Gillberg and other members of his group appeared in court again, this time charged with destroying government property. Members of his group, including his wife, Carina Gillberg, each received suspended sentences and fines.

Despite his conviction, Gillberg has kept his place at Gothenberg University and continued to appear as a prominent speaker on the international circuit. In what to some may appear like an attempt at 'revenge' the University of Lund asked the scientific council to investigate Karfve and her book on the DAMP/ADHD issue. During the period of investigation, which took approximately a year, Karfve was denied research funds (unlike the Gillberg group). However, the investigation, which was completed in early 2006, cleared her of all charges.

The story of Professor Gillberg reveals something of the David and Goliath struggle that critics of such prominent academics face when they try to raise legitimate, clinical, scientific and ethical questions. Throughout the controversy and during the investigation Gillberg had the support of: a large group of international academics who signed various petitions, continuing support from drug companies for his research, the University which employed him and various consumer pressure groups (who likewise had been receiving funding from the drug companies). Indeed, these various groupings, such as Riks Foreningen, of which his wife is a vice chairwoman, and the Riks Foreundet Attention, have carried out fundraising to help pay their fines. Like many around the world who achieve high status, prestige and power, it seems that, in our opinion, Professor Gillberg acted as if he was untouchable and somehow above the law of his country.

An interesting contrast to this story is that of Professor Gretchen Lefever, Professor of psychology at Eastern Virginia Medical School. In 2002, Lefever published a study that revealed that diagnosis of ADHD in the area of East Virginia she was studying had risen to 17 per cent in children in grades 2 to 5, with 84 per cent of those diagnosed with ADHD being on ADHD medication. These results, naturally, caused alarm in some sections of the scientific community and the media, but were dismissed by many prominent figures in the 'ADHD industry'. In early 2005, Professor Lefever, was suddenly informed that she was placed on administrative leave with intent to terminate her employment. Her employers filed charges of scientific misconduct against her and her computers and other equipment were seized. The investigation had started in May 2004, after an anonymous whistleblower charged Professor Lefever with scientific misconduct, pointing out a discrepancy in one question between Lefever's published report and the actual question used in her 2002 study. In the original survey, parents were asked: 'Does your child have attention or hyperactivity problems, known as ADD or ADHD?', and the published version of the question was 'Has your child been diagnosed with attention or hyperactivity problems known as ADD or ADHD?' It is notable that during this period of investigation several members of the much more powerful pro-ADHD lobby had not only questioned her claims, but also accused her of 'jeopardising the rights of children'. Fortunately, a campaign in support of Professor Lefever (including a group of psychiatrists and psychologists who signed a petition that they sent to the medical school's president) argued that, instead of threatening to fire Professor Lefever, the school should have commended her for having the courage to sound the alarm bells about the concerning trends with regard to ADHD diagnosis and stimulant prescriptions. It eventually succeeded and Gretchen Lefever was finally reinstated in her position at Eastern Virginia Medical School in late 2005.

The above two 'case studies' illustrate just how powerful the political forces at play are in either supporting or censoring academic and scientific opinion.Such a political climate makes it very difficult for critical perspectives, like those expressed herein, to be taken seriously, debated properly and be accessible in the public realm. While we all like to live in a world of moral certainties, there is a big question about what we do when we are faced with substantial gaps in our knowledge. It is our proposal that such 'substantial gaps' define our current state of knowledge with regards to ASD, and it is without apology that we wish to expose these gaps and propose that current theory and practice around ASD has more to do with socio-cultural processes than scientific progress. Further, we believe that this blindness is putting many of those diagnosed at risk of a poor outcome rather than helping them.

PERSONAL EXPERIENCE

While the 'meat' of this book is the critical analysis of scientific evidence and an exploration of the political context that allowed the concept to flourish, we also want to keep in mind the real experiences of real people. Here we again saw something vital missing from the current literature on autism. While we have books, articles and websites written or produced by individuals diagnosed with autism and their carers, some of whom protest at the current emphasis on the 'disabilities' of autism, little can be found that questions the diagnosis itself. In Chapter 2 we give voice to two people (authors NG and BM) and a clinician (author ST) who bring such a personal perspective. We think more people should know about this more radical, but evidence-based, voice of protest. In telling our stories in Chapter 2, we show that in the real world, there is much to be concerned about in current practice and a perfectly viable and perhaps preferable alternative to being diagnosed with one of the 'autisms'.

There is much more we could have said, not only about our own lives but other situations we have experienced that contributed to casting doubt about the concept. For example, at an informal meeting of a regional autism support group, one of the authors (NG) witnessed the interaction between a group of young men diagnosed in their teens with Asperger's and former students of a special needs school who were diagnosed with autism (and also had learning difficulties). The contrast between the groups was highly visible. The latter were confident and at ease, but spoke with a reduced vocabulary, often being unable to grasp some of the most basic concepts that arose in the group discussion, but always eager to stress the need for solidarity with other people with learning disabilities, such as friends who had Down's syndrome and Fragile X. The former group, far more capable in terms of eloquence and sociability, had a fairly average understanding of most social and medical issues discussed, but distinguished themselves mainly by their failure to 'integrate' into a mainstream society. Such experiences influenced NG as he began to question what such disparate groups of individuals have in common beyond their labelled status.

Labelling alone can do a great deal of harm. After all, given a choice, what profession would employ someone with an ASD diagnosis if they could employ someone without it? One of the authors (BM) qualified as a teacher in 1998 and was then diagnosed with Asperger's in 2000. He approached a local college to teach and disclosed his condition. They were happy to employ him with one proviso; having concerns about his capacity to empathise, they wrote to his psychiatrist to ascertain this psychiatrist's views on his suitability. The psychiatrist declined to reply, and the college declined to employ him. Another of the authors (NG) only met commercial success in his career as a Web programmer when he removed the disability clause from his CV where, up until then, he had been declaring his Asperger's diagnosis. For a while NG had naively believed that explaining his diagnosis to employers would better help them understand his situation.

There remain many similar untold stories and unheard voices in the new age of the autism epidemic; we now turn to some of these.

2
THE MISSING VOICES: OUR CASE HISTORIES

This book undertakes a largely technical review of the autism literature, while attempting to place this within the context of the broader cultural milieu and differing objectives societies have for the role of individuals. However, such technical accounts have a real problem. While it may be legitimate, important and even (sometimes) fun to joust with and ask searching questions of the current crop of ASD proponents, somewhere at the receiving end of these discourses are real people living through and trying to make sense of real problems. Here, at this most important level – the human level – the supporters of the autism construct claim to have brought tangible benefits to people who were otherwise struggling to make meaningful sense of their difficulties. Many personal narratives written by those who have been diagnosed as having an ASD have described, in moving and gripping terms, their personal struggles, often concluding that the diagnosis of an ASD helps them to make sense of their life. From a technical point of view, the scientific validity of this is no greater or smaller than using your star sign for this purpose. Millions, possibly billions, around the world use astrological charts to guide and provide meaning and purpose to their lives. We are, after all, meaning-seeking creatures. Thus, at the level of the person and their family, autism can provide this 'meaning-making' function, providing a reference point and framework within which some comfort can be derived, helping them through the messy business of negotiating the often turbulent waters of life.

However, a failure to reach beyond current mainstream beliefs and practices, not just at the scientific level, but at the human level too, leaves the field inclined to silence alternative narratives and accounts. Not everyone has found being labelled with an ASD makes sense or is experienced as liberating; indeed, for some the label creates meanings that can become problematic, creating unnecessarily limited autistic scripts. By writing our own personal narratives, we hope to create a space at the 'human', experiential level for other ways of making meaning of people's lives, ways that may be viewed as more rich and multilayered (or may not), but at least open up possibilities for a more genuine acceptance of the diversity of humans, rather than merely seeking to control such diversities by ever-more encompassing categorisations.

NEIL GARDNER

Outwardly I grew up in a fairly typical lower-middle-class or upper-working-class household, but never felt the same sense of belonging as most of my peers. My mother had spent the first four years of her life in an East London orphanage (the precise location has always remained a mystery and I only found out about this via my late grandmother), before her mother married and formed a new family with her new husband and his son. Growing up subsequently in Surrey, she acquired a 'Pigmalion-esque' pseudo-posh accent, itself probably a reaction to early stigma. She has always been extrovert with strangers, but obviously had many emotional issues of her own. This sometimes made it hard for us to integrate with neighbours in Edinburgh (where I spent the early years of my life), especially as my Scottish father often worked away from home for several weeks or even months. Both my brother and I were late talkers. My brother stuttered until he was around five years old and I did not utter full sentences until at least three, but by the age of four had become a little chatterbox. When I started school, my mother trained as a primary school teacher, giving a new meaning to her life, and through great professional dedication succeeded very well with nine- to 11-year-olds.

Many years on I observed her interaction with my own newborn children; I'd later contrast her relative emotional detachment, reminiscent of a school mistress, with the almost instinctive bonding that usually takes place between mother and child. Recent trends in psychiatry have tended to attribute differences in emotional and social development to genetic factors, but in the 1950s and 1960s John Bowlby and Mary Ainsworth pioneered research highlighting the importance of mother–child bonding in early socialisation. The latter's attachment theory can lead nominally to the conclusion that the infant and young child should experience a warm, intimate and continuous relationship with his mother (or permanent mother substitute) in which both find satisfaction and enjoyment. However, this hardly explains why many children grow into emotionally balanced and socially aware adults despite early hardships and familial disruptions, while others from relatively stable middle-class backgrounds experience significant problems bonding with their peers. Most parents try to do the right thing for their offspring, but subconsciously treat their children differently and instil their moods, anxieties and past experiences in the next generation.

At the age of nine I was a keen swimmer and diver, but hopeless at ball games. I'd happily play on the climbing frame or join in some playground activities – often unsuccessfully, but at least I tried! Unfortunately I then suffered a road accident. The collision chipped my neck and sent me into a coma for three days. On my return to school I was more withdrawn and would be seen walking around in a world of my own at break time. However, paradoxically, my academic performance improved in leaps and bounds. I hadn't mastered the alphabet until the age of eight and, at one stage, had been referred for remedial reading practice.

Just before my 11th birthday, we moved south to Luton (in the UK). My father began a new job and became involved in politics with the Labour Party. For several years most of my parents' friends and family contacts were political associates. Contact with my extended family was often remote, with occasional visits to aunts, uncles and cousins dotted around the country.

In my final year of primary education, I had my second road accident, this time fracturing my femur. As a result I took three months off school and had to continue to use crutches and sticks for a further six months. By the time I returned to school, a new comprehensive, I found myself the target of concerted bullying, with many acquaintances from the previous primary school turning against me. I must have come across as the uncoolest dude in the school, with greasy shoulder-length hair, a weird accent and limping along on sticks.

Perhaps partly because of these accumulated alienations, I experienced a deep identity crisis. Things turned around a bit for the better at about 13 years of age, as I developed a premature interest in rock music and radical politics, encouraged by my elder brother's involvement with the Labour Party's youth league and support for various leftwing causes. At one point he suggested I started a National Union of School Students (NUSS) group at my school and even helped me draft a five-point leaflet calling for the abolition of school uniform, corporal punishment, religious education and school records, calling for the establishment of an elected school council. When the head teacher got his hands on some of the leaflets, he had some of my new friends sent home and informed their parents before summoning me to his office and accusing me of political naivety. Nonetheless I continued to attend meetings with local activists, all over 17, who had set up similar students' union branches in two local colleges. I even went to the 1978 NUSS conference, dominated by Trotskyite Socialist Workers Party (SWP) and Communist Youth League activists. This proved quite an experience, replete with juicy titbits such as an embarrassing speech I attempted to give before being booed off the stage for repeating myself and my first intimate encounter with a girl two years my elder.

Back home I had lost interest in my peers (possibly a way of coping with their earlier rejection) and began to hang out with people involved in the Anti-Nazi League and SWP. On the last day of school that year I persuaded a classmate (who had begun to show more respect for the new 'cooler' Neil) to stage a protest against the school uniform. We turned up dressed as punks, prompting verbal warnings and suspension for the rest of the day. A few months later I distributed a few copies of the NUSS magazine, with a special feature on contraceptives, at school. I was called to the head teacher's office once again, immediately suspended and eventually expelled. The case reached the national media. A *Sun* photographer turned up at the door of our house, surprising my embarrassed mother.

I was eventually placed in a 'rougher' comprehensive school. At this, at the time, low-achieving school I felt less motivated to perform academically and (perhaps as a delayed reaction to earlier bullying about my alleged 'swottiness') regularly skipped school and failed to complete homework. My poor handwriting and idiosyncratic spelling worsened, leading me to have to re-sit my English O-level twice before passing. I bonded with few other students, except a latter-day hippie girl whose boyfriend I knew from the local SWP group. As my enthusiasm for radical politics waned, partly due to some unfortunate social experiences at gatherings, I once more drifted into self-imposed solitude, often daydreaming and even falling asleep in class. I struggled through sixth form college, occasionally attempting to make new friends, but felt increasingly alienated from the culture I saw around me.

When my parents noticed me sleepwalking (in an undressed state) shortly after my 18th birthday, they asked for me to be referred to a psychiatrist. I hate to think what would happen now, in the early 21st century, as any mention of insomnia and hallucinations could perhaps merit a diagnosis of psychosis. At the appointment, I explained some of my emotional problems and then bored the psychiatrist with a talk on politics. I think this psychiatrist probably thought my case was just a waste of valuable NHS time. I had committed no crimes and seemed pretty much of sound mind – nothing that at the time would have met the definition of a psychiatric disorder – so little came of this. However, I would have preferred to have been referred to a friendly psychotherapist rather than a 'white coat' psychiatrist.

Around 1981 the campaign for nuclear disarmament saw a huge upswing in support as Cruise and Pershing missiles were to be installed in the UK and elsewhere in Europe. It attracted a new range of activists, not just your run-of-the-mill leftwing types. We had Young Liberals, Greens and even Church of England followers, many in their 30s, 40s and beyond. I soon became involved in politics again, organising demos, videos, debates and printing leaflets. When a local organiser quit, I was unexpectedly elected as secretary (nobody else had the time) and attended the 1982 national CND conference in Sheffield in this capacity. My social life at the time revolved almost exclusively around local CND meetings. I refused to go to parties for fear of negative experiences, like being left in the kitchen all alone, or generally making a fool of myself. With this fresh boost to my self-confidence, I suddenly found myself interacting with 'interesting' people feeling more of an equal than an intruder. Inevitably, the assorted group of people I felt I had now bonded with retired to the pub after each day's proceedings and conversations moved into more personal matters. When someone commented on my weird accent (hard to pin down), I improvised a Dutch background and a convoluted story about being the product of an affair my father had had with a female Dutch heroin addict. I assembled this story from various strands of a 'what-if' scenario I had played in my mind after learning, at the tender age of 13, of my mother's 'illegitimacy'. My grandmother had confided her past misdemeanours to me the first time I ever visited her alone. I replayed her confession several times over in my mind, until it became obvious that she not only worked as a domestic in a stately home, but offered paying clients other services too. My new detachment from my family's preferred identity as an upstanding, but progressive British family was a cruel wound against my mother, who was coping at the time with a husband intent on pursuing a political career. I had effectively narrated her out of my life or demoted her to a mere stepmother. I consciously started to 'morph' my accent and on separate occasions experimented with variants of this story, choosing different origins. It became complicated to remember to whom I had told what story.

On a more positive note I had taken up a new interest – foreign languages. I jumped at the opportunity of visiting an anarchist German acquaintance in West Berlin. Anything seemed better than memories of rejection and alienation at school. I stayed there a while as I found life abroad easier. I could switch between various identities as long as I didn't claim to come from the locale and my attempts at conversing in the local tongue sometimes confounded natives, as I didn't have an English accent at all.

On my return that summer, now aged 19, I invited a group of SWP friends around while my parents were on holiday. This impromptu party attracted more revellers than expected and my inability to stop someone from raiding my father's drinks cabinet led to a violent outburst and conspicuous damage. I felt disillusioned by a lack of solidarity from those whom I counted as friends. They simply left after a half-hearted attempt to clear up some of the mess. Deeply embarrassed by the whole situation and fearing my parents' reaction, I accepted the offer of an acquaintance, who was in the SWP, to crash out on his bed and return later in the morning to clean the place more thoroughly. At six in the morning, after barely two hours' sleep, I discovered him fondling my genitalia and attempting to penetrate me. Owing to my extreme sense of vulnerability and guilt, I let him go ahead provided he agreed not to tell anybody about the inconsistencies in the accounts of my personal background.

After a year spending time on and off away from the UK, I decided to study modern languages. As many foreign language courses were at the time undersubscribed, I found two polytechnics (as they were then known) prepared to accept me after a test. I opted to read European Studies at what is now the University of the South Bank. This included politics, economics and two European languages. I quickly found myself thrown into a social jungle, populated mainly by female students eager to mate with 'alpha' males – which I was not! My time at university soon became an extension of the earlier miasma I had experienced at school, but I just couldn't resist morphing my identity and personal background to suit the scene. Interestingly few commented on the obvious inconsistencies in my tales. On one occasion, after a welcome disco for all first-year students, I had amused a female sociology student from Scunthorpe with my presumed South African background, taking care to pronounce pertinent proper nouns in the South African way. Unexpectedly, we later went to her flat, which she shared with a student in my Spanish class, who incidentally also shared a similar Anglo-Scots background to me and with whom I had been absolutely honest about my past. The latter only briefly poked her head in, but it was long enough for me to almost instinctively switch accents. After receiving an odd look I had to explain myself, claiming this was just a made-up persona and that in reality I just had a muddled accent which some people mistook for foreign, often South African. I can certainly recount a number of similar episodes in that year indicating a worsening of my identity crisis. This was manifesting itself not only in variations on my cultural background, but also in sexuality.

At high school I had been taunted for alleged homosexuality, but although I mixed with lefties who had a liberal attitude to sexual orientation (something that has since become orthodoxy sometimes in a rather illiberal way), I had consciously excluded this option. It only took a couple of pints of beer in a pre-Xmas student bash for me to claim bisexuality, something that appeared politically correct at the time, and find myself in bed with the epitome of a male hunk, an experience I found, quite frankly, a complete anticlimax. Despite my private reservations about the innate sexuality hypothesis, I continued to hang out occasionally with a bunch of students on the gay scene, including one SWP comrade, only to discover a highly commercialised, competitive and narcoticised lifestyle quite antithetical to my aspirations.

By the following summer I had saved up enough cash from my grant to go on a month-long train tour of Europe, known at the time as the 'Transalpine'. For just £200 I could explore most of Europe and parts of North Africa, a welcome break for a budding linguist with an identity crisis. I had a few addresses of people I had met here and there and hit the tracks. I had corresponded with an Italian girl who was eager to learn English and whom I'd met on my return from Germany a year earlier. When I turned up at her family's flat in Bari, south-eastern Italy, I was not only accommodated for the night, as I had originally planned, but for five whole days, mostly in the company of her female friends. While this was an excellent opportunity to try out my improvised Italian, it had the side effect of restricting conversation to simpler matters rather than my usual focus on politics.

The trendy student phase of my life came to an abrupt end when I failed my history exam twice at the end of first year of university, requiring me to repeat the first year and seek special funding to complete a four-year BA. Unwilling to face the emotional trauma of repeating a year, I opted to go abroad, this time heading to Cologne, Westphalia, to meet friends of a German friend. I soon ran out of resources after losing a job at the Berlitz School as a teacher of English as a foreign language. I committed the cardinal sin of correcting a German teacher of English who supervised my lessons and of not following the curriculum. I spent a couple of months crashing out on acquaintances' sofas before someone lent me enough to rent an attic room, earning a pittance with occasional English-language tuition and translations. Eventually I resorted to the German equivalent of a Job Centre, much better organised than in the UK, and obtained employment as a packer in a large warehouse serving supermarkets over much of northern Germany.

Most colleagues were either working-class Germans who had failed academically or Turkish and Eastern European guest workers. The money was not too bad if you could get yourself out of bed at 6am and methodically pack pallets for loading on trucks as the orders came in. I never progressed beyond the smallest size of forklift truck, seldom packed fast enough to earn myself a bonus, but at least I assembled orders correctly and had enough to live on. In the last three months there I joined a trade union and resumed my political activity. After nine months my contract, which had been extended every three months, failed to be renewed. This mattered little, as I had saved up enough money to move on, this time to north-eastern Italy to meet a young Italian woman I had met in Portugal the previous summer and had corresponded with over the previous year; we married 15 months later. I didn't quite cut it as a teacher of English as a foreign language, my main source of income for the first two years in Italy, and opted instead to specialise in the burgeoning technical translation business; I soon began to build large databases of previously translated terms and phrases. However, economic uncertainties led me to supplement my income as in-house translator-cum-export sales representative at a number of small manufacturing businesses, where my relative lack of diplomacy proved a disadvantage masked only by my quaint foreignness. An argument with one local entrepreneur led to four months' unemployment before my daughter's birth. Eventually, I returned to translating from home while learning the programming and database administration skills I needed to build a new career. Although initially very enthusiastic about the Italian way of life, noise – generated largely by traffic and cottage industries – proved too much for me to cope with and may have been a motivating factor in my decision to return to the UK, where, incidentally, I've encountered another form of noise pollution – piped music in offices.

I can think of many possible psychological explanations for my extended 'identity' crisis. My mother, who experienced her own emotional issues of not belonging, had, at least in my eyes, preferred my brother. By my mid-teens I had already experienced moving, serious road accidents that required extended periods of time out of school, bullying, expulsion, truancy and had become a 'problem' to both school and my parents. My parents' marriage had broken up, as my father sought solace in his secretary, 25-odd years his junior, and I sometimes felt responsible for this. I also often felt that my parents were impatient and intolerant of my psychological woes.

I became aware of the subject of Asperger's syndrome (AS) gradually between 1996 and 2001 via a series of documentaries that led to internet research and contacts with others who had been diagnosed with AS. Without the encouragement of internet acquaintances and problems at work, I doubt I would have taken the extra step to seek a referral for an assessment via my GP. The first psychiatrist I saw in 2001 had never heard of AS, but after two sessions she referred me to an autism specialist, a psychologist by training, who, after several sessions, diagnosed me as having AS. This set in train a period of self-reappraisal in which I began to see my social woes, identity crisis, other life history problems and lack of professional success in terms of this alleged disability. I imagined that such a diagnosis as a teenager would have helped me deal with alienation and bullying at school. As a long-standing advocate of social justice, I contacted local autism organisations, only to encounter the very duplicitous façade they claimed to combat. Superficially they sought to defend the rights of 'individuals with autism' and campaign for better services, but in reality I found them firmly wedded to a bio-genetic model that views the autistic continuum as pathological, focused more on the negatives than the positives of our culturally abnormal behaviour.

In the same period my marriage had began to collapse, triggered perhaps by an almighty row leading to a short outburst on holiday (resulting in a shattered glass door, although the only person injured was me and even that was accidental). My wife left with the kids without telling me and only agreed to return after her best friend persuaded her otherwise and I agreed to take medication to calm my nerves. Previously sceptical of psychoactive drugs, my attitude had changed largely due to contact on the internet with others diagnosed with AS, many of who were on SSRIs (a class of antidepressant), Zyprexia (a type of anti-psychotic medication), or Ritalin. This also coincided with a spell of partial unemployment and working from home on translation database projects. I was prescribed Venlafaxine (a type of antidepressant) but this made me lethargic, blunted my usually sharp faculties of creativity and critical thinking and made me sleep two hours extra a day. Luckily, I weaned myself off this debilitating drug amid a second bout of marital problems and have steered clear of any such medication since.

Around this time the new Autism Employability Advisor for the region where I lived contacted me to offer employment advice. I was struck by her enthusiasm and apparent empathy with my plight, but soon came to realise that hardly any of her clients had successfully secured permanent paid employment. She was desperately below target. However, in January 2003 I began work as a creatively titled 'community multimedia support worker' for people with learning disabilities. My task was to assist small groups of service users in the creation of multimedia projects, video editing, badge-making, printing newsletters and the development of a website. This began a two-year excursion into the diverse world of learning disabilities, where I met nobody with a personal profile similar to my own. I entered a parallel universe of key workers, service users and a culture of interdependence divorced from the normal laws of economics. Despite all too familiar rhetoric about equality and diversity, awareness-raising activities, injections of public money and bogus employment schemes, all but a few borderline cases had their lives organised in great detail by staff. To me care workers seemed unaware of the mixed bag of social consequences, such as reinforcing a culture of entitlement and pervasive monitoring, that their benevolent activities could produce.

Much of the promotional language used in the learning disability world is recycled in the autism sector with similar buzzwords and phrases, like 'the same but different', and often the same advice and apparent solutions. It struck me that the Council had invested copious resources into the promotion of services for the learning disabled. One such project, a local implementation of the Scotland-wide 'Same As You' recommendations, employed just 11 individuals with learning disabilities, including one diagnosed with AS, to do little more than staple newsletters, shred paper, work a badge-making machine, place CDs in sleeves and attend numerous conferences, which sometimes involved using camera equipment under close supervision. Nothing would ever happen without two permanent members of staff.

Every year the Council's 'Employability Team' held an event rewarding local employers for hiring staff with recognised disabilities. This involved an enormous range of people, including those with sensory impairments, physical disabilities, brain injuries, mental health problems, learning disabilities and those on the autistic spectrum. All these categories were happily assembled into one generic concept. Thus blind, but perfectly intelligent, workers were publicised alongside those with considerable learning difficulties. Recent recipients of the prize included a local McDonald's franchise and a 24-hour Asda supermarket. While employability advisers will flaunt their expertise in the issues their clients face, true success stories, leading to self-sustaining meaningful long-term employment were few and far between, and I only saw a handful of cases in which talented individuals with a sensory or physical handicap simply needed assistive technology and a little understanding to enable them to perform their job adequately. I wondered why the Council simply didn't lay off or redeploy their Employability Team and give the same number of intellectually capable disabled individuals guaranteed administrative jobs.

In some Scottish cities, besides the National Autistic Society and the Scottish Society for Autism, two other non-governmental organisations 'Into Work' and 'Autism Initiatives' jumped on the gravy train, receiving funds from European organisations and the Scottish Executive. As far as I could see, much of their time was dedicated to promoting autism as a concept and encouraging vulnerable individuals to seek a diagnosis.

I joined a group as part of a nominally independent Asperger's Society, facilitated by a charming professional from the Scottish Society for Autism, partly to meet others with a similar diagnosis and because I was convinced that such initiatives could only help the plight of the marginalised. My initial enthusiasm was greeted with a warm welcome, but three sacred cows would remain untouchable: the concept of the extended autistic spectrum as part of the galaxy of learning disabilities, the role of facilitators and other professionals in the group's organisation and the need to recruit new members by encouraging vulnerable adults to seek diagnosis. Shortly after I had joined, the group expressed its intention to produce an awareness-raising video, no doubt encouraged by the fact that one of its most active members had a special interest in video editing. The facilitator suggested the clichéd title of *The Same But Different*, which had, unbeknown to other participants, been used for numerous other similar promotional media projects. In my opinion we can hardly blame the public for confusing Asperger's syndrome with Down's syndrome, schizophrenia or ADHD, if so much pop psychology promoted by the mainstream media blurs the boundaries between intellectual handicaps, emotional stress, depression, addiction, personality disorders and psychopathy. More than perhaps any other psychiatric diagnosis, AS straddles the borders between these concepts, so for healthcare professionals we are simultaneously moody, awkward, in need of medication and potentially psychopathic. Outreach workers are trained to deal with us and usually make huge assumptions about our behaviour and likely reactions. A perceived deficiency in emotional intelligence may infer some kind of learning difficulty and thus lead to stress and depression. An obsessive interest in circumscribed subjects may infer dysfunctional addiction. An inability to understand the effects one's actions have on other people's feelings may require constant supervision to save us from ourselves and protect the community at large.

At the beginning of the 21st century, despite such huge advances in assistive and communication technology and such high-profile equality and diversity awareness-raising campaigns for all sorts of human conditions, I felt more alienated from mainstream society than ever and grew suspicious of the intent of the autism professionals who claimed to represent us, but inevitably imposed their preconceived ideas about AS on us. Did I need to attend group meetings just to watch an ASD awareness-raising video in which a prominent member of the National Autistic Society's committee revealed his obsession with eating multipack flavoured crisps in a specific order as if such habits could identify someone with high-functioning autism? On several occasions I felt coerced to reveal past experiences and reframe them in a new autism-friendly light. If I had been bullied at school, I could no longer blame my peers or societal values, but a lack of awareness of an alleged neurological difference. If I tended to acquire a passion for esoteric subjects without immediate prospects of financial gain, then that too was attributed to my new psychiatric diagnosis rather than to the broad diversity of human experiences and potential. Even my slight absent-mindedness and poor hand–eye coordination, previously attributed to a weak left eye and a childhood accident, were re-evaluated as dyspraxia, and explained as something often co-diagnosed with ASDs. My detour into the world of neurodiversity had served as a journey of self-appraisal, but had failed to provide the practical answers I needed. I can fully accept that my poor hand–eye coordination has biological roots, possibly with a strong genetic component, but that hardly explains my deviant personality profile in the way that, for example, sightlessness undoubtedly shapes the character development of a blind person.

Disillusioned with the 'autism scene' I decided to redouble my efforts to gain full-time employment as a Web applications developer, building on the experience I'd gained, mostly on my own initiative, through the creation of a Council-wide content management system. However, in the real commercial world, despite the huge demand for competent analyst programmers and Web developers at the time, I faced an obstacle. Most IT jobs require a modicum of people skills, not least to work alongside colleagues and project managers. Agile programming, requiring coders to write scripts in pairs, was all the rage, and relied on a hive mentality, to which a person with AS traits could be seen as likely to find it a struggle to adapt. That somehow the assets attributed to AS are an advantage in IT is a myth. They inhabit a microcosm teeming with consultants, project managers and marketing executives. In such an environment a worker unable to gauge the business requirements of the task assigned or liaise effectively with a multitude of colleagues would send shivers down the spine of any prospective employer. Thus, the carefully worded clause in my CV under the heading Disability Issues, which referred to having a diagnosis of AS, became an instant show-stopper. As I had now started to lose faith in the autistic spectrum paradigm, I decided to remove mention of AS from my CV. However, on reaching the final shortlist for an opening as a Web programmer at a prestigious IT company, I decided to mention my AS diagnosis in a routine questionnaire. Needless to say again, I didn't get the job. A week later, my work on an open-source on-line test management system won me a contract at a company based in England. With this short commercial experience in hand and no longer mentioning the AS diagnosis in questionnaires or interviews, I secured another contract for the development of the search engine behind a major London-based property website and have been in full-time employment ever since, finally earning an income commensurate with my age and ability.

BRIAN MCCABE

I am told that my delivery was normal and that I was not premature or late to any appreciable degree. I have few recollections of my early years but I am informed by my existing parent and relatives that, as far as they were concerned, there were no markedly impaired patterns of reciprocity and that I was a reasonably affectionate child. Likewise, both my parents were affectionate and warm. I had several friends but I do not think I could be described as a particularly gregarious child. I was not a clingy child and when my mother was having an operation I stayed with a friend of the family and did not manifest any obvious pattern of distress. I was reasonably well liked at school both by teachers and children. By no stretch of the imagination could I be called a 'little professor', nor did I show any precocity.

It would appear that I did, however, become 'prickly' and no longer welcomed physical reciprocity at around the age of ten. From puberty onwards this prickliness became more pronounced. I also manifested an increasingly poor concentration and high levels of 'sarcasm'. Possibly as a consequence of this poor concentration, at school I began to act the 'clown'. Laughter became a kind of positive reinforcement. I began to struggle in areas that required prolonged and sustained concentration or those that required one to learn by rote. I still had a few friends but I was not a great mixer. At the same time as I attracted attention and affection from my peers, I also began to rebuff them. This pattern of attraction and repulsion would follow me for the next 30 years. I left the school with no qualifications at 16, was persuaded to return to school, and finally left with two O-levels.

Sexually I had no doubt I was heterosexual. I found myself attracted to women and some girls and women were attracted to me. I am not 'blind' to the signs of female attraction; what held me back was a total lack of confidence, my prickliness and a certain physical squeamishness. Knowing that I felt unable to return girls' attraction, yet continuing to welcome to it, I began to derive a certain frisson from emotional cruelty.

My first job was with the Civil Service, where I was a filing clerk. I talked incessantly and exhibited many of the character traits that previously manifested themselves in my adolescence. Again I had friends in the office, but when a higher level of intimacy was required, I repulsed all those that came too close. I had a very high (some might say inflated) opinion of my intelligence at the same time as having a poor opinion of my physical appearance. When I went out with women I began to use alcohol as a kind of anaesthetic, but it was not sufficient to lower all inhibitions. Even when I had explicit requests from women I continued to decline.

At work my restlessness began to result in absenteeism. I was enjoying going into Liverpool and browsing round record shops. This obsession with music, particularly jazz, has stayed with me and I often feel has kept me sane. From my teens I had began to dislike all forms of authority, including that of my father, who died when I was 14. It probably influenced my nascent interest in Marxism, which has also stayed with me. I was never one to join any formal political group and doctrinaire orthodoxy of any kind put me off. I felt an affinity between jazz and the racism and sexism that minority groups often suffered. I felt this very strongly and remember being excited by pictures of riots in the 'Watts' ghetto in 1965. I found loud characters such as Mohammed Ali appealing for their braggadocio in and outside the ring.

I was sacked by the Civil Service and was lucky to secure temporary positions in clerical jobs. I had also obtained more qualifications at night school. I went to London for two years and was fine as long as I stayed in structured environments such as Civil Service hostels. I did a degree in Social Science and again I had no problems making friends – and by friends I mean friends (I know what friendship means and was insulted to be asked this question by the apparatchiks at a diagnostic clinic I attended). In my degree I got a 2.1 but left with no sense of direction. I thought I enjoyed academic work but, looking back, I may have been fooling myself. I do remember that intense concentration caused headaches and tension. At university I even began to gamble in the refectory and this led to quarrels that almost got me expelled. I also suffered a large panic attack, a phenomena that was to track me for many years. I now began to dread going to bed, as I would hear my heart ringing in my ears and develop a fear (in the existential sense) of an impending attack. As a result I now began to use alcohol in increasing amounts as a soporific.

I couldn't get onto a full-time academic course; instead I took a part-time course and worked as a hospital porter to pay for it. An all-male environment is not for the faint-hearted but my squeamishness was overcome by my anti-authoritarianism and the antics associated with this. In a heavy-drinking fraternity the increased ability to drink heavily myself was sufficient to achieve respect and entry to an inner coterie. We were all pissed and pissed off. Gradually the 'burnt ones', as I call them, were sacked and after three years my time came too.

Jobs now became harder to come by and I thought I could save myself by training to teach. I knew this to be folly, as standing up in front of people had always induced incredible anxiety in me. I was thrown up, like Jonah, into the swarthy streets of Cardiff (which is a book in itself). I hardly attended any classes and all my learning was now done in the pubs of the city. My few coping strategies were sufficient to earn the same kind of kudos as they had done when I was a hospital porter. I met a succession of interesting characters. I had for some time immersed myself in the bowery chic of the 'drunken' poet Charles Bukowski and fancied myself as a connoisseur of low life. I convinced myself there was romance on the streets, and to some extent there was. If there was violence there was also generosity of spirit (and spirits) the like of which I have not met since. I met people who had read Heidegger, Sartre and all the greats of modern and post-modern literature. I met and loved (at the same time as feeling repelled by the poor hygiene) proto-hippies and new-age travellers. I wouldn't say I was welcomed but I was tolerated and protected. I had arrived, spineless and with no nous, in Cardiff and when I left I had at least got a spine and a sense of direction. I overcame my fears of physical intimacy and my descent into the Underworld meant that if I had not returned with Eurydice, I had at least touched bottom and was on my way up.

'Was I cured then?' I hear you ask. Unfortunately I still had my bad temper, restlessness and poor concentration. I was also an alcoholic. I know that because of the withdrawals. In the early 1990s, the attractions of alcohol began to wear off and I began to think more seriously about my future. I had people who were prepared to back my application for teacher training. I got on a PGCE and left Cardiff never to return. I scraped through my PGCE, but I am not teaching (however, that is another story). I have resigned myself (without undue despondency) to my present situation and may never work. I can never seem to pass interviews and my past is a big hole that cannot be covered up.

In 1982 I sought help but found it impossible to motivate myself to attend or go to clinics. In 1985 I sought help again and it was the opinion of the consultant psychiatrist that I had a 'schizoid personality disorder'. I was prescribed an anti-psychotic and an antidepressant but these did no discernable good. Over the next 20 years I intermittently tried all kinds of drugs and therapies, all to no avail. I saw an article in the *Guardian* about Asperger's syndrome, which mentioned a leading professional in the ASD field whom I sought out. My mother and I were sent questionnaires, which I now recognise in the literature on screening. I was given an appointment and my parent and I travelled down to the appointment together. We were almost late and my mother arrived very flustered. This would have been apparent to anyone, but despite her advanced years she wasn't even offered some reassurance or a drink. The interview lasted an hour and I talked a great deal; the rationale for that was to provide as much information as I could as one hour is not a lot of time. The doctor and his assistant did not ask my mother anything, despite the fact that this is meant to be a childhood-onset disorder, nor did they enquire about my childhood. After the hour, we were told to go for lunch and return later that afternoon. When we did, we were seen by the assistant who passed on the diagnosis of 'Asperger's' to me. I have since procured my case notes and a great deal of what I did say was taken out of context, metaphorical statements being taken literally. I have wondered who it was that was supposed to be autistic! There were no treatment recommendations, no suggestions and no follow-up. Travelling home I felt let down and we both felt as if some dreadful deceit had been practised; after all, what was the point of the exercise?

I also sought a diagnosis of ADHD after I saw a different article in the *Guardian* (that paper has a lot to answer for!), which included miraculous stories of the efficacy of Ritalin. Again I sought a diagnosis at a national clinic mentioned. This clinic also requested that I bring my parent; my mother and I travelled the night before the appointment, to be on time for the interview. In the morning I was subject to a battery of 'tests' and then we were told to take a two-hour lunch break. When we returned, I was interviewed by a consultant psychiatrist and my mother was finally interviewed for ten minutes. We had been there for six hours and this elderly lady had sat there for all of that time, only to be interviewed for ten minutes. Towards the end I was very concerned for my mother but I was the only one who was concerned – but, hey, I am the autistic one! I was diagnosed with ADHD and prescribed Ritalin. I found Ritalin to be effective and people who worked with me saw a transformation in me. Unfortunately, I was foolish enough to exceed the one tablet and got some nasty side effects. I am also savvy enough to know that the effects of the tablets will not last a lifetime. I sought a referral to a local psychiatrist, with the stipulation that he should not be sceptical about ADHD in adults, although this subsequently proved not to be the case; he was of the opinion that I had a schizoid personality disorder. I had come full circle.

By this time I was doing an MA in Learning Disability and had the good fortune to have access to DSM-IV (*Diagnostic and Statistical Manual of Mental Disorders*, 4th edition, APA, 1994). I decided to look through it all and see whether I justified the diagnosis of schizoid personality disorder or whether, indeed, I warranted a different diagnosis. It struck me that dysthymia fitted my experiences most accurately, so I did a 'Psychinfo' search for dysthymia and found that Sertraline (a type of antidepressant) was a frequently prescribed medication. I had no problem persuading my GP to prescribe this and since then things have been a lot better. I no longer have chronic concentration problems and constant anger and my life is happier as a result.

What do I make of this long and protracted journey and the many diagnoses and treatments I have received? My view is that the labels I have received have been meaningless and useless. I am what Eysenck would have called an introverted neurotic; the type of person I am was recognised hundreds of years ago and immortalised by Burton in the *Anatomy of Melancholy*. Calling it autism or ASD, ADHD, schizoid personality disorder, dysthymia or anything else has not led to any clinical utility, quite the reverse. The issue is not just what to diagnose but who does the diagnosis. Drugs have helped but there is no value in seeing someone who cannot prescribe or someone who is fixated on one label.

When I saw the leading ASD professional, I had already filled out a screening questionnaire and many of the questions I answered in the affirmative bear an uncanny resemblance to Eysenck's personality inventory. I can see no real value in giving people like myself a specific label or labels. Examples and anecdotes from my life were ripped out of context and metaphors taken literally. I freely admit to sarcasm and verbal cruelty and I suppose that on the surface this indicates a lack of empathy. Conversely I have worked in the care sector and people who have known me have found me kind and considerate. It was my prickliness and insecurity that caused me to be verbally cruel and now that I am not so prickly I no longer have this problem.

I gave the leading ASD professional one example from when I was training to be a teacher. I had a mentor who I had rubbed up the wrong way. I had to keep a diary as part of my professional practice and much to my surprise she asked to see it. I knew of no one else who had been asked to show their diary and therefore had not given too much thought to what I had written in it. In one entry I had referred to her as 'Obergruppenfuhrer Jenny' as I found her manner overbearing. The well-known professional in the ASD clinic seemed to believe I told this to her face.

By the time I went to the ADHD clinic, I was keen to try and get the Asperger's diagnosis removed. The person at the clinic with whom I had initial contact appeared to have no grasp of the vicissitudes of life on the dole. I was expected to go to London on the first train available, stay overnight and then go home again. I was asked questions such as 'What is a friend?', as if I were Frankenstein's monster. I also know (for I submitted a Freedom of Information request) that I was 'scored' for using terms such 'go the extra mile' and 'on the sauce'.

These archaic expressions scored two out of the six points that went towards me reaching the cut-off score. As someone who was brought up a Christian, 'going the extra mile' has been part of my philosophy and 'going on the sauce' seemed to me preferable to saying 'on the piss', as well as being slightly tongue in cheek. Not only was the diagnosis of Asperger's not rescinded, but I was now given an additional diagnosis of pervasive developmental disorder – not otherwise specified (PDD-NOS). Again no recommendations were made, nor any follow-up suggested.

I am what is wrong with psychiatry in miniature. Each person I have seen has adhered to their little hobbyhorse; my interests, needs and preferences have been ignored. In each instance no one has done a follow-up and no one seemed interested in how I got on. What kind of a medical profession is that? Those improvements that have been made in my life have been made through my own endeavours and research. Sometimes it feels like the 'professionals' involved have stood like Mengele at Auschwitz and pointed to the left or the right, leaving me to my fate. From my perspective, their crass insensitivity towards my needs and that of my parent were more autistic than any of my own behaviours.

SAMI TIMIMI

I have come to realise that everyone has a story to tell. How accurate our personal narratives are is perhaps less important than the personal meanings these stories have to us and to those who recount their own meaningful versions of our stories (including mental health professionals' constructions of their patients' narratives). So the following is my abridged version of those aspects of my 'story' that come to my mind, once I came round to the task of writing my personal account for this chapter. In telling this story I am trying to appreciate what led me to seek and be sensitive to non-mainstream ways of understanding those my profession seeks to help. Obviously this is not as powerful as Neil's and Brian's accounts, for I have not found myself at the mercy of psychiatric services' preferred interpretations of my problems (although I did attend personal psychotherapy for a number of years). However, I hope there will be at least some people reading this book who sit on the other side of this human encounter between doctor/expert and patient/client. Hopefully, some of these clinicians may at least begin to consider that there may be another way to understand and be helpful to those who could be diagnosed with autism, without diagnosing them.

I believe that, like most people, my growing-up years had a profound effect on me and helped shape my attitudes, values and habits. I have an Iraqi father and an English mother. I love my parents dearly, see many irritating faults in each of them, but more strengths and characteristics that I admire. My parents met in Bristol, where my father had been sponsored by the then Iraqi regime to do a PhD. An interest in politics, through meetings of the Communist Party, brought them together (I am mindful as I write this that a background interest in leftwing politics and Marxism seems to be one thing that Neil, Brian and I share – perhaps Marx had Aspergers?!). I was born in Bristol, the second oldest of the three boys my parents were to have. We moved to Basra in southern Iraq when I was two years old, which I understand was a real challenge for my mother, as she not only had to cope with a radically different cultural milieu, but also living under the same roof as a hostile mother-in-law who was disappointed that her son had not only rejected a prospective bride she had in mind for him, but worse had gone and married a Brit! My father then worked at the university in Basra, but we did spend a year in Dunblane, Scotland, in 1970 and a year in Southampton in 1976, both due to my father arranging sabbaticals. However, my years in Iraq came to an abrupt end when, as a 14-year-old in the summer of 1978, my elder brother and I were sent to stay with relatives in England to avoid the rapidly deteriorating political situation in Iraq with the beginning of Saddam Hussein's Baath Party era, the war with Iran and compulsory military service age all looming.

Growing up in Iraq was a rich experience. Being embedded in an extended family system meant a ready supply of people, including children to play with and adults to nurture you, a sense of having more than one house that you experienced as 'home' and learning to experience and negotiate relationships with a variety of personalities. From a young age I remember struggling with questions of meaning, trying to get my head around concepts of infinity, distance in light years, and why some people had so little and others such riches. As I entered adolescence I found an environment that was wonderfully receptive to my quizzical mind. Long talks with my devout Shia Muslim cousins, about god, miracles and the Koran would be brought to my parents, who argued (from their Marxist perspective) for the non-existence of deities, arguments that would then be taken back to my cousins or friends, leading to new arguments with them trying to convince me about the existence of god. Looking back, I believe this to have been a strong influence (if you believe a more socio-cultural causative model) or first symptoms of a personality pattern (if you believe a more bio-deterministic model) or excellent training ground (if you don't care about establishing a 'cause') for a pattern that has since followed me into my professional life. Being exposed to strong, confident claims about knowing the 'truth', from polar opposite beliefs, has helped me to realise that quite contradictory meanings, indeed cosmologies, can make perfect sense to different people, and it also instilled in me a deep scepticism for any claims of knowing the 'truth' in the absence of physical proof.

My elder brother and I were told we were leaving to England seven days before we flew out from Iraq in 1978 (the short notice was to stop us, particularly me, from 'blabbing' to our friends, thereby potentially alerting the authorities, particularly as this was the era in which children were being encouraged to 'spy' on others, including their parents). I was initially excited as I saw England as 'modern' and so the thought of going to live there was appealing. I went to live with my grandmother and my brother went to live with my uncle and his family. The reality of my 'new' life began to sink in. My grandmother was a wonderful person, grounded, pragmatic and someone who lived by her Marxist ideals. She cared for me in what was a very difficult year of my life, but, however capable you are, it is hard to fill the gaps that emerge after such a radical change in life. I had not only lost my immediate family, but my extended one and so had gone from a large interconnected web of people who I knew and who knew me, to a small council flat which I shared with my grandmother. My contact with my family was reduced to a weekly phone call and I became increasingly concerned that I may never see my mother, father and younger brother again (and I still find making phone calls causes me anxiety).

Not only was I facing a radical change in lifestyle, but also the confusion of differing expectations and attitudes of my new mid-adolescent peer group. For example, back in Iraq socially constructed gendered expectations of the young formed some clear (if unwritten) rules about how boys and girls were expected to behave now that they were entering the age in which interest in sexuality and sexual drives emerges. Thus gender separation and more clearly defined differing expectations of each gender emerged. So, as a boy starting to turn into a man, having absorbed these cultural messages in Iraq, and following my peers' example, this meant spending time with other males (playing football, making catapults, sometimes falling out and fighting, etc.)

and not showing interest in the fairer sex (as this would be unmanly). As a 14-year-old in the UK, the opposite was now true – the new rule was that if I didn't show interest in girls then that was unmanly, making me a 'sissy' or a 'poof'. Much was different. Pupils were freer to answer back to teachers and punishments for misbehaviour were (by the standards I was used to in Iraq) more liberal (although at that time corporal punishment in the UK was still legal and used); paradoxically, however, peer group culture was a lot more cruel, competitive and hierarchical, with gangs and a pecking order for 'top dog' outside the classroom (which was often the opposite to the top-dog pecking order in terms of academic achievement inside the classroom). There was more 'project' work and less rote learning. In Iraq I was used to monthly exams, in the UK there was virtually none. I struggled to make friends and to find a place where I felt I fitted in, a struggle that has followed me ever since.

Of course my personal story has many, many chapters that trace this, from the time my parents and younger brother arrived in the UK in 1979, through to moving to Southampton, my struggles with school there, early exposure to illicit drug subculture, going to Dundee University (where I studied medicine and simultaneously learnt about surviving independently on a shoestring, excessive individualism, hedonism and deep camaraderie) and, finally, my 'settling down' into the world of work, marriage and family (helped along by seeing an analyst for a few years). But it is to the story of my professional life that I wish to now turn.

My first brush with psychology as a subject was as a first-year medical student. I found the subject vaguely interesting, but rather dry. At the end of the module we had to write an essay on the question 'Is psychology a science?' I recall with amusement that a good friend of mine failed after he decided to argue that it wasn't. A few years later during our psychiatry placement I recall, with less amusement, that I failed the third of four case write-ups we had to do. I had found the psychiatry textbook and lectures rather dull, but I was drawn to the stories the patients I met were telling me. For my first two case write-ups I stuck to the 'formula' we were provided: history, symptoms, differential diagnosis. But this third case moved something in me. She had a diagnosis of schizophrenia, but her story seemed 'pregnant' with meaning. She had developed her 'illness' some years earlier, after her husband had died young and before they had the children that they had wished for. As a childless widow she had then descended into a delusional world of miracle births, divine interventions and having hundreds of 'water-babies' growing unseen to the rest of the world in a river near a local power station. The standard case formulation we were meant to do for our write-up didn't seem to capture anything meaningful, so I went to our main hospital library and looked through their small collection of psychiatry books. Here I came across R.D. Laing's *The Divided Self* (1960). This was what I was looking for, a book by an author who was trying to make the apparently unintelligible and meaningless, intelligible and meaningful. I could see that he was critical of psychiatry as it was practised at the time he was writing (some 27 years prior to the time I was reading it), but, given that it was in the small collection of the main hospital library, I assumed that this famous son of Scotland's ideas were now accepted as relevant, particularly in Scottish universities and hospitals. How wrong I was; my essay was peppered with insights from Laing and quotes from him – the returned marked essay, which was failed, was equally peppered but with red marks and advice to steer clear of R.D. Laing, whose work, I was informed, was not relevant to modern psychiatry. If my 'toing-and-froing' between my cousins and my parents in arguments about god set the paradigm for my general attitude to systematised beliefs, then this first formal brush with psychiatry set the paradigm for my professional career since then.

Since deciding to pursue a career in psychiatry my professional development has been shaped by: my interest in meaning and trying to make sense (and help the people I see make sense) of people's diverse experiences; a quest and ongoing drive to search for answers – not just at the micro level of the personal, but also at the meta and macro levels of the political and cultural (I guess this is the age-old search to try to understand what it means to be human); and a strong scepticism towards claims for the 'truth' that rely on faith and ideology (this is where my scientific training is most valuable, as I refuse to accept lax standards for demonstrating proof). Thus, at various times, I have been drawn to psychoanalysis, systemic theory, post-modern approaches, behavioural approaches and even biological approaches (though the latter two were relatively short-lived interests compared to the former); with each approach, enthusiastic embracing has been followed by slow realisation of its short-comings, leading to scepticism, rejection (in the main), then slow acceptance of its utility (rather than grand narrative powers) in certain theoretical and clinical situations.

I have done lots of training to a certain depth, on each occasion stopping short of completing my course in that modality as my 'allegiance' to the specific school of therapy faltered. Thus, I have trained in psychodynamic psychotherapy, psychodynamic group therapy, psychodynamic child psychotherapy, family therapy, hypnosis and a variety of other briefer studies (such as solution-focused therapy and client-directed outcome-informed approach). I also read authors and attend conferences from a variety of perspectives, including those from 'allied' disciplines such as sociology, anthropology, cultural studies, philosophy, etc. I have met many wonderful colleagues and forged a large number of close ties with many like-minded people, both psychiatrists and non-psychiatrists. I have also encountered (and still do) some (here it is nearly all psychiatrists) who continue to wish to put red marks through my work, have hounded me in my day-to-day practice, to the point that some believe I should be 'struck off'.

This accumulation of experiences has, as always, many layers of interconnected meanings, but I have often wondered how my attitudes and behaviours could be categorised. So, recently, I sat down with my wife and asked her to fill in a screening questionnaire for autism (the autism-spectrum quotient [AQ]) about me. I asked my wife (a non-medical professional) to fill this in in such a way as to try to avoid any bias my knowing what would be rated as autistic symptoms could introduce. There are 50 questions and for each question the person being 'tested' rates the question as 'definitely agree', 'slightly agree', 'slightly disagree', 'definitely disagree'. Example questions include:

- If I try to imagine something, I find it very easy to create a picture in my mind.
- Other people frequently tell me that what I've said is impolite, even though I think it is polite.
- I tend to notice details that others do not.
- I would rather go to a library than to a party.
- When I talk, it isn't always easy for others to get a word in edgewise.
- I don't particularly enjoy reading fiction.
- I would rather go to the theatre than to a museum.
- I know how to tell if someone listening to me is getting bored.
- People often tell me that I keep going on and on about the same thing.

Kitty, my wife, struggled with many of the questions (e.g., I don't particularly enjoy reading fiction – well, it depends on the book!). Such decontextualised questions that seek to illuminate inner qualities, as if these can be separated from the web of meaningful relationships and the environment more broadly, are always open to such broad interpretations. Anyway, the average score for the AQ in the non-autistic general population is said to be about 16, with around 80 per cent of those diagnosed with autism scoring 32 or higher. My score (as rated by my wife) was 30. My wife's score (as rated by me) was 13. Make of that what you wish.

In my five or so years as a trainee in child psychiatry in the early to mid-1990s I came across two cases diagnosed as having autism. Both were more typical of earlier notions (such as Kanner's), had severe learning difficulties, little language, a lot of repetitive behaviours and had acquired little capacity for independence. By the time of writing this, having been a consultant for over 12 years now, most children who I inherit (who have previously seen another psychiatrist or paediatrician and are being referred for follow-up with me) these days, seem to have been diagnosed with autism at some point. To me there is little that these individuals share in their life histories, presenting behaviours, or types of therapeutic approaches required, beyond the label that they have received. Many had been also diagnosed with other 'disorders', most notably ADHD. My impression is that when treatment for (say) ADHD seems not to have helped or has worn off and the problems are returning, then some clinicians explain this by concluding that this is because the child is also 'co-morbid' for autism.

Thus, I have met charming young men, who are described as the life and soul of the party, but are disorganised daydreamers; sullen boys who have their struggling insecure single mother wrapped around their little finger excusing them from all sorts of responsibilities on the grounds of their son's 'disability'; anxious young lads who've witnessed severe domestic violence and cling on to their parent worrying what might happen to their mother if they let them out of their sight for too long; clumsy boys who are desperate to have friends, but for whom poor 'ball skills' mean that they are never picked to play in teams; sad and angry young women who have developed a close and dependent relationship with one parent, having survived together traumatic early childhoods; sons of mothers who have been sexually abused, with these mothers' being left with an understandable fear of touching and cuddling their sons; families attempting to gain a label for their perfectly ordinary son, having received disability living allowance for their other son after he was diagnosed with autism (and in these hard times who can blame them?); teens with a great sense of humour, but who were stubborn and enjoyed provoking their teacher; and so on. Everyone has a story, just as I, as a mental health professional have my own story to construct about their story, which, given the high status particularly of doctors, will have a large and, with autism conceptualised as a life-long disorder, a lasting impact. Of particular concern is the frequency with which I have come across young people who have been labelled with an ASD and who have a history of trauma and/or abuse. To me such practice, that renders not only the traumatic stories irrelevant, but also sometimes overtly (as well as covertly) blames the victim for their plight (e.g., because of his autism he was too difficult to parent, *causing* arguments, rejection and breakdown of life at home). To my mind, the desire to diagnose is therefore sometimes not only a distraction from talking about and understanding the more difficult things to talk about and understand, but renders clinical practice vulnerable to unintentionally blaming the victim. This means that the clinician should always think carefully about the ramifications of labelling someone as having a life-long 'disability' on the basis of an astrological (-style) questionnaire and a cursory examination. It's been so many years since I last diagnosed anyone with autism that I can't remember doing it.

By diagnosing autism the clinician who did the diagnosing has, in just about every case I have encountered, in my opinion, failed to discover the cause or meaning of the young person's problems – instead they created a new one. The diagnoses were not made following any supporting physical or other objective evidence; rather they were based on a subjective belief (as passed on by their professional training), which then constructs a meaning for the problems – in other words it provides a new story to explain the story the young person and their family told. When administering an autism rating questionnaire or tool to confirm this diagnosis, another story about the professional's story of the family's story is told – that this questionnaire/tool objectively measures something called autism. This questionnaire may claim to have validity and reliability as a result of being 'tested' on samples of 'autistic' subjects – another story saying that this questionnaire has been adequately tested to prove that it measures what it's supposed to measure. I could go on to talk about the literature on reliability and validity, the different sorts of reliability and validity there are, how useful each is and what they each mean – a story about a story about a story about the professional's story about the family's story. With each layer of story the professional moves one step further away from the original narrative.

This is the potential problem for autism at the human level and at the level of the clinical encounter. There is no state-of-the-art rocket science going on here; it is merely that psychiatry, being a branch of the high-status medical profession, has been allowed the cultural privilege to successfully claim that its own brand of mysticism represents a scientific truth in the same way that possession by demons is believed to be a true explanation for many mental health problems in cultures that privilege a more spiritual cosmology (although possession by fixed internal bad and evil genes gives less hope for recovery than possession by temporary external bad and evil spirits). The desire to categorise human behaviours into DSM categories, despite the lack of utility for such categories (in terms of them telling us anything about unique causes, treatments and outcomes), means that what is ultimately an academic exercise leaves a gap in the ability of the clinician to listen to the uniqueness of the patient's narrative. It also means a 'dumbing down' of diagnostic skills (in the broadest sense of diagnosis meaning to 'characterise' a problem), as real-life processes become irrelevant under the weight of the assumed explanatory power of a fictional concept (autism).

These questions about the social construction not only of subjective experience, but also of biology itself are the sorts of things I have felt need a lot more unpacking and understanding in my field (child psychiatry), as I feel labels like ADHD and autism have a life of their own, narrowing people's expectations of the labelled (including the expectations of the person with the label) into a kind of 'autistic' (if I can be ironic) tunnel vision and a place where, as far as I can see, it must be difficult at times to feel at ease and accepting of yourself, given that these are definitions of deficit. In my practice I now spend more time noticing the exceptions, those many bits of the story that don't fit with the 'autism' stereotype, rather than focusing on those small bits that apparently do. Not uncommonly this has eventually led to many under my care being 'un-diagnosed' (through their own choice) and losing their autism (hopefully for good).

I
AUTISM
THE HISTORICAL AND CULTURAL CONTEXT

3
HISTORY OF AUTISM

In order to understand what we think childhood isn't we need first to understand what we believe childhood is. Put another way, to appreciate how we define what makes an abnormal child (such as the ASD child) we need to understand how we define a 'normal' child.

WESTERN CHILDHOODS

To help us understand the background that made it possible for autism to be invented and become popular, we need to put a context around the history of autism and first need to look at the changing environment and changing beliefs about the nature of childhood within which it developed. This means examining how our beliefs about what constitutes a 'normal' childhood in the culture that invented autism – Western culture – developed (see Timimi, 2005, for a more detailed and fully referenced account).

While the immaturity of children is a biological fact, the ways in which we understand this immaturity and make it meaningful is a fact of culture. Members of any society carry within themselves a working idea about childhood and its nature. They may not openly talk about their ideas, or write about it, or even think of it as an issue, but they act upon their assumptions in all of their dealings with, fears for and expectations of their children. Our ideas about what makes a normal or disordered child can, therefore, be seen as connected to current political, economic, moral or indeed health concerns.

Each historical period creates its own ideas about what normal childhood and child-rearing methods should be like; in other words each historical period creates its own novel version of the child. The developing images of childhood are not simply abandoned over time; fragments from each period are included in the next period's ideas of childhood. Looking at the history of childhood in any culture (as well as between cultures) we can see that our ideas about what makes a normal or abnormal child and/or child-rearing practices are neither timeless nor universal but instead rooted in the past and reshaped in the present.

Philippe Ariès's 1962 book *Centuries of Childhood* had a major impact in developing a new understanding of how ideas about childhood have changed in Western culture over recent centuries, particularly because of the boldness of its basic conclusion – that in medieval society the idea of childhood did not exist. Norbert Elias had already anticipated Ariès's arguments in his 1939 book *The Civilizing Process*, in which Elias argues that the visible difference between children and adults (psychologically and socially) increases in the course of the (as Elias saw it) 'civilising' process. However, Ariès went further and illustrated the great variability of human society's attitudes to children and child-rearing practices, not just by examining non-Western cultures, but also by referring to the familiar Western European past.

Ariès argued that the modern idea of childhood as a separate life stage emerged in Europe between the 15th and 18th centuries, at the same time as modern ideas of family, home, privacy and individuality were developing. Ariès believed that before the 15th century children past the dependent age of infancy were seen simply as miniature adults and their socialisation took place within such an environment. Ariès was not saying that this is necessarily a bad thing, if anything he was suggesting the reverse, that modern Western culture insists on a period of quarantine (for example through education) before allowing young people to join society. Even if we modify Ariès's bold idea and acknowledge that every known society has its own beliefs and practices that in some respect mark off children from adults, the importance of his book is the understanding that there are many forms of childhood and that they tend to be socially and historically specific.

When we look at the history of childhood in the West we can see changes occurring in all aspects of childhood and child-rearing. For example, in medieval Europe, child-rearing was seen as being a mother's responsibility for the first seven or so years of that child's life. However, during the Renaissance period in 15th-century Italy, the emphasis began to change and the father–child relationship came to be seen as the most important in child-rearing. It was the father's responsibility to choose and hire a wet nurse, to watch over their children's development and to thoughtfully interpret their child's actions so as to understand and shape their future. An influential writer at this time was Dutchman Desiderius Erasmus. Erasmus placed considerable emphasis on early education and attacked those who, in his view, allowed children to be pampered by their mothers or wet nurses out of what he saw as a false spirit of tenderness. Instead he thought fathers had to take control of their children's (in particular their son's) upbringing, in order to develop their child's character in a way that would, in his view, bring them closer to reflecting the divine.

Then, in the 18th century, the followers of Rousseau (see below) attacked the traditions of the time that encouraged fathers to take charge of child-rearing, insisting that the father's ambition and harshness were more harmful to a child than the blind affection of mothers. Rousseau asserted that children have a right to be happy in childhood and even went on to suggest that childhood may be the best time of life. With this Rousseau-inspired 'romantic movement' gaining a foothold in popular culture by the end of the 18th century, mothers regained the predominance they held in the Middle Ages and child-rearing once again became a predominantly female occupation.

So, in the example above, we can see that in the space of a few hundred years the dominant belief about who should be the most important parent changed from mothers to fathers and then back to mothers again. There are many similar examples of beliefs switching from one pole to the other. But let us return now to following a rough time-line of Western history.

After the medieval period when, according to historians like Ariès, children were viewed as miniature adults, a new attitude towards children began to emerge in the late 17th century and early 18th century in Europe. The story of European childhood in the 18th century is framed by the writings of John Locke at its beginning and Jean-Jacques Rousseau and the 'romantic movement' towards its end. During this century the cultural discourse began to see childhood not just in terms of preparation for something else, whether adulthood or heaven, but as a life stage to be valued in its own right.

Historians believe that modern, Western ideas about children can thus be traced to the late 17th century, when Locke (1693) published his influential book *Some Thoughts Concerning Education* (see Locke, 1989). In this book Locke proposed that children should be viewed as individuals waiting to be moulded into shape by adults. In the mid-18th century, Rousseau (1762) published his highly influential book

Emile in which he argued that children were born with innate goodness that could be corrupted by certain kinds of education. These two books were crucial in paving the way for a new focus, in European culture, on childhood, which was now being viewed as having separate needs and expectations than adulthood. By the mid-19th century, childhood was viewed as a distinct life-stage, requiring protection and fostering through school education.

Through the second half of the 19th century, this growing idea – that all children need to be in schools – began to take root for several reasons. First, many children were at that time being forced to work long hours in poor conditions for little reward. The scale and intensity of exploitation of 'factory children' appalled many critics, and campaigners began to promote a new idea of childhood, where children were not exploited in this manner and where work was no longer viewed as a normal expectation of children. Second, there was the development of the first mass working-class political movements that were also complaining about the dehumanisation of their children. This resulted in the middle and upper classes becoming concerned about the potential for social unrest and thus more focused on the task of keeping public order. Lively debates occurred, with middle-class campaigners voicing the fear that the natural order of parents, and particularly fathers, in supporting their children, was being undermined by the demand for child labour in factories at the expense of adult males. This led to a fear in the ruling classes that the neglect of children could easily lead, not only to damnation of souls, but also to a social revolution. Third, the growing economic success of industrial capitalism had resulted in a growing demand for a semi-skilled, skilled and educated work force, which lessened the economic need for child labour and increased the economic need for education.

So, for the reformers the idea of effective schooling now became important, not just for the new idea about what children 'need', but also for economic and political reasons. These changes also paved the way for an important new development; that of introducing the state into the parent–child relationship. Not only had the reformers put aside the financial hardships many working-class families would suffer as a result of the ending of the child labourer, but, in addition, by changing our ideas of what children were thought to 'need', the parents of families who continued to send children to work were now seen as exploiting their own children. In other words, the message this produced was that if children were useful and produced money, they were not being properly loved.

By the beginning of the 20th century children in Western, capitalist states were now seen as individuals on whom the state could have a bigger influence than their families. Now that children were all in schools they also became readily available to a variety of professionals for all sorts of 'scientific' surveys. Professional interest in the idea of child development grew and the scientific study of the individual child was encouraged so that 'guiding principles' could be offered to parents and teachers. This now began to give the medical and psychological professions greater authority in defining what childhood is, which in turn began a process that helped popularise the view that childhood is marked by stages in 'normal' development, and that it is to such professionals that we must turn in order to define these stages. Thus, doctors and psychologists began to build a new set of assumptions about what constituted normal childhood development and normal parenting. At the same time the state was becoming more powerful and more able to interfere in family life through new laws that followed a debate about children's rights and an assumption that only the state could enforce these rights.

Before the onset of the Second World War, Western society still viewed child-rearing mainly in terms of discipline and authority of the parents (particularly the father). This pre-war belief was grounded in behaviourism and stressed the importance of parents controlling their children's instincts (children's instincts were seen as dangerous to society if not properly controlled) in order for children to grow up with the 'good' habits of behaviour that were believed to be necessary for a pro-social and productive life. During and after the Second World War anxiety about the effect on children of discipline and authority increased, the concern being that authoritarian discipline could lead to the sort nightmare society that Nazi Germany represented. Medical and psychological professional groups that spoke about the child as an individual and which favoured a more open and sympathetic approach to child-rearing, encouraged humane discipline of the child through guidance and understanding, helped popularise new ideals for child-rearing, eventually resulting in the ideals of the 'permissive' culture influencing mainstream approaches to child-rearing.

The 'permissiveness' model saw parent–child relationships more in terms of pleasure and play than discipline and authority. Parents now had to give up their traditional authority in order for children to develop individuality, autonomy and self-esteem. In addition, while the pre-war model prepared children for the workplace within a society of rations and economic depressions, the post-war model prepared them to become pleasure-seeking consumers within a prosperous new economy.

Childhood had now become a key metaphor through which adults spoke about their own social and political concerns. Thus permissiveness as regards child-rearing was allowing not only new identities to be given to children, but also to adults. Mothers and fathers were responding to these changing ideas about childhood and child-rearing and seeing this as a way for them to 'express' themselves more fully. Parental obligations were now giving way to the culture of fun and permissiveness for all.

Changing economic circumstances also led to enormous changes in the organisation of family life. More mothers were working and thus a renegotiation of power within the family was taking place. The economic demands of successful market economies were resulting in greater numbers of families moving, less time for family life and a breakdown of extended family networks. Many families (particularly those headed by young women) were now isolated from traditional sources of child-rearing information (such as direct advice and support from older generations). As a result child-rearing guides and books took on a greater importance, allowing for a more dramatic change in parenting styles than would have been likely in more rooted and stable communities. This resulted in greater 'ownership' by professionals of the knowledge base about children, childhood and the task of parenting. For advice on how to bring up children, people were now turning to professionals (including books written by them) as often as their own families.

The new child-centred permissive culture was also good for consumer capitalism. An industry of children's toys, books, fun educational material and so on developed. With the expansion of this consumerism and a more affluent population, permissive beliefs about children and child-rearing embraced pleasure as a positive motivation for exploration and learning.

In the 1980s and 1990s, the monetarist policies of Ronald Reagan and Margaret Thatcher had a big impact on many aspects of Western culture. Children and families were often the losers in the new policies that emphasised a more aggressive version of free-market capitalism at the same time as reducing and cutting back on social supports for those at the bottom end of the financial hierarchy. This new political ideology has since affected not only Western culture but has been exported worldwide and was (and still is) in service of capital following a period of decline in Western economies. More parents were now forced to work for longer hours, and state support, particularly for children and families, was harshly cut resulting in widespread child poverty and the creation of a new under-class. We are still digesting the impact and effects of the recent global 'credit crunch' and will have to wait and see what impacts it will have on children and their families.

With the increase in the number of divorces and of two working parents, fathers and mothers are around their children for less of the day. As kids are forced to withdraw into their own culture the free market exploits this, preying on their boredom and desire for stimulation. In such an environment poor children are constantly confronted with their shortcomings by media that tells them they are deficient without this or that accessory. In this unhappy isolation Western children respond to the market's push to 'adultify' them (in other words turn them into miniature adults), at the same time as the culture of self-gratification can turn adults towards what some consider more 'childish' pursuits. Thus, children respond to these new cultural conditions by entering into the world of adult entertainments earlier and often without adult supervision. This is confirmed by studies that find that the modern Western child (or some might say the post-modern Western child) is sexually knowledgeable and has early experience of drugs and alcohol.

Some commentators argue that as a result childhood in the West is being eroded, lost or indeed has suffered a strange death. Thus, our traditional ideas about childhood are disappearing as children have gained access to the world of adult information resulting in a blurring of boundaries between what is considered adulthood and what is considered childhood, leading to children coming to be viewed as, in effect, miniature adults once again. For example, we now have a fashion industry of children's clothing modelled on adult ranges and the gradual replacement of traditional street games by organised junior sport leagues, such as football leagues starting with the under-sevens.

One result of these changes in families and lifestyles has been the development of some core tensions and ambivalent feelings about children. The children's rights movements see childhood as being at risk and needing safeguarding against 'abuse' by adults (often without noticing how much the children's rights movement has already blurred the boundaries between what is considered adulthood and childhood), at the same time as seeing childhood as needing strengthening by developing children's character and ability to socialise, empathise and reason. In other words, on the one hand childhood needs to be preserved and on the other hand children have to be made older than their years. This contradiction runs through our modern beliefs about childhood innocence; we desire to keep children 'innocent' and we want to help children to move beyond it, we want to 'coddle' the child and we want to 'discipline' the child.

At the same time there has been a growing concern that children themselves have become the danger, with children being viewed as deviant and violent trouble-makers, despite coming from a generation who are perceived to have been given the best of everything. Thus, by the beginning of the new millennium our vision in the West of childhood is a polarised one: on the one hand we have victimised 'innocent' children who need rescuing; on the other we have impulsive, aggressive, anti-social and sexual children who are a threat to society. Just as children are polarised, so are parents, who are now set impossible standards by many professionals including the 'child savers', with many parents finding themselves afraid they will be viewed as potentially abusive parents by child welfare professionals. Being viewed as a 'normal' child and a 'normal' parent has arguably, become, harder than ever to achieve.

The common thread through both these visions of 'childhood at risk' and 'children as the risk' is the suggestion that modern society has seen a collapse of adult authority (both morally and physically). This collapse is reflected in the growth in parental spending on children and the endless search by parents for emotional gratification for their children. As we repeatedly hear these increasing concerns about children's development in the media and from parents, teachers, doctors and governments, so different potential causes for this are identified and blamed. Fingers have pointed towards the role of the family, particularly mothers, the genetic make-up of the child and the nature of schooling environments. Negative judgements about children and their families have become harsher; such that parents and children feel ever more closely observed and 'under the microscope'.

While parents are feeling the pressure to constantly scrutinise their parenting in order to measure up to these high expectations, schools have also had to respond to these double pressures. The result at the individual child level has been a mushrooming of explanations locating the cause of these perceived problems with children's behaviour, within the individual child. This results in the development of a new belief about the cause of the worries we have about children – that they are caused, not by our changing ideas about childhood, parenting, schooling and a narrowing of what we consider to be a 'normal' childhood, but instead by something going wrong in the child's genes that causes a 'chemical imbalance' in the child's brain or a 'neurodevelopmental' disability affecting the development of their brains.

It is within this contextual background that we wish to situate the history of the development of the concept of autism, and it is to this history we now turn.

AUTISM BEFORE KANNER

Any 'history' of autism is complicated by a lack of clarity of just what it is. In reviewing the history of autism before 'autism' was first formally defined, three strands at least are worth mentioning: retrospective diagnosing of historical figures, what services dealt with those who may have had (by today's standards) an ASD and the development of the concept of autism prior to becoming a diagnosis.

Retrospective diagnosing of historical figures

The retrospective diagnosing of historical figures such as Einstein and Newton as being autistic is based on the idea that we have always had people with ASDs, it's just that in the past it was not recognised as such. There are many authors and websites who have claimed that autism as a condition has afflicted people for centuries, with speculation on various historical figures who may have been autistic becoming rife. In books such as Fitzgerald's (2003) on creativity and autism, *Autism and Creativity: Is there a Link Between Autism in Men and Exceptional Ability?*, all kinds of individuals are brought out from the cupboard of history and given a retrospective diagnosis of autism or an ASD. In these books and articles, apart from the fact that they cannot have been considered gregarious, in our opinion, little evidence is forthcoming to substantiate the existence of the kind of impairments that were said to be indicative of autism in the childhoods of the individuals concerned. For example, Sir Keith Joseph is one of the individuals deemed to be autistic, yet Joseph is reported to have suffered a great deal of guilt over the ramifications of his economic policies (see Denham and Garnett, 2001), which is more than can be said for Margaret Thatcher! It is only now that we have dreamt up ASD that we can look back and start labelling all manner of those previously deemed to be part of the 'great and the good' as having been afflicted with a 'neurodevelopmental' disorder. ASD simply didn't exist until very recently and was therefore an irrelevant way of interpreting what happened in these people's lives.

What services dealt with those who may have had (by today's standards) an ASD?

In looking at state and healthcare practices that existed prior to the creation of the descriptive category of autism we may be able to speculate about what used to happen (regarding service involvement) in those who could be diagnosed with an ASD. By the early 20th century, despite the advent of mass education, autism as a concept was still a long way off. As Jones (1972) has argued, prior to 1880 the 'lunatic' and the 'idiot' (terms of that era) were largely lumped together. A whole raft of legislation was enacted from 1880–1913 as a result of the challenges faced by the new forms of democracy; part of this was to gain a greater sense of social control over a section of society deemed to be 'deviant' but not criminal. The 1913 Mental Deficiency Act concerned itself mainly with the administration of the 'Mental Deficient'. The 1913 Act had four categories: idiots, imbeciles, feeble-minded and moral defectives. The latter category had a particular focus on girls and young women (e.g., those who got pregnant out of wedlock). The male moral defective in the culture of the time was of little interest or importance for legislators. It was the naivety of the girl and the links between her progeny and social problems that were of concern to the reformers of the day. The 'idiots' were deemed the least educable and the 'feeble-minded' the most educable of the mentally deficient. Separate schools were created for the 'mental deficient' whom, it was felt, could be educated, while others were often put in homes. However, there was something of a trade-off between the interventionists and the non-interventionists and although regulation of family life by the state was growing, the state's interference in the family at this time was mainly where the domestic hearth had decided that it could no longer nurture its young. Thus, prior to the creation of the diagnosis of 'autism' and the subsequent mass marketing of this concept, apart from those with moderate to severe learning difficulties, governments and services had little interest in this group.

The development of the concept of autism prior to becoming a diagnosis

It was Bleuler (1911) who coined the term 'autistic' to denote schizophrenic individuals who were catatonic and evidenced no interest in other human beings:

> The...schizophrenics who have no more contact with the outside world live in a world of their own. They have encased themselves

with their desires and wishes...they have cut themselves off as much as possible from any contact with the external world. This detachment from reality with the relative and absolute predominance of the inner life, we term autism. (http://www.pubmedcentral.nih.gov/ articlerender.fcgi?artid=1489853, accessed 10 December 2008)

Autism and autistic stem from the Greek word 'autos', meaning self. Thus the term autism originally referred to a basic disturbance found in schizophrenia (another term introduced by Bleuler) characterised by an extreme withdrawal of oneself from the fabric of social life.

In the early 1900s, psychologist and psychoanalyst Carl Gustav Jung (who, early in his career, worked with Bleuler) introduced the well-known personality types, 'extroverts' and 'introverts'. Jung saw the activity of the extrovert as being directed towards the external world and that of the introvert towards the inward world. The extrovert is characteristically the active person who is most content when surrounded by people – carried to the extreme such behaviour appears to constitute an irrational flight into society, where the extrovert's feelings are acted out. The introvert, on the other hand, is normally a contemplative individual who enjoys solitude and the inner life of ideas and the imagination. Severe introversion was now believed to be characteristic of autism in some forms of schizophrenia (Jung, 1923). Jung, however, did not suggest strict classification of individuals as extroverted or introverted, since he believed each person has tendencies in both directions, although one direction generally predominates.

KANNER, ASPERGER AND THE EARLY DEFINITIONS

Autism, as we think of it today, was first used by the psychiatrist Leo Kanner in 1943 to describe a group of children who had previously been depicted as emotionally disturbed and intellectually impaired. Kanner observed the behaviour of 11 children (eight males and three females) at the Johns Hopkins Hospital in Baltimore, and suggested that their symptoms formed a unique 'syndrome', which he termed 'autistic disturbances of affective contact'. He characterised the children as possessing, from the very beginning of life, what he thought of as an extreme 'autistic' aloneness. The following year, another psychiatrist, Hans Asperger, published 'Autistic Psychopathy in Childhood' (Asperger, 1944). The article presented case studies of several children whom he described as examples of a particular and recognisable type of child. Asperger's definition of autism or, as he called it 'autistic psychopathy', was far wider than Kanner's, and included many children with no easily recognisable intellectual impairment. Both Kanner and Asperger believed that the children they were describing suffered from a fundamental disturbance that gave rise to highly characteristic problems. At the time of writing it, Asperger's paper, written in German during the Second World War, was largely ignored.

Kanner believed that he had delineated a new syndrome which he described as characterised by 'extreme autistic aloneness'. All of the children he described appeared to have little or no interest in other human beings. Kanner (1943) reported that as the children approached puberty their lack of sociability diminished to some degree. He also reported that some of the parents also lacked expressive affect, noting that some had reared their children in a formulaic way using child-rearing textbooks. However, he noted that the size of the sample was too small to make any substantive generalisations.

By 1955 Kanner had reported a total of 120 cases of what he described as 'infantile autism'. He differentiated this condition from childhood schizophrenia as he felt autism was evident almost from birth. He included a sub-group of children who appeared to have an initial normal development followed by regression. Kanner alludes to cases in other countries but reports a lack of agreement over definition. He also reported that in one third of cases the prognosis is better, than it is for the rest and found a gender ratio of 4:1 in favour of males. Kanner, writing with Eisenberg (1956), concludes their article by hypothesising about aetiology, stating:

> There is little likelihood that a single etiologic is solely responsible for the pathology of the behaviour. Arguments that counter pose 'hereditary' versus 'environmental' as antithetical terms are fundamentally in error. Operationally, they are interpenetrating concepts. The effects of chromosomal aberrations can be mimicked in the phenotype by environmental pathogens, and genetic factors require for their complete manifestation suitable environmental conditions.
> (Kanner and Eisenberg, 1956: 563)

One might have hoped that the caution regarding the cause of autism, as expressed by Kanner and Eisenberg in 1956, might still be found nowadays. Kanner was keen to differentiate autism from childhood schizophrenia on the basis of age of onset and a lack of hallucinations. Psychiatrists, at least in Britain, however, who were well aware that such symptoms could manifest themselves in childhood, believed some of these behaviours might be risk factors for the subsequent development of schizophrenia.

In 1951 Mildred Creak, a British psychiatrist, wrote a seminal article on childhood psychosis. In it she describes 16 cases of 'childhood psychosis', which she believed were comparable to Kanner's cases. She states that all of her cases are 'autistic', but at this stage, for her, this is a description rather than a diagnosis. Creak's descriptive criteria were subsequently used as being coterminous with autism.

Meanwhile, during the mid-1940s, American psychiatrist Bruno Bettelheim who directed the Chicago-based Orthogenic School for children with emotional problems, put forward the idea that children who presented with 'autistic'-type symptoms, had been raised in non-stimulating environments during the first few years of their lives, when language and motor skills develop. He saw parents' unresponsiveness to their child as an underlying cause of autistic behaviour (Wing, 1988). Bettelheim's psychological explanation, resulted in the theory commonly referred to as the 'refrigerator parents' (particularly the mother) theory of the cause for autistic symptoms, a thesis that remained popular throughout the 1950s and 1960s (Gardner, 2000).

The first epidemiological study of this new diagnosis was published in 1966 and used the term 'autistic conditions' (Lotter, 1966a and b). The criteria used to diagnose 'autistic conditions' was that developed by a working party headed by Mildred Creak (*British Medical Journal*, 1961). Creak had continued to write about 'autistic' children, but referred to them as having 'childhood psychosis'. Her detailed description of 'childhood psychosis' led to the adoption of these criteria and eventually their acceptance as being good descriptions of 'autism' once 'childhood psychosis' was abandoned as a diagnostic term. It is not clear how much these children had in common with each other or with Kanner's children. By the time that Lotter had conducted his epidemiological study, it seems apparent that the issue of classification constituted something of a problem. In determining what constituted a case of 'autism' Lotter (1966a) utilised Creak's criteria for childhood psychosis as being coterminous with autism although he also makes it clear that his 'cases' were not necessarily comparable with Kanner's cases.

Lotter (1966a and b) screened all children aged eight, nine or ten years (78,000) on a chosen census day (1 January 1964), who were living in the former English county of Middlesex. He identified 35 children he considered had 'autistic conditions'. Of the 35 children,

15 were described as having 'nuclear' autism; that is, they had social aloofness and elaborate repetitive routines, both to a very marked degree. The remaining 20 were said to have 'non-nuclear' autism, having similar symptoms but without key characteristics being present to the same degree as in the nuclear group. A third group of 26 children, who had some autistic behaviour but not sufficient to be diagnosed as nuclear or non-nuclear autism, were retained for comparison. Sixty per cent of the parents of the nuclear group were in the Registrar General's social classes I and II. Two-thirds of children had IQs below 55 and only five had IQs above 80. From this study, Lotter arrived at a prevalence figure of 4.5 per 10,000 (2 per 10,000 for 'nuclear' autism) with a gender distribution of 2.4 to 1, males to females (compared to 1.7 to 1 for those classified as 'mentally subnormal').

Also in 1966 a book called *Early Childhood Autism*, edited by J.K. Wing, was published. Wing presents some case studies of children who had a plethora of severe developmental issues, but when some of these children developed speech they are described as becoming more sociable and affectionate. The issue of whether the children being described in the literature (for example by Kanner, Creak, Bettelheim, Lotter and then Wing) as 'autistic' represented a distinct grouping (such as having a characteristic aetiology, course, outcomes or particular interventions that they require, compared to others such as the mentally subnormal group as a whole) is of relevance to the question of reliability. It seems that from its conception, and despite being a much rarer and more carefully defined syndrome, even in the early days it is difficult to know how much the cases defined as 'autistic' represent a discrete group with some common (presumably biologically based) processes that differentiated them from other children.

As we have mentioned, in 1944 Hans Asperger described a number of children whom he labelled as having 'autistic psychopathy'. Few of them had the stereotypies of the cases described by Kanner. The children described by Asperger were all separated from their parents and were institutionalised. Unlike Kanner, Asperger's paper provoked little interest in academic circles of the time. That was soon to change.

FROM AUTISM TO ASD

In the 1970s Lorna Wing, a London-based epidemiological psychiatrist, observed that autistic traits could occur in varying degrees of severity, and saw a similarity in children who presented with less severe or obvious forms of autism to the children described by Hans Asperger back in the 1940s. This revisiting of Asperger's ideas led to the expansion of the category of autism through the notion of the 'autistic spectrum' (Wing, 1981, 1991). Dr Lorna Wing's new direction intersected with Michael Rutter's and the basis for the expansion of the concept of autism far beyond its original status as a rare and serious condition associated with multiple impairments, was built. Given these two academics' role in setting up the type of discourses necessary in order for autism to 'develop' from a rare disorder to one that is now regarded as affecting about 1 per cent of the population or more, it is worth spending a little time analysing these two authors' contribution and arguments.

Dr Lorna Wing

Lorna Wing is the daughter of J.K. Wing (a key figure in schizophrenia research and an advocate for the notion of the schizophrenia spectrum). Whether her father's interest in the notion of a 'schizophrenia spectrum' played any part in Dr Wing's similar enthusiasm for the autism spectrum is open to speculation. Dr Wing gave birth to a child, later diagnosed with autism, in the 1950s and so, understandably, she would have been particularly sensitive to any notion that autism was caused by having 'refrigerator' parenting, a notion that was to become popular in the 1960s (see above). Dr Wing joined with other parents of autistic children to found the National Autistic Society (NAS) in the United Kingdom in 1962. In 1976 Dr Wing conducted one of the first epidemiological surveys on autism and in 1979 she wrote (together with her colleague Dr Judith Gould) a seminal piece entitled 'Severe Impairments of Social Interaction and Associated Abnormalities in Children: Epidemiology and Classification' (Wing and Gould, 1979). It is in this paper that reference is made to three behaviours (the now familiar triad of symptoms) that she believed differentiated one group of people with severe abnormalities from another.

Wing and Gould (1979) begin by pointing out that the history of classification of these behaviours has been unsatisfactory (at least to them). Interestingly, they make no reference to the work of Mildred Creak (see above), an important figure in the history of child psychiatry and the study of autism, or to the standard works on 'mental deficiency' (the term in use at that time). A cursory glance through books of that era on mental deficiency (such as Clarke and Clarke, 1965) would have provided an alternative insight into the disparate range of behaviours associated with mental retardation or mental deficiency, which included most of the behaviours now being proposed by Wing and Gould for the new autistic triad of symptoms.

Wing and Gould (1979) articulated three objectives for their research. These were a) to estimate the prevalence of the three types of abnormality (the triad of symptoms), b) to assess whether these abnormalities could be sub-grouped and c) to investigate how these related to mental retardation. In devising a system of classification from this they appeared to minimise the importance of physical or cognitive disability in the screened population. They also chose to ignore age of onset. These latter criteria had been deemed to be important in earlier papers by, for example, Rutter (1972). The study looked at all children under 15 in an area of London. After screening, children were split on the basis of the extent of their social impairments. A 'socially impaired' group (more than half of whom were severely retarded) and a comparison group of 'sociable severely mentally retarded' children were identified. Mutism (not speaking) or echolalia (repeating what is said to you), and repetitive behaviours were found in almost all the 'socially impaired' children, but also, although to a less marked extent, in the 'sociable severely mentally retarded' group. Organic conditions were found more often in the 'socially impaired' group. The relationships between mental retardation, autism and other conditions involving social impairment were then discussed, and a system of classification based essentially on quality of social interaction was proposed. The division into 'sociable' and 'non-sociable' as the new basis for categorisation seems to us based on rather circular reasoning. Finding a group of mentally disabled children who are not as sociable as others doesn't seem like a terribly profound discovery; however, sociability was now imbedded in the new discourse about 'autism' and it was this new emphasis that lay the basis for the subsequent expansion of autism into the family of ASDs.

It was no clearer than it had been in previous papers whether the three types of behaviours belonged together, whether they could be sub-grouped or how accurately they could be used to differentiate 'autistic' children from others. Given that all of the children with the triad of symptoms had some degree of mental retardation, the hypothesis should, in our opinion, have been refuted as this becomes a major complicating factor. Unfortunately, this standard of scientific reasoning soon became the norm in the autism research arena, with the desire to cling on to a hypothesis regardless of evidence (usually contorted to fit the new ideology) bedeviling much of the literature on autism. Further, it is very difficult to establish 'face' validity on this subject as our beliefs on what might constitute abnormality in social interaction or language or what might constitute repetitive patterns of behaviour is very much subjective, particularly as we move out of the arena of moderate and severe learning difficulties.

In 1981 Dr Wing gave birth to her second child, later diagnosed with Asperger's. At least at this stage researchers such as Dr Wing include case histories in their papers, a practice that has all but disappeared. In her 1981 paper Wing alludes to Asperger and his 1944 paper and adds to the range of behaviours that she states is commensurate with those of Asperger. In her paper, Wing (1981) describes six case histories (five of whom are male). Four of the six are of individuals in their adult years. The difficulty of determining that abnormalities in behaviour were occurring in the first three years when interviewing someone in their 30s is all too obvious. Dr Wing does discuss alternative diagnoses but these are 'straw men' such as schizophrenia. From the case histories presented it is difficult to determine what all six cases have in common. All are described as being 'slow' to develop, some have a learning disability, including one adult who is described as mentally retarded and not able to achieve independence in adulthood and one boy who attended a special school. Many of them are described as clumsy and as having coordination problems and one had a history of illnesses, operations and poor eyesight. It is not clear how all of them would qualify as having the now established 'triad' of impairments. Furthermore, none of them bear an obvious relationship to Asperger's cases. Two of the six cases have some degree of learning disability, whereas none of Asperger's were reported to be learning disabled. Most of Wing's cases spoke late whereas most of Asperger's spoke early. Most of Wing's cases were described as having little capacity for analytical thought whereas Asperger's cases were thought by him to be highly analytical. None of Wing's cases could be described as manipulative, mendacious, cheeky, confrontational or vindictive (terms of description used by Asperger about his cases). It might be said that both Wing's and Asperger's cases lack some degree of social reciprocity, but there seems little else in common, nor any clear reason why such a lack should warrant a diagnosis, or if it did, why it might not include just about every child who had some degree of learning disability or mental health problems (see Chapter 7). The range of their social problems could only be deemed to be autistic using a definition of autism that is circular.

With Asperger's syndrome having been brought in out of the cold, the creation of an 'autistic spectrum' was now under way. This spectrum as imagined by Dr Wing could now, in our opinion, include most children with some sort of developmental peculiarity and many beyond. By 1997, Dr Wing (1997) is arguing that the spectrum runs from normality to severe mental disability and that the cut-off point that differentiates eccentricity from autism is an essentially arbitrary one. In her depiction of the spectrum, Wing (1997) argues against adhering to any diagnostic rules and instead falls back on clinical experience as the guide. In terms of reliability and validity the shortcomings of that approach are all too obvious, particularly when it is not at all clear just what clinical experience a professional needs in order for them to be able to make an 'accurate' differentiation between 'normal' and 'autistic' children. Without any evidence to suggest that these professionals have an interest in tackling the questions of the ethical or political ramifications of such a process, we remain highly concerned about such developments.

In her 2005 paper 'Reflections on Opening Pandora's Box', Wing (2005) looks back at what she helped create. She reflects upon those who assign diagnosis on the great and the good, such as Einstein, without any trace of irony. We can only wonder what might have happened to the Einsteins or Wittgensteins of this world if they were subject to early screening, identified as autistic, channelled into years of special needs help at school, given psychiatric medication and then, together with their parents, 'psycho-educated' about their lifelong disability. Indeed, how many of tomorrow's Einsteins or Wittgensteins are being sent along this path today with who knows what consequences for them or indeed our culture more broadly? Dr Wing would like to present the past 25 years as representing untrammelled success, with the promise of more to come. As we might expect, Dr Wing appears to us blind about the pitfalls, incongruities and poor science that support the notion of autism to which she contributed.

Dr Wing's contributions have thus been key to the widening of autism into a spectrum. However, the person who gave the concept respectability and clout is the paterfamilias of child psychiatry – Sir Michael Rutter – and it is to him that we now turn.

Sir Michael Rutter

Sir Michael is the pre-eminent child psychiatrist of the past few decades, his knighthood being a testament to this. Autism and the autistic spectrum are unlikely to have had the profile they do, either in the UK or worldwide, without the patina of scientific respectability that Sir Michael Rutter has given them. I hope we are not doing Sir Michael a disservice by calling him an empiricist, but he frequently refers to evidence and the implicit and explicit need for 'facts' as providing a solid foundation for a scientific approach to childhood psychiatric disorders. Rutter has been particularly influential in convincing both the scientific community and the general public that autism is a primarily genetic disorder.

Sir Michael Rutter's contributions to the discourse on autism are many and varied. In addition to supporting the hypothesis that autism is genetic and that these genes act on an 'autism spectrum', he also provided early support for Wing and Gould's proposal that autism is characterised by the 'triad' of symptoms. In Rutter's influential 1978 revision of the definition of autism, three related terms – autism, infantile autism and childhood autism – were used somewhat interchangeably. Rutter (1978a) reinforced the now familiar 'triad' of symptoms by defining autism as being: 1) impaired social development which has a number of special characteristics out of keeping with the child's intellectual level; 2) delayed and deviant language development that is also out of keeping with the child's intellectual level; and 3) 'insistence on sameness' as shown by stereotyped play patterns, abnormal preoccupations or resistance to change. In addition, he added an age of onset of before 30 months to the criteria.

Despite the claims that Sir Michael Rutter makes for the great advances child psychiatry has made over the past 25 years, we argue that the 'evidence' for autism and its spectrum having a strong biological and genetic basis (as with the rest of child psychiatry) is no more than vapid rhetoric. We are here not stating that autism or the spectrum is 'caused' by the environment; rather we are scientifically sceptical about the concept and more than prepared to accept its existence when the proof is provided. Sir Michael Rutter lays a great deal of importance on the need for rigour in definition. In order to define what something is, by implication one has to establish what it is not. Sir Michael Rutter accepts the necessity for such conceptual clarity and critiques dyslexia, for example, as lacking such conceptual clarity. This 'lack', he claims, is a hindrance to empirical research (Rutter, 1998.)

When it comes to causation, if one reads standard child psychiatry texts or mainstream newspapers, one might believe that the proof that autism or the spectrum is caused by a number of genes is irrefutable. One might think that someone with Sir Michael Rutter's credentials would want to establish whether the evidence for the role that genes play in autism is either sufficient or necessary to establish causation, but this seems a long way off. The debate over intelligence conducted more than 20 years ago has many similarities to the current debate over social competence, with the proviso that the measurability of the former is considerably greater than that of the latter. Twin studies in autism have been carried out only with what might be called 'core' autism and the numbers involved are minute compared to the numbers now included in the diagnostic category. Furthermore, these studies have not considered twins reared apart or adoptive cases to bolster the argument that the role the environment plays is minimal (see Chapter 5).

Although Sir Michael Rutter is careful not say that genes 'cause' autism, he seems to owe some of his approach on this issue to the 'Dawkins' school of thought, where genes have an almost teleological propensity. In such an approach selection, and more importantly human selection of environment, are determined by the action of genes. Thus, even though we know that almost all psychopathological disorders are disproportionately clustered among the poorer sections of society, there is (according to this perspective) a strong suggestion that this is through genetic selection. So it is not the environment that is causing the behaviour but the genes acting through the environment.

A typical example of this approach can be found in his book *Genes and Behaviour* (Rutter, 2006). Sir Michael Rutter sets out to examine the relationship between nature and nurture (genes and environment) in relation to a variety of behaviours. He approaches the task with admirable care to attend to and mention counter arguments and critiques of, in particular, genetic theories. He is open about gaps in knowledge and stresses the importance of the so-called 'new' genetics needing to develop in cooperation with other branches of science. Such a calm and apparently objective approach can easily seduce the reader into accepting what ultimately turns out to be an ideological position (e.g., 'Any *dispassionate* critic would have to conclude that the evidence in favour of an important genetic influence on individual differences is *undeniable*' [Rutter, 2006: 6, our emphasis]). A more careful reading of the book finds that Sir Michael Rutter often uses generalised (and often contradictory) statements to cover up for a lack of evidence (e.g., after discussing how the evidence on genes suggests that genetic influences do not concur with the boundaries of current mainstream psychiatric diagnosis, he goes on to state 'these considerations *definitely* do not mean that we should abandon concepts on the *distinctiveness* of different psychiatric syndromes' [Rutter, 2006: 37, our emphasis] without any further evidence put forward to justify such a definitive position). In other places he gives appearance of trying to engage with social and ethical issues only to subsequently ignore them in his interpretation of the evidence (e.g., he defends the importance of individual variation but then talks about 'deficits' in individuals' cognitive, emotional and behavioural functions, including in those in the general population with no diagnosis, when discussing the evidence for disorders that occur on a 'spectrum').

As regards the autism spectrum disorders, Sir Michael Rutter concludes that

> the estimate of heritability is something of the order of 90 percent. Because the twin and family studies provide the same conclusions, there can be *considerable confidence* that the heritability is very high with genetic factors accounting for the majority of the population variance in liability to develop the disorder. (Rutter, 2006: 68, our emphasis)

This quite deterministic approach to autism contrasts with other more general statements, for example

> It is of little value to attempt to quantify the relative influence of the two [genes and environment] in any precise way, because it will vary by population and over time. Moreover, the precise estimates for the strength of genetic and of environmental influences have few policy or practice implications. (Rutter, 2006: 221)

Other crucial issues in interpreting the evidence, such as the problem of the equal environment assumption (EEA) (see Chapter 5) in twin-based research is simply dismissed:

> Although it is important to recognise that there is likely to be some violation of the EEA with respect to some traits, the effect is unlikely to be of *sufficient magnitude* to jeopardize the overall twin strategy. (Rutter, 2006: 43, our emphasis)

Overall this book turns out to be similar to many others on the subject, offering lots of platitudes and little convincing evidence leading to rather clichéd and generalised conclusions that suggest little if any useful knowledge is emerging from the field of behavioural genetics. 'Any *dispassionate*, but critical, review of the research leads to the *clear conclusion* that there are substantial genetic and environmental effects on *almost all types* of behaviour and *all forms* of psychopathology or mental disorder' (Rutter, 2006: 60, our emphasis) is typical of the rather unhelpful (to both science and clinical practice) 'we'll bet on everything (and throw in the kitchen sink too)' type of conclusions.

Another area in which Sir Michael clings to scientific terminology and hypothesis testing, at the same time as, in our opinion, excluding hypotheses that might undermine his own presumptions, is in the area of ethnicity and psychopathology. Sir Michael Rutter acknowledges the disproportionate clustering of many disorders in certain ethnic groupings. In this respect it is not uncommon to find theories going around in the autism lobby that have already been discredited in the schizophrenia arena. One such theory is that of viral causation. The fact that second-generation Afro-Caribbeans had much higher levels of diagnosis of schizophrenia than the population in general led to a theory that this was caused by a specific viral epidemic that had affected the immigrant community. Sir Michael Rutter appears to endorse a similar explanation for higher rates of autism in second-generation Afro-Caribbean children (Rutter and Nikapota, 2002). Understanding that the higher rates of 'disorder' might have something to do (at least in part) with the political and social realm (and its effects on certain communities) is not seriously considered. It seems that with some categories (such as autism and its spectrum), defending its validity and constructing it as unquestionably biological can take on a fundamentalist zeal rendering it closed to any critical scrutiny. The classifying of human behaviours into those that are deemed worthy of a medical diagnosis and those that are not is subject to the shifting sands of the political climate (such as removing homosexuality as a diagnosis when such practice was no longer considered 'deviant'), a reality that Sir Michael Rutter seems unable to take into account in his analyses. Similarly, Sir Michael Rutter does not appear to have considered how the question of gender affects the idea that autism is a genetic disorder (unless it is considered to be due to a defective sex-linked chromosome). All this sadly considerably weakens the credibility of Rutter's otherwise meticulous approach to examining the evidence.

LATEST DEVELOPMENTS

Once autism started to 'expand', new definitions for what constitutes a 'case' of autism began to emerge and trickle into diagnostic manuals.

In 1980, the third edition of the *Diagnostic and Statistical Manual of Mental Disorders* (DSM-III) (APA, 1980) used 'infantile autism' as the core descriptor, but also placed autism in the context of the 'pervasive developmental disorders' (PDD) for the first time. In 1987, a revised edition, DSM-III-R (APA, 1987), abandoned the term 'infantile autism', in part to recognise cases in which the onset of symptoms did not occur in early infancy. DSM-III-R also included a new category of pervasive developmental disorders; that of PDD not otherwise specified (PDD-NOS). In 1992, the World Health Organization published the International Classification of Diseases (10th revision, ICD-10), which uses the term 'childhood autism'. Just over a year later, DSM-IV (APA, 1994), whose definition is in most respects identical to ICD-10, used the term 'autistic disorder'. Even in the nomenclature being used to define 'autism' agreement seems hard to come by (see Chapter 6).

By the 1980s much research was under way to try and find the biological cause of autism. This necessitated that psychiatrists and psychologists develop new theoretical concepts to give researchers a practical way forward for their investigations. Thus it was proposed that a lack of 'theory of mind' (ToM) was the central deficit found in autism. ToM refers to the ability to understand that other people have their own plans, thoughts, beliefs, attitudes and emotions. It was suggested that there was an underlying cognitive structure responsible for ToM, which was viewed as an innate 'module' that is activated around three years of age. The ToM module (ToMM) was seen as dedicated, specific, fast, automatic, at least partly encapsulated, and its functioning as being largely independent of the general intellectual capacities of the individual (Baron-Cohen, 1995). Autistic children were found to have a significantly lower performance on certain measures of ToM compared to other cognitive tasks for testing intelligence and language capacities. This led to the hypothesis that autism was the consequence of a specific (biological) deficit in the ToMM.

However, by the late 1990s, interest in ToMM was waning as the diagnosis of autism was increasing, no genes responsible for the ToMM had been found, the diagnosis was being made mainly in males and interest in behavioural and biological continuums was increasing. Moving away from the idea that autism is caused by a discrete pathology, Professor Simon Baron-Cohen put forward the 'extreme male brain' theory of autism. His new theory was the first to at least recognise that a theory of causation must be able to explain the gender disparity. Professor Baron-Cohen's theory is that people with autism simply match an extreme of the male profile, with a particularly intense drive to systemise and a low drive to empathise. In other words, autistic traits are biologically male, normally distributed, found as a continuum in the population; autism is simply the extreme end of this (male) continuum (Baron-Cohen, 2003). Given the importance of Professor Baron-Cohen's theory to our arguments, it is worth reviewing his specific contribution to the field.

Professor Simon Baron-Cohen

Perhaps the most radical theory put forward by those considered to be mainstream thinkers on this subject is that put forward by Professor Baron-Cohen. In his book, *The Essential Difference: The Truth About the Male and Female Brain* (2003), Professor Baron-Cohen argues from a biological perspective that men and women's brains function differently. He characterises men's brains as being geared towards 'systematising' (needing to understand 'systems', organised conditions, mechanics and technology –'how things work') and women's towards 'empathising' (having the power to quickly assess others' emotional states, more readily identifying feelings in others, responding appropriately when sympathy is required and 'reaching out' empathically when dealing with people). Through his subsequent analysis of the research evidence, he concludes that those individuals diagnosed with ASDs are best understood as having a constitution that puts them at the extreme end of the systematising (i.e., male) brain. This, he suggests, is the reason why ASDs are so disproportionately diagnosed among boys and men. Professor Baron-Cohen seems to be aware of the radical potential of this theory and, indeed, seems to have been concerned that as a result it would receive a hostile reception among other researchers, academics and campaign groups from the autism field. However, it is our opinion that Professor Baron-Cohen does not fully realise just how radical his theory could be, as within it lie the seeds for exposing the socially constructed nature of ASDs and, indeed, the academic and theoretical foundations for dismissing autism as a scientifically and clinically valid category. Because Professor Baron-Cohen takes an a-historical and a-cultural approach he does not, in our opinion, conduct or even attempt to conduct an analysis of the relationship between gender and what we regard as psychopathology. Thus, for example, he fails to comment on how, in much of the last century, an excess of 'empathising' (as opposed to systematising) was a far more common reason for ascribing psychopathology.

In order to illustrate how his theory exposes the socially constructed nature of autism, we need to take a step back from this theory to try and contextualise the interface between developing categories for classifying mental phenomena and the social processes that produce these classifications. In this respect, of the common social groupings used in analytic discourses, gender is particularly interesting as it is the one where significant biological differences are present. Other common social groupings, such as class and ethnicity, have differences more obviously located in the sociological, rather than biological, realm. This does not, of course, mean that when it comes to matters of health and society, biology becomes redundant. What it does mean is that we have to attempt to understand the specifics of how biological and sociological influences interface in order to be able to construct and deliver effective healthcare to all sections of society. For example, it is well known that the majority of major diseases, such as heart disease, cancer and airways disease, occur far more frequently in the lower social classes in industrial, relatively wealthy countries, although these patterns do vary with other social, economic and political factors such as national dietary patterns, levels of wealth, access to universal healthcare and so on. Similarly, significant differences in prevalence and outcome of mental disorders by social grouping have been known about for some time (Pilgrim, 1997). For example, we know that psychosis and psychotic diagnoses such as schizophrenia occur more frequently in the lower social classes. Indeed, it is one of the strongest of the social grouping associations. However, in mental health, the relationship between these social variables and biological ones is much more difficult to disentangle, as the majority of disorders diagnosed as psychiatric disorders do not have any known, testable pathological or physiological features.

There are two predominant models that are used to provide an explanatory framework for this association between lower social class and major mental illness. The one that has been favoured by mainstream psychiatry privileges biological processes over social ones. This is known as the 'drift hypothesis' and suggests that it is the effects of the biological disorder on a person's intellectual and social functioning that causes those afflicted with the disorder to drift downwards in their earning capacity and, therefore, social status. In other words, biological disease causes the adverse social class profile found among those diagnosed with psychosis. The alternative model privileges social processes over biological ones and proposes that the social processes have a causal role and thus psychosis is, at least, in part caused by adverse social circumstances (Pilgrim, 1997; Cohen and Timimi, 2008). Current available evidence is compatible with either interpretation. Indeed, a third framework would propose a more interactional model that suggests both the above processes (i.e., the biological and social causation) are important, with essentially the whole being greater than the sum of the parts; in other words it is the interaction of these biological and social processes that produces the higher rates of psychosis among the lower social classes, with either factor alone being insufficient to account for this distinctive epidemiological pattern.

The interpretive framework you decide to privilege has cultural, legislative and professional implications. The drift hypothesis – which suggests that early intervention and effective 'treatment' could not only spare individuals from the long-term ravages of a mental illness, but in addition play a significant role in social equality and, thus, a more psychologically and economically just society – would give psychiatric treatment an important political role as well as a therapeutic one. The 'adverse environment as cause' hypothesis, on the other hand, would cast psychiatry's relationship to politics very differently, effectively putting the boot on the other foot, as it were; in other words, political and economic policies that increase social inequality would also prove to be detrimental to mental health – conversely the psychiatrist's ability to prevent and treat psychosis is aided by progressive politics that fights social and economic systems that support wide gaps between the classes.

One social category where there are known and significant biological differences is, of course, gender. Baron-Cohen (2003) adds to the knowledge about anatomical and hormonal differences (for example) by summarising some of the cognitive and emotional ones. Knowing that there are significant biological differences does not eliminate the enormous importance of the cultural and political factors that come into play in both interpreting the significance of these differences and the degree to which we can also culturally construct differences between men and women. Thus, at the macro level we can see that the lives of men and women and the types of roles that they occupy vary enormously globally, a variation that could not be accounted for by differences of gender biology alone.

While our social construction of gender in terms of our beliefs, values and practices around masculinity and femininity is important and highly relevant, much of the literature on the subject has avoided an engagement with biology, leading to somewhat polarised discourses – one focusing on the biological differences between men and women, the other on the social construction of masculinity and femininity. However, we believe the task is not to avoid biology but to radicalise it. If there are important features of gender differences that are biologically based then apparently enlightened approaches to changing our cultural attitudes to men and women and their roles may well fall short of their aims if they come to be experienced as, for example, attempts to feminise men or masculinise women in biologically incongruent ways.

While this debate sometimes gets unhelpfully reduced to a chauvinistic 'nature v nurture' argument, the current evidence base is simply unable to disentangle some core questions, such as 'How different are boys and girls biologically?', 'How does this affect their psychology?' and 'How adaptable are they to different sets of expectations?'. Indeed, within the confines of the current knowledge base, how useful is it to search for answers to these types of questions within the (rather masculine) linear framework that seeks to place causality (often in concrete terms, such as percentages) for the outcomes in terms of masculinity and femininity to either biology or nurture (see Chapter 9 for a more detailed discussion of gender)?

Recent trends in Western culture have moved child-rearing beliefs and practices towards an 'assimilationist' model, where the needs and wants of boys and girls are perceived to be similar and any differences between them minimised. To the 'assimilationist', the eventual goals of rearing and educating children are the same regardless of the child's sex. This means that boys should be taught in the same way as girls, and that boys will learn and be interested in the same things as girls because they will eventually work and occupy the same societal roles as girls (and vice versa).

One of the proposals of this book is that this assimilationist, 'biology blind' approach with regard to gender, while it has brought many important and progressive social advances, has also produced a number of drawbacks (particularly for boys). One important drawback associated with this is the increasing medicalisation of boys' behaviour, as it is boys who are increasingly unable to fulfil the cultural expectations of an essentially non-gendered childhood and thus it is boys' behaviour that is increasingly perceived to fall outside the norm (Timimi, 2005). There are, of course, many other interesting and complex interactions between male and female, masculinity and femininity, at various levels of cultural organisation, which are rendered invisible by a cultural approach that seeks to minimise differences between men and women (see Chapter 9).

Coming back to Professor Baron-Cohen's theory and the implications of this, it seems obvious to us from the above brief analysis, together with his theory that ASD is the result of being at the extreme end of what he is referring to as the male or systematising brain, that categorising ASD as a 'neurodevelopmental' (meaning a disorder in the development of the nervous system) disorder (as it currently is) is thus a category fallacy. Instead, we believe ASD has become a category that reflects current cultural preoccupations and thus its existence and increasing popularisation owes little to scientific advancement and functions much more as a 'commentary' on how masculinity and femininity are being constructed and how this plays out in the social processes that assign roles to men and women in neo-liberal or late capitalist societies. In such societies the concern is more with policing men (particularly loners) and having good face-to-face (marketing) skills. This contrasts with the types of concerns other cultures and other times have and have had. For example, in Sigmund Freud's time, Western society was less interested in the empathy skills necessary for selling and marketing and more interested in 'systematising' to solve 'scientifically' a whole variety of problems. At that time 'systematising' had a high social value and 'empathising' a low one. Indeed 'over'-emotional/hysterical women were seen as a problem worthy of a medical gaze, so that much of Freud's writing and clinical practice involved analysing and treating 'hysterical' women.

There are also other more challenging interpretations of the 'extreme male brain' hypothesis. Could this be an attempt to produce a biological explanation for the new concept of the extended autistic spectrum, an explanation furthermore that could 'save' autism's claim to a biological base and one many would feel is more appealing than that of 'disorder'? In this world of marketing there are many ways to sell your product. The idea of a psychiatric condition, disorder or illness is arguably less appealing than defining something as a 'difference' that requires particular types of 'support'. Once people accept the need for support for their biological 'difference', the path is cleared then to start defining these 'deficits' that afflict diagnosed individuals and thus they can more easily brought into defining their condition as being within the remit of psychiatric/psychological disorder 'by the backdoor' so to speak. Extreme male brain may be more appealing as it produces a 'difference' perspective, but that leaves all of us vulnerable to reconstructing essentially 'cultural' pathology as being bodily pathology.

Furthermore, despite the evidence presented by Professor Baron-Cohen, the degree to which differences between men and women are biologically defined remains hard to establish. Can women really multitask better than men? Are men really better at maths? While Professor Baron-Cohen's theories about the gendered nature of the emergence of specialised mental functions make sense from a number of perspectives, from others they do not. In some way, like the systematising brain he is commenting on, his arguments seem to wish to follow a nice 'systematising' pattern, by getting rid of competing data in order to arrive at a nice neat, tidy, fully coherent, and complete theory. Unlike the 'empathising' brain he talks about, Professor Baron-Cohen seems unable to conceptualise interactively and at multiple levels of experience (at least in what he has written).

Why are the Dutch so good at learning foreign languages? Is it because so many Dutch citizens have genetic markers for learning new languages or is it because they are more motivated to learn other languages as few foreigners with whom they regularly come into contact speak Dutch? What do monoglot English speakers do with the parts of their brains that others would reserve for second or third languages? The body, along with its hormones, forms part of the eco-system in which our mind operates. Differences in the more primitive parts of the brain responsible for motor and sensory coordination, also affect the development of our personalities. So, in the same way as a monoglot Anglophone fails to develop skills to learn other languages, a slightly 'clumsy' teenage boy who is at a natural disadvantage at most ball games and activities that require good coordination skills would fail to learn important socialising techniques acquired in team sports and may prefer to focus more on individual pursuits. But this does not mean that being clumsy 'causes' a-social behaviour any more than 'being ASD' does when living in a culture that constructs 'masculinity' in competitive ways that are often focused on physical prowess (see Chapter 9). If male socialisation were based on pursuits at which a clumsy child excels, it would be a different ball game (excuse the pun). Sadly, many such kids find themselves isolated with only video games and the computer or TV as companions. We are thus concerned about the degree to which Professor Baron-Cohen's analysis becomes too simplistic and just a more 'respectable' form of pop psychology.

Other areas of concern

In the past few years, there has also been public interest in a theory that suggested a link between the use of thimerosal, a mercury-based preservative used in vaccines and also the measles-mumps-rubella (MMR) vaccine, and autism. A number of large-scale studies have failed to show a link between thimerosal and autism (e.g., Madsen *et al.*, 2002). However, campaigners point out that such large-scale studies are unable to detect individual cases of children whose immune system may be particularly sensitive to these vaccines.

Another recent preoccupation has been early diagnosis and early intervention. In the UK this has led to the development of the 'Early Bird Programme' designed to provide support, training and encouragement to parents of autistic spectrum children, as well as developing communication and behavioural skills in their children. Early Bird begins when a child is in pre-school and is part of a wider national autism plan in the UK, which suggests that all professionals in contact with pre-school and school-age children should have training in autism and the alerting signals that indicate possible autistic impairment (Le Couteur and Baird, 2003).

With interest in autism growing at the same time as a rapid increase in the numbers being diagnosed with ASDs, it is now regarded as a neurological disease that has reached what some consider to be 'epidemic' proportions (Autism Research Review, 2000). According to this view, there could be as many as 60 million people with ASDs worldwide, of whom about 48 million would have average or above average intelligence. In the UK, the National Autistic Society, using an approximate prevalence of 91 per 1,000 of the population, estimate that there are around 535,000 people with autistic spectrum disorders in the UK and claim that the majority of those go undiagnosed (National Autistic Society, 2006).

HISTORY OF AUTISM IN CONTEXT

How do the above two histories about our changing notions of the 'normal' child and the 'autistic' child relate to one another?

The concept of autism has wound its way through the pages of history starting with Bleuler, who coined the term to denote schizophrenic individuals who were catatonic and evidenced no interest in human beings into an epidemic that has apparently affected some of the most brilliant minds of recent centuries. How this 'mutation of constructs' emerged requires us to examine the wider context in which our changing ideas about childhood and parenthood reflect our changing ideas about when we think something is wrong with children and what to do about it, as well as having a direct impact on children's experience, behaviour and other outcomes.

The emergence of autism as a diagnostic category in the 1940s must be understood in relation to the socio-political context of professional and parental practices that marked the cultural and economic transition of the time, in the same way that the emergence of wider autistic spectrum must be understood in terms of the matrix of practices that mark the late 20th century in the industrialised north. The conditions of possibility for diagnosing a child as autistic or high-functioning autistic are ultimately less rooted in the biology of their conditions than they are rooted in the cultural practices and economy of their times.

For example, in the 1800s, practices of classifying individuals as psychologically or psychiatrically disordered were much less developed, the standards of normality much broader and the mechanisms for social and individual surveillance that we take for granted in the Western world today simply did not exist. Prior to the late 1800s, children, in particular, would have not have been subject to any form of 'developmental' or 'psychological' examination unless their conditions were severe and their parents particularly economically privileged. Indeed, it was not until the 1930s that developmental guidelines were created and used in tracking children's progression.

Thus, a distinct medical/psychiatric disease called autism could not have emerged until standards of normality had been formalised and narrowed and standards of paediatric screening extended to a child's earliest years so that children with ASD could be 'identified'. This is not to say that there haven't been people throughout history who have displayed the symptoms we now group and define as autism, but to remind the reader that calling this 'autism' is simply a 'trick' of classification, as opposed to being the result of new biological knowledge.

As discussed earlier, from the late 19th century the state in the West has taken an increasing interest in child welfare. Nineteenth-century governmental practices included expansion of compulsory education, resulting in more social and expert surveillance of children. Investigations and interventions were now tailored to increase the numbers of children deemed to be educable to prepare them for an economy that was requiring increasing numbers of skilled workers and reduce the proliferation of the 'dangerous classes', among whom street children were considered particularly malevolent. This not only increased the opportunity for ever-greater state control over parents but also, now that children were all in one place (school), they were readily accessible to all sorts of 'scientific' surveys. This resulted in the growth of new professional groups (from teachers to doctors, and psychologists to social workers) tasked with the purpose of studying, surveilling and intervening in children's lives and, by implication, in their parents' lives. As the last century moved on, children's failure to learn (academically and socially) was increasingly seen as attributable to a bio-genetic deficit or poor parenting rather than a failure of the state or their education systems.

As new educational and psychological authorities were developed to meet the new imperatives of social adjustment, the boundaries between normality and pathology were problematised. Psychologists, psychiatrists and paediatricians began 'discovering' apparent manifestations of a range of disorders among the children they surveyed. Cognitive psychology, in particular, replaced the psychoanalytic framework for understanding 'developmental disorders' and so autism was reconceptualised, from an ego shipwrecked on the shores of object relations, to a computer with modular dysfunctions (Nadesan, 2005). These developments in the way we think about childhood and its problems interact with the rapid political, economic and social changes seen in the last few decades in the West, some of the hallmarks of which are: the movement into smaller family and social networks, decreasing amounts of time spent by parents with their children, aggressive consumerism preying on children's desire for stimulation, greater involvement of professionals in child-rearing activities (and advice on child-rearing) and a sense of panic about boys' development (Timimi, 2005).

Thus, a few decades ago autism was though of as a rare disorder estimated to occur in about four per 10,000 children (Lotter, 1966a) – with the criteria being used identifying, almost exclusively, children with moderate to severe learning difficulties – whereas now it is thought to affect about 1 per cent of children (National Autistic Society, 2006), a phenomenal increase in prevalence. This means that a young person with virtually no language and unable to carry out even the most basic self-care, can receive the same *behaviourally* defined diagnosis as another young person who is articulate, goes to mainstream school, is academically capable, but struggles to make friends. It is obviously absurd to have a spectrum stretching from speechless residents of day centres who need constant care to Einstein (who has been retrospectively diagnosed as autistic). We might just as well replace the term 'autistic spectrum' with 'human spectrum'! Indeed, many of the symptoms identified by Kanner and Asperger are no longer regarded as the primary symptoms that demarcate 'autistic' children. For example, we are no longer concerned about identifying 'flat affect' as vital (something that was observed and remarked upon by both original researchers) with much more emphasis now being placed on 'social communication' (Hacking, 1999).

Thus, autism is a disorder of the early to mid-20th century, while the high-functioning variants of autism such as Asperger's syndrome and pervasive development disorder that helped give rise to the idea of an 'autistic spectrum' are fundamentally disorders of the late 20th and early 21st centuries. The idea of autism could not have emerged as a distinct disorder prior to this because, within the discourses of the 19th century (and earlier), autism was simply missing from the doctors' and the public's imaginations. It was not until standards of normality had been formalised and narrowed and standards of paediatric screening extended to a child's earliest years that children with 'autistic spectrum' symptoms could be identified, labelled and given 'therapy'. The scientific search for understanding the essence of autism in the late 20th century must also be contextualised within the set of hegemonic beliefs and practices that seek to explain social behaviours in terms of genetic markers, which are seen as entities that will ultimately be linked (deterministically) to the whole repertoire of human behaviours.

4
THE CULT OF CHILD DEVELOPMENT

ASDs are viewed and categorised as 'developmental disorders' (in other words, a disorder in the development of the child). So, in addition to contextualising the study of autism by relating it to our changing ideas about childhood, we also need to critically examine theories and findings that pertain to the subject of child development and the goal of development (i.e., what type of people does 'normal' child development turn us into). It is to this that we now turn.

DEVELOPMENTALISM AND ANTI-DEVELOPMENTALISM

As discussed in the last chapter, by the late 19th century, partly under the impact of schooling and partly as a result of a growing concern about poverty and its possible political consequences, a prolonged and unprecedented public discussion about the physical and mental condition of children began in the UK. One development above all others turned children into attractive research subjects, namely the opportunities afforded to investigators by mass schooling. School made children available to professionals like sociologists, psychologists and doctors, all of whom sought to do scientific surveys of pupils (Sutherland, 1984). Now children found themselves being examined under the influence of science, whose main institutional forum was the Child Study Movement. Mass schooling revealed the extent of mental and physical handicap among pupils which, together with a growing anxiety about racial degeneration and the effects of poverty, led a variety of professionals and middle-class parents to become anxious about the quality of the child population, leading to a great interest in the subject of human development (Wooldridge, 1995).

The Child Study Movement developed in the late 19th century, from two important organisations. The first, the Child Study Association, argued for a scientific study of individual children by psychological, sociological and anthropometric methods and for the examination of the normal as well as the abnormal (Keir, 1952); its emphasis was on the individual child, to try and gain an insight into the processes involved in the unfolding of the human mind. The second group was the more medically orientated Childhood Society, formed largely under the influence of the British Medical Association, whose main interest lay in studying the mental and physical condition of children, with a special emphasis on racial characteristics. These child study organisations helped popularise the view that a child's normal development was marked by stages and that there were similarities between the mental worlds of children and so-called 'primitives' (Woolridge, 1995).

By the early 20th century child welfare was achieving a new social and political identity, with a shift in emphasis towards maximising children's potential (Baistow, 1995). This was thought to be in the national interest. At that time in Western society, policy was being developed that stressed the importance of national efficiency, with an emphasis on education, racial hygiene, responsible parenthood, social purity and preventative medicine (Hendrick, 1994). In each of these areas the state was becoming more interventionist through legislation. Both the state and charitable welfare organisations were now making a number of assumptions, mainly derived from the rise of 'psycho-medicine', about what constituted a proper childhood. There was a growing concern with children's rights and an assumption that it was the state alone that could enforce these rights. Protecting children and their rights was in harmony with the larger purposes of the state, which was of securing the reproduction of a society capable of competing in the new harsh economic conditions of the 20th century (Cunningham, 1995). These developments not only consolidated the idea that childhood is a period essentially different to adulthood and marked by vulnerability that required protection, but also began the trend towards a universalised idea of childhood and child development. Children in middle-class Western society were viewed as approaching this new ideal for childhood, with other childhoods (e.g., in colonised countries) being seen as primitive and in need of civilising.

Much of the energy of this relatively recently created psycho-medical discourse (often referred to as the 'psy-complex') has gone into a powerful 'story of our time', that of an apparently natural and universal way in which children are supposed to develop from birth through to adulthood. As an inevitable consequence of a rather unique focus on child development that is found in Western culture, our professional and everyday ways of understanding and making sense of when things go 'wrong' in children's lives is framed with reference to 'psy-complex' beliefs about normal child development. One of the author's (ST) child and adolescent psychiatry training consisted of a four-year course in 'developmental psychopathology', which is the 'science' that studies mental disease processes (psychopathology) with reference to normal development (developmental).

In traditional writing on development and developmental psychopathology, a particular approach to knowledge is taken which, for historical and cultural reasons, is based on Western beliefs regarding the 'knowability' of the physical world; a form of science that is modelled on the physical sciences (Habermas's positivist knowledge or approach – see Chapter 1). Experimental research is carried out under controlled conditions and where possible statistical analysis of samples is expected. An underlying assumption is that the general laws of developmental change are present in the world and can be discovered by appropriate research (Karmiloff-Smith, 1992; Morss, 1990). Systematic experimentation, observation and appropriate measurement are taken to represent the means to this end. When directed towards issues of development, this 'positivism' tends to be accompanied by the belief that developmental change is part of a natural, biological process that should occur in all children (Morss, 1990).

The line of argument is also a functionalist one; that is it treats the activity of children as an adaptation to a relatively stable environment. 'Developmentalism' might therefore be said to be born out of a positivist, naturalist and functionalist view of children (Burman, 1994), a way of viewing that is derived from the success of the physical sciences and application of this philosophy to the study of the inorganic world. These are also the underpinnings that drive developmental psychopathology. Both child development and developmental psychopathology set themselves the tasks of uncovering universal and natural processes by which human infants are transformed into fully adapted adults (or not).

Developmental psychology was one of the first branches of psychology to be established, precisely because childhood was seen as the prime location to investigate how nurture impinged on nature. The assumptions that have developed within developmental psychology and psychopathology are deeply embedded in Western philosophy and thought. The development of a biosocial science of psychology took place in an atmosphere where the natural sciences had already achieved some very compelling accounts of the inorganic world. It is hardly surprising, therefore, to find that psychological reasoning drew heavily upon ways of thinking already found fruitful in those contexts. However, unlike the natural scientists, psychologists and psychiatrists have never had any clear idea of how the processes they study actually operate and how the moulding together of nature and nurture happens. What we are left with is a metaphor for a process and not the process itself. Psychologists and psychiatrists therefore can only speculate in rather vague terms about the way their theories work (Stainton-Rogers and Stainton-Rogers, 1992). With the powerful assumption of a natural blueprint for development, genetics came to play an ever-bigger role in developmental theories. Borrowing ideas from the natural sciences meant that genetic material was now held to have the power to specify not only how things are made (e.g., having blue eyes or tall stature) but also behaviour (so-called behavioural genetics) and a whole host of experiences and beliefs.

One of the strongest stories of modernism is that if we want to know about something all we need to do is measure it. Guided by this recipe, developmental psychologists and psychopathologists have employed those direct means of investigation – for example, by using psychometric tests (such as those used to measure a child's intelligence) and diagnostic questionnaires (for example, to diagnose anxiety, depression or autism). The answers to these questionnaires cannot tell us anything directly about any quality of the child, only about a hypothetical property of the child (e.g., the child's intelligence) as constructed by the designer of the test (Stainton-Rogers and Stainton-Rogers, 1992). Yet psychological tests are purported to be direct indicators of fixed and stable properties (traits) of a child or to diagnose 'real' medical conditions in a child (such as autism). The use of measurement has beguiled many into assuming that they are finding out some essential truth about what the child being tested is like. Yet all such tests achieve is to replace one unknown (the child) with another set of unknowns (the traits out of which the child is assumed to be constituted). As soon as we probe further to find out about what these tests and traits mean, we find that they too are subjects about which more tests and debates are written. What often happens is a movement further and further away from the original matter of concern – finding out about the child. Basically, what this means is that there is no device that can tell us the 'truth' about what a child is supposed to be like, although that does not mean that all such questionnaires are of no meaning or practical use. What we need to appreciate is that they are maps and not the territory, metaphor and not the thing itself.

In the same way that the inability of psychiatry to prove the material reality of the constructs it uses has left it open to justifiable and continued criticism not only of its concepts but also the way it uses them; so developmentalism too is having to face up to some powerful criticism. The Western story of development simply does not stand up to rigorous inspection. Far from offering, as is often assumed, an explanation for the changes that children undergo between birth and adulthood, it merely reclothes this transition from a ragbag of carelessly borrowed garments and accessories; 'what modern developmentalists measure, investigate, even perceive in their subject-matter is, therefore, still defined by outdated illogical concepts. What developmentalists discover may be determined in advance' (Morss, 1990: xiii).

According to Geertz (1983) all human knowledge is, to some extent, local knowledge relative, in many respects, to the culture in which it makes sense. Thus, Western developmentalism should be seen as one of the 'great stories of our culture' (Morss, 1996: 28). It can be thought of as one of the grand narratives by which modern, industrialised societies regulate themselves. After all, much of the state intervention into its citizens' lives is rationalised in terms of the 'developmental needs' of particular age groups. At the same time, much of the entrepreneurial effort of the private sector is directed at the redefinition of those needs in terms of the products and services it wishes to sell. That children have certain characteristics, that adults have others and that it is natural to grow from one to the other are messages that we receive from all forms of modern communication (Burman, 1994). Morss (1996) points out not only the limits and constraints of child developmental knowledge, but also its cultural specificity, its bio-determinism, the huge impact it has had upon how our culture deals with children (e.g., the impact of developmental theories in education and social-work practice) and the constraints it puts upon our ability to develop a broader understanding of children and their problems.

One branch of criticism has come from the so-called 'social construction' perspective. Ron Harre has consistently argued that psychologists should take seriously the social processes through which their objects of study are constituted, insisting that human mental life is socially produced through processes such as interaction, language and the sharing of values (Harre, 1983, 1986). Harre argues that stage-based accounts of childhood are, at best, a description of a particular way in which some person is obliged to behave. He knows that there are always alternatives. Instead of the hierarchical account of children's growth being a set of stages, Harre sees them as a set of alternatives, recognising that traditional developmental psychology failed to positively acknowledge diversity and the full range of people's capacities.

Likewise, as far back as the 1970s Shotter (1974) emphasised the role of interpretation in the study of human development; that is the interpretation of children's actions by adults, by each other and by themselves. Once able to use language, children are described by Shotter as living in a world of shared representations in which they play a part in constructing their own development. Another social constructionist, Kenneth Gergen (1985, 1991), emphasises the negotiated, social-collective nature of human knowledge and the historically relative status of childhood and of developmentalism. In a similar vein, Kessn (1979) notes the historical dimension involved in how we situate the knowledge that we use. He notes that if adult treatment and perception of children in the Middle Ages or in the 19th century was in any way historically dependent and a product of those times, then it must also be historically dependent today. It is inconsistent, for example, to treat child labour in the 19th century as somehow a historically dependent, unnatural state for children, while at the same time neglecting the role of present-day circumstances in defining childhood. If child labour happened as a consequence of economic conditions, then it follows that present-day treatment of children must also be relevant to present-day economic and social circumstances. Kessn was, in essence, arguing that modern-day perceptions of childhood cannot be the be all and end all of a science of human development. In fact, Kessn was also proposing that the scientific study of child development is itself an accident of history in that what we study, how we study and how we formulate our conclusions is relative to our historical circumstances. Kessn linked those notions by a discussion of the importance of individualism in Western thinking, showing that a focus on the individual is central to Western psychology of development.

For Gergen, a valid psychology would accept a plurality of stories, whereas modernist psychology has been dominated by the narrative of scientific progress. The assumption of progress in developmentalism is little more than a literary device. Progress is a way of framing a story about psychology; indeed, for Gergen storytelling is an unavoidable aspect of what we might prefer to call science. For those who tell the story, according to Gergen, should never forget the constructed and negotiated character of that story. For Gergen, globalisation has meant we are increasingly exposed to diverse alternative lifestyles, to stories that we can see making sense for other people and that we can less and less easily dismiss as deviance (Gergen, 1991). In Gergen's postmodern world, the post-modern self is thus saturated with possibilities as the number and variety of persons with whom it is in conversation expands, seemingly without limit. Gergen sees these diverse possibilities as being inhibited by professional cultures sticking to a narrow Western 'scientific' view about development.

From a Marxist perspective, what psychologists call development can be thought of as socially produced:

> If people's thinking is, like consciousness in general, the reflection of their social and political status, then changes in that thinking must be thought of in the same way. There is some regularity in the way adults of a certain class think, and if this kind of thinking seems different from the thinking of those people's children, then one might expect the explanation of change to be sought in the social circumstances. If the way the adults think seems desirable from the point of view of the owners of wealth, then it would be misleading to describe it as 'mature'...Instead the different kinds of thinking observed, and the fact that individuals tend to move from one state to the other, would be interpreted as a consequence of the social and political situation. (Morss, 1996: 57)

According to the Marxist critic Adorno, conceptual systems always perpetrate violence towards reality. They aim at completeness, at closure and try to explain everything. At the same time Adorno felt there was no other easy way to grasp reality and that reality cannot be known outside of that violent and unending and struggle with some conceptual structure (Buck-Morss, 1987). According to Adorno, thought is not developing either in the individual, the species or society towards a closer connection with reality. Therefore it cannot be assumed that adult thinking is in any sense more valid or truthful than that of children. Adorno's analysis is connected with the Marxist account of 'commodity fetishism', by which process phenomena constituted through social relations come to be treated as 'real' (in this case current mainstream views of child development). By implication, development can be looked upon as 'commodification', that is to say, changes in people's lives that are social and contingent might come to be looked upon as if they were natural and necessary. The social function of the so-called science of developmentalism is, from a Marxist perspective, that of serving the best interests of maintaining the social stability of a particular society, in this case Western capitalist society (Broughton, 1986). The claims and theoretical formulations of developmental psychology are then seen as distortions or incomplete representations of reality. Developmentalism is viewed as typically treating change that is actually produced socially as if it were natural.

At the same time, developmental psychology is itself seen as being produced by larger social forces and hence as representing those forces in some way. For example, isolation and loneliness, which could be seen as inevitable features of subjective life under capitalism, can be redefined in developmental terms as autonomy and independence (Lichtman, 1987). Similarly, the Piagetian glorification of abstract modes of thinking can also be seen as an ideological construct that is more congruent with the intellectual ideals found readily in industrialised rather than non-industrialised cultures (Buck-Morss, 1987). This is entirely predictable as the ideals towards which developing children should reach in Piagetian theory are those of the favoured modes of interaction of a money-based, capitalist economy. Similarly development of 'emotional intelligence' becomes part of an individual's expected developmental tasks, as a culture of marketing and selling values the ability to understand and manipulate people's emotions in order to convince them that they require whatever it is that is being sold.

We see flaws in the whole developmental project when we view developmentalism through a cultural or a Marxist lens; furthermore, there was a considerable anti-developmental edge to much Freudian psychoanalytic theory. Although Freud is credited with developing the highly influential psychoanalytic theories of emotional and psychosexual development, much of the more systematised way of organising Freud's theories into a developmental perspective was done by other psychoanalysts interpreting his work. Freud himself appears to have become less and less confident in his developmental analysis the more he developed his theories (Morss, 1996). Thus, much of Freud's writing contains anti-developmental as well as developmental formulations: 'it is often merely a question of our own valuation when we pronounce one stage of development to be higher than another'

(Freud, 1922: 51). Many of Freud's theories developed out of therapeutic work with patients; Freud described the phenomena of transference, where the patient's present actions and thoughts appear to be a repetition of actions, thoughts and feelings that occurred in that patient's past, usually their childhood. In this sense the past may exist in the patient's head not as a resource for personal growth but as a tyrannical compulsion where repetition may be the truth behind the illusion of development. In this view of psychological reality, humans are condemned to repetition because they are continually trying to do something right that is impossible for them to do right. What might look like progress in a human life is simply the replacement of one doomed strategy with another.

But Freud makes an even stronger anti-developmental point in *Beyond the Pleasure Principle* (Freud, 1922). Here, Freud begins to see repetition as an inherent tendency in psychic life and part of all organic life's compulsion to return to the inorganic state from which it once emerged. Freud, thus, introduces his notion of the 'death instinct', a drive that he feels is part of the one goal which all organisms share, 'the goal of all life is death' (Freud, 1922: 47). In this light development is seen as a distraction, a grand irrelevance and the higher the organism the greater the irrelevance. At the same time, Freud also introduces the idea that to balance the death drive there is another general instinctive tendency to build up, combine and reproduce life. This drive he calls 'Eros'. From this perspective, what might appear to be regularity in development is little more than a series of side effects of the conflict of these larger forces that are constantly operating within an organism.

From a post-structuralist perspective there is a much deeper loss of faith in any approach that could be described as positivist. Even though there are criticisms of developmental perspectives in both Marxism and psychoanalysis, their analytic claims still have a positivistic element; in other words, they are still saying this is how things are. In the post-structuralist (often called post-modern) approach science is no longer treated as relevant to the search for answers to problems that arise outside science. Nor can science be seen as generating objective forms of knowledge that can be used to inform practice. Instead, scientific procedures are seen as playing a part in producing the objects that they study and the interventions that they sanction. Thus, although Foucault suggests that governmental and scientific scrutiny has come to focus on matters of population surveillance and population control, he is careful to avoid the suggestion that all these state systems work together in a smoothly functioning way, as a Marxist analysis might assume. Foucault suggests that scientific and medical studies of populations are closely related to changes in the regulatory role of the state – for example, in education, welfare and health provision – but not in an obvious way such as wielding power through deliberate manipulation of population. Foucault sees the way power typically functions in modern, Western society as having more subtle elements that interact with the way people define themselves and thus it is hard for most professionals and the populations they serve to recognise the subtle ways in which power and control operate within everyday discourse (Parker, 1992; Foucault, 1981).

This is the same in Foucault's discussions of the family and childhood in that he sees them as also constituted through interactions with social processes. Thus the same person who is treated as a child in some circumstances may be treated as an adult in others. It becomes difficult to pin down what childhood is or what childhood should be in any definitive sense. Such matters seem to be consequential on cultural values, beliefs and practices and people's behaviour tends to be a reflection of that activity. Thus, human subjectivity is seen as socially produced; individuals retain some personal agency and choice but their beliefs, choices and practices tend to be highly influenced by the prevailing cultural discourses of the time (Foucault, 1981). In this way of looking at things, universal stages of development can be thought of as no more than bodies of knowledge, forms of scientific, professional and lay discourse of a particular culture.

Walkerdine similarly insists that what we call development – what parents and teachers, for example, may treat as inherently, naturally regulated change – can only be an effect of normalising and regularising practices (Walkerdine, 1993). She sees, for example, teachers' recognition of developmental achievements of the individual child as a subtle kind of regulation. Although this regulation may be less obvious than the more formal old-fashioned classrooms with rigid rows of desks, control is still being exercised. She notes how schooling practices rely on certain kinds of so-called expert knowledge about children in general on which the curriculum is based. Furthermore, within the classroom, teachers' observations and the types of behaviours and achievements that they privilege contribute to making up this expert knowledge defined as it tends to be in terms of developmental achievements (Walkerdine, 1984).

Bradley (1989), meanwhile, concentrating on theories about infant development, describes how the general discourse of our time tends to blame and devalue women in their role as mothers. As with psychiatric and psychological literatures' pathologising of mothers, developmental theories are set up for blame in that there is an expectation that mothers should be capable of providing a hypersensitive, interactive partner for the young baby, a partner who is at the same time meant to be natural, educational and constructive (but non-directive), and who must at all costs enjoy what she is doing. He illustrates how theories of infant development assume quite specific caretaking conditions and functions that they treat as natural in the same way that development itself is seen as natural.

In this brief summary of some of the criticisms of the naturalistic, pre-determined theories of development, we have tried to illustrate why developmental ideology and developmental psychopathology are simply this culture's way of interpreting how children are expected to mature rather than a scientific endeavour that is leading us ever closer to the 'truth' about the nature of childhood and its development. In discussing how, he believes, Foucault would have questioned these practices, John Morss reflects:

> [W]hat, he asks us, is actually going on? What are people doing to other people when that word development is used? What happens as a result of its invocation? How is developmental knowledge spawned? Foucault urges us to maintain the questionings of the discipline. (Morss, 1996: 150)

For within the developmental discourse there is a constant subtext that is saying there is a superior and inferior position. Development says to the child, the parent and the teacher: this is your future and if you do not reach it you are, in some senses, inferior. It is not just children who are said to develop but also peoples and economies (Sachs, 1992). Development is about modern hierarchies of superiority and inferiority – it has trouble coping with diversity. Developmental explanations instil the notion of individual competitiveness; from the moment you are born you will have developmental milestones thrust upon you. As parents we are desperate to see our children achieve these age-bound expectations. Development of our children is under constant professional surveillance, starting with health visitors and community paediatricians and moving on to general practitioners, nursery nurses, teachers and a whole range of specialists. We are concerned when our children seem to be falling behind and we are constantly encouraging them to achieve these expectations. If we are not concerned and not encouraging, presumably we are neglecting.

How do these affect children themselves? If there is a belief that these are natural, unfolding processes, which professionals must be involved in helping children achieve, does this not encourage competitiveness from a very early age? How much do children get caught in these parental and professional anxieties? How relaxed can children, from the moment they are born, be to just be, as opposed to having to do something to ease these cultural anxieties? When these anxieties cannot be comforted and there is a perception that a child has strayed from their predestined development path, who is to blame? In this blame-ridden culture that needs an explanation for everything, much of the developmental psychopathology literature has pointed at the mother in terms of blame, and more recently at the child's genes. In a culture where families have shrunk and fathers seem to disappear and relinquish duty and responsibility in ever-increasing numbers, mothers have to shoulder not only the responsibility for caring for their family (a role given much lower status in Western culture than many non-Western cultures), but also have to shoulder responsibility for things going wrong. In a final stab from the developmental discourse, mothers are then denied credit for their work when things do go well, as children are then simply seen as achieving their biological destiny.

Within this context the more bio-deterministic aspects of the developmental and developmental psychopathology culture have, at least, appeared to provide a get-out clause for the beleaguered mother. Now problems can be viewed as being the result of a fault in the genetic programme for development and thus intrinsic to the child. But this approach to understanding the problems of children is equally guilty in its simplistic theoretical assumptions (masquerading as truth), in denying alternative possibilities, and it never solves the nagging doubt in the back of a parent's mind that it is their fault.

Nor does it tackle the question of what impact such a system has on children themselves. Why is it boys who consistently outnumber girls by somewhere between two to one and ten to one in most of these apparently developmental disorders? Why does our view of development appear to discover such massive genetic fault in boys as opposed to girls? It would seem that modern, Western society has developed a set of beliefs and expectations about development and its problems that girls are better able to live up to than boys (see Chapter 9).

These beliefs heavily influence the education system our children grow up in. Special needs resources in schools go to a much higher proportion of boys than girls (Timimi, 2005). Furthermore, the defining of a disability requiring special needs help at school is shaped by the disciplines of medicine and psychology. The adherence of these two fields to measuring physical and mental competence in order to determine normality inevitably conveys assumptions about deviance and failure and these labels then become attached to both individuals and groups which have failed to measure up/conform. Special needs practice within schools rests on within-child explanations and on the whole is focused upon reading ability or acting-out behaviour (Timimi, 2005). More recently there has been an increasing focus on social and emotional competence, with the growth of ASD-specific special needs teaching programmes and vigorous campaigns to increase funding and provision for those labelled as having an ASD (e.g., Batten *et al.*, 2006).

Like the professions of psychology and psychiatry, teaching has fallen victim to rationalist, scientific, market values and has moved towards a more 'technicist' approach, with greater emphasis on specialisation and less acknowledgement of the human social exchange nature of a teacher's activity; this has led to deskilling and greater emotional detachment from their work (Skelton, 2001), and the return of more didactic beliefs and practices in school that revolve around concepts derived from a child development perspective. The language of development has far-reaching consequences with regard to how we deal with children in our culture, how we define childhood deviance and how we then interpret the meaning of their perceived deviance.

SOCIETY AND SUBJECTIVITY

To understand what ideas about child development become hegemonic, we need to understand a little about what the society in which children are growing up wants them to be once they are adults. Knowing what your society wants you to develop into provides a further context within which to understand the ultimate goals of any child development theory and the way it is applied and regulated in any given society. In this section, therefore, we want to further explore the relationship between the subjective experiences of a person, family and the wider social and cultural (including economic and political) climate in which they live. This not only helps us understand why particular theories of child development and particular concerns about development become widespread, but also lays a theoretical foundation for understanding some of the common cultural preoccupations we have about personality and its development.

The Marxist subject

Since Marxism emerged a century before modern neo-colonial, globalised world markets, we would expect Marxist ideas to be both incomplete and flawed when it comes to understanding the impact of current political and economic systems on the person in modern 'late capitalist' societies. Nonetheless, certain aspects of Marxist analysis of the nature of capitalist economy and its impact on people's lives remain pertinent. Capitalist market economies lead to such enormous monetary and social inequality that conflicting interests emerge between different groups of people that have an important role to play in shaping both the experience and beliefs of these groups.

According to Marx, commodities appeared at the dawn of economic activity and became generalised with the advent of capital. Capital is inserted into each commodity and can be released only through exchange. Every commodity is a conjunction of a 'use value' and 'exchange value'. 'Use value' signifies the commodity's place in the ever-developing manifold of human needs and desires, while 'exchange value' represents an abstraction that can be expressed in quantitative terms as money. Broadly speaking, capital represents that regime in which 'exchange value' predominates over 'use value' in the production of commodities; the problem with capital is that once it is installed this process becomes self-perpetuating and ever-expanding. With 'exchange value' dominating, production of commodities comes to revolve around production for profit, with prices having to be kept as high as possible and costs as low as possible. Competition between commodity producers becomes endemic to the system, so cutting costs is also a paramount concern in capitalist economies (Kovel, 2002; Bottomore and Rubel, 1961).

There are a number of effects of this mode of economic organisation on subsequent cultural values and the personal experiences of those living within it. This system produces hierarchical social groups with conflicting interests, both between each group and within each grouping. Thus, Marx saw a fundamental conflict of interest between the ruling classes who owned the means of production and the working classes whose labour is bought and sold by the ruling classes. Second, the central place of commodities and production for profit results in a 'commodification' of all aspects of society, including the commodification of nature, which includes human beings and their bodies.

Marx also observed that capital is quantitative at its core and, thus, imposes a regime of quantity upon the world. This is evident throughout Western culture and its institutions, where there seems to be an underlying belief that in order to 'know' something one has to measure it. This has supported a particular way of organising our institutions and the technologies they adopt, fostering a reliance on positivist materialist science, often to the exclusion and belittling of the importance of spiritual and ethical orientations. We see this in the practice of mental health that has come to be dominated by quantitative approaches through use of 'tick list' methods of arriving at psychiatric diagnoses and reliance on quantitative questionnaires in both research and practice.

Another aspect of market economies is that they constantly seek to go beyond the limits in existence at any moment in time. While this provides capitalism with its inherently dynamic quality, constantly pushing development in new directions as new markets are opened up and exploited, it also means that one of the characteristics of modern, market-dominated societies is that they are gripped by what Hamilton (2003) has called a 'growth fetish'. Here the obsession is to continually produce economic growth, where every quantitative increase becomes a new boundary, which is immediately transformed into a new barrier to push growth beyond. Thus, a core value required for continuous growth is a disregard for boundaries except as barriers to be surpassed. We are currently digesting the social and economic consequences of such an economic psychology as we come to terms with the consequences of the global credit crunch.

The penetration of this value into everyday life may shed some light on the behaviour of certain social groups (e.g., in youth culture, the music industry and the visual media, where one can see the boundaries of what was acceptable, even just a generation ago, repeatedly transgressed). It may also shed light on the observation, that, despite becoming richer in the West, levels of happiness and satisfaction are decreasing and rates of mental disorders and psychosocial disorders, particularly among the young, are increasing (Hamilton, 2003). In other words, like our economies, our expectations from life are continuing to expand, leading to a mismatch between what we wish for and what we can get.

While Marxist analysis is correctly criticised for its economic reductionism and as being too simplistic, thus failing to grant cultural practices any specificity of their own, the fundamental inequalities that underlie market capitalism remain as relevant today as they did 100 years ago. This can be seen both within societies of the industrialised North and when comparing the industrialized North with the poorer

South of the world. Thus, while absolute levels of income have grown in all sections of the populations in the industrialised North, the wealth gap between the rich and the poor in most Western societies has continued to grow. For example, in the USA in the 1980s the top 10 per cent increased their income by 16 per cent, with the top 1 per cent increasing their income by 50 per cent. In contrast the bottom 10 per cent lost 15 per cent of their income (George, 1999).

We see this even in countries with apparently left-leaning political parties in power. Under a Labour government in the United Kingdom, the gap between the rich and poor continued to grow even after eight years in power (Inland Revenue, 2005). A wealth of statistics attests to the fact that the gap between North and South has similarly increased and absolute levels of income in some countries (most noticeably in Africa) have actually decreased. In the last three decades of the 20th century third-world debt increased by a factor of eight and the gap between rich and poor nations increased from 44/1 to 72/1 (Kovel, 2002).

Such stark economic realities are bound to have an effect on a large population's everyday experiences as well as their beliefs and values. As the economist and philosopher Samir Amin (1988) noted, Western capitalist ideology has necessarily led to the domination of market values, which penetrates all aspects of social life and subjects them to their logic. This philosophy pushes to the limit an opposition between humankind and nature. The goal of finding an ecological harmony with nature disappears as nature comes to be viewed as a thing to be similarly manipulated for selfish ends. The ability to manipulate people, particularly by exploiting their understandable emotional desires for something 'more' in their lives (which in conjunction with the capitalist values dominating their culture usually means something more materially), becomes a desirable quality, necessary for competing successfully in the cut-throat marketplace.

One significant theorist who used Marxist ideas (at the same time as criticising some of them) is Althusser. Marx believed that capitalist societies produced 'false consciousness' in its citizens. He argued that the dominant ideas in any society were the ideas of the ruling class and that populations within society were thus taught to accept the idea that we are free to sell our labour and that we get a fair price for it, because that is the way the ruling classes wish the social world to appear to us. Althusser, in agreeing with this, saw ideology and, in particular, ideological state apparatuses as the central arena through which such false consciousness is produced (Althusser, 1969, 1971). For Althusser, subjects formed as a result of such ideological discourses, will always be 'fragmented' subjects. Consequently, such a thing as 'class consciousness' is neither an inevitable nor unified phenomenon. Classes, while sharing some common conditions of existence, do not automatically form a core, unified class-consciousness; instead, they are cross-cut by conflicting interests (e.g., questions of gender, race and age). While an appreciation and understanding of the fragmented nature of individual subjective identities seems highly relevant in modern culture, particularly when noting the diversity of social groupings with very different attitudes, beliefs and practices within economic classes, it remains open for criticism as it stresses the discursive 'outside' at the expense of explaining the affective 'inside'. It will enhance our understanding further if we are able to explain why particular subject positions are 'taken up' as the target of emotional investments by some subjects and not others (Hall, 1996).

The post-modern subject

The most influential thinker in the development of the post-modern paradigm was Foucault. He argued that discourse and history are discontinuous, being marked by historical ruptures in understanding. Different configurations of knowledge shape the practices and the social order of specific historical periods. Thus, in place of truth, Foucault speaks instead about 'regimes of truth' (Foucault, 1972, 1973). Foucault explored how meanings are temporarily stabilised and regulated into a 'discourse'. This ordering of meaning is achieved through the operation of power in social practice. The resulting discourses regulate not only what can be said under particular social and cultural conditions but also who can speak, when and where.

Foucault used these ideas in examining the disciplinary character of modern institutions and practices (Foucault, 1977). For example, Foucault's (1961, 1973) study of the discourses of madness illustrated how our current concepts of 'mental illness' and 'madness' are highly influenced by the European enlightenment movement's preoccupation with reason and the individual subject. According to Foucault, the birth of psychiatry and the dominance of the medical model in how we understand mental distress and deviance was not a result of progressive medical/scientific progress illuminating our understanding of how the mind/brain works, but an act of social exclusion of subjects who the culture of the time deemed as needing to be segregated from the rest of society. He also notes that, just as practices in past historical epochs are socially and culturally constructed, so the same can be said for current practices. This means that different discourses about, for example, madness, will appear at later historical moments, producing new ideas and new social practices (Bracken and Thomas, 2001).

Thus, for Foucault the subject is historically produced, with power not simply a negative mechanism for control, but also, through discourse, productive of the subjective itself. The disciplinary power of particular social groupings – such as educational and medical – results in their having significant influence on how we construct our own subjectivities as well as others'. Although this argument fits with the idea that identities are fractured, discursive, cultural constructions, it is not without its problems. In particular, if subjects and identities are social and cultural 'all the way down', how can we conceive of persons as able to act to engender change in the social order?

Foucault turns his attention to this question in some of his later works, which focus on 'techniques of the self'; he introduces the possibility of resistance and change. Here subjects are viewed as involved in practices of self-constitution, recognition and reflection. This concern with self-production as a discursive practice is centred on the question of ethics as a mode of 'care of the self' (Foucault, 1981). Thus, in everyday life, people are concerned with the ethics of what it means to be a 'good' person, a 'self-disciplined' person, a 'creative' person and so forth. These ethical discourses that are in common circulation are partly culturally constructed, but also allow the subject a position, which enables agency to occur. In addition, where discursive power operates, so resistance becomes possible, not least through the production of 'reverse discourses'. For example, medics and clerics put the idea of homosexuality into cultural discourses in order to condemn it. However, the very act of producing a public discourse about homosexuality allowed homosexuals to create the space for resistance and eventually to be heard and to claim rights. Arguably, the opening up of a space for an assertive homosexual identity may not have occurred had those in the position of power not sought to make an issue of it in the first place. A similar process has begun to take shape in the politics of those labelled with 'autism' or an 'ASD', with active campaign groups asserting that autism is best understood as a neurological difference rather than a disorder and likening their movement for the right to be 'autistic' to that of gay rights.

Many other post-modern theorists have expanded on the themes that Foucault first developed. In summary, these post-modern-orientated thinkers argue that the institutions of modernity are associated with social and cultural processes of individualisation, differentiation, commodification, urbanisation, rationalisation, bureaucratisation and surveillance; further, that the experience of living within such societies and its institutions involves life at a faster pace, constant change, ambiguity, risk, doubt, fragmented identities, blurring of cultural boundaries and the requirement for high levels of reflexivity (Barker, 2000). Thus, post-modernism provides some conceptual tools that are suited to analysing the development of subjectivity within diverse social groups, the influence of power on knowledge systems at the micro level and a more flexible approach to examining the dynamics and experiences of specific cultural groups and modern institutions (such as medicine, psychiatry, the family and childhood).

Affect, hegemony and pragmatism

A discussion about the nature of subjectivity and personality development would not be complete without mention of psychoanalysis. For Hall (1996) psychoanalysis has particular significance in shedding light on how identifications of the 'inside' link to the regulatory power of the discursive 'outside'.

This line of thinking is explored by Judith Butler (1993), for whom the link between the affective 'inside' and the discursive 'outside' is through identification. The unconscious develops a series of symbolic subject positions, which are then taken up, partly through idealisation and partly under threat of punishment. Thus, the unconscious develops a series of normative injunctions that secure the borders of a socially produced position (for example, what constitutes normal gender behaviour) through the threat of psychosis and/or abjection. This identification is understood as a kind of affiliation and expression of an emotional tie with an internalised, fantasised object (usually person or body part) or normative ideal. She is at pains to argue, however, that these identifications are never complete or whole. Identification is with a fantasy or idealisation; consequently it can never be co-terminus with real people and bodies. This perspective highlights the instability of identity and how easily it can become fragmented in a milieu of disjointed and often contradictory social discourses.

Timimi (1996) has highlighted how mutual, projective identification between groups – whereby healthy aspects of the self are split off and projected into a cultural group that is socially more powerful, at the same time as undesirable aspects of the self can be split off and projected by cultural groups in a more powerful position onto those in a less powerful one – operate at the interface of the individual and their group affiliations. Much of this emanates from an inability to accept and acknowledge difference without attempting to dominate the object felt to be different (Tan, 1993). These unconscious processes thus have the potential to maintain social hierarchies and embedded power relationships at the emotional level.

The concept of hegemony, first articulated by Gramsci (1971), has proved useful as a way of conceptualising and talking about the effects of power on discourse regulation. Hegemony refers to a strand of meaning and practice that is dominant. For example, we can say that free enterprise and free trade philosophies have economic hegemony in the world. We can also speak about hegemonic masculinity (referring to the dominant ways in which we construct our beliefs about masculinity), hegemonic psychiatry (in reference to the dominant models used in psychiatry) and so forth. For Gramsci, hegemony implies a situation where a historical block of ruling class's actions exercise social authority and leadership over the rest of the population, which he believed is achieved through a combination of force, but more importantly, consents. Indeed, attempts would always be made to ensure that force appears to be based on consent of the majority through the influence that hegemonic opinions have on the organs of public opinion, such as newspapers and associations. For Gramsci, all people reflect upon the world and, through the 'common sense' of popular culture, organise their lives and experience, thus common sense becomes a crucial site for ideological conflict and ideological struggle because it is the terrain of the taken-for-granted that in a practical way guides actions in the everyday world.

Another influential thinker, Rorty (1989, 1991), argues that we do not require universal foundations or ideologies to pursue a pragmatic improvement in the human condition. He believes that it is desirable to open ourselves up to as many possible descriptions and re-descriptions of the world as possible. He is particularly concerned with finding pragmatic ways forward and argues that knowledge is not a matter of getting a 'true' or 'objective' picture of reality, but of learning how best to cope with the world. He believes that our best chance for transcending our acculturation is to be brought up in a culture that prides itself on not being monolithic, on its tolerance for plurality of subcultures and its willingness to listen to other worldviews and other cultural perspectives. This approach of 'politics without foundations' stresses the importance of finding pragmatic opportunities to bring about change in limited areas often revolving around specific issues rather than grand meta-narratives (like that of Marxism). By this approach, truth becomes a pragmatic question of what is 'to count as truth' and, as a result, truths and actions are formed within and through social values. Thus, in order to help us focus on what specific aspects of our cultural conditions we should seek to change and why, we must first engage in debate and reflection on what values it is we wish to adopt, both as individuals and as a collective (including the political/policy level).

What's missing?

In the above very brief description of some dominant strands of thought on the subject of the relationship between society, culture and subjectivity we have summarised a few relevant themes that provide useful conceptual tools for analysing the significance and meaning of the data in relation to children, families, the development of the self, and the interface between our beliefs about the self and the institutions that produce and regulate these beliefs. What is often missing is the non-Western perspective. While the above concepts are all useful, diverse and take in a wide spectrum of opinions and thinking from a rich tradition of philosophical, psychological and sociological thought in Western culture, the thinkers and thought traditions referred to above originate from Western societies. In his book *Mining Civilizational Knowledge*, Goonatilake (1998) points out that there is a wealth of knowledge held in non-Western cultures that has been almost completely overlooked as the assumption of the inherent superiority of Western culture, has deemed non-Western knowledge 'backward'. Similarly, Saunders *et al.* (2008) point out that the dominant view in most of the world's population tends to be more 'pre-modern' and based on principles of totality, unity, continuity and community, with a belief in the human lifespan as part of a larger narrative determined by either a 'cosmic law' or deified entities. The self and concepts of disorder of this self (including what we in the West would call mental illness/psychiatric disorder) cast through this prism look very different indeed.

For example, there are many different ways of conceptualising the 'unconscious'. South Asian philosophies have for centuries had a wide-ranging and vibrant set of ideas on the nature of the unconscious, in contrast to Western culture, which has only really grasped at trying to understand this in the last century or so. Theories of mind, personality and the human condition from these perspectives are familiar with notions of a many-layered unconscious affecting our perceptions of reality. Indeed, for many South Asian theories (such as Buddhism and the Upanishads) our perceptions are always distortions of reality and recognising this is the first step towards 'true' knowledge of the nature of reality (Goonatilake, 1998).

Another example relates to ideas on child development, which have long-established theories and practices in many non-Western traditions. In traditional Indian thinking the human life cycle is conceptualised as unfolding in a series of stages, each having unique tasks. Traditional Indian medicine and philosophy in the form of Ayurveda describes childhood Samskaras (which are expressive and symbolic performances), including rites and ceremonies that are held over the child to mark her/his transition from one stage to another (Kakar, 1994, 1997). Middle Eastern culture is heavily influenced by Islamic ideas on child development, which has been debated by Islamic scholars over many centuries (Gil'adi, 1992). Emphasis is placed on learning about the social values of Islam such as cooperation, truthfulness, helping the elderly, obeying parents and the importance of cleanliness of the body. Various stages of cognitive development are identified, which revolve around sophisticated concepts such as *Tamyiz* (facility for discernment), *Addab* (respect/public manners) and *aql* (mindfulness or social intelligence), the development of which in a child are seen as evidence of readiness to progress to the next developmental phase (Davis and Davis, 1989; Gregg, 2005; Timimi, 2005).

This ignoring of non-Western theory and practice is a somewhat hidden form of institutionalised racism (or more accurately, institutionalised cultural hegemony) that has infected Western academic and political endeavours for a long time. Not only does this present real dangers to the traditions and knowledge bases in existence in the non-Western world, it also means that populations of the Western world are being denied the opportunity to benefit from the positive effects that embracing non-Western knowledge, values and practices may bring. Edward Said (1978, 1981) illuminates this 'structural' and societal character of racism in his discussion of 'Orientalism'. Orientalism is a set of Western discourses of power that have constructed an 'Orient' in ways that depend on and reinforce the positional superiority and hegemony of the West – a general group of ideas impregnated with European superiority, racism and imperialism that can be found in a variety of Western texts, media and practices. Even before the current crisis, which has led to panic about and demonisation of Islam in the West, Said (1981) argued that the Western media represents Islamic people as irrational fanatics led by messianic and authoritarian leaders, with Islamic women portrayed as oppressed, not allowed to speak for themselves and lacking a sense of personal agency.

SUMMARY

What these discourses highlight is that when we try to understand how a phenomenon such as ASD has come to occupy an increasingly prominent place as an explanatory story – couched in a scientific/medical framework, for a set of human behaviours/experiences that just a few decades ago avoided the gaze of doctors – we also need to understand the broad context that promotes such a change. In setting this broad context, we first discussed how our concept of what constitutes a normal childhood and what constitutes autism have never been static and have changed over time (Chapter 3). In this chapter we have discussed the cultural- and political-specific nature of our ideas about child development and the goal of child development – in other words the types of 'selves' that are deemed desirable for us to develop into, how we come to acquire these ideas and how they affect how we live our lives. Our beliefs about how children should develop reflect the preoccupations of our culture; the concept of the selves we are meant to become is heavily influenced by the ideologies of the ruling classes. Various conscious and unconscious processes mean that people identify with and often willingly absorb some of these values and practices of the ruling classes, accepting them as being the 'normal', natural way the world works. Thus, current mainstream beliefs about ASDs became dominant not as the result of scientific breakthroughs but as a result of economic, political and cultural conditions that promoted them as a means of furthering the dominant political ideology.

Dominant ideologies in other cultures have sometimes radically different ideas about how children are meant to develop and the nature of the selves they are meant to become. Autism and its expansion could only have developed in modernist Western culture and can only be popularised around the world through the export and imposition of Western ideology onto other cultures.

Setting this context allows us to concentrate, in the following chapters, on the scientific evidence (or rather the lack of it) that supports the notion that autism and the ASDs are categories that can be given a natural boundary. Without understanding the role political, economic, social and psychological processes play in our changing ideas on how to categorise and regulate children, and how this relates to the type of 'selves' we are meant to acquire, it would indeed appear strange that autism has the high profile it does despite being based on what we believe is such flimsy scientific evidence.

It is hard to picture the wider consequences of the construction and then expansion of autism without analysing other concomitant trends within current systems of people management found in Western neo-liberal societies. Whatever the causes, functionality or social acceptability of the behaviours associated with ASDs may be, the solutions (treatments) offered seem to lead to greater social control through psychiatric screening in early childhood, greater monitoring of children's and young adults' daily activities and more interventions of a plethora of social, medical and educational services, both public and private. The concept of ASDs is but a small part of a much larger picture, with multiple phenomena contributing to ever-growing networks of social control. It is a 'small part', however, that reveals much about our current cultural preoccupations.

II
AUTISM
THE SCIENCE

5
BIOLOGICAL EVIDENCE

Having set the broad context into which autism as a concept emerged and then expanded, we now turn to examining what science has discovered about the concept. In this chapter we will look at the crucial subject of what biological evidence there is to justify conceptualising autism as a 'neurodevelopmental' (development of the nervous system) and genetic disorder.

GENETICS

In many ways the argument over genes versus environment replays that of earlier epochs on free will versus determinism. It is not our intention to suggest that ASD is 'caused' by the environment, rather to suggest that the proponents of genetic 'causes' for psychopathological behaviours have misrepresented the evidence. What we suggest is that recourse to genetic determinist arguments not only rests on poor science but that it is ultimately also ideology masquerading as science. What we have is closer to science fiction, as various authors in the field 'look forward' to that day when the genetic causes for this or that psychopathological condition (including autism) will be found.

What would it mean if we discovered the genes that 'cause' or played a significant part in increased susceptibility to autism? Even a confirmed convert to the genetic proposition such as Sir Michael Rutter (see Chapter 3) recognises that although identification of susceptibility genes may be helpful in shaping the biological research that could discover the neural basis of autism, it is much less clear that the genes themselves will be of much practical utility in terms of screening or diagnosis (Rutter, 2006).

In 2000, Rutter proposed seven benefits that might accrue from genetic research into autism:

1. It might alleviate the previous stigma associated with the inference that autism was caused by affectionless parenting. (However, it is unclear whether knowing that one or one's partner is carrying genes for disorder Z will be viewed as reassuring.)
2. It may lead to genetic counselling.
3. It should benefit research, although Rutter concedes that 'the connection between autism and the broader phenotype may prove to be quite complex and difficult to determine' (Rutter, 2000: 11).
4. Knowing the genes involved may lead to research that might shed light on the pathways from the cell to the neurological.
5. Such research may also uncover the existence of protective genes that might explain why women are less prone to autism.
6. Discovering the pathways from gene to neurobiology might lead to appropriate and rational interventions, particularly pharmacological. (Conversely, this could be seen as an admission that current approaches do not have a 'rational' basis.)
7. Identification of genes might lead to the discovery of environmental risk factors. What we might do if we discovered that specific environments proved risky or, indeed, why we need to know the genes to discover the environmental risks, is not discussed.

What, to us, is obviously missing from the above is a discussion of the ethics involved; thus, there is little acknowledgement of the potential dangers involved in moving towards identifying the 'genes' associated with (or that are believed to cause) autism, particularly in the context of an autism that now has such a wide and 'fuzzy' definition.

The Nuffield Council on Bioethics has looked at the question of *Mental Disorders and Genetics* and concluded that:

> The Working Party recommends that genetic testing for susceptibility genes which offer relatively low predictive or diagnostic certainty be discouraged, unless there is clear medical benefit to the patient. The genetic testing of children requires special safeguards and the Working Party recommends that predictive genetic testing and testing for carrier status for mental or indeed other disorders in children be strongly discouraged. (Nuffield Council on Bioethics, 1998: xiii)

The Working Party had already concluded in its executive summary that genetic tests will not be particularly useful, even if 'a number of susceptibility genes were identified for a particular disorder', and that 'without an understanding of their interaction, they would not be adequate for predicting individual risk in a clinical setting' (Nuffield Council on Bioethics, 1998: xiii). The report also states quite unequivocally that science and values cannot be separated and that the abrogation of moral responsibility is incompatible with good science.

One very obvious issue that autism genetic research has consistently failed to address satisfactorily is that of the over-representation of autism and ASDs in boys. Pickles *et al.* (2000) hypothesise that because autism is rarely diagnosed in girls without an accompanying learning disability there is a link to the X chromosome, particularly as some of those girls who had been previously diagnosed were subsequently identified as having Fragile X. However, given that very few males with 'core' autism will marry, just how is autism being transmitted? One might expect that autism has a random transmission very much like Down's syndrome, in which case it should not be so disproportionately found in any one class, gender or specific ethnic background. Outside of child psychiatry – where other so-called 'neurodevelopmental' disorders (such as ADHD) also have an excess of males – there are no genetic disorders that affect children's development that come near to being so linked to the male sex. These important gender issues seem to have passed most autism academics and researchers by.

The argument that autism is a strongly genetic condition rests primarily upon twin and family studies (see below). These studies generally focus on what might be called 'core' autism rather than broader ASD diagnoses such as Asperger's or PDD-NOS (Freitag, 2007), thus the findings cannot be generalised as there is little direct research into the genetics of other major categories of PDD or the hypothesised spectrum. In addition, autism twin studies do not have the luxury of having studies with twins reared apart and there are no adoption studies (studies comparing the biological families with the adopted families of adoptees adopted early in life and who are subsequently diagnosed with autism). There is one study that included subjects who had been adopted (Szatmari *et al.*, 2000); however, this was a familial aggregate study comparing what the authors called the 'lesser variant' of PDD (i.e., traits that do not amount to a diagnosis) among the relatives of adopted children with a diagnosis of a PDD with the relatives of non-adopted children with a PDD diagnosis; thus, it is not a true adoption study.

Twin studies

Twin studies are the most often-cited research methodology used to provide evidence for genetic causation. As identical (mono-zygotic – MZ) twins share all their genes, whereas non-identical (di-zygotic – DZ) on average share half their genes, higher rates of concordance (i.e., both twins having the same feature being studied) in MZ than DZ twins for condition X is taken as providing good evidence that condition X has a strong genetic component. Joseph (2006) suggests that the twin method rests on three basic assumptions:

1. That there are two types of twins – identical (MZ) and fraternal (DZ) – and that researchers can distinguish between the two.
2. The results from twins can be generalised to singletons.
3. That the environments of identical (MZ) and fraternal (DZ) twins are the same. This assumption is called the equal environment assumption (EEA). EEA does not hold if, for example, the environments of MZ twins were more alike than DZ twins (such as, for example, that MZ are parented significantly differently than DZ).

With regard to the first issue – that researchers can reliably distinguish between MZ and DZ twins – Joseph (2004) identifies three methods for twin identification:

1. The resident hospital method. Here a researcher will sift through the records of people with a diagnosis, locate any who have a twin and assess the twin.
2. National registers. Some countries, notably the Scandinavian countries, keep a database of all twins.
3. Consecutive admissions method. This involves identifying twins from a sample of consecutive admissions to a hospital over a specified time period.

One of the problems with the selection of twins in many countries (including in the UK) is that selection of twins is done through at least one of the twins having already come to the attention of a hospital or clinician. The problem here is that if a researcher knows that twin A has condition X, then if she/he is already committed to the belief that condition X has a genetic basis then the researcher may already have a bias about what they will find in twin B, which may lead to the diagnosis of condition X in this twin, particularly as conditions such as ASD rely on subjectively defined criteria. In such a situation where the twin 'appears' identical it is hard to imagine that diagnoses would be made blind.

With current genetic testing it is quite easy to settle the zygosity (i.e., MZ or DZ) of the twin. However, it may not have been so in the past and identification was usually based upon parental reports on a questionnaire, raising some concerns about the accuracy and comparability of early twin studies.

In relation to the second assumption – that the results from twins can be generalised to singletons – there are number of problems. Studies have found that a whole host of health issues are more frequent in twins, including low birth weight, poor language and reading skills, conduct disorders, obstetric problems and congenital anomalies. With an increased use of *in vitro* fertilisation, decreasing infant mortality and increasing ability to keep very premature and low birth weight babies alive, there are more surviving twins and multiple births than ever before. As health issues are more common in twins, an increase in the number of twins could also to lead to an increase in the prevalence of certain conditions, making generalisation from this rather specific population to singletons complicated.

However, of the three basic assumptions identified by Joseph above it is the third (that the environments of MZ and DZ twins are the same) that is the most problematic and has caused the most controversy. It is now well established that MZ twins are treated more similarly and experience more similar environments than DZ twins or singletons. To conclude that a concordance rate difference between the two sets of twins is the result of genetics one must first assume that both sets of twins are treated similarly by their parents, friends, teachers, etc. – the equal environment assumption. If society treats identical twins more similarly than non-identical twins then any, or all, of the difference in concordance rates could be explained by environmental stimuli. In addition being one of an identical twin produces its own psychological dynamic with identity confusion and swapping roles occurring more commonly (Joseph, 2006). Therefore the assumption that the higher incidences of psychopathological conditions found in MZ twins *can only be* attributable to genetics is not sustained. This is not the same as saying that such data is incompatible with a genetic theory of causation, as clearly the data is compatible with a theory of genetic causation. However, the data is also compatible with an entirely non-genetic explanation. Essentially this undermines the theory of genetic causation; twin studies can tell us very little and probably nothing at all about the role of genetics in autism and ASD, given that these are behaviourally defined conditions with no physical markers.

Joseph (2004) points out that twin researchers have largely accepted this criticism, but some have reacted by trying to stand the criticism on its head. They do this by suggesting that genetic factors lead twins to 'choose' their more identical environments (e.g., Rutter, 2006). With such an argument (that genes are responsible for disrupting the EEA, therefore the difference in rates between MZ and DZ twins is still genetic) it is difficult to see how evidence could ever settle this, unless clear pathological pathways are identified from specific genes to specific behaviours – and we are a long way from that.

In the largest twin study done to date (of twins in general), the Minnesota Twin Study (Bouchard *et al.*, 1990), all kinds of behaviours, including dressing alike, are deemed to have been found in twins. Are we to assume that there is a fashion gene? Church attendance and political persuasion are found to be 'identical' in identical twins. What is it that we are inferring is genetic from this? When it comes to drawing any conclusion about what role genes play in behaviours we are in agreement with Sadler (2005) who concludes that when we ask what is genetic we would be as well to ask what isn't. How are we to evaluate our assumptions that some things are more genetic than others and what relevance does this have to autism research?

The autism twin studies

In their study, Folstein and Rutter (1977) identify a number of problems they associate with previous twin studies of autism, which presumably this study is meant to rectify. The authors refer to a previous review by Rutter (1968) of twin studies, some of which referred to childhood psychosis or childhood schizophrenia. Folstein and Rutter (1977) identified a further three studies that had been published since that review and concluded that these subsequent studies had similar findings as the 1968 review – that is that no firm conclusions can be reached about the role genes play in autism. One of the deficiencies they identify was the disparity of MZ to DZ twin pairs. In the previous studies there were more MZ twins in the studies than DZ pairs, despite the fact that in the general population DZ outnumber MZ twins, roughly in the ratio 2:1. In this study, Folstein and Rutter (1977) identify 11 MZ pairs and ten DZ twin pairs, therefore retaining the disproportionate imbalance. They also state that one of the other problems in previous studies was a significant lack of clinical information on how zygosity was determined. In this study zygosity was determined by physical appearance, fingerprints and blood grouping. The authors state that in eight of the twin pairs DZ status could be determined solely on physical appearance – that is they looked dissimilar to each other – leaving some questions about whether zygosity was determined in a reliable fashion for all the twins. Given that the twins were selected from clinics where they had already received a diagnosis of autism, one also has to wonder just how representative a sample this was.

However, in relation to the clinical information provided, this study cannot be faulted. There is a wealth of information on parents, backgrounds, birth weight, obstetric and peri-natal complications, as well as information on social, cognitive and linguistic functioning. Each pair is laid out in detail, with clear information on whether the twins were concordant for autism or some other form of social and cognitive disorder. A considerable attempt was made to make diagnosis in a 'blind' fashion, using Kanner's criteria and Rutter's criteria of the time.

What can be said about all MZ pairs in this study is that no pair was free of a social, cognitive, or communication disorder, even if some of the social problems had dissipated, at least in those with a 'normal' IQ. Folstein and Rutter state that about half of the individuals had an IQ in the severe learning disabled range, although they don't comment on whether the MZ twins had a greater/lesser proportion of individuals in the severe range than the DZ twins. Only about one third of the twins were deemed to have IQs in the normal range. A number of obstetric complications were reported and where both twins had a low birth weight they also had 'mental retardation'. In the majority of cases where only one twin was autistic, it was the twin who had the lower birth weight and mental retardation who also had autism. No twin had a high IQ and autism. In addition, 82 per cent (nine of the 11) of the MZ twins were concordant for other problems of a cognitive, social or linguistic kind. The vast majority of the MZ cases cited in the study had considerable problems irrespective of whether they were also diagnosed with autism. In conclusion, they report a concordance rate for autism of 36 per cent for MZ twins and 0 per cent for DZ twins. This difference forms the basis for arguing that autism is a strongly genetic disorder.

In 1989, Steffenberg *et al.* carried out what they call the second 'acceptable' twin study. They criticise previous studies as flawed because their numbers were too small or they included mixed-sex pairs, which they argue is not appropriate because of the high ratio of boys to girls in autism. They criticise the Ritvo *et al.* (1985) study as flawed due to the method of recruitment using those who had already accessed services. One wonders whether this same criticism could also be laid at the previous 'acceptable' study – that of Folstein and Rutter (1977) – given the fact that recruitment of twin samples were also achieved via those who had already accessed services. In this study the authors contacted professionals across Scandinavia. In addition, the Danish, Norwegian and Swedish autistic societies were contacted to identify twins. Diagnosis was established using a number of checklists but the authors go to great pains to point out that these were not the sole basis for diagnosis, with interviews being undertaken with the caregivers and the child before establishing diagnosis. The authors make the point that the Folstein and Rutter (1977) study did not do this. The diagnostic criteria used were those of DSM-III-R. Zygosity was established in 82 per cent of cases, although it is not clear why it was not possible to do so in 100 per cent. What is remarkable is that, despite the fact that the authors had an extensive trawl of all Scandinavian countries, they were left in the end with no more than 22 pairs, ten of whom were female. One of the aspirations of the authors, to yield a greater number of twins than previous studies so that conclusions about the genetic basis for autism could be made on greater numbers than the Folstein and Rutter (1977) study, seems to have failed.

The subjects of this study (Steffenberg *et al.*, 1989) had lower IQs than the Folstein and Rutter (1977) study and, unlike the later Le Couteur *et al.* (1996) study, three-quarters came from social class III. The boy–girl ratio was comparable to that found for mental retardation (MR) (among the learning-disabled population the ratio of boy to girl is about 1.3 to 1 and the ratio of boy to girl for autism in this study is 1.3 to 1) and nearly all of those children who were rated autistic also had MR. They suggest that peri-natal stress could be a complicating factor, but hypothesise that this could be an effect not a cause (of having an autistic child). The presence of a high level of cognitive problems in 88 per cent of MZ twins begs the question as to what exactly it is that is being 'inherited' and how one is supposed to disentangle social communication difficulties resulting from more global learning difficulties as opposed to autism. Given the existence of problems in all twins (but which are more severe in MZ twins), is it really valid to make extrapolations from twins to singletons without obvious learning difficulties? What seems to differentiate those diagnosed with autism from those who were not was the existence of stereotypies, adherence to routines, finger twirling or hand flapping. It was unusual for these problems to be manifest in twins who had normal IQs, were not second born, or didn't have a low birth weight.

In the UK there are two subsequent important studies (Bailey *et al.*, 1995; Le Couteur *et al.*, 1996). If we take the Folstein and Rutter (1977) study as a 'gold' standard thus far, then these studies are base metal, despite the fact that Rutter is a co-author. Many of the criticisms made of previous studies are to be found here. Diagnosis is not 'blind', very little clinical and case information is given and no details of cognitive impairments or peri-natal events are provided. Despite the fact that new cases are discussed, the paucity of clinical information makes it impossible to share the conclusions across studies with any degree of confidence. As diagnosis was made using the ADI-R and ADOS-G (see Chapter 6), it is likely to have dealt with very different individuals and definitions of 'caseness' to the other studies, making comparisons between these and previous studies problematic.

The Bailey *et al.* (1995) study consisted of a follow-up of the twins from the Folstein and Rutter (1977) study (19 pairs), as well as a study of 28 new pairs. The companion study by Le Couteur *et al.* (1996) looked at the existence of the broader phenotype in the same twin sample. Three areas of dysfunction were now deemed to be commensurate with the wider autism phenotype: apart from repetitive interests (gone was any allusion to stereotypies), there were now social deficits and social and communicative delays (these included delays in reading and speaking). The criteria they use bore little relationship to ICD or DSM criteria and there was no age of onset criteria. In fact, the authors say they were stepping outside ICD criteria in order to identify these impairments. Some of the original twins from the Folstein and Rutter (1977) study were in their 40s or 50s; it is not clear if any attempt was made to establish whether these so-called impairments were contemporaneous or had been manifested from infancy. The criteria were probably extrapolated from either the ADI-R or the ADOS-G as functioning was determined in adult terms. The authors quote a number of studies used to establish the wider phenotype. Some studies purport to find cognitive difficulties in relatives, whereas others find social difficulties in relatives. Even if cognitive problems or social problems were found on their own, it is still argued that this would constitute an example of the autism phenotype. The authors also take issue with the Scandinavian study, which purported to find a link between autism and obstetric complications, and argue that obstetric complications where they occur may be a symptom of carrying an autistic child.

No twins who had a 'recognisable' medical aetiology for a medical disorder were included in the Bailey *et al.* (1995) study. What might have constituted 'recognisable' is not defined. Included in this study were female twin pairs, for reasons that remain unclear. The Folstein and Rutter (1977) study had originally ruled out the inclusion of female twin pairs on the basis that autism was a disproportionately male phenomenon. In terms of social functioning, none of the original MZ twins (irrespective of whether they had an autism diagnosis) were functioning well as adults, but given the level of cognitive impairments this is hardly surprising.

The authors mention that two twins did not meet ICD-10 criteria and were excluded. Does that mean that they were deemed autistic in the original study but were not deemed autistic in 1995? This is not explored further. The authors also state that it was established that one female twin pair who had been concordant in the original study were found to be Fragile X. Surely this means that in the original study this would lower the concordance further. Twins who had recognisable medical disorders were excluded in the Bailey *et al.* (1995) study, but included in the Le Couteur *et al.* (1996) study.

In the new studies the concordance for MZ was 69 per cent and 0 per cent for DZ, and the ratio of MZ to DZ twins was almost 3:2. Folstein and Rutter (1977) had said, prior to their paper, that having a disproportionate number of MZ twins in a study was sufficient to invalidate research; it seems a little strange that this is no longer an issue. It is no surprise to find that the more behaviour one labels as autistic, then the more autistic behaviours one discovers. There is insufficient data on obstetric and other demographic factors to warrant the conclusions the authors provide. The authors state that the average gestation age of both MZ and DZ twins was 36 weeks. However, collapsing the data in such a fashion is duplicitous as the close correlation between being an MZ twin and being diagnosed as autistic renders the gestational period of the MZ twins most salient, yet this is not specified.

It should be recalled that the vast majority of the MZ cases cited in Folstein and Rutter (1977) had considerable problems, whether they were diagnosed with autism or not. No twin who did not also have a low IQ merited a diagnosis of autism. In the Le Couteur *et al.* (1996) study, any person diagnosed with autism also had social and language problems, although these differed in severity. The fact that most of the MZ twins were not free from any of these impairments is then used by Le Couteur and colleagues to argue for the existence of an autism phenotype. Irrespective of whether a twin in the first study or in the subsequent study by Le Couteur *et al.* (1996) had impairments in only one dimension of the triad of impairments, it is now argued that these are manifestations of the phenotype. Whether a child would merit no diagnosis or an alternative diagnosis was not properly explored. This raises the question of whether any childhood disorder manifesting communicative or social impairments would be deemed to be part of the phenotype.

Previously, Rutter (1978b) argued that a valid diagnosis of autism relied on differentiating it from other comparable disorders. With the current diagnostic criteria, including those used in the Le Couteur *et al.* (1996) and Bailey *et al.* (1995) studies, this differentiation becomes a near-impossible task, leaving the distinct impression that their interpretation is born not of science but of ideology. The Le Couteur *et al.* (1996) study looked at the broader phenotype in twins and whether MZ twins rather than DZ twins had more impairments in autism symptoms (although not necessarily sufficient for a diagnosis). It should come as no surprise that MZ twins were much more likely exhibit the full phenotype and parts of it than DZ twins. Social functioning posed the greatest problems: far fewer of the MZ twins were in employment or relationships than their DZ counterparts. The study contains a number of case vignettes where details such as class, zygosity and birth complications have been removed, in order (according to the authors) to protect confidentiality. We are left to accept that (on trust) there was nothing unusual to differentiate these twins from the overall population.

Family studies

Many of the criticisms above apply to family studies, particularly as most families share the same socio-economic environment. Health issues tend to 'run' in families and are disproportionately clustered in lower socio-economic groups. There have been few twin studies of autism and none of sufficient scale for many of the ASDs such as Asperger's syndrome (AS). There have been a few family studies of AS, but as it is not clear that the authors of these studies have any consensus over 'caseness' these studies are of limited value. Gillberg and Cederlund (2005) and Ghaziuddin (2005) both purport to find evidence of AS and autistic traits in family members but in the absence of case histories it is difficult to interpret the meaning of their findings. Both papers talk of relatives having such behaviours, but no details are provided with regard to crucial information such as age of onset or level of functioning. As no evidence is presented to suggest that the adults concerned are not productive members of the community, one has to wonder what the relevance to both researcher and clinician of finding an 'Asperger' trait is. But let us look in more detail at a couple of the other family studies in order to illustrate these methodological failings.

A family history study was conducted by Bolton *et al.* (1994 to investigate the existence of the broader phenotype in relatives and to establish whether the presence of this phenotype was more likely due to genetic or environmental factors. The study used 101 probands (those with the diagnosis). The authors chose a control group of what they deemed a comparable disorder – Down's syndrome – although no empirical evidence was used to justify this choice of control. The filtering process employed by the authors resulted in there being a ratio of autism probands and families to that of Down syndrome probands and families of 3:1. ADOS-G and ADI-R, used to study the relatives, were initially meant for observing children in multiple settings (see Chapter 6 for further information about these assessment 'tools') and one has to wonder how relevant they are for adults. The authors also state that 'blind' diagnosis was not feasible and a 'case vignette' method was therefore used. The function of the case vignette was to obtain a second set of researchers who were deemed 'blind' to the study to double check the diagnosis of the autism probands.

In their results, Bolton *et al.* (1994) point out that among the siblings of the autism probands, two already had a diagnosis of autism and another two met ICD-10 criteria for a diagnosis. A further four had a 'developmental disorder', did not meet ICD criteria for autism, but did meet the criteria for 'atypical autism' and, in one case, AS. None of the siblings of the Down's children met any of the criteria for a developmental disorder. The authors then go on to examine the prevalence of minor 'phenotypic' behaviours. The authors state that minor variants were found in first-degree relatives, but not at a statistically significant level. They then added that if a less stringent definition of what constituted stereotyped behaviours was adopted, then statistically significant results could be achieved. This seems a rather lax level of scientific reasoning where it appears that when you don't get the results you like, you change the hypothesis to achieve them. Bolton and colleagues (1994) go on to define the lesser variant and examine its boundaries. The mere presence of deficits in the 'triad' of impairments (irrespective of whether it was in only one or two domains) is now deemed to constitute the lesser variant of the phenotype. Relatives of the autism probands manifested six times the incidence of this 'lesser variant' than those of Downs probands. It is argued that this constitutes proof for the phenotype and evidence of a genotype regardless of how many of the 'triad' appeared. It is not stated whether the manifestation of this lesser variant would warrant a diagnosis of anything, never mind a PDD or ASD. No details of current level of functioning or employment or relationship status is given; this makes speculation about this or that phenotype or variant of little scientific or clinical relevance.

In their discussion the authors take issue with the question of representative sampling. They state that the rarity of the disorder prohibited a wider sampling – but one might have thought that by the early 1990s this was no longer the case. It is also unclear just what is being asserted in the research. Even if we accept that there is such a phenotype, does this mean it is an 'autism' phenotype? Even if the existence of an autism phenotype is adequately demonstrated, can this be translated to an autism genotype? Given that siblings are the primary study group here, such research cannot disentangle genetic from environmental causation.

Starr *et al.* (2001) sought to determine if the family loading for either the broader autism phenotype or for cognitive impairment differed according to whether or not autism was accompanied by severe learning difficulties. This study examined families recruited from the Children's Department at the Maudsley Hospital in London. Forty-seven probands were selected, of whom 39 were male. It is stated that all those selected had IQs less than 50 and were between the ages of four and 34. Family histories were taken but much of the information was anecdotal, particularly in relation to second- and third-degree relatives, none of whom were seen by the researchers. The probands had a high proportion of communication problems, which is not surprising given their low IQ. Of the 49 'eligible' siblings, two met ICD-10 criteria for autism. A further six were deemed to have impairments in at least one of the 'triad', although none of these had impairments in two of the three prongs of the triad and none of them manifested problems in the social dimension. No information is given on the IQ of siblings or other relatives. None of the parents had the full triad: four manifested impairments in two dimensions and nine manifested impairments in one dimension; of these 13, eight were male. Three second-degree relatives had impairments in two dimensions. The authors report that 17 families (roughly one quarter) had no other affected relative; two families had six affected individuals. One would have liked to know a great deal more about those families. The authors also report that what they term 'scholastic difficulties' was found in families of probands. They do not say whether these were disproportionately found in first- or second-degree relatives or any particular families. This study included a large number of half-siblings and, according to the authors, many of the families had experienced considerable disruption, raising questions about the ability of this data set to differentiate genetic from environmental causation.

Genes and autism in summary

So, on the basis of a few twin and family studies we are now told that there is good evidence for an autism phenotype and that previous diagnostic classifications must be re-evaluated. This seems a rather skewed form of reasoning – a bit like arguing that because one member of a family had bronchitis and others had colds that there was a bronchitis phenotype

The results raise a number of questions about the 'phenotype' and its nature. In these studies it is rare to come across the presence of a relative who has or would warrant a diagnosis of autism, AS or PDD-NOS, which one might think you would find if these are regarded as autistic spectrum disorders. In the Starr *et al.* (2001) study any problems in probands and their families could be attributable to cognitive impairments. Learning difficulties and behavioural disorders (such as ADHD and conduct disorder), which are often associated with social problems that are found in those with an IQ above 70, also tend to cluster in families. Throwing a heterogeneous mish-mash of behaviours together under the rubric of the autism phenotype or ASD may thus have little scientific or clinical utility. It is also legitimate to wonder, if the 'affected' parents in these studies can marry and work, how severe can their impairments be? If these first- and second-degree relatives can look forward to becoming like their parents, then is the course of autism or autism-like disorders necessarily gloomy?

If we are at the stage when we assume that there is no longer any age cut-off when autism can manifest itself, then the concept needs a dramatic rethink as the number of comparable disorders that autism would have to be distinguished from would become intolerable. This danger is one that Rutter (2000) is alive to, but, like so many dangers to the concept that he realises, he shirks from exploring its full ramifications. He alludes to the fact that others have posited a spectrum that would include affective disorders – after all the lack of affect was one of the original defining features of the condition. Rutter (2000) raises the possibility that the concept may suffer from over-inclusion, as more and more disorders are swallowed up in its maw. He goes on to suggest that, contrary to earlier impressions, cognitive deficits such as reading or spelling are not part of the genetic liability. Of course, this rather depends upon one's definition of 'cognitive'. When the Le Couteur *et al.* (1996) study was undertaken the concordance of 82 per cent for cognitive disorders was deemed to be one of the main strands for defining the phenotype. However, Rutter (2000) believes that language impairments do constitute an important part of the phenotype. It would seem naive, however, not to expect social impairments to result from language problems and that circumscribed interests might then follow from these.

In their paper *Genetics and Child Psychiatry: II Empirical Research Findings*, Rutter *et al.* (1999) present an overview of research on the role genetics plays in child psychopathology. The authors provide some useful observations, in the context of other disorders, which they might have also applied to autism. For example, in the context of affective disorders, they point out that an emphasis on current research may occlude the fact that diagnosis of depressive disorders in young people have increased in recent years (although they don't discuss the implications of this 'historical' perspective for the role genes may or may not play in affective disorders). They also point out that in research on affective disorders among second-degree relatives researchers relied on second-hand accounts, which is of questionable reliability. These potential problems are equally true of research on the autism phenotype. In the context of schizophrenia research the authors point out that family studies have revealed the presence of schizoaffective and schizotypal disorders: 'the problem, however, is that it has not proved possible to end up with diagnostic criteria that can be informative at the individual level as regards whether the disorder in one particular case reflects a genetic liability to schizophrenia' (Rutter *et al.*, 1999: 24). It seems clear to us that the same applies to autism.

Is it possible that autism researchers have stood the phenomena on its head? Having devised tools from studying autistic people, they then applied these to other diagnostic groups and many previously regarded as 'normal' and found that they too are autistic. The idea came before the evidence, and the evidence has been 'shaped' to fit the idea. The 'discovery' that families with children considered autistic have an increase in autistic traits has led to the creation of the autistic phenotype and from there a strong belief in the autistic genotype. It should be no surprise to find that people who have certain personality characteristics have children with similar characteristics. However, we are still not even close to knowing what having a child with more severe autism (as it used to be defined) means for subsequent generations of children in that family's gene pool.

There are a number of additional factors that pose a problem for the genetic explanation – for example, the difference between genders. How could genes account for the case that autism is more prevalent in males than females or that the ratio of male to female for AS could be as high as 10:1? Why should a genetic disorder become more prevalent in males as we get into the outer boundaries of the spectrum? Why should there be a disproportionate number with ASDs found among members of ethnic or immigrant populations?

Even if we do reach the point of elucidating the genetics behind autism, how useful would such information be? If we examine one strongly genetic condition, Phenylketonuria (PKU), we can see that knowing that it is a genetic condition adds little to our knowledge or to the relevance of any specified intervention. Controlling PKU requires a number of dietary measures. Even if we know that something is genetic (and in the case of most mental conditions, including autism, we are a long way from reaching such conclusions), what difference will it make? If we are to follow Rutter's (2006) formula that genes (G) × environment (E) = condition X, then even if we know gene G we will still need to find any or all of the E factors and (as in PKU) we do not necessarily need to know G to find E. Surely, it is easier to find therapeutic solutions through changing E than changing G.

Rutter *et al.* (1999) report that Romanian children who have been severely deprived have 'quasi-autism'. If they have all of the descriptive criteria to meet a diagnosis of autism, surely there is no quasi about it. Whichever way we turn we continue to find evidence that challenges the genetic theory of autism, with authors using all sorts of semantic and interpretive devices to try and avoid facing this. In truth the cupboard is bare – no genes have been found for autism, perhaps because no genes for autism exist. As Sadler (2005) suggests, little of this is of relevance to psychiatry. People approach doctors primarily for treatment and at the moment the disproportionate time and money that is going into genetic research is adding nothing to either scientific knowledge or clinical utility.

The lack of any clear undisputed evidence that autism is 'genetic' is reflected in the lack of any 'genes' for autism being discovered in molecular genetic studies. Thus, various candidate genes, linkage studies, genome scans and chromosome studies have failed to produce or reliably replicate any particular genes for autism. The more failures that pile up, the more 'complex' autism genetics becomes, such that in a 2004 textbook chapter L.Y. Tsai identified the majority of the human chromosome as potentially harbouring autism genes (Tsai, 2004). Others have come to the more honest (and predictable) conclusion that, 'Though numerous linkages and associations have been identified, they tend to diminish upon closer examination or attempted replication' (Wassink *et al.*, 2004: 272). And 'No major genome scan has produced significant and reproducible results.. no candidate gene from a genome scan has shown a reproducible and statistically significant association with autism... no candidate gene that has inspired multiple studies has shown a robust and reproducible connection to autism' (Blaxill, 2005, quoted in Joseph, 2006: 251–2).

AUTISM AND NEUROIMAGING

Neuroplasticity

The social construction of many diagnostic categories has long been a problem that has plagued mental health professions. For a number of the diagnostic categories with which clinicians work, no conclusive evidence exists of a physical problem, such as a neurological deficit or abnormality in the endocrine system. In some cases minor physical abnormalities have been noted by researchers, but no one has yet been able to link these physical differences in a convincing way to the individual's behavioural problems. Part of the reason for this is 'neuroplasticity', which refers to the remarkable ability of the nervous system (particularly in children) to grow and change in response to environmental stimuli. This remarkable plasticity of the human brain makes it difficult to determine precise cause and effect when individuals with differential life experiences subsequently show what appear to be differences in neurological functioning.

For example, Sadato *et al.* (1996) reported activation of the primary visual cortex by Braille reading, when studying participants who became blind early in life. Using positron emission tomography to assess activation in blind and sighted participants during tactile discrimination tasks, this research team discovered that blind subjects showed activation of primary and secondary visual cortex areas during these tasks, while sighted controls showed deactivation. This finding fits well with the results of an early investigation by Merzenich (reported by Baringa, 1992) in which an adult monkey was trained to use its middle finger repeatedly, and after a relatively brief period of learning, a significantly larger region of the somatosensory cortex began to respond to the middle finger.

What these and other similar studies suggest is a profound ability of the brain to remap its own contours, based on differential life experience. While these findings have opened new avenues of investigation for neuroscience, they make efforts to link neurological differences with behaviour disorders more difficult. When a group of individuals with aberrant behaviour are found to have different brain functioning from normal controls, we must ask ourselves if the neurological discrepancies are a cause or an effect of the disordered behaviour. In trying to deal with the inconvenience this causes for researchers trying to 'pin down' behavioural aberrations into neurologically valid and clinically meaningful categories, lines have been drawn into the sand and diagnostic categories for behavioural problems created. As has been outlined in this book and elsewhere (for example, Timimi, 2002, 2005, 2007a; Timimi and Maitra, 2006), efforts to discover underlying neurological substrates to behavioural disorders have proved frustratingly unfruitful, a state of affairs that we predict will continue to be the case.

The fruitless search for the biological 'endophenotype'

Where biological theories of causation for human experiences (thoughts, feelings and behaviours – primarily investigated through genetics and neuroimaging) have repeatedly failed, is in pinpointing any specific 'substrate' to which a human experience considered socially deviant or transgressive can be attributed.

For example, one of the most potent areas of discourse around the social deviant/normal variation borders has been that of sexual orientation. In 1952, the original *Diagnostic and Statistical Manual of Mental Disorders (DSM)* (APA, 1952) listed homosexuality among the sociopathic personality disturbances. In 1966, *DSM II* removed homosexuality from the sociopathic list, categorising it with other sexual deviations (APA, 1966). Then in 1973, after a concerted campaign, it showed the most striking change of all: after a vote among psychiatrists, homosexuality was removed from the *DSM* and was no longer considered a psychiatric disorder. In his analysis of the American Psychiatric Association's reversal of the diagnostic classification of homosexuality, Bayer states, 'The result was not a conclusion based upon an approximation of the scientific truth as dictated by reason, but was instead an action demanded by the ideological temper of the times' (1981: 3–4). The combined effects of the sexual revolution and the civil rights movements had finally produced sufficient political pressure on the American Psychiatric Association to force through a change on primarily ideological rather than scientific grounds. Such a change would not have happened had the political climate not been supportive to this. This example is instructive, not least because 'autistic pride' campaigners have compared their struggle for wider acceptance of being 'autistic' to that of the gay rights movement.

Through out its short history, psychiatric diagnoses from 'Drapetomania' (diagnosis given to black slaves who attempted to flee captivity) to 'sluggish schizophrenia' (often used on 'dissidents' in the old Soviet Union) have reflected socio-political concerns of the time. As psychiatry, unlike the rest of medicine, has been unable to develop an aetiologically based diagnostic framework, then we see no reason why today's diagnoses should not also be reflective of current socio-political concerns, particularly for those (like autism) that are undergoing rapid change.

In 1993 Dean Hamer and colleagues published a paper in *Science* reporting on a study with a small number of families, with the claim that they had identified a gene marker, on the tip of the X chromosome (Xq28), which was common to gay men, but not their straight siblings. Following the press release accompanying the publication, the media confidently announced to the world that the 'gay gene' had been discovered. Hamer became an overnight celebrity and his findings were understandably welcomed by gay organisations, particularly in the USA, with them using this finding to argue that 'gayness' was therefore a natural condition, not a disease, and therefore gays should not be criminalised (interestingly, in psychiatry the finding of genes is seen as important in order to prove the opposite, i.e., that psychiatric disorders are biological 'diseases' caused by genetic 'abnormalities'). As is the rule of thumb now with such claims, Hamer and his group's results were not replicated (Rice *et al.*, 1999) in other studies and the 'discovery' joined the large pool of behavioural genetic gene 'discoveries', all of which thus far have come to nothing.

We shouldn't be surprised by this. Like most human experiences, to take sexual orientation as something that could be defined by biology alone, one must begin by assuming that sexual orientation is fixed by our genes and that historically it appears as a fixed stable category subject to varying degrees of socially mediated oppression/tolerance. Cultural studies reveal a variety of models operating in different cultures over time, including differing ideas about the development of sexual orientation and differing socially sanctioned practices, that make such simplistic formulations (like sexual orientation being driven by biology *alone*) simply untenable, however attractive such a simplification may appear. Furthermore, it is such scientifically unsustainable simplifications that arguably render issues such as sexual orientation most susceptible to 'eugenic' approaches, should society loose its tolerance, as it is frequently prone to do when searching for scapegoats at times of crises.

A second example comes from neuroimaging studies of a disorder that is increasingly seen as tied to ASD. This disorder also afflicts primarily boys, is conceptualised as being a genetic, neurodevelopmental disorder, and is increasingly diagnosed alongside ASD in those children troublesome enough not to make progress in their lives once they have the ASD label, or the opposite (i.e., children originally diagnosed with this other disorder who are not making progress, rendering them vulnerable to being given an ASD label in addition in order to try and explain this lack of progress). This disorder is, of course, attention deficit hyperactivity disorder (ADHD).

Support for the neurobiological underpinning of ADHD relies in large part on neuroimaging studies. Critical inspection of these studies not only reveals a complex picture, it actually casts strong doubt on the premise of an underlying neurological abnormality being responsible for ADHD, as the studies demonstrate that there is no characteristic neurophysiological or neuroanatomical pattern that can be found in children diagnosed as having ADHD. Brain scan studies have not uncovered a consistent deficit or abnormality, with a wide variety of brain structures being implicated: for example, left prefrontal cortex; left thalamus; right paracentral lobule; frontal, temporal and parietal lobes; the striatum; splenium of the corpus callosum; right caudate; total cerebral volume; right cerebral volume; and portions of the cerebellum (see Timimi, 2005; Timimi *et al.*, 2008). The sample sizes in these neuroimaging studies have all been small and in no study have the brains of the ADHD diagnosed children been considered to be clinically abnormal, nor has any specific abnormality been convincingly demonstrated (Baumeister and Hawkins, 2001).

The most problematic comparison, in terms of interpretation, would be between medicated ADHD children and controls, because any anatomical differences could be due to a medication effect, an organic deficit, or some combination of the two. Yet, for 30 years, and in over 30 studies, this comparison has been a mainstay of ADHD-imaging researchers. This has been pointed out by critics for many years; yet, for the most part, ADHD researchers have ignored this confounding variable and declared that their results show a biological basis of ADHD, although one could just as easily interpret their results as confirmation that stimulant medication is harmful to the developing brain.

More recently, ADHD-imaging researchers have finally acknowledged that prior medication use in the subjects is a confounding variable, and have started to use children who haven't taken ADHD medication in their studies. While this would seem to simplify their studies, somehow it has made them more complicated. A comparison between two recent studies, both funded by the US National Institute for Mental Health (NIMH), is illuminating. One study, with the first author being Xavier Castellanos, was published in 2002. The second study, with the first author being Elizabeth Sowell, was published in 2003 (Sowell *et al.*, 2003). Both studies had three groups of children: medicated ADHD children, unmedicated ADHD children and controls. Yet only the Castellanos study reported results about the comparison between the unmedicated ADHD children and medicated ADHD children. A major finding of the study, according to the authors and the corresponding NIMH press release, was that the researchers found no neuroanatomical differences between the unmedicated ADHD and medicated ADHD children, thus concluding that stimulants are not harmful to the developing brain. However, it is highly unusual for a drug to be declared safe on the basis of a single study, particularly as this study also failed to provide any details about the specifics of medication history (see Leo, 2006).

But just a year later, all of a sudden, the specifics about medication history were problematic. Variable medication histories were now the very reason given by the Sowell team for *not* reporting on the comparison between medicated and unmedicated ADHD children – even more problematic, they cite the Castellanos study as support for not reporting the data. Is it possible that Sowell's team did the comparison and found evidence that stimulants are associated with neuroanatomical changes, and then decided not to publish the data? At this point no one knows, but if so, the results would certainly run counter to NIMH's message (and academic psychiatry in general) that children diagnosed with ADHD should be medicated (Leo, 2006).

There are other major problems with the Castellanos study (Castellanos *et al.*, 2002). For example, his group of researchers had an opportunity to do a simple comparison of unmedicated children diagnosed with ADHD with an age-matched control group; however, numerous methodological inadequacies, such as choosing a control group whose age was on average two years older than the unmedicated ADHD group, meant that this straightforward comparison was never done (Leo and Cohen, 2003).

In addition to these methodological problems, interpreting the significance of any positive finding is far from straightforward. Neurological differences could be the result of environmental factors (like psychological trauma) on brain development, differential maturation rates and variations resulting from a more inclusive definition of normality. Making the leap of logic required to conclude that ADHD is therefore a disorder causing a neurological disturbance is suspect until we have established what this neurological disturbance looks like and how to test for it.

The idea of separating nature and nurture in the arena of human subjective life (thoughts, emotions and behaviours) and creating artificial hierarchies to explain causality is hugely problematic. The old eugenics has been criticised for being based on poor science, while the new eugenics peddles essentially the same beliefs (about the relationship between the health of a society and its gene pool) but has new toys (like the various neuroimaging scans) to play with (see Chapter 11). Nonetheless, as before, the science is week and a solid scientific basis for carving up and categorising humanity on a neurological basis is as absent as it was during the old eugenics. Therefore, claims that we know or understand enough in order to create scientifically valid categories based on naturally occurring neurodevelopmental or neuropsychiatric processes (as in ASD or ADHD or schizophrenia) should be viewed with scepticism.

The new phrenology

Early in the 19th century a new 'science' came into existence called 'phrenology'. Phrenologists believed that by examining the shape and unevenness of a head or skull, you could discover facts about a person's intelligence and character traits. They thought that the brain was the location of the mind and that the brain is composed of distinct areas (which they called 'organs'), each of which had a different function (for example, an 'organ' for intelligence). They believed that the size of an 'organ' was a measure of its power. Finally, they thought that the shape of the brain is determined by the development of these various brain 'organs' and that the skull takes its shape from the brain. Therefore they thought that by measuring the surface of the skull, you could get an accurate picture of a person's psychological abilities and tendencies.

Most phrenologists would run their bare fingertips over a head to distinguish any elevations or indentations. Sometimes callipers, measuring tapes and other instruments were used. A skilled phrenologist knew not just the layout of the head according to the latest phrenological chart, but also the personality traits associated with each of the 35-odd 'organs' (the number of brain 'organs' gradually increased over time). Like so many popular sciences, the phrenologists were only interested in evidence that confirmed their ideas. Phrenologists spent considerable time and effort defending themselves and their 'science' from criticism – always ready to portray themselves as Galileo-like defenders of natural 'truth'. Any evidence or anecdote that seemed to confirm that their 'science' was accurate was promoted by them as 'proof' of the 'truth' of phrenology. What phrenologists never accepted was that a psychological characteristic could be independent of the size of its 'organ'.

Phrenology societies were established and 'scientific' journals were developed. At the dawn of the 20th century, nearly 100 years after phrenology was first described, phrenologists were still attracting mass audiences to their lectures and 'skull-reading' sessions. Phrenologists campaigned for their beliefs, that the protuberances on the skull provided an accurate index of talents and abilities, to be applied to education and criminal reform and they suggested that phrenology could be used to determine the most suitable career for the young.

Phrenology, as all popular fads, eventually became unfashionable, gradually degenerated into a sect of zealous extremists and the practice slowly disappeared. Nevertheless, the British Phrenological Society (founded in 1887) was only disbanded in 1967. A legacy of phrenology lived on in other projects of measuring and comparing human heads – most notoriously the attention given to cranial size and forehead shape (which houses the frontal lobe) which was used by late 19th- and early 20th-century racial anthropologists (and later Nazi anthropologists) to confirm their belief that Europeans were superior to other humans.

In its heyday phrenology was seen as a robust science that measured 'real' qualities in people – in other words, a science that could tell you some 'truth' about the person under study. What is not surprising, when poor science comes to be seen as factual beyond dispute, is that its conclusions sat comfortably with the social values and beliefs of the society within which it developed. Thus, phrenologists' claim that their science 'proved' that non-Europeans had lower intelligence found support in the racist beliefs of the time, that perpetuated the idea that their empires reflected a 'natural' hierarchy. If phrenology's conclusions were in opposition to that of the society, it is unlikely that an idea with such a slim scientific basis would have lasted as long as it did.

Many professionals and academics are, like us, concerned that we are today witnessing the creation of a 'new phrenology'. In the last couple of decades various inventions have given us a new window on the brain. We have computers that can generate a three-dimensional picture of x-rays of a person's brain, allowing us to measure the size of different structures and different parts of the brain. We have totally new kinds of brain imaging devices that allow us to see the brain in action. Thus, we can measure blood flow to different parts of the brain, or see which parts of the brain are using more energy while someone is doing an activity (like trying to solve a puzzle).

These new brain scans have caused much excitement in the psychiatric community and researchers have set about measuring the brains (and its internal structures) of people with a variety of psychiatric diagnoses in an attempt to find evidence of differences compared to the rest of the population. No markers in the brain have been found for any of the psychiatric diagnoses studied. Despite this disappointing failure, it has not stopped some academics making wildly exaggerated claims about these brain-scanning studies.

The problem when professionals and academics draw conclusions not supported by scientific evidence and, further, insist that their conclusions are the truth and only truth, is that you end up in similar situation to that of the (so-called) science of phrenology. If the conclusions fit with the beliefs and interests of those in powerful positions in society, then the question of the strength of the scientific evidence can be overlooked. All that is needed is for a group of high-status individuals to say that their pet theory is not simply an idea, it is a 'scientific fact', and the path for this idea to become viewed as 'scientific fact' is cleared. Furthermore, in the absence of objective methods to verify these theories (such as medical tests) there is an ever-present danger that such speculative concepts like ASD will be misused by those in a position of power (as happened with phrenology).

The story of phrenology is also interesting in the context of the 'holy grail' for neuroscientists, working within a culture built on enlightenment values of scientific rationality fused with the focus on the individual, unravelling the mysteries of how the brain works. Here the idea of locating specific regions in the brain, as responsible for specific human experiences, remains understandably attractive (its more 'modern' form is to refer to specific brain 'circuits' as well as regions).

The problem of tying specific brain regions with specific functions has had many notable successes, starting in 1861 with Broca's discovery that a left inferotemporal lesion interfered with the ability to articulate speech, an area of the brain still referred to as 'Broca's area' in medical literature. By the late 1950s, using a variety of research methods (including direct stimulation of the brain through electrodes inserted during operations), it had become possible to map out the motor and sensory areas in the cortex of the brain. However, the available techniques have yet to lead us any closer to producing similar maps that go beyond our perception and direct motor control, to reach into that complex that makes up our thoughts, feelings and social behaviours. Even mental processes more easily quantifiable, such as memory, have proved difficult to pin down, as researcher Karl Lashley (1950) discovered much to his frustration, when rats trained to run a maze, still managed to find a way through no matter where he cut their brains.

So it seems that trying to locate hypothesised brain 'modules' such as the theory of mind (ToM) module, much discussed in autism literature, may be misguided. To seek localisation of thought, emotion and associated actions is to commit a category error if the biological processes involved in shaping the sum of the individual 'psyche' are not held in specific locations but in a pattern of dynamic interactions between multiple brain regions and, indeed, between the being and its environment. Further, the brain as machine model behind the attempt to localise personality 'deficits' or even 'differences' does not sit comfortably within a paradigm that suggests that what makes us human is that our minds work with subjective meaning rather than on purely objective information.

Neuroimaging studies in autism

Has the current state of knowledge from neurobiological research led us any closer to uncovering the underlying biological pathology of autism?

Here's a typical press release from 2005:

> New research from Melbourne's Howard Florey Institute helps to explain why children with autism spectrum disorders (autism) have problem-solving difficulties. Using functional magnetic resonance imaging technology (fMRI) the Florey scientists have shown that children with autism have less activation in the deep parts of the brain responsible for executive function (attention, reasoning and problem solving).
>
> 'Specifically, we found that activity in the caudate nucleus, a critical part of circuits that link the prefrontal cortex of the brain, is reduced in boys with autism.'
>
> 'These findings have important implications, since prefrontal brain circuits play a critical role in maintaining and focusing attention, planning and setting goals, and keeping goals in memory during problem-solving and decision-making.'
>
> 'Our neuroimaging findings showing dysfunction in these prefrontal brain circuits now explain why children with autism have problems with learning and problem-solving,' he said. (Rafferty, 2005)

Interestingly, frontal and pre-frontal dysfunction leading to poor 'executive functions' (such as setting goals, keeping goals in memory during problem-solving and decision-making) is the current dominant theory of causation in ADHD (Barkley, 2001), thus adding to the confusion about whether ADHD and ASD are separate disorders.

Here's another press release from 2004 making similar bold claims based on the results of a single study (Spice, 2004):

> Since the late 1990s, a succession of high-functioning autistic people have submitted to brain-imaging studies by researchers at Carnegie Mellon University and the University of Pittsburgh. The results are beginning to change their understanding of what autism is.
>
> The first major research paper to emerge from the studies, published this month in the British journal *Brain*, suggests that different areas of the brains of autism patients don't work with each other in the coordinated manner necessary for most high-level thinking.
>
> Though this first study focuses on only how brains perform during tests of sentence comprehension, Just and his co-author, Pitt's Dr Nancy Minshew, use the findings to propose a biological theory of autism they call 'underconnectivity'.

A lack of connections between brain areas, or a surplus of connections, which results in inefficient communication, could explain the disordered thinking of autism patients, they said.

'Dr Just's work suggests the first plausible brain mechanism that may be able to explain all of the deficits seen in autism,' said Dr Janet Lainhart, an autism researcher at the University of Utah.

'I think that there's a new paradigm emerging in autism research,' said Dr Martha Herbert, a pediatric neurologist at Massachusetts General Hospital. Autism has long been defined by its behavioral symptoms, but now researchers are getting closer to understanding what goes haywire in the brain to cause those behaviors.

'It opens up a whole new universe of research,' she added, 'and I think people are beginning to realize this.'

However, as countless similar claims are regularly announced in the media, others suggest caution (Spice, 2004):

As exciting as the findings might be, Dr Helen Tager-Flusberg, who heads a collaborative program at Boston University, counseled a wait-and-see approach.

'For the last 25 years, the field of autism has been filled with people who announce spectacular findings that other groups have been unable to duplicate,' she said.

Many researchers have looked for structural brain abnormalities that might explain these characteristics. 'That hasn't been all that fruitful,' Mass General's Herbert said.

Schultz is busy trying to replicate the Pittsburgh work, using the fMRI technique for studying face perception by autistic people, one of his specialties. 'It's tricky. With fMRI, you have to keep in mind that we're measuring blood flow,' and so the effects of the pumping heart have to be considered.

Uta Frith, deputy director for the Institute of Cognitive Neuroscience at the University College London and an influential player in autism research, said the findings of underconnectivity were consistent with her own theory of autism, called weak central coherence. But she said similar findings have been found in studies of dyslexia, a learning disorder that involves problems with word recognition, and so underconnectivity probably does not explain autism.

Lainhart, however, contends Frith's theory, which suggests that people with autism have a heightened focus on details, explains only some of the nonsocial aspects of autism. Underconnectivity, she said, appears to explain all autism symptoms.

Minshew expressed confidence that the evidence would eventually support the underconnectivity theory. 'This is one of the major papers that will stand the test of time. They'll refer to this paper forever.'

In a similar manner to Minshew's confident declaration that this time we really have hit the jackpot, we can equally confidently declare that, 'this is one of the major papers that will not stand the test of time. It will be forgotten like the rest of them.' Like all other theories, 'underconnectivity' seems to have slowly dropped off the radar.

Clues as to why we seem to be getting nowhere are easy to find. For example, in local processing and visual search (exemplified by the embedded figures task – EFT), people with autism have been reported to demonstrate superiority over normal controls. A study that employed fMRI (a device that shows what areas of the brain are active when the subject is performing a particular task) scans of subjects during the performance of the EFT found that several cerebral regions were similarly activated in the two groups. However, normal controls, as well as demonstrating generally more extensive task-related activations, additionally activated pre-frontal cortical areas that were not recruited in the group with autism. Conversely, subjects with autism demonstrated greater activation of ventral occipitotemporal regions. These differences suggested that the cognitive strategies adopted by the two groups are different (Ring *et al.*, 1999). In other words, the fMRI scans showed how different people may use different regions of the brain to solve the same task, making the idea of localising functions or of 'grand narratives' such as 'underconnectivity' very difficult to support from such a diverse set of findings.

Let's take the caudate nuclei as another example. Several studies have suggested abnormalities of the caudate nuclei are present in autism (Turner *et al.*, 2006). Reduced correlation of resting cerebral glucose metabolic rates between the caudate and frontal regions has been seen in a study of children with autism (Horwitz *et al.*, 1988). Sears *et al.* (1999) and Hollander *et al.* (2005) found that enlargement of the caudate nuclei was associated with stereotyped behaviours in autism. However, a study using MRI scans (Hardlicka *et al.*, 2005) showed that reduced caudate size was correlated with greater impairment on the Childhood Autism Rating Scale, again pointing to inconsistent anatomical findings. With regard 'functional' MRI (fMRI) studies of autism, a number of studies have shown decreased levels of activation in the caudate nuclei (compared to controls) for a variety of tasks, such as spatial processing (Haist *et al.*, 2005), finger tapping (Müller *et al.*, 2001) and face perception (Pierce *et al.*, 2004) (these three studies were carried out by the same research group). Other studies, however, have shown significantly more fMRI activation in the caudate nuclei (Turner *et al.*, 2006). While the authors of this latter study suggest that methodological difference may account for the very different results in their study, it reveals many of the problems that beset interpretation of the significance and meaning of findings in such research. Apart from methodological problems, such as small sample sizes and confounds resulting from issues such as how autism is defined and IQ, we are also left with the question of direction of causality when such disparate patterns are found.

Thus, we must ask if the differences found (scientifically known as an association) are part of the biological cause of autism, or whether we are just seeing what a brain that thinks or feels differently looks like. This is sometimes referred to as the 'state v trait' argument. Is this the picture of a personality 'trait' – something fixed and hardwired – or is it a picture of a 'state' – a brain that approaches a problem in a different way. In an acknowledgement of the possibility of the latter, the authors of the last study (Turner *et al.*, 2006) speculate that their increased fMRI effects in their autism group may have been affected by non-specific states, such as levels of general arousal.

Other brain structures that have been the focus of attention in autism neuroimaging research have suffered from a similar mixed bag of results. For example, the cerebellum has been the focus of much interest. Studies with magnetic resonance imaging (MRI) and positron emission tomography (PET) scanning have produced a divergent range of findings. Some studies have documented an increase in cerebellar volume among autistic children (Buitelaar and Willemsen-Swinkels, 2000; Abell *et al.*, 1999), while others have found smaller than average cerebellar volumes (Gaffney *et al.*, 1987; Courchesne *et al.*, 1988; Levitt *et al.*, 1999); yet others have reported no significant differences between cerebellar volumes in autistic people and 'normal' controls (e.g., Piven *et al.*, 1992). Further problems become apparent when we take into account the 'heterogeneity' of the subjects being studied (heterogeneity refers to the large mix of characteristics in the individuals under study). For example Cody *et al.* (2002) found that in the case of the cerebellum most of the evidence does not establish that there are significant differences in cerebellar size between autistic individuals and normal controls once confounds such as the volume relative to total brain size and IQ are taken into account.

Other lines of research have examined associations between brain structures and cognitive processes associated with autism. Functional magnetic resonance imaging (fMRI) has allowed the investigation of the neural networks underlying cognitive impairments in autism, including face and emotion processing, which has been one of the most extensively explored areas. Hypo-activation of the so-called 'face area' in the right fusiform gyrus has repeatedly been reported in adults with ASD while looking at faces (Critchley *et al.*, 2000). However, more recently it has been identified that this response can be modulated, depending on the familiarity and personal emotional content of the faces presented (Toal *et al.*, 2005; Hadjikhani *et al.*, 2004; Pierce *et al.*, 2004). Like other areas of biological autism research, a dead end has appeared.

From the above examples one can safely characterise current neuroimaging literature in autism as having two predominant features: first, over-inflated claims of a major breakthrough; and, second, subsequent studies that cast doubt on the specificity of these claims. Indeed, the vast majority of people diagnosed with autism, when their brains are scanned, do not display any overtly discernable brain abnormalities that a neurologist or radiologist would consider clinically significant (Rapin, 1998). When these dead ends keep being hit and specific, consistent findings are totally absent, what usually starts to take shape next are theories that paint things as more subtle and complex, thus requiring more of the same research but in larger quantities. Thus, more recently the focus has turned instead into trying to elucidate 'subtle' brain abnormalities.

One area where it is claimed there is a consistent finding is the replication of Kanner's original observation of increased brain volume (megalencephaly) in 'core' autism (Toal *et al.*, 2005). It has been proposed that people with ASD have an early period of accelerated brain growth followed by a period of decelerated development. This led to a line of research exploring the idea that abnormal patterns of brain growth in early childhood may be linked with or cause autism. However, the results of several studies suggest a more complex picture not easily reduced into a uniform pattern. A number of other factors also need to be taken into account.

For example, a finding in a number of studies is that children diagnosed with autism were born with normal head circumferences, but by the ages of two to three years old, as a group these children have statistically significant larger than average head circumferences and brain volumes; however, by the time they reach adulthood their brains are no longer larger than average (Courchesne *et al.*, 2001; Toal *et al.*, 2005) – although there is a suggestion that in adulthood brain ageing is significantly different in people with ASD compared with controls (McAlonan *et al.*, 2002). However, some studies have found no bulk regional brain volume differences between the ASDs and controls and speculate as to whether the finding of increased brain volume reported in the literature may therefore reflect an effect of disease severity (as illustrated in degree of generalised learning difficulties) (McAlonan *et al.*, 2002). The problem thus arises of interpreting the significance of these findings, particularly given that we are not talking about clinically abnormal brains. The picture is consistent with a number of alternatives (to the genetic/neurodevelopmental disorder hypothesis) including: a difference rather than abnormality in neurodevelopment, differential rates and times of development (just as milk teeth fall out at different ages in different children), environmental causes and within-group differences in the study due to confounds such as IQ, diagnostic criteria and specific learning difficulties.

Thus there are many problems associated with how we interpret the significance of the neuroimaging findings. Nadesan (2005) summarises as follows:

1. The problem of representation. Essentially neuroscience has developed a distinct linguistic set of representations that stand for what they are studying in the brain. However, these linguistic representations of subsystems in the brain describe theories and it is not at all clear to what extent the categories they have created reflect the real 'natural' brain. In the natural world these categories may simply not exist as distinct categories and the brain may well function in a manner that lacks any clear demarcations between the subsystems that neuroscience has 'created'.
2. The data generated by neuroimaging requires interpretation. We know that each individual's brain changes over time in response to all sorts of developmental and environmental stimuli. This variety and plasticity of the human brain makes it difficult to work out how to achieve reliable and valid methods for distinguishing between what should be considered 'normal' from that which should be seen as 'abnormal'. Furthermore, the neuroimaging tests themselves are riddled with a multitude of confounds that makes 'reading' the results problematic. For example, it is difficult to control for the

effects of an experiment involving noisy functional neuroimaging scans where the subject is expected to complete a task while being scanned, when the subject may or may not be interested in the task and may or may not find the conditions of the experiment distracting or emotionally stressful.
3. The third problem is that of 'heterogeneity'. Heterogeneity refers to cultural, social, biological, or other differences within a group. This means that a diverse variety of factors within the group we now define as autistic could lead to a similar outcome (a similar set of behaviours that we now call autism). The neuroimaging studies have little possibility of disentangling the relative contributions of multiple causal pathways to whatever brain morphology is being pictured. This is a significant issue in autism research as we are not talking about brains considered to be clinically abnormal.

CONCLUSION

The 'genotype' of an organism represents its exact genetic make-up; that is, the particular set of genes it possesses. Two organisms whose genes differ at even one locus (position in their genome) are said to have different genotypes. The transmission of genes from parents to offspring is under the control of molecular mechanisms. The 'phenotype' of an organism, on the other hand, represents its actual physical properties, such as height, weight, hair colour and so on. While the inheritance of physical properties occurs as a secondary consequence of the inheritance of genes, it is the organism's physical properties (phenotype) that directly determine how the organism appears and functions. The organism's genotype may be a large influencing factor in the development of its phenotype but it is not the only one. The level of determination depends upon what is called phenotypic plasticity. Where an organism has little phenotypic plasticity then it is possible to infer its phenotype from its genotype. With complex organisms it is simply not feasible to infer a mono-causal relationship between the genotype and the phenotype. Rose *et al.* state:

> There is no one-to-one correspondence between the genes inherited from one's parents and one's height, weight, metabolic rate, sickness, health, or any other non trivial organic characteristic. The critical distinction in Biology is between the phenotype of an organism, which may be taken to mean the total of its morphological,

physiological, and behavioural properties and its genotype; the state of its genes. It is the genotype, not the phenotype that is inherited. (Rose *et al.*, 1990: 95)

Furthermore, 'The phenotype of an individual cannot be broken down into the separate contributions of genotype and of environment, because the two interact to produce the organism' (Rose *et al.*, 1990: 97). Thus, we must not succumb to the temptation to make phenotype and genotype one and the same, nor do we support the idea that it is possible to arrive at estimates of how much autism and the broader ASDs are the result of genetics or environment. As we have argued in this chapter, the evidence on the genetics of autism is week, based on poor methodology, open to disparate interpretations and provides scant material to support the genetic hypotheses for autism and ASDs. It is not even clear what help finding 'autism genes' would provide to those thus labelled.

Like many other branches of biological psychiatry, psychiatric (or behavioural) genetics has increasingly turned to determinist and reductionist views of what genes do, probably in an effort to bolster the position of biological causation in the absence of empirical support for such a model. Boyle (1990) points out that before the modern determinist view of genes there was that of the eugenic movement's concept of the 'germplasm' as causing all sorts of mental and social ills. It would appear that certain researchers are trying to infer the genotype from the phenotype from a set of ill-defined behaviours. Yet it remains unclear why we should assume that minor 'autistic traits' are worthy of admission into an 'autistic phenotype' and from there into an 'autism gentotype'.

The attempts to give a patina of scientific respectability to 'folk' beliefs seem to us no more than that. Studying the relationships between genotype and phenotype might prove useful if we were about to engage in selective breeding! In the absence of clear genetic markers, genetic counselling for disorders such as autism are seriously misguided, as it will be based on an almost complete absence of empirical 'evidence-based' data. We know that both physical and mental problems run in families and that such problems are disproportionately found in people from poorer backgrounds. It is not feasible to argue that poverty 'causes' ill health because what constitutes poverty and ill health are essentially normative (in other words they are largely dependent on our understanding of how 'normal' should be defined). What constitutes mental dysfunction is even more normative than what constitutes physical dysfunction (in other words, much larger variations across cultural groups exist regarding the definition of 'normal' in the mental arena than the physical/bodily arena). Thus, conceptually the idea that either genes or the environment *cause* autism becomes increasingly difficult to articulate, given no obvious genetic or environmental causative agent has been found. To then argue that gene + environment = autism, is a bit like betting on every horse in a race and then celebrating your efficacy as a pundit. Nobody doubts that genes and environment play significant parts in all human behaviour.

Not only are we unable to conclude more broadly that autism is a genetic and 'neurodevelopmental' disorder, but, in addition, the diagnosis does not provide us with any way of differentiating causal or contributing factors in any individual person – in fact it is likely to hinder our ability to do so. As a result we have the absurd situation where someone with severe learning difficulties, very little language, suffering with epilepsy and requiring full-time care can receive the same 'neurodevelopmental' diagnosis as someone who has an above-average IQ and is holding down a prestigious post at a top university.

The notion that we have established autism as a genetic, neurodevelopmental disorder is simply false. Neuroimaging is not leading us towards identifying any distinct 'endophenotype' (biological marker) for autism, nor have any of the genetic studies. Indeed, it is entirely plausible that it is (paradoxically) leading us in the opposite direction, as the consistent failure to find a distinct abnormality lends strong support to our proposal that autism as a genetic/neurodevelopmental construct simply lacks validity and that autism is thus best understood as a cultural construct.

Despite years and millions of pounds of expensive research with sophisticated machines, we seem to be no nearer to discovering the biological basis for autism. What is disappointing is the continued insistence of many researchers and writers in this field that biological causation for autism (as we define it today) is already a known given. As with many other psychiatric disorders, researchers have to employ increasingly mysterious hypotheses to keep the biological construct alive in the face of an absence of evidence to support it. This often results in rather broad and somewhat meaningless conclusions about the role of biology: Brambilla and colleagues (2003: 566) conclude that 'a disturbed neural network probably involving the tempora-parietal cortex, limbic system, cerebellum, pre-frontal cortex, and corpus callosum, appear to be involved in patho-physiology of autism' (translation: autism involves disturbances in the brain), while Hyman (2003: 99), reviewing neuroimaging research in autism, concludes 'because the overall shapes and sizes of peoples brain differ so much, researchers must employ complex computer algorithms to define normal values for various populations and compare the brains of individuals against these group norms. Moreover, the boundaries between brain structures may be very subtle' (translation: the reason we aren't finding anything specific is because the brain problems in autism are too subtle for our brain scans to find them). One can't help thinking that conclusions such as the above and many more like them are elaborate excuses for the obvious failure of this line of research to produce anything of value to aid our understanding of the biology of autism and ultimately to help us improve the lives of those with or destined to receive an ASD label.

The most scientifically appropriate conclusion that we can draw from the evidence (or lack of it) so far is that *there is no characteristic genetic or biological brain-based abnormality that corresponds with our current definition of autism and the broader ASDs.*

In science we generally set out to disprove a 'null hypothesis' as the starting point for generating objective data to help support a particular theory. The 'null hypothesis' refers to the hypothesis that there is nothing going on; in other words, when we put forward a theory (such as autism is caused by disorder in the development of the brain) we start with the assumption that this is incorrect (the null hypothesis). We can only accept evidence to support this new theory when we have proved that the null hypothesis cannot be true. Thus far, we have found that the null hypothesis on this subject (i.e., of ASD not being caused by or associated with a characteristic abnormality of the brain) is stubbornly resistant to being disproved. The only legitimate scientific conclusion we can therefore reach is that – according to the evidence that we have at this moment in time – autism and ASDs are not caused by or associated with a characteristic abnormality in the genes or of the brain. The fact that this possibility is now consistently overlooked seems to us to be positively negligent.

If, indeed, this null hypothesis is correct and there is no discernable, pathognomic (medical indicator of a disease) and characteristic abnormal biological process taking place in the brains of those who would currently attract one of the 'family' of autism labels, then current research merely provides an active ongoing distraction from the task of trying to understand what may be happening in the lives of that diverse group of people and how we may best go about the task of improving their lives. Furthermore, this distraction may contribute to failures in developing not only appropriate ways of helping them, but also paradoxically contribute to greater stigmatisation, a narrowing of our beliefs about what can be considered as normal, and lesser understanding of and tolerance for diversity.

In the current state of evidence the only thing we can say with any certainty about autism as it is defined today is that it is a social construct whose meaning is being created rather than discovered. Without having any identified patho-physiological abnormalities or characteristic 'markers', we are left with a construct that does not stand up to even a cursory critical appraisal, let alone the more rigorous scrutiny we are attempting in this book.

This does not mean that there is no significant physical component involved in the development of what we today call autism. After all absence of evidence does not necessarily equate with evidence of absence. We know certain physical conditions are associated with symptoms of what some refer to as 'core' autism (e.g., PKU, tuberous sclerosis, Fragile X, blindness, epilepsy) just as environments that lead to severe emotional neglect are also associated with autism (e.g., institutionalised Romanian orphans). We are also aware that the effects on the body of interacting with the social and physical world is an issue for all of medicine; for example, there are well-known relationships between social class, gender, race, culture, geography and the types and severity of diseases members of different groupings suffer. Thus, the medical model has its limitations in the rest of medicine too. However, a 'diagnostic' system built in the absence of an identifiable objective scientific basis is, we believe, anything but 'diagnostic', if we use the broad meaning of diagnosis, which is that of characterising 'what is going on'. Far from it, in fact, it may well be leading us further and further away from accurate and useful diagnostics to help understand the life circumstances of those currently receiving or who will receive an ASD label.

Scientifically, the only conclusion compatible with the evidence is that *autism, as it is defined today, is a myth.*

6
CLASSIFICATION

THE CURRENT STANDARD 'MAINSTREAM' VIEW OF AUTISM

As we have already explained, autism is presented, in both mainstream scientific and popular literature, with the foundational premise that it is a neurodevelopmental condition that will, ultimately, be known and rendered transparent through the ceaseless efforts of scientific authorities. It is a behaviourally defined disorder, characterised by qualitative impairments in social communication, social interaction and imagination (the core triad of symptoms). Sensory hypo-sensitivities or hyper-sensitivities to the environment are also said to be common features. Criteria for the diagnosis of autism are set out in the ICD-10 (International Classification of Diseases, 10th revision) (WHO, 1992) and DSM-IV (*Diagnostic and Statistical Manual of Mental Disorders*, 4th edition) (APA, 1994).

In DSM-IV autism is classified as belonging to the 'pervasive developmental disorders' (PDD). There are five subcategories listed under PDD:

- Autistic disorder: see below.
- Asperger's syndrome: relatively good verbal language, with milder non-verbal language problems, restricted range of interests and relatedness.
- PDD-NOS (not otherwise specified): non-verbal language and other problems that do not meet the strict criteria for other PDD disorders.
- Rett's disorder: rare neurodegenerative disorder of girls.

- Childhood disintegrative disorder: another rare neurodegenerative disorder.

In common practice, Rett's disorder, and childhood disintegrative disorder are considered mainstream medical disorders and are not usually dealt with within services for ASDs.

The triad of symptoms that are thought to be indicative of autism are as follows:

- First, an inability to engage in reciprocal social interaction. A popular idea is that the autistic child fails to develop a 'theory of mind' (see Chapter 3) and cannot imagine what other people may think or feel; thus, they lack empathy. Humans, animals and objects are treated alike. The child may become solitary, avoid eye contact and display little of the interested curiosity and exploratory play seen in normal infants and young children.
- Second, there are communication problems, both verbal and non-verbal. Rather than having a problem with spoken language per se, the autistic child appears not to grasp the point of communication. The affected child may not babble, is often late to speak and has difficulties in understanding what is said to them. This defect in understanding spoken speech may be almost total, or may be subtle and merely take the form of literal interpretation of language. If the autistic child does develop spoken language, then there is sometimes an abnormality in the way it is used, such as echolalia (repeating back what someone has said word for word). Volume, pitch and tone of speech are said to be peculiar. Sometimes the affected child may remember and repeat endlessly whole conversations, but be incapable of explaining the content.
- Third, there is evidence of restricted imagination and a predilection for rigid routines. The autistic child may form strange attachments to certain everyday objects, such as pieces of plastic or stones, or become fascinated with flicking paper or running water from taps. An obsessive need for routine is often found, with temper tantrums resulting from any small change in the usual pattern of their life.

In more severe cases first presentation with symptoms such as delayed language and solitary play is apparent before the age of three years. Higher-functioning children tend to have a behavioural presentation at around four or five years or subtle social problems in later childhood. Concerns about more able children, or those with Asperger's syndrome, may not develop until children are exposed to the greater social demands of the school environment. Some children may even have been considered well advanced in their development, because of their special interests or precocious vocabulary.

The prevalence of the broad spectrum of autism (determined with current diagnostic tools) is approximately five to nine per 1,000 and is three to four times more common in males than females.

Asperger syndrome (AS) is defined in the *Diagnostic and Statistical Manual of Mental Disorders* (DSM-IV) as:

Qualitative impairment in social interaction, as manifested by at least two of the following:

- Marked impairments in the use of multiple nonverbal behaviours such as eye-to-eye gaze, facial expression, body posture, and gestures to regulate social interaction.
- Failure to develop peer relationships appropriate to developmental level.
- A lack of spontaneous seeking to share enjoyment, interest or achievements with other people (e.g., by a lack of showing, bringing, or pointing out objects of interest to other people).
- A lack of social or emotional reciprocity.
- Restricted repetitive and stereotyped patterns of behaviour, interests, and activities, as manifested by at least one of the following:
  1. Encompassing preoccupation with one or more stereotyped and restricted patterns of interest that is abnormal in either intensity or focus.
  2. Apparently inflexible adherence to specific, non-functional routines or rituals.
  3. Stereotyped and repetitive motor mannerisms (e.g., hand or finger flapping or twisting or complex whole-body movements).
  4. Persistent preoccupation with parts of objects.
- The disturbance causes clinically significant impairments in social, occupational, or other important areas of functioning.
- There is no clinically significant general delay in language (e.g., single words used by age two years, communicative phrases used by age three years).
- There is no clinically significant delay in cognitive development or in the development of age-appropriate self-help skills or

adaptive behaviour (other than in social interaction) and curiosity about the environment in childhood.
- Criteria are not met for another specific Pervasive Developmental Disorder or Schizophrenia.

The development of diagnostic criteria

In 1956 Kanner and Eisenberg provided the first formal set of criteria for the diagnosis of autism. The criteria focused on two dimensions of the condition: a profound lack of affective contact and repetitive, ritualistic behaviour, which must be of an elaborate kind. Some practitioners found these criteria too narrow, in particular because they omitted the unusual language and communication patterns that seemed to them a core element of the condition. Rutter's (1978a) refinement introduced the concept of simultaneous deficits in three behavioural domains: impaired social relationships, impaired language and communication skills, and insistence on sameness. In 1976 L. Wing conducted one of the first epidemiological surveys on autism and in 1979, together with Gould, she wrote her seminal piece entitled 'Severe Impairments of Social Interaction and Associated Abnormalities in Children: Epidemiology and Classification' (Wing and Gould, 1979). This paper was the first epidemiological study using the now-familiar triad; it is Rutter's and Wing and Gould's papers that lay the foundation for the triad (impaired social relationships, impaired language and communication skills, and restricted imagination) in its various forms becoming the accepted operational definition for autism ever since (see Chapter 3).

The shift away from the Kanner criteria appears to have broadened the scope of the diagnosis. For example, age of onset is one criterion that has changed over time. Kanner and Eisenberg (1956) implied an age assumption by using the term 'early infantile autism'. Rutter (1978a) (followed by DSM-III) set a specific age of onset limit of earlier than 30 months. The DSM III-R (APA, 1987) criteria relaxed this limit, requiring only that the age of onset occur during infancy or childhood. ICD-10 (WHO, 1992) and DSM-IV (APA, 1994) set an age limit at 36 months, in part as a reaction to the problem posed by the expanded age definition introduced in DSM-III-R.

At that time of ICD-9 (WHO, 1978), autism appears under 'Childhood Psychoses' and was characterised by an age of onset before 30 months. Also included under 'Childhood Psychoses' was the subcategory of 'Disintegrative Psychosis', which was said to be characterised by a regression in development. There was also an 'Atypical Childhood Psychosis' category and a final unspecified category. It is worth mentioning that under 'Emotional Disorders Specific to Childhood' ICD-9 suggested that this can be characterised by 'shyness and withdrawal'.

In Rutter's influential modernisation of the definition in 1978, three related terms – autism, infantile autism and childhood autism – were used somewhat interchangeably. The third edition of the *Diagnostic and Statistical Manual of Mental Disorders* (DSM-III) (APA, 1980) used 'infantile autism' as the core descriptor, but also placed autism in the context of PDDs for the first time. DSM-III helped the move towards the concept of a spectrum of autistic disorders through classifying autism under PDDs, and also introduced the term 'atypical PDD'. DSM-III had five classes of what it described as 'Infancy, Childhood or Adolescence Disorders'; these were: intellectual (mental retardation), behavioural (ADD and conduct disorders), emotional (anxiety disorders and other disorders of childhood), physical (eating disorders, stereotyped movement disorders and other disorders with a physical manifestation) and developmental disorders (PDD and specific developmental disorders). It introduced a new way of classifying those who didn't quite reach diagnostic criteria such that each of these subcategories terminated in an 'atypical' category, described as a 'residual' class. It was to be used whenever a person did not quite meet the descriptive criteria for any of the other disorders in that subcategory, but shared features with them. With regards the developmental disorders, what differentiates PDD from a specific developmental disorder is that in the case of the former every aspect of development is assessed as being affected. Within the category of PDD there were a further three subcategories: infantile autism, childhood onset PDD and atypical PDD. What appears to differentiate the first two categories is the age of onset – if onset was before 30 months then infantile autism was to be used; after 30 months childhood onset PDD. Atypical PDD was to be used when a person did not meet the full criteria for the other two, but shared some similarity to them.

In 1987, a revised edition of DSM-III, DSM-III-R (APA, 1987), abandoned the term 'infantile autism', in part to allow for cases where the onset of symptoms did not occur in early infancy. DSM-III-R also included a new category of 'pervasive developmental disorder – not otherwise specified' (PDD-NOS). PDDs now had just two disorders: autistic disorder and PDD-NOS. When DSM-III was compiled there were no representatives from the UK involved, but in the revised manual a number of UK practitioners had some input. What effect their views on the triad of impairments and age of onset had on the construction of 'autistic disorder' is unclear. Infantile autism and childhood onset PDD had now gone, to be replaced by autistic disorder. It is likely that the broader criteria for autistic disorders led, in time, to a substantial increase in the numbers being diagnosed.

In 1992, the World Health Organization published the ICD-10, which uses the term 'childhood autism'. ICD-10 (WHO, 1992) criteria for PDD have eight subcategories: childhood autism, atypical autism, Rett's syndrome, childhood disintegrative disorder, hyperkinesis associated with mental retardation, Asperger's, other PDDs and PDD-unspecified. The latter is similar to PDD-NOS and the penultimate category, together with 'hyperkinesis associated with mental retardation', has no DSM equivalent.

The fourth DSM edition (DSM-IV, APA, 1994) which took a similar approach to ICD-10, used the term 'autistic disorder'. DSM-III-R had introduced the term 'PDD-NOS' and this was retained in DSM-IV. By DSM-IV the PDDs now had three new diagnoses; 'Asperger's syndrome', 'childhood disintegrative psychosis' and 'Rett's syndrome'. DSM-IV has five categories for the PDDs: autistic disorder, Asperger's, PDD-NOS, Rett's syndrome and childhood disintegrative disorder (see above).

The continuous mutation of constructs raises a number of issues with regards obtaining valid and reliable information on the time trends and prevalence rates for autism. Given the changing definitions of autism, accurate comparisons of changing prevalence over time are difficult to make. The three sets of DSM criteria for autism have varied in breadth. Some have argued that the move from DSM-III to DSM-III-R broadened the concept of autism, contributing to an apparent increase in prevalence over time; however, others believe that in the shift from the DSM-III-R criteria to the DSM-IV/ICD-10 criteria, a 'corrective' narrowing occurred, although this is unlikely to have compensated for changing trends in clinical practice as it came to take seriously the expanded notion of the autistic spectrum.

ASPERGER'S SYNDROME (AS)

In 1981 Lorna Wing, who is usually credited with the bringing of the concept of AS into mainstream research and clinical practice, wrote her seminal paper on the subject. Wing (2005) contends that the syndrome delineated by Asperger was first brokered by a Russian psychiatrist in a paper in a German journal that was then translated by Dr Sula Wolff. Wolff had earlier written a book called *Children Under Stress*, first published in 1969. Wolff originally used the phrase 'schizoid personality of childhood' in her translation, although later Wolff (1995) stated that she preferred the term 'Asperger's' as it had few of the connotations of the term 'schizoid'.

It is difficult to assess how much of a similarity any of the descriptions of children's behaviour and criteria for 'caseness' have with each other as the diagnosis of AS began to catch on and was subsequently developed by different authors. When we examine Wing's initial cases, later use of the term by Gillberg (1989), Szatamari *et al.* (1989), Tantam (1988) and those formalised in DSM IV and ICD-10, the cases described appear to have very little in common with each other or with that of Asperger's. A degree of consensus over what constitutes a case is imperative if research is to focus on cause, course and treatment. Frith (2004) recognises this when she states: 'Of course, we can only know how many cases there are if we know what a case is! There is reason to believe that in current clinical practice the label Asperger syndrome is used rather indiscriminately' (Frith, 2004: 673). This point is also made by Klin *et al.* (2005), who correctly argue that the definition of AS should be considered tentative and in need of empirical validation. Wing (2005) also mentions that Asperger was against the idea that the children he described were autistic. Asperger died in 1981 and thus we will never know what he thought about the way the concept he first articulated was being developed.

Hans Asperger wrote his study in 1944 with the first full English translation appearing in the book *Autism and Asperger Syndrome*, edited by Uta Frith (1991). In his paper Asperger describes a number of cases. The first child, Fritz L, was described as a late developer who nevertheless spoke early and like an adult. Asperger describes him as restless, fidgety, destructive, very familiar and confrontational. He also described his gaze as 'odd', often appearing to be staring into a void, apart from when his eyes were lit up by a 'malignant glimmer'. Asperger states that he lived in an interior world (interestingly Lotter [1966b] alludes to the children described as lacking 'interiority'). Fritz is described as someone who did not play with either children or toys. Occasionally Fritz would pick on other, usually smaller children and took pleasure in this, a feature which Asperger says is characteristic of the 'autistic psychopath'. Despite his lack of social engagement, the child's parents described Fritz as being an excellent judge of people.

The second child Asperger describes is Harro L, a child who refused to cooperate, was cheeky and fought a lot. Harro's gaze is also described as 'far away'. He responded poorly to teasing and would act aggressively. His facial expression is described as sparse and rigid and he is rarely friendly in his attitude. Both Harry and Fritz are said to 'intellectualise'. Asperger goes on to describe two other children; Ernest K and Helmut L. Asperger's children seem disinterested in others unless they were engaged in malicious acts; when their eyes would, according to Asperger, 'light up'. One wonders whether their behaviours were related to the broader social context of the time, given that these were children from war-torn Austria, but unfortunately details about the content of their attitudes and beliefs are lacking. Asperger (1944) also differentiates these children from children who 'know all the tramlines of Vienna' and thus he appears to be aware of cases that may later be called autistic and wants to differentiate 'his' children from those kinds of children.

In her 1981 account of Asperger's syndrome Lorna Wing presents six case histories. The case histories outlined by her were procured from adults and it is not clear from the paper whether evidence beyond individual or parental recall of childhood history was obtained. These case histories appear to have little similarity to the cases presented by Asperger. None of Wing's cases appear to manifest any malice. Two of the cases appeared to have some degree of learning disability, whereas none of Asperger's were reported to be learning disabled. Most of Wing's cases spoke late, whereas most of Asperger's spoke early. Most of Wing's cases had little capacity for analytical thought, whereas Asperger's cases were thought by him to be highly analytical. None of Wing's cases could be described as manipulative, mendacious, cheeky, confrontational or vindictive. It might be said that both Wing's and Asperger's cases lack some degree of social reciprocity, but there seems little else in common, nor any clear reason why such a lack should warrant a diagnosis or, if it did, why it might not include just about every child who had some degree of learning disability or mental health problems. Wing goes on to discuss diagnostic categories and suggests that the term 'Asperger's' is to be preferred to that of possible others such as autism or schizoid personality disorder. Wing (1981) does not discus the issue of other diagnostic or developmental delays/disabilities as alternatives. She suggests that the following are characteristics of the syndrome Asperger described, even though these bear slender similarities with the behaviours found in the original Asperger paper:

- *Speech*: Reversal of pronouns. Content of speech is pedantic and overly formal. Words or phrases are repeated in a stereotyped fashion. Verbal jokes are not understood unless they are simple.
- *Non-verbal communication*: Little facial expression. Monotonous intonation. Limited gestures and motor clumsiness. Poor interpretation or misunderstanding of others' facial expressions, verbal and non-verbal communications.
- *Social interaction*: No, or little, understanding of social rules. Social behaviour is naive and peculiar. Relationships with the opposite sex are characterised by inappropriate behaviour or inappropriate advances.
- *Repetitive activities and resistance to change*: Adherence to routines and attachment to particular objects or even people.
- *Obsessive interests*: Excellent rote memory and intense interest in a very narrow range of subjects, such as history of steam trains, bus timetables or dinosaurs. Little ability to grasp underlying facts of subject and little ability to understand when people are bored. Special skills, for example, at chess or jigsaws.
- *Experiences at school*: Children may be bullied at school and deemed 'little professors' by their peers. They may be hyper-sensitive to criticism but also insensitive.

It is easy to see that such 'symptoms' are rather subjective in nature and it appears to us difficult to comprehend how such symptoms should take precedence over other features in these individuals lives (such as family circumstances, childhood experiences, social support, etc.) and form the basis for a new diagnostic category. Of the six cases Wing describes in her paper, two had moderate learning disabilities; apart from this and their apparent social impairments it is difficult to see how one could argue for 'caseness' on such a basis. The heterogeneity of her cases means that to say they all had the triad of impairments seems like saying a man in a coma had the triad and was therefore autistic. This paper would, however, prove to be key in promoting 'looser' definitions and expanding the remit of psychologists and psychiatrists, with greater incorporation of psychiatry into an arguably more political agenda of surveillance and intervention for those deemed by current cultural standards to be socially inadequate in some manner.

Asperger's, as a diagnostic term, was brought back to life by Wing in this paper, which was written at a time when controversy was gaining ground about what should and should not be categorised as autistic. Many believed the then-current definitions were leading to a considerable number of false positives, while others believed they were too narrow. The rehabilitation of Asperger's thus caught the attention of academics and clinicians, as this construct appeared to provide the 'get out of jail card', given the problem of the narrowness of the formal 'autistic disorder' category. Thus Lorna Wing's paper was written at a time when there was a receptive professional audience, thus resurrecting a long dead paper. Throughout the 1980s Wing's Asperger's (as opposed to Asperger's Asperger's!) started being taken seriously in various countries and by various professionals before eventually becoming incorporated into DSM and ICD.

One of the next important milestones in establishing AS as a scientifically valid diagnosis was 'Lifelong Eccentricity and Social Isolation, II: Asperger's Syndrome or Schizoid Personality Disorder', written in 1988 by Digby Tantam, a British psychiatrist. By contacting colleagues he was able to procure details of 110 adults, of whom 60 were included in the study. All of the people were over the age of 16. In the paper, Tantam provides two case histories, In neither case history is any evidence provided to substantiate a lack of social reciprocity in the first three to five years.

In 1989 Szatmari and colleagues wrote an article entitled 'Asperger's Syndrome: A Review of Clinical Features'. This study at least had the virtue of using children as the subjects of their research. The authors define AS as a clinical picture characterised by social isolation in combination with odd and eccentric behaviour. They do not say why children who present such a 'picture' should warrant a diagnosis or if they do why AS should be the only diagnostic label considered. They state that Wing's triad of impairments were adapted to produce the following criteria:

1. a 'solitary' child;
2. impaired two-way social interactions;
3. one of: odd patterns of speech, impaired non-verbal communication, or an interest in repetitive activities; and
4. onset in the pre-school years.

Twenty-eight children with their version of AS were then compared with 28 controls. The AS group differed from the controls by the degree to which they satisfied the above criteria only. The authors conclude that the AS subjects tended to approach others only to have their needs met, engaged in one-sided interactions and were indifferent to the feelings of others. They also decide that AS subjects were more likely to have 'bizarre' preoccupations and differentiate these from appropriate preoccupations (such as sex, drugs and rock'n'roll presumably?). These 'bizarre' preoccupations included the occult, Nazis, floor plans and complex electronics. The issue of how this fits into global functioning is not addressed and one is left with the impression that these interests are in and of themselves difficult to translate into indicators of malfunctioning. The authors also discuss the previous diagnoses some of the AS group had received; these included ADHD (or hyperactivity), anxiety disorders, obsessive compulsive disorder and conduct disorder. They differentiate these from AS by concluding that none of the other diagnoses have a clear social reference. They also suggest that AS, as conceptualised by them, differs from the criteria for autistic disorder found in DSM-III-R and then put forward their own criteria for AS.

Also in 1989 Swedish psychiatrist Christopher Gillberg wrote about 23 children with what he deemed was AS, producing yet another set of diagnostic criteria. He states that his criteria were in 'good accord' with that of Asperger, but that is not our impression. Gillberg compared his AS children with 23 other children who were diagnosed with infantile autism (IA). Of the 23 in the AS group, 21 were boys, a slightly higher proportion than in the IA group. With regards IQ, only two AS and two IA had IQs less than 70. Compared to findings in the epidemiological studies of the time, this is very unusual, particularly for IA (where usually a much higher proportion will have low IQs). Gillberg concludes that the AS group differed only by degree from the IA group in their social and communicative competence. He does, however, go on to suggest that an important feature of the AS group is that they had poor motor coordination (motor coordination is, of course, a particular preoccupation for Gillberg as he is the inventor of the diagnosis 'DAMP' – disorders of attention, motor control and perception). Gillberg has since continued to argue for the validity of his criteria for AS against that of the diagnostic manuals.

In *A Guide to Asperger Syndrome* Christopher Gillberg (2002) criticises the 'no significant delay' clauses of the DSM and argues that they represent a misunderstanding or oversimplification of the syndrome. He believes that although there may well be significant delay in some areas of language development, it is often combined with exceptionally high functioning in other language-related areas, and argues that this combination superficially resembles, but is in reality very different from, normal development in language and adaptive behaviour. Using Gillberg's definition, a 1993 study carried out in Sweden found that, at a minimum, 3.6 per 1,000 school-aged children 'definitely' meet the criteria for AS. If merely 'suspected' cases are included, the prevalence becomes 7.1 per 1,000, in other words close to 1 in 100 (Ehlers and Gillberg, 1993).

It is difficult to see what, if any, similarities the behaviours described by the different authors as indicative of AS, have in common, particularly as it is now rare to find any case histories described. If none of the diagnostic frames have much in common then it is hard to argue that AS as a concept has any diagnostic validity or reliability.

DIAGNOSTIC PRACTICE

Although autism 'experts' are fond of claiming that diagnostic tools are highly reliable and valid and that clinicians using these can be trained to become 'accurate' diagnosticians, there is much reason to doubt this. Given the widening of the diagnostic frame since the notion of ASD became popular, it seems more likely that clinicians have subscribed to the notion of a spectrum that is wider even than the category of PDD as defined in diagnostic manuals. It is not surprising that some of the leading clinicians and researchers in this subject have no desire to adhere to diagnostic criteria that could undermine the validity of the wider spectrum that has become embedded in routine practice.

Rutter and Schopler (1987, 1992) discuss some of the thorny issues surrounding diagnosis and classification of autism and PDDs. They disagree with a system that might stipulate a minimum number of symptoms as they feel this might tie the hands of clinicians, but they do not address the issues of ethics, global functioning, or levels of impairment and how diagnosis may be viewed in relation to these. When considering diagnosis without proper reference to the extent and limit of impairments, could this not lead to unnecessary pathologisation, with all the subsequent implications of ascribing disability? The authors refer to the importance of cause, course and response to treatment as factors to be considered in the identification and classification of disorders, but come across as untroubled by the lack of any solid evidence to support current ASD categories having developed as a result of clear differences in any of these areas. They also suggest that within a group of disorders it would be better to have too many (even unsubstantiated diagnostic categories), which could later be collapsed with or into each other, than vice versa. This, however, avoids engagement with surrounding problems of what should be the basis on which a variety of aberrant behaviours are grouped together to make a set of disorders and how to differentiate these from other groupings of disorders. They make a case for differentiating autism and related disorders from learning difficulties, specific language disorders and other developmental disorders, though the grounds for doing this rests on a belief in the uniqueness of autism and PDDs, a belief that seems to us based more on circular reasoning than scientific evidence, as establishing where the spectrum begins and ends is just as difficult as differentiating one condition from another within the spectrum.

Rutter and Schopler (1987, 1992) reject the proposal that a lack of 'theory of mind' is the main deficit of autism and related conditions. They also (correctly, in our opinion) reject the idea that clinical judgement is a necessary or sufficient criterion for ascribing diagnosis, as all that would yield would be consensus, thus not residing in strong scientific foundation. In other words, lumping together disparate behaviours, with possibly different causes and courses, is unlikely to result in good research into cause or interventions or to lead to the sort of scientific foundation necessary to support a system of classification that will be useful for developing a scientific evidence-based approach, as found in the rest of medicine. It is our contention that current theory and practice lacks such a scientific basis and is, as a result, based on ideological developments reflecting a variety of academic's and clinician's opinions, which have gradually developed into a series of (often disputed) consensus-based approaches. By Rutter and Schopler's standards, then, we have failed to achieve an adequate scientific basis to current classifications and therefore practice in this area is anything but evidence-based.

Despite none of the ASDs having this solid scientific foundation on which to build sound and ethical clinical practice, the belief that early screening and early diagnosis is essential became increasingly popular in the last decade (e.g., Howlin and Moore, 1997; Baird *et al.*, 2003). Given that there are numerous references to famous people who are deemed to have been (or are) sufferers of some form of autism (looking at the website http://www.geocities.com/richardg_uk/famousac. html [accessed 22 January 2009] it's harder to work out famous people who did not have features of autism than those who, according to this site, do!), then if the prognosis for some children with ASD is to be able to look forward to joining tomorrow's greats, then why not leave well enough alone? One might think that the variability of symptom expression and course and prognosis might be sufficient to allow a note of caution to creep into the professional discourse. One further good reason for early screening tools and early diagnosis would lie in the reliability and efficacy of this leading to successful interventions; however, there is little evidence to support this (see Chapter 8). If symptoms are subject to such variability whether or not 'technical' interventions are applied, then what is the purpose of such a system of classification and attempts at early diagnosis?

Charman and Baird (2002) wonder how accurate and stable the diagnosis of an ASD might be. Although arguing for the stability over time of the syndrome, it is worth noting that in two studies, one by Gillberg *et al.* (1990) and the other by Lord (1995), both written by strong advocates of the 'lifelong' disorder hypothesis, one child out of 28 and 30 respectively were found to be no longer autistic, according to their criteria, by the age of three years, a year after the first assessment. Standing this on its head, if this child had been assessed for diagnoses at the age of three rather than earlier, they would not have received that label. Was this label rescinded in those two who no longer were deemed autistic? What might be the heartbreak, stress and confusion caused to the parents? Given that the authors are strong advocates of the diagnosis, how many other children at the tender age of three were on the path to a more ordinary development (as children develop at different rates, evidenced by the two who were 'autistic' at two but 'normal' at three)? In addition, Stone *et al.* (2000) report much lower time stability for those accorded a diagnosis of PDD-NOS. The variability of infant behaviour and development would seem to argue against a blind adherence to preconceived notions of social and emotional development. It might well be the case that a certain type of 'core' autism has a unitary course with a poor prognosis, but by lumping disorders such as AS and PDD-NOS all under ASD, with the current practice being to call all of these ASDs just 'autism', a great disservice could be done to those in receipt of such a diagnosis. If the prognosis for some of those diagnosed is good enough to allow entry into the halls of fame for their accomplishments, then what benefit accrues from diagnosing such individuals, particularly as those people may never have their diagnosis rescinded as autism is conceptualised as a 'lifelong' disorder?

The issue of diagnosing at the other end of the age spectrum – that of diagnosing childhood disorders in adults – is also highly problematic.

Children with 'autism', as it used to be defined, are unlikely to have escaped diagnosis by the time they reach adulthood given the accompanying range of disabilities (physical and mental) associated with this previously rare diagnosis. There is a considerable paucity of material on diagnostic procedures in adults. There is also a great difficulty in using contemporaneous symptoms as being indicative of childhood problems, or using an adult's retrospective recall of childhood functioning to assess their childhood. The difficulties in detecting symptoms, which may have occurred many decades ago, are all too obvious; but just what kind of behaviour is worthy of scrutiny? Wing (1981) began the trend of using adults to study childhood onset 'autistic' disorders. The case histories outlined by her were procured from adults and it is not clear from the paper whether evidence beyond individual or parental recall of childhood history was obtained. This not only began a trend of using adults to retrospectively investigate possible ASD symptoms in childhood, but the clinical practice of diagnosing adults (who had not received such diagnoses in childhood) with ASDs.

Diagnostic questionnaires

Tools such as the Autism Diagnostic Interview-Revised (ADI-R) (Lord *et al.*, 1994) and the Autism Diagnostic Observation Schedule-Generic (ADOS-G) (Lord *et al.*, 2000) are increasingly being used in the diagnostic process. If one gets a high score on one of these this usually results in a diagnosis of autism. If a lower score is found, but still above the threshold, then a diagnosis of either AS, PDD-NOS, or ASD may be given.

The ADI-R (Lord *et al.*, 1994) is marketed as a 'clinical diagnostic instrument' for assessing autism in children and adults. It consists of a standardised, semi-structured clinical interview for caregivers. The interview contains 93 items and focuses on behaviours in three content areas or domains: quality of social interaction (e.g., emotional sharing, offering and seeking comfort, social smiling and responding to other children); communication and language (e.g., stereotyped utterances, pronoun reversal, social usage of language); and repetitive, restricted and stereotyped interests and behaviour (e.g., unusual preoccupations, hand and finger mannerisms, unusual sensory interests). Responses are scored by the clinician based on the caregiver's description of the person in question. Questions are organised around content area. Within the area of communication, for example, 'delay or total lack of language not compensated by gesture' is further broken down into specific behavioural items, such as pointing to express interest, conventional gestures, head nodding and head shaking. Similarly, the area of 'reciprocal social interaction, lack of socio-emotional reciprocity and modulation to context' includes the following behaviours: use of other's body, offering comfort, inappropriate facial expressions, quality of social overtures and appropriateness of social response. In addition to asking about current behaviour, each question focuses on the time period when the behaviours were likely to be most pronounced – generally, between the ages of four and five years. The interview then generates scores in each of the three content areas (i.e., communication and language, social interaction and restricted, repetitive behaviours). Scores are essentially based on the clinician's judgement following the caregiver's report of the child's behaviour and development. For each item, the clinician gives a score ranging from 0 to 3. A score of 0 is given when 'behaviour of the type specified in the coding is not present'; up to a score of 3 for 'extreme severity' of the specified behaviour. A diagnosis of autism is given when scores in all three content areas of communication, social interaction and patterns of behaviour meet or exceed the specified cut-offs. The ADI-R is said to require substantial training in administration and scoring, and a 'highly trained' clinician is thought to be able to administer the ADI-R in approximately 90 minutes. There is no requirement for the assessor to observe any of the behaviours the caregiver is reporting.

The ADOS-G (Lord *et al.*, 2000) is marketed as a semi-structured assessment for individuals suspected of having autism or other pervasive developmental disorders (PDD). It is a combination of two earlier instruments: the Autism Diagnostic Observation Schedule (ADOS: Lord *et al.*, 1989), a schedule intended for adults and children with language skills at a minimum of the three-year-old level, and the Pre-Linguistic Autism Diagnostic Observation Scale (PL-ADOS) (DiLavore *et al.*, 1995), a schedule intended for children with limited or no language. It also has some additional items for verbally fluent, high-functioning adolescents and adults. The ADOS-G consists of four modules. Each module is aimed at children and adults of differing developmental and language levels, ranging from no expressive or receptive language to verbally fluent adults. The examiner is allowed to observe the occurrence or non-occurrence of behaviours that are deemed to indicate a diagnosis of autism or other PDDs across developmental levels and chronological ages. The examiner selects the module that is most appropriate for a particular child or adult on the basis of his/her expressive language level and chronological age and then uses structured activities and materials, and less structured interactions to provide 'standard' contexts in which social, communicative and other behaviours are observed. Within each module, the participant's response to each activity is recorded by the diagnostician, with overall ratings being made at the end. These ratings are then used to formulate a diagnosis. The ADOS-G essentially provides a 30- to 45-minute observation period during which the examiner presents the individual being assessed with planned social situations in which it has been determined in advance that behaviour of a particular type is expected to appear.

The focus of the ADOS-G is on observation of social behaviour and communication with the goal of the activities being to provide 'standard' contexts in which interactions occur. Standardisation lies in the hierarchy of behaviour employed by the examiner and the kinds of behaviours taken into account in each activity during the overall ratings. The examiners have a difficult task, as what the examiners do not do (such as deliberately waiting to see if the participant will initiate an interaction or try to maintain it) is as important as what they do, thus there is implicit acknowledgement that in setting up 'social' scenarios the person and personality of the examiner is unavoidably part of the mix. As such the goal of 'standardisation' seems difficult to achieve. The impact of the observer in any human situation under study is well recognised in the humanities. Thus, anthropologists, in developing the ethnographic method of investigation, recognised the impact the investigator had not only on an individual, but a whole community and as a result developed a methodology that required the investigator to live among those they were studying for months and sometimes years.

Thus, both the ADI-R and ADOS-G provide a superficial and highly subjective way of diagnosing an individual with an ASD. They are examples of judging a book by its cover and in the case of ADI-R someone else's book by a description of its cover. Although supporters of the use of such rating scales in establishing diagnosis claim that reliability and consistency in scoring can be established by training in use of these instruments, in the real world, however, this rarely translates into practice, which is not surprising given that the so-called 'symptoms' being rated are open to highly subjective interpretations. Thus, one of the authors (ST) has found that even within the boundaries of a rural county, in one town the numbers diagnosed with an ASD are plentiful and exceed those that are diagnosed with ADHD and in the next town there are hardly any – all down to the differential diagnostic habits of two clinicians using similar instruments. In his practice, ST has found that when clinically working with those who have been previously diagnosed with 'autism', it only takes a few meetings before far more meaningful narratives have emerged than those attached to the superficial focus of 'symptoms' and 'diagnosis'. Working in this way, without the distraction of trying to categorise behaviours, ST has found that diagnostic-type conversations ascribing experiences to 'autism' (as in 'this is because of his autism') usually disappear and become of little relevance to therapeutic work.

In addition, both tests require considerable time to administer, which has led some (such as Williams and Brayne, 2006) to suggest that this undermines their efficacy and practicality in clinical settings, arguing, instead, that we should use shorter screening tests. Others suggest these 'instruments' should not be used in isolation because they cannot capture the presentation of stereotyped behaviours, meaning a more complete diagnostic history is required. De Bildt and colleagues (2004) specifically looked at the ability of ADOS-G and ADI-R to discriminate between those with autism and learning disability; they conclude that the level of agreement between the two tools was 'fair' but both had poor ability to discriminate between PDD and learning disability in general. Like other authors, they emphasise that neither should be used in isolation; use of both, augmented by as much personal historical detail as possible, is desirable. If that is the case and consensus is arguing that these 'instruments' should be supplemented by thorough history taking and clinical judgement, one wonders why the well-trained clinician can't just use historical data, without recourse to cumbersome, superficial tools, open to subjective interpretation and poor discriminators of conditions within the spectrum and between other potential diagnostic categories.

In 2002 Wing and colleagues devised the Diagnostic Interview for Social and Communication Disorders (DISCO). The authors explain that the purpose of developing the DISCO was to assist clinicians in the diagnosis, differential diagnosis and management of ASD and other development disorders affecting social interaction and communication. Thus, they suggest that the autistic spectrum is wider than that of PDD and accept that this means widening the spectrum further; as a result the list of behaviours in the DISCO exceeds that of the other two tools. The authors are astute enough to point out that any attempt to devise a tool of this nature falls prey to the 'insoluble' problem of 'circularity', but no attempt is made to solve it! We wish to suggest that this circularity is only a vicious one as long as one is committed to both the spectrum and a pre-determined view of what constitutes autism, the spectrum or normal behaviour. It matters little whether any of these tools have specificity, reliability or validity if the premise (face validity) upon which they are based is flawed. In what appears a self-serving view, the authors suggest that rigid adherence to diagnostic categories will prove detrimental to parents and caregivers.

For those who seek a referral for a diagnosis of AS, some services (and one author, BM, can attest to this through personal experience) send out the Autism-spectrum Quotient questionnaire (AQ) (Baron-Cohen et al., 2001). Baron-Cohen and colleagues argue that this instrument has been piloted over several years on adults with AS or high-functioning autism (HFA). In their study (Baron-Cohen et al., 2001), the authors report that of the 11 individuals who exceeded the 32 cut-off score, all were male and of these seven were deemed to be eligible for a diagnosis of HFA or AS. It is not clear what differentiated these seven from the other four who exceeded 32. However, none of these seven had previously received a diagnosis of HFA or AS and as all taught at university it seems likely that they were functioning adequately. One might ask therefore, what the point of the exercise was. The authors conclude that the AQ has reasonable validity and also decide that their results show that HFA and AS are found disproportionately among scientists, mathematicians and engineers, which to them suggests a link between these professions and the autistic spectrum.

It is well worth looking in further detail at the AQ, to see what behaviours it sets out to try and capture. Here are some of its questions:

- I prefer to do things on my own rather than with other people.
- If I try to imagine something, I find it very easy to create a picture in my mind.
- I often notice small sounds when others do not.
- I usually notice car number plates or similar strings of information.
- I am fascinated by dates.
- I would rather go to a library than a party.
- I find myself more strongly drawn to people than things.
- I don't particularly enjoy reading fiction.
- I notice patterns in things all the time.
- I am not very good at remembering phone numbers.
- I enjoy social occasions.
- I enjoy meeting people.
- I am not very good at remembering people's date of birth.

One may wonder what these questions have to do with the 'core' feature of a lack of empathy. It is also worth pointing out that this list bears more than a passing resemblance to Eysenck's Personality Inventory (Eysenck and Eysenck, 1975) which has questions such as: do you like mixing with people? Do you like working alone? Do you like planning things carefully, well ahead of time?

SCREENING FOR ASDS

In 2003 a UK National Plan for Autism was published. This plan was implemented by the All Parliamentary Group on Autism, and was developed by the National Autistic Society in collaboration with the Royal College of Paediatrics and Child Health and Royal College of Psychiatrists (National Autistic Society, 2003). The plan had ten 'key' action points:

- Easy and transparent access to assessment within a specified time frame.
- Discussion of the diagnosis, taking into account a sensitive framework for sharing information.
- Easy access for families to information and support and relating it to their needs.
- Multi-agency, multidisciplinary assessment and working.
- Appropriate intervention.
- Immediate appointment of a key worker for the family.
- Care plan developed with and for the family.
- Care management for complex situations and ongoing needs.
- Regular ASD-specific training of all professionals working in assessment and provision of services.
- Strategic planning and coordination of ASD services for local populations must be undertaken.

In addition, under the subheading 'Identification' the plan recommends 'Training of all involved professionals in 'alerting' signals of possible ASD both at pre-school and school age.' And 'Regular opportunities (at least at 8–12 months, 2–3 years and 4–5 years) to discuss a child's development with parents as part of "surveillance" to detect and respond rapidly to any developmental concerns.' And 'Age of detection/diagnosis of all developmental problems including autism/ASD as a specified disorder to be audited in each local area.' Although whole population screening was not recommended, this represents a sea change in our approach to autism even though it is acknowledged in the document that these recommendations come from professional opinion with little research being available to support its producing positive benefits to the lives of those 'identified' as autistic at such a young age. The lack of evidential support and the clinical, ethical and potential lifelong implications for those diagnosed was not discussed.

In the UK, as in other parts of the world (such as California), we have, in a very short space of time, moved from the realms of vague unsubstantiated hypotheses to political ideology. There are no 'national plans' for dyslexia, ADHD or dyspraxia, so why autism? Does autism somehow fit into the government's plans for children who lack social competence and have relevance, therefore, for initiatives such as Sure Start (see Chapter 10)? In the plan there is reference to behavioural features that rarely appear in the academic literature, such as biting/hitting peers and being oppositional to adults, but also an acknowledgement of what we have been arguing in this book – that, given the available evidence, autism is best understood as a social construct – even though, of course, this cannot be admitted as overtly as that would undermine the whole idea behind a 'National Plan':

> The identification of an ASD is through behavioural 'symptoms'...Yet behaviour by itself is a poor guide to diagnosis and certainly there is no single behaviour or even set of behaviours that unequivocally denote autism, although missing behaviours may be a better guide. Making a diagnosis is, therefore, a clinical judgement, with behavioural 'symptoms' as a guide to that judgement. This task is made more problematic by the fact that most behaviours that are seen as 'characteristic' of an ASD can be seen in other (including normally developing) populations, albeit at times of particular stress or in isolation. A further difficulty for the categorical model of ASD is that the three behavioural domains (communication, social understanding and skill, flexibility in thinking and behaviour) vary dimensionally across both the normally developing and the ASD populations. There is no point (other than an arbitrary one) at which behaviour along any one of these three dimensions can be divided into 'autistic' versus 'non-autistic'...It is also the case that many people with ASD view themselves as part of normal human variation, rather than as having a pathology...The two views of ASD can be reconciled by viewing ASD as a broad category sharing certain developmental characteristics within the three dimensions

within which there is normal variation, but it is only when someone is situated beyond a certain (necessarily arbitrary) 'cut off' point along all three of these dimensions that they would be categorised as having a disorder. (National Autistic Society, 2003: 76)

If you screen a population it is likely to be the case that 'hidden' numbers of people with a disorder will be detected. How many largely depends upon how specific the definition of a case is. It is the lack of case specificity that undermines the argument for the use of screening and screening tools. Unless you can reliably distinguish a case of X from that of Y then the possibility of large numbers of false positives is strong. Once you start with the presupposition that certain behaviours are worthy of diagnosis and are likely to be indicative of a specific condition it is likely that you can get caught in a process of circularity. Using criteria of refutability one should instead start by questioning whether certain behaviours are worthy of diagnosis and if so which ones. That is why both the DSM and ICD have criteria for 'global' functioning that should be addressed before considering diagnosis and why they recommend not using a 'cook-book' approach to their manuals .

According to the National Screening Committee (2000) certain criteria have to be fulfilled for a population screening tool to be valid. For example, the second criteria states:

> The epidemiology and natural history of the condition, including development from latent to declared disease, should be adequately understood and there should be a detectable risk factor, or disease marker, and a latent period or early symptomatic stage. (National Screening Committee, 2000: 26)

Criteria number 13 states: 'The benefit from the screening programme should outweigh the physical and psychological harm (caused by the test, diagnostic procedures and treatment)' (National Screening Committee, 2000: 27). It is highly dubious whether even the diagnostic screening for autism, let alone the broader ASDs, could meet either of these criteria, or indeed some others in the list. Williams and Brayne (2006) take an alternative approach, arguing that when screening for ASDs a test should be reliable, repeatable and valid, and its sensitivity, specificity and positive predictive value must have been assessed in the general population; they make no mention of the National Screening Committee (NSC) criteria. It is not clear why the latter should not be used, other than that of needing to find a way for the various screening tests for ASD used in the UK to aspire towards having criteria that they could meet.

Many concerned parents and professionals have been exposed to literature and programmes from lay and professional sources that talk about 'autism' and autistic symptoms and how to recognise them. The authors of this literature and these programmes therefore have a considerable interest in the expansion of behaviours that necessitate interventions from 'experts', who then become vital in oiling the wheels of 'screening'. Parents may be caught in a trap of thinking that the diagnosis will lead to access to goods and services that their child would otherwise be denied. Indeed, many of these (well-intentioned) 'experts' contend that that is one of the rationales behind their proselytising. To us it seems that the people who have most obviously benefited from the increase in the use of tools for screening for and diagnosing of ASDs have been the professionals themselves.

Screening questionnaires

The Checklist for Autism in Toddlers (CHAT) was devised by Baron-Cohen and colleagues in 1992. The CHAT is a screening instrument which seeks to identify children aged 18 months who are at risk for an ASD. It is a short questionnaire used by primary health workers (such as community paediatricians) during the 18-month developmental check. The following are examples of questions asked by the CHAT:

Section A – Ask Parent:
Yes or No?
- Does your child take an interest in other children?
- Does your child enjoy playing peek-a-boo/hide-and-seek?
- *Does your child ever pretend, for example, to make a cup of tea using a toy cup and teapot, or pretend other things?
- *Does your child ever use his/her index finger to point, to indicate interest in something?

Section B – GP's observation
Yes or No?
- *Get child's attention, then point across the room at an interesting object and say 'Oh look! There's a (name a toy)!' Watch child's face. Does the child look across to see what you are pointing at?

- *Get the child's attention, then give child a miniature toy cup and teapot and say 'Can you make a cup of tea?' Does the child pretend to pour out the tea, drink it, etc?
- *Say to the child 'Where's the light?' or 'Show me the light'. Does the child point with his/her index finger at the light?

* Indicates critical question most indicative of autistic characteristics

Baron-Cohen and colleagues (1996) pinpointed protodeclarative pointing (pointing at an object of interest), gaze monitoring and pretend play as key items to screen for with the CHAT. The conclusion that these, above any other features, when seen at such a young age, are indicative of potential future autism seems to have been arrived at without any robust research evidence to substantiate this idea.

Robins *et al.* (2001a) decided to modify the CHAT. The M-CHAT does not require physicians' observations, just parental self-report. The questionnaire is simply given to parents of a 16–30-month-old infant as a screening tool. The following are examples of questions found in the M-CHAT:

- Does your child take an interest in other children?
- Does your child like climbing on things, such as up stairs?
- Does your child ever pretend, for example, to talk on the phone or take care of a doll or pretend other things?
- Does your child ever use his/her index finger to point, to ask for something?
- Does your child ever use his/her index finger to point, to indicate interest in something?
- Does your child look you in the eye for more than a second or two?
- Does your child smile in response to your face or your smile?
- Does your child imitate you (e.g., you make a face – will your child imitate it)?
- If you point at a toy across the room, does your child look at it?
- Does your child walk?
- Does your child look at your face to check your reaction when faced with something unfamiliar?

Each question is marked by a yes/no answer and the questionnaire can be completed in a couple of minutes. If the child fails two to three items (or more) they should be referred for a diagnostic evaluation. It is not clear whether or why a 16-month-old child not exhibiting these behaviours should raise concerns about developmental delays or problems that are worthy of diagnosis or in what way such behaviours constitute specific risk factors for the development of autism or an ASD. Those of us who are parents can imagine our children 'failing' this 'test' quite easily at 16 months of age or older, particularly our boys (who often develop the type of skills being rated later than girls).

The Robins *et al.* (2001a) M-CHAT produced a critical response by Charman and colleagues (2001), among whom Baron-Cohen is listed as a co-author. Whatever the respective merits of the CHAT and M-CHAT, there appears to have broken out something of a turf war. In neither the Robins *et al.* (2001a) article nor in the subsequent articles of Charman *et al.* (2001) and Robins *et al.* (2001b) do either side spend any time addressing the kinds of ethical criticisms that could be made if they had attempted to judge the merits of their screening tools by the criteria established by the NSC. Given the current state of case definition and knowledge (then and now), it is hardly surprising that they chose not to do so.

In a 2001 paper by Baird and colleagues (that also includes Charman and Baron-Cohen as co-authors) there is a limited discussion of the case for and against screening for autism. Although there is some reference 'caseness', sensitivity, specificity and reliability, there is little acknowledgement of the implications of poor case definition and the problem of producing potentially large numbers of false positives. Instead, the authors choose to highlight the importance of parental concerns as if the scientific questions should be dictated by a demand and supply equation. In answer to the question of 'Why screen?' they point to parental concern and early intervention and treatment, although, as they admit, evidence for the efficacy of such intervention is poor to absent. This admission should effectively undermine the whole argument for screening but Baird *et al.* (2001) blithely skate over it. Further they suggest another reason for early screening is genetic counselling:

> The risk of a second child having autism when the first has the diagnosis is 5% (one hundred times the reported prevalence), and the chances of a more general problem in social communication or cognitive development are several times higher still. There is no prenatal diagnostic test but parents need to have this information as soon as possible if they are to make personal choices about extending their family based on existing knowledge rather than ignorance. (Baird *et al.*, 2001: 469)

As with many papers on this subject the terms autism and ASD are used interchangeably. This is particularly unfortunate, when they appear to argue that the prognosis for what had hitherto been called 'autism' is dismal.

Let us now turn to the Childhood Asperger Syndrome Test (CAST), which was devised to screen for possible AS. This screening tool was devised by Scott and colleagues (2002a) and includes Baron-Cohen as a co-author. Initially a pilot was devised where 13 children already diagnosed with AS were compared with 37 'typically developing' children aged four to 11 years. The CAST consists of 37 questions with yes/no answers. There are six 'control' questions, so the maximum score is 31. The 37 questions on the CAST were based on ICD-10 and two other screening tools: the Pervasive Developmental Disorders Questionnaire (PDDQ) and the Autism Spectrum Screening Questionnaire (ASSQ). One tool was devised in the USA (the PDDQ) and the other in Scandinavia. The authors deemed these questionnaires problematic as the ASSQ has only been validated on a clinical sample, and the PDDQ was in very early stages of development and neither had been designed to focus specifically on AS. They conclude that, as all of the AS sample scored equal to or greater than 15 on the CAST, while none of the controls did, choosing a provisional cut-off of 15 would not generate many false positives or lead to many cases needing an assessment for a possible social and communication condition, in a typical mainstream primary-age population. The authors then argue that as a result CAST was suitable to administer as a screening to a wider population, when perhaps more appropriate questions might have been whether such a tool could differentiate from other comparable conditions, and the appropriateness of generalising from a small population of already diagnosed individuals to other populations.

In the subsequent study (Scott *et al.*, 2002a, 2002b) the CAST was sent to the parents of 1,150 primary school-aged children in the Cambridge area. An additional screening tool called the Social Communication Questionnaire (SCQ) was also sent to families who returned the initial CAST questionnaire, and this acted as a comparison tool. Further assessment using the ADOS-G was undertaken in those above or near the cut-off scores on the CAST or SCQ. Any individuals who were 'discovered' but were not already in receipt of an AS diagnosis were not automatically given one, but were given sufficient information to procure one if they wished. Out of the 1,150, 199 replied. Of these 199, 25 withdrew consent, leaving 174 of who 139 also returned the SCQ. Of the 199, 6.5 per cent scored at or above the cut-off point on the CAST. Given that the authors assume that an expected level in the population was 0.5 per cent, this led the authors to conclude that either the score of 15 was too low or that only those parents who already had concerns replied. If one adopted the former view one might have thought that this seriously undermined the validity of the tool as a screening measure. Were one to assume that the tool was a valid one, then it would yield an epidemiological result for AS that far exceeds all current estimates for ASD prevalence, let alone AS. Yet the authors conclude: 'In summary, these preliminary results indicate that the CAST may be an effective tool for the early screening of primary-school-age (4–11years) children at risk for AS and related conditions, in a non-clinical sample' (Scott *et al.*, 2002a: 30), but only if the CAST cut-off point is raised to 17.

The papers do not discuss whether those identified did pursue a diagnosis. Serious ethical issues are involved in identifying need where none had hitherto been discerned, but this is not raised as an issue by the authors, who instead conclude that with ongoing development CAST could be established as a UK screener to act

> as an early indicator for those children likely to be at risk for AS or related conditions, who are not achieving their educational potential and who have clinical or educational needs. It needs to be developed using a non-clinical sample as these children may not yet be in touch with clinical services, but it is likely that such children will be the ones for whom there is already parental and/or teacher concerns, but who may be struggling to have their needs recognised, or who are being misclassified as lazy, naughty, disruptive, etc. (Scott *et al.*, 2002a: 30)

In addition to questions about the appropriateness of such conclusions, given the unacceptable mutation of the original study hypothesis (that CAST with a cut-off of 15 is a suitable screening instrument for AS), which clearly (and unsurprisingly) produced unacceptable rates of false positives, it also begs the question of just whom the tool is devised for if 'lazy', 'naughty' or 'disruptive' children are the target population.

The possibility of profound consequences of using CAST as a screening tool make it worth examining further. The following are examples of questions are as they appear in the CAST:

- Does s/he come up to you spontaneously for a chat?
- Does s/he enjoy sports?

- Does s/he appear to notice unusual details that others miss?
- Does s/he find it easy to interact with other children?
- Can s/he read appropriately for his/her age?
- Does s/he mostly have the same interests as his/her peers?
- Does s/he have an interest which takes up so much time that s/he does little else?
- Does s/he enjoy joking around?
- Does s/he have difficulty understanding the rules for polite behaviour?
- Does s/he appear to have an unusual memory for details?
- Does s/he often do or say things that are tactless or socially inappropriate?
- Can s/he count to 50 without leaving out any numbers?
- Does s/he often care how s/he is perceived by the rest of the group?

Are we in McCarthy's America? Should any of these behaviours warrant concern, never mind diagnosis? One is left with the view that the authors have a predetermined view of AS that essentially becomes circular. In other words 'What is causing X to find it difficult to interact with other children?' Answer: 'Because X has AS'. 'How do you know X has AS?' Answer: 'Because X finds it difficult to interact with other children.'

In a subsequent paper Williams and colleagues (2005) (not surprisingly Baron-Cohen is again a co-author) go on to screen a slightly larger population, with those screened positive subsequently being diagnosed. In this study, the parents of 1,925 children were given questionnaires. Those children, who were selected for possible diagnosis, were diagnosed by either of the 'gold-standard' tools (ADOS-G or ADI-R) and/or clinical judgement. Three of the authors of the study were involved in the diagnostic process, which raises some concerns about possible conflicts of interest interfering with their objectivity. There is no discussion in the paper about whether children should have any rights in a process rendering them passive recipients of such diagnoses. In their conclusion, the authors now see CAST as having properties that go beyond that of being a screen specifically for AS and they recommend that CAST can now be used in epidemiological research for identifying ASD in general.

Among the benefits they claim for this approach are access to genetic screening and the possibility of early intervention. They fail to point out that neither of these could be considered viable options for ASD at present or at any time in the near future. All of the children in this study, who were subsequently diagnosed, were given a diagnosis of an ASD. It would appear that many of the children had pre-existing diagnoses and disabilities. Advocates of the spectrum approach argue that the spectrum can co-exist with any other condition. It remains to be seen whether this is a case of special pleading. In this study three groups were differentiated: those who scored less than 12, those who scored between 12 and 14 and those who scored 15 and above (on the CAST). Of those who scored less than 12, 5 per cent were selected for assessment, but it remains unclear whether any were subsequently diagnosed. It is also unclear what percentage of those who scored 12–14 were subsequently diagnosed. If individuals who scored less than 12 could still be diagnosed and those (particularly when compared to the previous study) who scored less than 14 are now also potentially eligible for diagnosis, then how specific and reliable is this tool? The authors do record that there is 'much anxiety' associated with false positive screening results. That is a major understatement! Diagnosing a child incorrectly with a condition for which no improvement is foreseen is, in our view, positively negligent. The response on the part of the authors to this calamity is that this question merits 'further investigation'. A more apposite conclusion arises from the NSC criteria – that no autism screening tool is fit for purpose.

Williams and Brayne (2006) make a distinction between primary and secondary screening for ASD. They define secondary screening as an early diagnostic screen for children with a known developmental problem. The authors also report that in a survey they found 9 per cent of child health teams were already using primary screening (screening all children for potential developmental difficulties). As we have mentioned, once you start with the presupposition that certain behaviours are worthy of diagnosis and are likely to be indicative of a specific condition, you are likely to be caught in a process of circularity; unless you are aware of this, ethical concerns about such a process will pass unnoticed.

Let us take the Webb and colleagues (2003) paper as an example. All mainstream primary schools in Cardiff were invited to participate in a prevalence survey of ASD. Teachers of each class filled in a questionnaire based on ICD-10 criteria for autistic disorders (primary screening). The ASSQ (secondary screening) was completed on children identified with problems from the first questionnaire. A total of 11,692 were screened and 234 (2 per cent) children were identified as requiring an ASSQ – with 151 of 234 (65 per cent) ASSQs returned. Of the 151, 60 children (52 male, eight female; 40 per cent) scored 22 or more on the ASSQ (i.e., deemed above the cut-off for ASD). Their notes and the involved professionals were then consulted. From this 35 children, unknown to specialist services before this time, had an additional assessment. From these, 17 children (all male) were diagnosed as having an ASD. The authors note that they discovered a diverse population who 'had' an ASD, including some who did not fit into the ICD-10 classification they were meant to be using (which makes one wonder what the point of the study having ICD-10 criteria was in the first place). In this situation what differentiates the secondary screening method from the primary one is largely a matter of size (involving smaller numbers being screened with slightly longer instruments). Some children whose symptomology appeared not to have given previous cause for concern were, by the end of the study, in receipt of a diagnosis; a diagnosis, moreover, of a condition considered lifelong and disabling. It is not clear whether the researchers saw any of the children and the ethics of such a process are not discussed.

This is particularly worrying as the authors describe having a protocol that was agreed with the local education authority, who liaised with individual schools. Parents were informed of the survey in writing by their child's school and advised to inform the school if they did not wish to participate. School staff and parents were advised that this was a survey of emotional, behavioural and communication problems, as the authors did not wish to introduce observer bias towards autistic behaviour in the screened population. Given that this eventually led to diagnosing children who had, up until that time, not been candidates for an ASD diagnosis, this raises major ethical concerns. The process that led to diagnosis was not initiated through requests for help from the children or their parents. Instead they found themselves swept along in a process for which initial consent was procured in a way that deliberately obscured a possible outcome – a potentially devastating label being applied to the child.

CONCLUSION

In this chapter we have described the current mainstream approach to the classification of ASDs and recounted some of the history behind this. We then critically examined how this relates to the development of diagnostic practice, diagnostic tools and approaches to screening for autism. The literature can be characterised as suffering from concepts with fuzzy boundaries, widening of diagnostic boundaries as behaviours that are difficult to view as pathological per se became included, a poor evidence base to support such changes, and classifications and practices that are subject to relentless circularity (with experts defining behaviours that become the sole criteria for confirming their theories – the behaviour becoming simultaneously symptom, syndrome and cause). Such an ideological basis for classification and practice has led us to conclude that current classifications lack validity and current questionnaires should not be used for diagnosis, screening, or clinical practice more generally.

7
THE PROBLEM OF HETEROGENEITY

So far in this book we have critically reviewed the development of the biomedical model of autism, situating this development within the broader cultural milieu. What we have uncovered is that autism is a disorder, field – of study and concept built on an ideological basis and, given the rapid expansion of its boundaries, it is of little surprise that it has become beset with the problem of heterogeneity.

'Heterogeneous' is an adjective used to describe an object or system consisting of multiple items having a large number of variations. In relation to autism we are taking it to mean that the boundaries are now so wide that it's hard to characterise 'autism' as it can be used to define a wide variety of presentations.

MAINSTREAM ACCEPTANCE OF HETEROGENEITY

Heterogeneity is widely accepted as an issue in 'mainstream' publications about autism. However, far from seeing this as a major problem with regard the validity of the concept, it is explained away as a reflection of the 'complexity' of autism. For example, genetic research in autism has been plagued with a failure to replicate findings and with regions of linkage seemingly occurring on the majority of chromosomes (Ring *et al.*, 2008). Genetic heterogeneity refers to multiple origins causing the same disorder in different individuals. Thus, this finding (or lack of it) is viewed as a product of autism having a heterogenic genetic origin; that is, lots of different genes acting together or separately can cause autism. Unfortunately, the most obvious conclusion and the most scientifically valid until positive evidence is found – that the reason we can't find them is that genes for autism don't exist – seems unacceptable to those who have staked their careers and reputations on the belief that autism is a genetic condition.

Since Kanner first defined autism, the field has been plagued by a desired to 'pin down' a more specific and scientifically supportable definition. Lack of success in developing this led to a growing problem of 'heterogeneity' as different authors argued for different conceptualisations and systems of categorisation. In 1968 Sir Michael Rutter argued against the view that autism was a form of childhood schizophrenia, but avoided any conclusions as to the cause/nature of autism. Over the following three decades the field experienced a rapid increase in interest in autism research, with attempts at defining the concept and linking this to an idea of a 'core' deficit being a prominent feature of this effort.

Wing and Gould (1979) set the ball rolling for an expanded notion of autism by classifying PDDs on the basis of lack of sociability. Allen (1988), in contrast, classified PDDs on the basis mainly of deficits in communication and play. Others turned to cognitive differences as their basis (e.g., Fein *et al.*, 1985) or specific language deficits (e.g., Allen and Rapin, 1992). However, the confusion as to what constitutes autism doesn't finish with these four distinct approaches. Tsai *et al.* (1985) suggest using the presence or absence of EEG abnormality as their basis for classification, while Prior *et al.* (1975) and Volkmar (1992) suggest age of onset/developmental course as the basis for a rational distinction between different types of autism. Yet others identify specific behaviours such as anger, hyperactivity and speech type as the basis for discriminating sub-types of autism (Overall and Campbell, 1988). But we are still not finished; some have suggested the presence of known aetiological factors (such as chromosomal abnormalities, epilepsy) as the basis for subdivisions (Gillberg, 1992), others have argued for using IQ level and level of overall functioning (Dihoff, 1993; Cohen *et al.*, 1987). Given that the field has been so split on how to carve up this expanding entity, heterogeneity being a more strongly defining feature than any of these proposed systems should surprise no one.

Rutter and Schopler argue in favour of the validity of autism, suggesting that it can be differentiated from the 'ordinary run' of emotional and behavioural disorders of childhood by its 'strong association with mental retardation and with organic brain dysfunction, as well as in its worse prognosis, and its persisting differences in symptomatology' (Rutter and Schopler, 1987: 162). They identify a number of areas of continuing controversy surrounding the boundaries of autism and other comparable disorders. Obviously identifying a boundary would help to minimise problems of misdiagnosis, thus aiding research that might potentially identify core deficits, aetiological pathways and specific treatments. At this stage Rutter and Schopler are pinning their hopes on the identification of a 'brain deficit' that 'defines' autism. Although Rutter and Schopler return to this issue in 1992, by then DSM-IV was on the way and the number of comparable diagnostic disorders and systems for classifying autism had increased, bringing with it new problems of how and whether different autistic spectrum disorders could be differentiated from each other, from other similar childhood disorders and from more ordinary or 'normal' children. Unfortunately, since then the issue of the reliability and validity of autism and disorders in its spectrum has not been given the attention it merits, subsequent publications (including those of Michael Rutter) having come to simply accept the validity of this construct, no longer feeling the need to ask serious questions about it.

Similar problems of developing diagnostic specificity have bedevilled the study of other PDDs. Szatmari (1992) argues that diagnostic criteria must have some essential internal consistency in order to be differentiated reliably from other comparable cases. Without such internal consistency diagnosis becomes unreliable as well as having questionable validity. The ability to differentiate one case from another is dependent upon training a clinician who is able to properly differentiate a diagnosis from all prospective alternatives. In relation to PDDs, Williams and Kerfoot (2005), argue that the ease with which poorly validated diagnoses can be made has been one of the causes of the rapid increase in Asperger's diagnoses in recent years:

> Wide dissemination of information about these conditions, particularly Asperger's syndrome, has led to a diagnosis or treatment recommendation being offered by non-specialists on the basis of checklists or media articles, without clinical experience or even basic knowledge of medical classification, rules and treatment being applied. (Williams and Kerfoot, 2005: 216)

Szatmari concludes that AS is of 'limited external or internal validity' (Szatmari, 1992: 596). The literature he reviews only seeks to differentiate AS from autism or so-called high-functioning autism, as there had been no studies that sought to differentiate AS from other developmental disorders.

HETEROGENEITY IN DIAGNOSTIC SYSTEMS

At the time of the studies that led to the expansion of autism into a spectrum the predominant diagnostic system in use was DSM-III. Under 'Conduct Disorders' in DSM-III, there is an attempt to differentiate several 'types' of conduct disorder. Under-socialised types are characterised by the inability to form bonds with peers. It goes on to say 'Egocentrism is shown by readiness to manipulate others for favours without any effort to reciprocate. There is generally a lack of feelings for others' (DSM-III: 45). Age of onset is described as pre-pubertal. This description bears (arguably) a closer resemblance to the descriptions of the cases Hans Asperger wrote about than Lorna Wing's cases (see Chapters 3 and 6). One of the core features of the autistic spectrum is meant to be a lack of empathy, a lack that is meant to cause enduring difficulties in social interactions. How is this type of 'lack of empathy' to be differentiated from the lack of empathy of the under-socialised conduct disorder or, indeed, the 'personality disordered' criminal (particularly as later definitions removed the age of onset criterion)? The literature on differential diagnosis of autism from conduct disorder/personality disorders is at best ambiguous, at worst avoidant, leaving it essentially to the individual interpretation of the 'expert'.

Other disorders of infancy, childhood and adolescence in DSM-III include 'reactive attachment disorder of infancy', which also describes children who lack empathy and have dysfunctional patterns of social interaction. Reactive attachment disorder is described as often associated with some form of neglect, abuse, or trauma; however, in the absence of robust evidence on aetiology in autism (then and now) making the distinction between social dysfunction in the context of conduct disorder, reactive attachment disorder or ASD, becomes little more than a matter of the subjective opinion of the diagnoser. DSM-III goes on to mention schizoid disorder of childhood or adolescence. As one might expect, the areas of dysfunction are primarily social and children in this category are described as 'loners'. Also mentioned are 'bizarre' interests, such as violence and the occult; interests which are now thought to be typical of the AS child or adolescent. What appears to differentiate the 'schizoid' child from the 'un-socialised conduct disorder' child is the lack of anti-social behaviour on the part of the former. So it seems that at the time the concept of the autistic spectrum was being invented, there were several other possible diagnostic categories into which these children could be placed. As we have already discussed, this change in nosology was not the result of any new discovery but a gradual recasting of definitions. Existing deck chairs were rearranged, no new ones had been found.

The problem of this overlap continued to cause researchers a headache. For example, Szatamari (1998) observed:

> Reading the clinical descriptions of children with atypical personality development (Rank, 1949), schizoid and schizotypical disorders (Wolff, 1995), semantic pragmatic disorders (Bishop, 1989), right hemisphere syndromes (Weintrub & Mesulam, 1983), Learning Disabilities (Klin, Volkmar, Sparrow, Cicchetti & Rourke, 1995), and more recently, multiple complex disorders (van der Gaag *et al.*, 1995) makes one wonder whether the same children are being described under very different diagnostic labels. (Szatamari, 1998: 65)

The kinds of behaviours which subsequently merited the diagnosis of ASDs (such as AS), could already have been categorised as one of many viable alternatives in the literature, including the diagnostic manuals (although, like the ASDs, it is likely that similar deconstruction of these concepts could be made).

Not only was there a great deal of overlap in the boundaries of the new ASDs and other psychiatric disorders, similar confusion also arose about the boundaries of each ASD, particularly whether AS can be distinguished from autism, especially high-functioning autism (HFA). When autism was first announced, the idea of HFA would almost have been a contradiction in terms (see Lotter, 1966b). Whether autism (higher functioning or not) could be differentiated from AS depends to a large degree on the diagnostic validity of the latter, a point Volkmar and Klin make when they state:

> Premature notions of seeing Asperger's Syndrome and autism as either the same or different, though deceivingly clear-cut to some are in fact quite complex and ultimately begging the availability of good data. To say that the conditions are the same, or on a continuum, implies our knowledge of the continuum on which these conditions place themselves. (Volkmar and Klin, 2001: 85)

Furthermore, it is not clear how a meaningful differentiation between AS and autism can be made when there is little consistency in the degree to which studies that focused on 'autism' also included cases that could be diagnosed with AS.

This might all seem like a storm in a teacup to many. Does it matter, as long as children get access to treatment and services? However, without some uniformity one cannot estimate prevalence, monitor just how serious a condition is and develop a cohesive framework to assess specific interventions. As a result, many authors find themselves falling back on their own clinical opinion, a far cry from the sort of scientific knowledge required if we are to develop an evidence-based approach:

> The lack of generally accepted diagnostic guidelines for AS means that, at present, it is impossible to provide more than an estimate of its prevalence. In our clinical experience, the condition is very frequently misdiagnosed and, if a strict definition of AS is adopted, it is certainly less common than autism. (Volkmar and Klin, 2001: 100)

HETEROGENEITY IN SYMPTOMS

It is obviously absurd to have a spectrum stretching from speechless residents of day centres who have little voluntary control over the most basic bodily functions to Einstein, but that is precisely the position we now appear to have reached. In some ways the autistic spectrum spans the divide between more traditional notions of learning difficulties/mental retardation and psychiatric disorders. Of course, some unfortunate individuals have crippling neurological deficits causing significant learning difficulties and associated disabilities in many aspects of their social and emotional functioning. It is also reasonable to assume that biochemical factors can affect behaviour and that there are genetically mediated variations in our relative susceptibility to a given pathogen, contaminant, hallucinogenic agent, brain insult and so on. While we can reliably identify those with gross brain pathology who usually have multiple disabilities, the task of reliably identifying the source or cause of the difficulties in those receiving the wider spectrum of ASD diagnoses is currently almost impossible. The illusion that a diagnosis such as 'autism' gives, of having identified that the person with the diagnosis does indeed have a neurologically based disorder, has many ramifications in self-concepts, others' treatment of that person, services, institutional practices and so on.

If it could be conclusively proven that individuals with any range of communication handicaps, out of step with their intellectual age and who are disinterested in the social world, despite otherwise favourable circumstances, are victims of a biological disorder, then a diagnosis and 'treatment' according to more traditional linear medical model seems legitimate and desirable. However, none of these early symptoms affected two of the co-authors (NG and BM) who received an ASD diagnosis or, for that matter, any of the other AS-diagnosed adults either has met. Nor should the existence of a communication or other social problem provide enough evidence to justify turning this problem into a diagnostic category or using this as a basis for an autism diagnosis regardless of what else is occurring in that person's life. For example, we've all met some 'simple-minded' people from humble backgrounds who, from a culturally biased perspective, may seem intellectually limited. Indeed, they may seem to share many personality traits with individuals at the higher-functioning end of Down's syndrome. Yet few would suggest that because they shared these personality traits these people were somehow at the higher-functioning end of the Down's spectrum. The similarities are merely apparent and insufficient to be used as a basis for a diagnostic grouping.

With such a potentially diverse group receiving an ASD diagnosis, it is simply impossible to identify a consistent causative route. The same person may show different degrees of autistic-like traits at different stages of their life, traversing periods of relative withdrawal and extroversion.

One of the flaws in the autistic spectrum theory lies in its primary focus on the identification of symptoms, followed by the interpretation of data to match a very restricted pool of neurological evidence with an enormous diversity of behavioural symptoms. It is thus highly probable, given the current failure to identify a cluster of genes linked to a broad range of autism spectrum conditions, that multiple causative pathways may induce outcomes with some superficial similarities. Traits that are currently considered secondary (such as dyspraxia) do not exist in isolation; they merely make affected persons more vulnerable to the psychosocial influences that may interfere with that person's integration into mainstream socialisation and thus contribute to alienation and the emergence of culturally atypical and sometimes obsessive interests. Other traits associated with ASD, such as an odd gaze and the avoidance of eye contact, may be observed to varying extents in most people suffering from depression or a lack of self-confidence. It stands to reason that someone who has developed a poor body image would avoid direct face-to-face contact with acquaintances they cannot fully trust for fear of revealing their perceived aesthetic inferiority. This avoidant behaviour hampers a person's integration into any new social environment, leading to further alienation. Given the growing number of young people receiving different diagnoses at different stage of their lives, we may reasonably ask where we draw the boundaries between depression, social anxiety disorder, AS and ADHD, etc. (see Table 7.1). The fluidity of these diagnostic categories

Table 7.1 *Heterogeneity of common ASD 'symptoms'*

Trait	Overlapping psychiatric and other presentations
Lack of eye contact	Depression, anxiety, social anxiety disorder, shyness, low self-esteem. A lack of eye contact can result from lack of self-confidence. The same person may exhibit widely different degrees of reciprocal eye contact in different social situations. Many cultures have practices that prohibit or limit eye contact (for example, in hierarchies such as between children and adults).
Poor 'reading' of non-verbal communication	Language disorders, ADHD, anxiety, depression, personality disorder, attachment disorders, bipolar affective disorder, psychosis, learning difficulties. As with most behavioural traits its importance is always relative to what you're comparing it to. Other overlaps include side effect of medications, disinterest, a sense of alienation and normal variation. Apparent poor reading of non-verbal communication could also be the result of deliberate provocation, boredom, a strong desire for attention, love and so on.
Preoccupation with one or more stereotyped and restricted patterns of interest (restricted imagination)	OCD, obsessional personality disorder, schizoid personality disorder, ADHD (such as with computer games), depression (morbid preoccupation with negative aspects), eating disorders (fixation with food and/or weight). Most men (e.g., with football!). Sportsmen and women. Humanity: obsessive interest in a restricted sphere is characteristic not only of a depressed state of mind, but also of a phase of discovery and exploration. If someone had not fixated long enough on the tendency of logs to roll down slopes, the wheel may never have been invented! Most high achievers/perfectionists 'fixate' on their area of interest/expertise.

Continued

Table 7.1 *Continued*

Trait	Overlapping psychiatric and other presentations
Failure to develop peer relationships appropriate to developmental level	ADHD, language disorders, learning difficulties, attachment disorder, personality disorders, conduct disorders, social anxiety and other anxiety disorders. This refers to an important reason why many parents, teachers or social workers to seek to have children under their care diagnosed in the first place – a failure to fit in. Failure to fit in can have many more ordinary associations such as clumsiness (particularly in boys), different interests to peers, unhappy home circumstances and other traumas that preoccupy the young person.
A lack of empathy	Depression, conduct disorder, psychosis, ADHD, personality disorders, attachment disorder. A lack of self-confidence in social situations and a preoccupation with one's own problems tends to reduce interest in other people's lives and interests. The extent to which one can feign interest in all subjects or empathise with all predicaments is limited. As expectations for social empathy (e.g., in school and in the workplace) increase, so more may appear to lack this capacity. For isolated immigrants, a lack of familiarity with cultural expectations may also be a factor. Poor achievement or a sense of inferiority in a competitive culture may also lead people to turn away from a range of common interests.
Hyper-sensitivities and/or hypo-sensitivities	Depression, anxiety disorders, ADHD, personality disorders, attachment disorder. There is a range of 'sensitivities' among the population. Some hate loud noises, others crave them. These change from situation to situation, with cultural etiquette, familiarity, age and so on.

may lead (and arguably has already led) some ASD proponents simply to extend the autistic spectrum even further.

HETEROGENEITY IN THE THEORY OF MIND

Theory of mind (ToM) is defined as the ability to attribute mental states – states, intents, desires, pretending, knowledge, etc. – to oneself and others and to understand that others have beliefs, desires and intentions that are different from one's own. Premack and Woodruff's 1978 article, 'Does the Chimpanzee have a Theory of Mind?', first sparked an interest in the idea of ToM as an object for scientific study, although, earlier in the 20th century, Piaget had articulated a view with similarities to ToM; that in early childhood a child does not understand that others' views and thoughts differ from his or her own – which he referred to as 'egocentrism' (Piaget and Inhelder, 1948). Even though there has been considerable disagreement regarding which behaviours indicate the presence/absence of a developing theory of mind in the young, behaviours considered to indicate ToM include joint attention, gaze following, proto-declarative pointing, comprehending objects' animacy and awareness of others as intentional agents (Falck-Ytter *et al.*, 2006).

Testing for ToM ability has usually been through a 'false-belief' task test. This is based on the idea that one of the most important milestones in ToM development is gaining the ability to attribute a false belief – that is, to recognise that others can have beliefs about the world that are wrong. To do this, it is suggested, one must understand how knowledge is formed, that people's beliefs are based on their knowledge, that mental states can differ from reality and that people's behaviour can be predicted by their mental states. Numerous versions of the false-belief task have been developed, based on the initial one developed by Wimmer and Perner (1983).

As individuals with ToM impairment are thought to have a difficulty in determining the intentions of others, a lack in understanding of how their behaviour affects others and a difficult time with social reciprocity, autism research became interested in investigating whether children with autism had a specific ToM impairment. In 1985 Simon Baron-Cohen, Alan M. Leslie and Uta Frith published research which claimed to show that children with autism do not employ a ToM, and suggested that children with autism have particular difficulties with tasks requiring the child to understand another person's beliefs. This led them to suggest that a ToM deficit is a key feature and cause of autism.

Over the following years the idea that a lack of ToM (which some authors started to call 'mindblindness') was a deficit that was at the heart of autism (a core deficit) became popular. One of the most vocal supporters of this theory, Professor Simon Baron-Cohen (1995), for example, believes that our ability to 'mindread' is the result of four separate modules/mechanisms working together in order to produce beliefs about what others know. According to him, the mindreading system can be broken down into the following four modules: the intentionality detector (ID), eye direction detector (EDD), the shared attention mechanism (SAM) and, finally, the theory of mind module/mechanism (ToMM). He believes that each of these four mechanisms line up, roughly, with properties in the world, which are: volition (desires), perception, shared attention and epistemic states (knowledge and beliefs). For Baron-Cohen, the autistic deficit arises within the SAM. Here there is a 'massive impairment' in the functioning and this then feeds forward into the ToMM, ultimately causing the mindblindness that we see in persons with autism. The autistic deficits are thus the result of related processing difficulties in both the SAM and ToMM. This theory, built on a cognitive psychology framework, explained (at least for Baron-Cohen) why people on the autistic spectrum have difficulties interpreting the behaviour of others (such as 'pretend' tasks, especially those involving deception).

The ToM view of autism sparked a great deal of research; however, it soon became apparent that it had many problems. Some of the critiques of ToM were internal and general in nature, arguing that the theoretical framework of modularity it uses as a background for the ToMM is unsuitable; Fodor, for example, states, 'what our cognitive science has found out about the mind is mostly that we don't know how it works' (Fodor, 2001: 100). Specific critiques have concluded that one of the more troubling problems for ToM is its reliance on the false-belief task, as this is increasingly seen as unlikely to tell us anything important about ToM development or autism in general (Bloom and German, 2000). The general thrust of these critiques is that the false-belief task taps into developing cognitive abilities that do not use a special type of knowledge base in order to work. That is, the capacity to process all the relevant information in the false-belief tasks requires a host of abilities that develop prior to and independently from social cognition. It is not a specific capacity to represent knowledge of other minds that is used in the false-belief task, rather it is the blending together of more basic abilities such as holding multiple representations in mind and the additional ability the child has to maintain certain bits of information in a particular social situation (a test) that allows them to recognise false beliefs. Failure indicates non-specific processing problems rather than ToM difficulties specifically.

Another critique argues that ToM approaches require that lower-level perceptual abilities are intact. The account of autism offered by a ToM-centred view, takes autism's root problem to be a higher-level cognitive deficit in forming representations about the epistemic states of others. According to Baron-Cohen (1995) eye-gaze monitoring behaviour occurs because we know that seeing leads to knowing. The higher-level representation is the cause of the behaviour. To allow a basic perceptual problem to be the root cause makes the explanation proffered by Baron-Cohen superfluous. Any theory of modular function must have the proper perceptual input in order for the modules to carry out the functions they are responsible for. Any type of perceptual deficit would threaten the proper working necessary for the modular architecture Baron-Cohen espouses. In Baron-Cohen's account the basic perceptual functions of the autistic are assumed to be, and must be, intact. If the basic perceptual deficits persons with autism have are more far-reaching than simply an inability to monitor eye-gaze, then ToM being the root problem is challenged. As a result, for those who believe that a disturbance of perception is the basic problem in autism, then the inability to monitor eye-gaze is the result of pre-existing perceptual deficits rather than ToM deficits (Cundall, 2007).

Others go further. For example, Hacking (1999) rejects ToM in general, not only in the ToM deficit theory of autism. He replaces it with a Wittgensteinian 'form-of-life' (FoL) theory of language and social knowledge. In this view, language and social interaction is a 'norm-based' practice; such practices cannot be analysed in terms of internal, language-like 'theories' about the domain governed by these norms. Practices cannot be reduced to theories; you cannot learn to roller-skate by reading a book about it. The ToM notion that we infer people's intentions based their behaviour (such as the direction of their eye-gaze) is a mistake; instead we intuitively *and* directly see people's intentions. He calls these intuitions of mentality 'Köhler phenomena' (after the gestalt psychologist who, Hacking says, inspired Wittgenstein), viewing them as relying much more on a reading of the 'totality' of the situation, that cannot easily be reduced to parts available for study. These intuitive skills of most people are not described by ToM, so autistics are falsely described as having a deficit of ToM.

McGeer (2004) poses some further philosophical objections to the ToM deficit view of autism. One is the fact that the ToM deficit theory creates a one-sided asymmetrical view of two people failing to understand each other; in other words a ToM-centred concept of autism assumes 'normals' would understand autistics, but not vice versa. Following on from this, if you have a ToM deficit then your self-narratives cannot be taken seriously; autistic self-narrative may be deemed unreliable because the authors, lacking a ToM, are assumed not to be able to understand what subjectivity even is. This would seem to be contradicted by the copious, often moving and gripping, personal accounts by those with an ASD diagnosis.

However, the controversy and increasing heterogeneity found in ToM deficit accounts are not limited to autism. A lack of a ToM has become increasingly popular as a proposed core deficit in schizophrenia (Firth and Corcoran, 1996). A recent meta-analysis concluded, 'This meta-analysis showed significant and stable mentalising impairment in schizophrenia. The finding that patients in remission are also impaired favours the notion that mentalising impairment represents a possible trait marker of schizophrenia' (Sprong *et al.*, 2007: 5). As well as bringing us full circle back to the origins of the concept of autism as a description for a state of mind found in those diagnosed with schizophrenia (see Chapter 3) it raises some interesting and rather circular questions (we apologise that we keep arriving at this statement; unfortunately, it seems unavoidable). If the core deficit of both autism and schizophrenia is a lack of ToM, then how do we differentiate the two? Is schizophrenia really adult autism in another guise (perhaps expressed differently) or vice versa? Without a robust attempt to refute the basic assumptions underpinning any aspect of the spectrum, we are left with little science and copious ideology. Theorists seem to have a remarkable capacity and tenacity to want to cling on to their theory in a way that is, well, one might say 'autistic'.

AUTISM AND THE FAMOUS

With the increase in rates of ASD diagnoses, its image has continued to shift from that of a disease in the more 'traditional' medical model sense to a more complex view of a syndrome, sometimes described as having both advantages and disadvantages. Although its supposed biological basis remains largely unchallenged, the widening of its net has sparked something of fight back against the 'disability' model, with a model based on the idea of a biological 'difference' rather than disorder (see, e.g., www.neurodiversity.com). Partly as a result of this, there are increasing numbers of adults, who have become quite successful in their fields, and who have been deemed to be diagnosable with an ASD (usually by some 'expert' who hasn't met the person in question). Of course, this means that questions about what exactly is the nature of the deficit, disorder, or disability arise. The list of famous people deemed to have ASD features is quite astonishing and a more apt question after reading these lists is who from the male great and good didn't have ASD features. For example, the website http://www.geocities.com/richardg_uk/famousac.html (accessed 2 February 2009) lists the following among those believed to have had autistic traits: Jane Austen, Ludwig van Beethoven, Alexander Graham Bell, Thomas Edison, Albert Einstein, Henry Ford, Carl Jung, Wolfgang Amadeus Mozart, Isaac Newton, Bertrand Russell, George Bernard Shaw, Mark Twain, Vincent van Gogh, Isaac Asimov, John Denver, Alfred Hitchcock, Woody Allen, Tony Benn, Bob Dylan, Bill Gates, Al Gore, Michael Jackson, Michael Palin, Keanu Reeves, Oliver Sacks and James Taylor. So diverse is the list that it includes past and present scientists, inventors, comedians, musicians, politicians, actors, philosophers, authors and entrepreneurs. It is hard to know what any of them have in common beyond being human, talented and (nearly all) male.

Many well-known researchers/academics in the autism field, such as Michael Fitzgerald, Simon Baron-Cohen, Christopher Gillberg and Ioan James, have spurred this trend on. For example, Michael Fitzgerald has written several books in which he speculates on a whole variety of famous historical figures having Asperger's syndrome (e.g., Fitzgerald, 2003, 2005) including: Hans Christian Andersen, Lewis Carroll, Bruce Chatwin, Arthur Conan Doyle, George Orwell, Jonathan Swift, William Butler Yeats, Baruch de Spinoza, Immanuel Kant, Bela Bartok, Ludwig van Beethoven, Bob Dylan, Glenn Gould, Wolfgang Amadeus Mozart, Vincent van Gogh, L.S. Lowry, Jack B. Yeats, and Andy Warhol. The arguments for alleged autism spectrum disorders in famous people vary from person to person. For example, Albert Einstein (one of the most frequently cited as allegedly autistic) was said to be a late speaker, a loner as a child, had violent temper tantrums, repeated under his breath sentences he uttered and needed his wives to act as parents when he was an adult, factors that are alleged to be stereotypical of autistic people.

To really confuse matters there is also a long list of famous people such as Albert Einstein, Isaac Newton, Hans Christian Anderson,

Thomas Edison, Leonardo da Vinci, Winston Churchill and so on, who are said to have had ADHD (for example, see http://www.adhdrelief.com/famous.html, accessed 2 February 2009). The same people often inhabit both lists (and sometimes those for other psychiatric disorders too). This is a peculiar situation; not only does this demonstrate how non-specific symptoms of ASD and ADHD are (and how gender-specific they are), but also it raises questions as to why we are now so concerned with finding diagnostic labels for anything that doesn't conform to an increasingly dull homogeneous middle ground, as well as what may happen if we try to 'treat' those who lie outside this middle ground. Had we done this in the past, what would the impact have been on those who ended up contributing so much to our culture? For many of the above famous names, their main issue as children was surviving the school system, where some attracted labels like stupid, lazy and un-teachable. If the problem here is not these individuals' innate abilities, but a mismatch between them and their schools, is it the kids or their schooling environments that we should be changing, or, indeed, need we get so concerned about changing anything at all?

The speculated social and cultural contributions of people who are supposed to 'have' some form of autism, has contributed to a shift in the perception of autism spectrum disorders, with some now viewing ASDs as a 'difference' rather than as diseases that must be cured. Proponents of this view reject the notion that there is an ideal brain configuration and that any deviation from the 'norm' must be considered pathological. Drawing on an analogy with gay rights, they demand tolerance for what they call their 'neurodiversity'. This has resulted in the creation of 'autistic rights' and 'autistic pride' movements. While we have sympathy with this movement and their views, which correctly calls attention to social tolerance of diversity as being a more important focus for intervention than the individual, we would go further and state that the case that those currently attracting an ASD label are in some essential way neurologically different simply hasn't been made (see Chapter 10 for a further discussion of the autistic rights movement).

In 2001, *Wired* magazine, ran an article entitled 'The Geek Syndrome' (Silberman, 2001). Silberman interviewed kids, parents, doctors and autism 'experts' and concluded that AS was more common in Silicon Valley – a haven for computer scientists and mathematicians:

> These days, the autistic fascinations with technology, ordered systems, visual modes of thinking, and subversive creativity have plenty

of outlets... Many children on the spectrum become obsessed with VCRs, *Pokémon*, and computer games, working the joysticks until blisters appear on their fingers. (In the diagnostic lexicon, this kind of relentless behavior is called 'perseveration.') ... Echoing Asperger, the director of the clinic in San Jose where I met Nick, Michelle Garcia Winner, suggests that '*Pokémon* must have been invented by a team of Japanese engineers with Asperger's.' Attwood writes that computers 'are an ideal interest for a person with Asperger's syndrome ... they are logical, consistent, and not prone to moods.'... The chilling possibility is that what's happening now is the first proof that the genes responsible for bestowing certain special gifts on slightly autistic adults – the very abilities that have made them dreamers and architects of our technological future – are capable of bringing a plague down on the best minds of the next generation... The genetics of autism may turn out to be no simpler to unravel than the genetics of personality. I think what we'll end up with is something more like, 'Mrs Smith, here are the results of your amnio. There's a 1 in 10 chance that you'll have an autistic child, or the next Bill Gates. Would you like to have an abortion?' (Silberman, 2001)

The journalistic interpretation of a science that has found little conclusive evidence coupled with an ideology that has pushed the boundaries of autism to an absurdity, is there for all to see. After the article the reader was invited to fill in Simon Baron-Cohen's 50-question Autism-Spectrum Quotient test (AQ), which appeared on the next page. The 'Geek Syndrome' article caused a storm, bringing the concept to a whole new audience and helping to popularise a notion that 'geeks' and other single-minded (often talented) individuals have AS. As ASDs (largely through AS) were now sold as a new way of thinking about a large part of the community, particularly those with gifts for developing, understanding and using the new technologies, and with pop psychology tests (like the AQ) that read more like a horoscope than a scientific instrument, so the expanded notion of ASD encompassing a whole variety of people (mainly men) has caught on in popular culture, opening whole new markets for the rapidly expanding 'autism industry' to exploit.

8
TREATMENT

There is very little evidence that any treatment alters the core symptomatology of ASD... There are anecdotal reports suggesting that certain interventions, such as vitamin or psychopharmacological treatments, may benefit some children, and yet they may be entirely unhelpful for others. For these reasons no definite recommendations can be made about individual therapies. There is also emerging evidence that some therapies previously advocated by professionals and parents, such as auditory integration therapy, are no more effective than placebo whilst others (such as Facilitated Communication) are now discouraged because of adverse side effects or other risks to the child. (National Autistic Society, 2003: 47–8)

No cause, no diagnostic markers, no 'characteristic' symptoms, no uniform course and no specific treatments. So what is the point of diagnosis? As summarised above by the leading UK autism advocacy organisation, there are no specific treatments for autism, despite the various claims that are made for this or that treatment. 'Treatment' for autism is largely geared towards management and support of associated difficulties the individual and/or their family experience, as there are no particular treatments that cure or otherwise ameliorate autism. Therefore, in respect of treatment, the label of autism adds little to what you actually decide to do to help those with the label.

Behavioural, educational, dietary and psycho-pharmaceutical interventions are widely used. Applied behaviour analysis is the best-known behavioural intervention (Lovaas, 1987) and is particularly popular in the USA. The goal of this behavioural management technique is to reinforce desirable behaviours and reduce undesirable ones. It is based on early identification of autism, intensive one-to-one instruction and a focus on teaching early communication and social interaction skills. Educational interventions are geared towards altering teaching strategies to take special account of the different ways children with an ASD are supposed to learn (when compared to non-ASD children). Dietary interventions are based on the idea that some food sensitivities or insufficiency of a specific food-group, vitamin, or mineral may be causing some of the symptoms of autism, and include interventions such as a gluten-free diet and supplements of essential fatty acids, gut bacteria and particular vitamins or minerals. Medications are often used to help families manage behavioural problems, such as aggression, self-injurious behaviour, obsessive-compulsive symptoms and tantrums. Medications used for this purpose include stimulants (such as Methylphenidate), anti-psychotics (such as Risperidone) and selective serotonin reuptake inhibitors (SSRIs) antidepressants (such as Flouxetine). The use of such medications remains controversial, as many are not licensed for use with children, none are licensed for use in autism, they have not been demonstrated to have any long-term effectiveness and may cause serious side effects (stimulants may cause growth retardation and stroke; SSRIs may cause suicidal ideation and paradoxical aggression; and anti-psychotics may cause movement disorders and diabetes).

DRUG TREATMENT FOR PSYCHIATRIC DISORDER IN CHILDREN AND ADOLESCENTS

There is a long history in the field of psychiatry of exorbitant claims being made for a variety of practices, from inducing insulin comas to performing radical brain surgery such as lobotomies. Each new wave brought enthusiastic claims of 'miracle' cures, which, over time, rigorous objective research showed not to be as effective as first claimed, with risks having been unduly minimized. In recent decades, waves of optimism about 'curing' and 'treating' mental illness through modern psycho-pharmacology has popularised the use of psycho-pharmaceuticals, changing the prescribing habits of doctors and the health-seeking behaviour of patients. Sadly, closer scrutiny of the scientific evidence reveals that the new age of the mass use of psycho-pharmaceuticals is the result more of good marketing than good science, through a confluence in the interests of neo-liberal policies, the profit motive of pharmaceutical companies and 'guild' interests of psychiatrists (Moncreiff, 2008a). Closer scrutiny of the science shows that, as in previous eras' physical treatments for psychiatric disorders, claims for psycho-pharmaceuticals' curative properties have been exaggerated and their dangers minimised (Whitaker, 2002; Moncreiff, 2008b).

The alliance between drug companies and doctors

The treatment of children with psychiatric drugs is even more contentious as most of the drugs are meant for, and have been researched in, adults. In a context in which no objective tests exist to verify the 'diseases' being diagnosed, pharmaceutical companies realise that a bigger market for their product can be created by 'disease promotion'. Here the task of the pharmaceutical company becomes that of convincing the medical profession and the public that young people's emotional and behavioural problems are the result of under-diagnosed and under-treated 'brain' disorders (which, of course, sets the context for their products to then be marketed as 'treatments' for these alleged physical disorders). They do this by sponsoring or producing material for doctors' and their waiting rooms that alerts the medical and lay community to the existence of these conditions, producing 'educational' material for parents and teachers, and funding parent support/campaigning groups.

One favoured means of promoting new illnesses is for pharmaceutical companies to invest in consumer support groups. For example, the National Alliance for the Mentally Ill received over US $11 million from 18 pharmaceutical companies between 1996 and mid-1999 (Medawar and Hardon, 2004). It is cost-effective for pharmaceutical companies to invest in such groups without any direct promotion of their product, as support groups can increase the number of patients who present to doctors with ready-made diagnoses. This also allows them to present what they are doing as a 'service'. However, the problem is not just that of the profit motive of pharmaceutical companies; the profession must take responsibility for the issue of professional identity, which makes child psychiatry vulnerable to manipulation. The discipline should sit at the confluence of many different systems of knowledge – medical, psychological, social, paediatric, anthropological, cultural and so on – but increased focus on biological models and physical treatments has allowed sections of the profession to carve out a clearer territory that bolsters a more 'doctory' image of what they do, in preference to the more diffuse, hard-to-define role of a more complex approach spaning several disciplines' 'territories'.

The above dynamics (pharmaceutical company marketing and profiteering combined with some child psychiatrists' willing collusion with this) has subsequently distorted the evidence and ultimately practice for all psycho-pharmaceuticals currently used with children. Two examples, illustrate this.

The case of children and antidepressants

In 2003 evidence was uncovered indicating that Selective Serotonin Reuptake Inhibitor antidepressants (SSRIs) are largely ineffective and may be dangerous in under-18s (Jureidini *et al.*, 2004). It appears that published studies on the effectiveness of newer antidepressants in childhood depression had exaggerated their benefits and downplayed their adverse effects with none of the studies having, on measures relying on patient- or parent-reported outcomes, showed significant advantage over a placebo. It was also discovered that unpublished trials conducted by pharmaceutical companies found these newer antidepressants to be less effective and more harmful (particularly causing a very worrying increase in rates of suicidal thoughts and behaviours) for under-18s than had been suggested by the published trials (Craig *et al.*, 2004).

Despite this rather damming picture that should have caused professionals and their governing bodies to pause to stop and reconsider use of all SSRIs in the under-18s, one SSRI antidepressant, fluoxetine, was spared. In the UK, National Institute for Clinical Excellence (NICE) guidelines for depression in children and young people repeated the earlier Committee on the Safety of Medicines (CSM) conclusion that the only antidepressant with a favourable balance of benefit over risk was fluoxetine. Given its similar pharmacological properties to other SSRIs, there is no theoretical reason why fluoxetine should achieve a significantly different profile – and indeed it doesn't.

The fluoxetine studies carried out in children and adolescents were designed to give the drug the best chance of coming out ahead. For instance, the first two fluoxetine studies (Emslie *et al.*, 1997, 2002) included a placebo washout phase, which involved putting all the patients on a placebo for a specified period and then removing from the trial those patients that got better. The use of placebo washout has become widespread in many drug trials, as some of those who have agreed to participate in a trial need to be taken off their previous medications, and because of a belief that anyone who responds to placebo is either not 'ill' enough or has already recovered. However, this practice with psychiatric drugs has been criticised on the grounds that there is a high placebo response to many psychotropics (particularly antidepressants), and withdrawal of previous psychiatric drugs can induce a discontinuation syndrome (misinterpreted as a deterioration of the illness) that is halted on restarting the trial drug. Thus, placebo washout causes artificial inflation of the numbers apparently responding to the active drug and reduction of the numbers apparently responding to placebo (Jackson, 2005).

The second of these two fluoxetine studies also had a unique twist, which consisted of a run-in phase to pre-select for drug responders (Emslie *et al.*, 2002). All the fluoxetine-treated children in this study were given 10mg for the first week; children who did not respond, or who had negative responses, were then dropped from the study. At the start of week two, the dose was increased to 20mg. The subsequent statistical analysis used only children who had had at least one week of treatment with 20mg. Even with these advantages, for the prospectively defined primary outcome measure (the Children's Depression Rating Scale) there was no statistically significant difference between the active drug group and the placebo one. It was only by looking at other measures that clinical significance was found and even then this was only on one of the clinician-rated scales (on the patient- and parent-rated scales there was no statistical advantage) (Leo, 2006).

The Treatment for Adolescent With Depression Study (TADS) (Treatment for Adolescent Depression Study Team, 2004) is the most influential pro-fluoxetine study and provides a good example of how the publicity (of efficacy and safety in treating childhood depression) for this study does not match the published findings. While the study was funded by a US government agency, investigators who had received significant industry funding conducted it. The investigators claimed to show an advantage for fluoxetine, especially when combined with cognitive-behaviour therapy (CBT). However, there were many fundamental flaws in the way they designed the study and reported their data.

TADS consisted of two separate 12-week randomised studies: a double-blind comparison of fluoxetine (109 participants) and placebo (112 participants); and an unmasked comparison between CBT alone (111 participants) and fluoxetine plus CBT (107 participants). The lack of patient-blinding and placebo-control in the latter two groups is likely to exaggerate the benefit seen in the fluoxetine with CBT group, who received more face-to-face contact (and thus a higher 'dose' of active treatment) and knew (as did their doctors) that they were not receiving placebo. Furthermore, the authors found a poor response in the CBT alone group, a finding that is inconsistent with the rest of the psychotherapy outcome literature for childhood depression, raising questions about the quality of the psychotherapeutic intervention in this study. Comparing results across all four groups is therefore misleading. The one valid finding from TADS is the lack of a statistical advantage for fluoxetine over placebo on the primary endpoint, the Children's Depression Rating Scale, a finding that was not even mentioned in the abstract. Despite the exclusion of known suicidal behaviour, TADS found a trend to more suicidal behaviour (six attempts in the fluoxetine groups, versus one in the no-fluoxetine groups), consistent with other trials of SSRIs. In the first study to follow up young people on antidepressants for 36 weeks after the start of treatment, the TADS group found that the outcomes for CBT-alone, fluoxetine-alone and combined treatment groups converged (Treatment for Adolescent Depression Study Team, 2007), with those in the flouxetine-only group experiencing significantly higher rates of 'suicidal events'. Thus, even their own findings suggest that any extra benefit from adding fluoxetine does not appear to be an enduring one, but that there are increased (and serious) risks associated with it. Putting together these results, the obvious conclusion is that the profile for fluoxetine is similar to all other SSRI antidepressants – it has little efficacy and is potentially dangerous (Timimi, 2007b).

Distorted reporting has meant that some academic journals have contributed to the circulation of myths about the benefits of antidepressants for the young that had little to do with the truth. Indeed, child psychiatry as a profession had already endorsed the use of SSRI antidepressants well before any of the major studies in children were even published (e.g., Koplewicz, 1997). The scene was thus set for marketing spin to take precedence over scientific accuracy. As a result it appears that one reason for doing the studies in the first place was to justify already well-established prescribing patterns. It created a trend of 'because everyone else is doing it', which has become difficult to reverse despite the evidence. This has raised some serious questions about the inaction of child psychiatry as a professional group, many of whom appear to have been complicit in allowing this misrepresentation of the evidence to go unchallenged. Why, as a profession, were they not asking the questions about the science, risks and benefits?

Why was it left up to journalists, campaigners and individual doctors to blow the whistle? What role did the intertwining of child psychiatric theory and practice with the interests of pharmaceutical companies play in giving the profession a blind spot when it came to critiquing the literature? Why have they continued to cling on to the misleading conclusions of a few studies as a basis for continuing to recommend prescription of fluoxetine to young people? Such searching questions are needed if the profession is to be treated as trustworthy by both the scientific community and the general public (Timimi, 2008a).

The case of stimulants

In November 2004, an article containing several interviews was published which highlighted the fact that questions about the scientific credibility of psychiatric drug research of stimulants were widespread (Hearn, 2004). Gene Haislip, the now-retired director of the US Drug Enforcement Agency (DEA), set production quotas for controlled substances such as the federally restricted stimulant methylphenidate. During that time, he fought hard to raise public awareness about the drug's high rate of non-prescription use/misuse and about its long-term health impact on young patients. He notes:

> When I was at the DEA, we created awareness about this issue. But the bottom line is we didn't succeed in changing the situation because this – prescribing methylphenidate, for example – is spiralling... A few individuals in government expressing concern can't equal the marketing power of large companies. (Quoted in Hearn, 2004)

Haislip suspects that the dubious marketing tactics of big pharmaceutical companies, supported by a small group of prolific researchers in attention-deficit hyperactivity disorder (ADHD) whose work is funded by corporate producers of ADHD drugs, fuelled the spiralling use of stimulants. He also suspects that one or more ADHD patient advocacy groups that receive pharmaceutical company donations have essentially become fronts to push the prescribing of stimulants to children.

William Pelham, a prominent ADHD researcher and former member of the scientific advisory board for McNeil Pharmaceuticals, was also interviewed for the article (Hearn, 2004). Between 1997 and 1999, he was paid by McNeil to conduct one of three studies used to get

US Food and Drug Administration (FDA) approval for a long-acting slow-release version of methylphenidate and, according to Hearn, the company now uses these three studies to claim that 96 per cent of children taking this drug experience no problems with appetite, growth, or sleep. But Pelham says the studies were flawed and this claim is misleading because his study started with children who had already been taking the drug and who had experienced no significant side effects – children who exhibited side effects were not included in the study to begin with. Pelham mentions that the company pressured him to change the final article, saying, 'It was intimidating to be one researcher and have all these people pushing me to change the text' (quoted in Hearn, 2004).

In the world of ADHD advocacy, Children and Adults with Attention Deficit/Hyperactivity Disorder (CHADD), a large US-based 'parent support group', engages in lobbying and claims to provide science-based, evidence-based information about ADHD to parents and the public. Pharmaceutical companies donated nearly $700,000 to CHADD in the fiscal year 2002–3 (Hearn, 2004). Pelham, listed by CHADD as a member of its professional advisory board, came face-to-face with what he says are the group's glaring conflicts of interest. In 2002, after he received the CHADD Hall of Fame Award, he was subsequently interviewed for *Attention* the organisation's magazine. In the interview, Pelham said, among other things, that stimulant drugs have serious limitations. Eight months later, *Attention* published Pelham's interview but with a large part cut out, particularly his comments about the limitations of the stimulants. Commenting on this Pelham says:

> In recent years, I have come to believe that the individuals who advocate most strongly in favour of medication – both those from the professional community, including the National Institutes of Mental Health, and those from advocacy groups, including CHADD – have major and undisclosed conflicts of interest with the pharmaceutical companies that deal with ADHD products. (Quoted in Hearn, 2004)

In a world run by those with the power to buy media attention, it is not uncommon for single studies to become the basis on which practice develops. One such study was the Multimodal Treatment Study of ADHD (MTA), a large multicentre trial in the USA testing the efficacy of the stimulant methylphenidate (MTA Co-operative Group, 1999). This publication led to widespread publicity claiming that we should be treating children who have ADHD with stimulant medication as the first line and possibly only treatment. In the years since the publication and popularisation of this study there has been a sharp rise in the rates of stimulant prescription all over North America, Northern Europe, Australasia and beyond (Timimi and Leo, 2009) In the UK this had resulted in a prescription rate for stimulants of over 550,000 per anum by 2006 (Department of Health, 2007), a staggering rise of over 7000 per cent in a decade.

The MTA study compared four groups of children who were given: medication only; intensive behavioural therapy only; combined behavioural therapy and medication; and standard community care. The study lasted 14 months and concluded that the medication-only and combined behavioural therapy and medication groups had the best outcome, with the 'combined' group having only a marginally better outcome than the medication-only group. A closer look inevitably brings up important questions of methodology and the hidden question of conflict of interest (Boyle and Jadad, 1999; Breggin, 2000). Methodologically this was not a placebo-controlled double-blind clinical trial, and the parents and teachers who participated were exposed to pro-drug literature at the start of the study, thus potentially putting them in a mindset of positive expectation for change in the children receiving medication. There are also many question marks with regard to the selection and recruiting process, the behavioural interventions used, the placebo effect of the active medication arm continuing until the end of the 14 months but the behaviour therapy component finishing many months prior to that, the lack of attention to the number of children experiencing side effects and the dismissal of some reported side effects as probably being due to non-medication factors (Breggin, 2000). In addition, two-thirds of the community-care group were also receiving stimulant medication during the study, yet the community-care group was the poorest outcome category (Timimi, 2005).

The three-year outcome for the MTA study was finally published in 2007 (Jensen *et al.*, 2007) – eight years after the results of the study at 14 months were published. All the advantages with regard to symptoms of ADHD for the medication-only and 'combined' groups had been lost, whereas the improvements in the behavioural-therapy-only ('therapy-only') group had remained stable. At the end of the original 14-month-long study, participants had been free to pursue whatever treatment they wanted. Some children had started taking medication and others on medication had stopped. The therapy-only group remained the group with the lowest use of medication. When the researchers analysed outcomes for those who had used medication in the previous year they found that they had a worse outcome than those who had not. Furthermore, those who had taken medication continuously had higher rates of delinquency at three years, and were significantly shorter (by an average of over 4cm) and lighter (by an average of over 3kg) than those who had not taken medication. The likelihood of ending up being prescribed medication was not related to initial severity of symptoms. The three-year outcome data, therefore, shows that the study that is repeatedly quoted as providing the scientific basis for prescribing stimulants to children (MTA Co-operative Group, 1999), actually demonstrates that there is little advantage (compared to behaviour therapy) associated with its use, but considerable risk. According to Pelham, who is on the steering committee for the MTA studies, 'No drug company in its literature mentions the fact that 40 years of research says there is no long-term benefit of medications [for ADHD]. That is something parents need to know' (Pelham, quoted in Hearn, 2004).

Children and psychiatric drugs

The above two examples show the extent to which the so-called scientific literature on the use of psycho-pharmaceuticals for childhood behavioural and emotional problems has demonstrated that it is quite simply unreliable and compromised, in particular by conflict of interest issues. Psychiatry appears to be the top 'offender' among medical specialities with regards use of and sponsorship from drug companies. Perhaps this is not surprising given the enormous potential markets that can be (and have been) developed if psychiatry is successful in medicalising people's emotional responses and behaviour, in a field so reliant on subjective interpretations of normality and deviance. Child psychiatry seems particularly vulnerable (Timimi, 2008a), with, most recently, an influential group of child psychiatrists at Harvard, extensively involved in research promoting the use of psycho-pharmaceuticals (particularly for ADHD and paediatric bipolar disorder), being found to have received millions of dollars of income from pharmaceutical companies, most of which they had not disclosed. These types of problems have resulted in a growing distrust of the claims made for the use of psycho-pharmaceuticals with children, not only among the general public, but also within the medical profession. For example, an editorial in 2008 in one of the world's oldest and most respected medical journals concluded:

> We know little about the long-term effects of psychiatric drugs in children. Side-effects of anti psychotics include shaking, damaged bones, reduced fertility, obesity, and increased risk of heart attack, diabetes, and stroke. Stimulants can damage the heart and stunt growth. Antidepressants can increase the risk of suicide in children. Do these drugs work? Evidence is often scant – and, where it exists, is largely discouraging... Many patients have argued for years that psychiatric drugs are often more harmful, and less effective, than doctors believe. Increasingly, these patients are seen to be right. If psychiatry is to retain its claim to rationality, it must allow patients, including children, to be heard, and not merely drugged. (*Lancet* editorial, 2008: 1194)

PSYCHO-PHARMACEUTICAL TREATMENTS FOR AUTISM

As far back as 1973, Ornitz commented that:

> Almost every conceivable psychotropic medication has been used with autistic children. The classes of medication have included sedatives, anti-histamines, stimulants, major and minor tranquilizers, anti-depressants, psychomimetics and anti-Parkinsonism drugs... As with psychotherapy, behaviour modification, special modification and speech therapy, no single medication or class of modification has made an autistic child any less autistic. Nor has any medication or class of medication proven successful in removing any particular symptom of the autistic syndrome. (Ornitz, 1973: 40).

These decades' old observations are as true today as they were then, despite his comments referring to a much narrower group of children, as this was prior to the concept of ASD taking hold. However, this is not the impression you get if you observe current practice in child and adolescent psychiatry. A good example of this comes from an article entitled 'Antipsychotic Drugs in Children with Autism' (Morgan and Taylor, 2007) that appeared in the world's most read medical journal – the *British Medical Journal*. Use of anti-psychotics, particularly risperidone, for 'treating' children with autism who have concurrent behavioural problems has become popular in recent years, well before any evidence for the safety and efficacy of such practice was available. As with the case of antidepressants and the young outlined above, studies in this area appear to have the purpose of trying to justify an already-established practice.

In this article, 'opinion leaders' Susan Morgan and Eric Taylor (2007) take an apparently moderate stance suggesting that antipsychotic drugs should not be used indiscriminately in children with autism but reserved for those with more 'serious' behaviour problems. This apparent moderation is possibly more dangerous than a more overtly stated position, as it effectively sanctions the use of anti-psychotics for 'aggressive' behaviours in those diagnosed with autism without presenting sufficient evidence that such practice is either safe or effective, yet it is written in a style that suggests they are being evidence-based and cautious. They state, 'We consider off label use [of anti-psychotics] is justified when other approaches fail or are unfeasible' (Morgan and Taylor, 2007: 1069). This effectively leaves the door open for the continued increase in the use of (off-label) anti-psychotics as the reading doctor is left to wonder what other approaches to use and for how long before deciding they have failed. Furthermore, unfeasibility of other approaches is near universal as the increasing popularity of the diagnosis of autism, together with this diagnosis becoming more often than not the responsibility of busy community paediatricians, means 'other approaches' are thin on the ground. They further recommend 'Diagnosis should distinguish between aggression and other seriously challenging behaviours (which may justify an antipsychotic agent) and lesser levels of irritability (which may not)' (Morgan and Taylor, 2007: 1069). However, they don't explain how a clinician is supposed to differentiate between what one should consider 'seriously' challenging behaviour and irritability. Not only is the conceptual basis of the article shaky, in addition the authors fail to approach the evidence with anything like sufficient rigour.

In support of their recommendation to use anti-psychotics for challenging behaviour they refer to two studies only (McCracken *et al.*, 2002; Shea *et al.*, 2004). A more critical review of these two studies reveals anything but encouraging news for this practice. First, both studies were of only eight weeks in duration, far off the many years that drugs' prescribed to pacify behaviour are usually used for. Second, one of the studies (McCracken *et al.*, 2002) reviewed their subjects at six months and found a familiar pattern seen with drug treatment for behavioural problems – that of diminishing returns, with less than half of the group that had received risperidone (the anti-psychotic) now rated as 'improved' (interestingly they do not provide the data for how the placebo group were doing after six months). Third, a decrease in challenging behaviour in those receiving an anti-psychotic at a sufficient dose is really a foregone conclusion, after all anti-psychotics are not classified as 'major tranquillisers' for nothing. Whether this is viewed as a therapeutic effect or side effect depends on your perspective. Reflecting this fact, both studies rated high levels of somnolence (sleepiness or drowsiness); for example, Shea *et al.* (2004) recorded a 72 per cent rate of somnolence in the group receiving risperidone, leading to the rather peculiar scenario where arguably the same pharmacological effect is simultaneously rated as therapeutic (decrease in aggressive behaviours) and an adverse effect (somnolence) – after all you can't get up to much mischief if you're drowsy. So much for efficacy then. What is most shocking, however, is Morgan and Taylor's minimising of the serious adverse effects of the anti-psychotics, which were prevalent in both studies. To give just one example, both studies found the group receiving risperidone put on more weight than the group with the placebo; in McCracken *et al.* (2002) this was an average of 2.7kg as compared to 0.8kg, and in the Shea *at al.* (2004) study this was an average of 2.7kg as compared to 1.0kg. Remember, this was after only eight weeks of 'treatment'. Thus, these children were being put at a greatly increased risk of serious illnesses such as cardiovascular disease and diabetes.

The article revealed that Morgan and Taylor are most certainly not the moderates they wished to present themselves as. Indeed, they note that Janssen-Cilag withdrew their application for risperidone to be licensed in the UK for use in behavioural problems associated with autism. As a result they actually outdo a drug company in their keenness for the use of psycho-pharmaceuticals in controlling autistic children's behaviour and go on to suggest doctors should carry on using anti-psychotics for this (off-licence) indication. As influential clinicians and researchers writing in an influential journal, their position effectively encourages the use of powerful, risky and probably ineffective medicines to control the behaviour of a group of citizens (children) who have never really had a say in what is being imposed upon them, with scant evidence to back up the validity or utility of such practice.

PSYCHOLOGICAL APPROACHES TO TREATING AUTISM

Several decades ago, Ornitz (1973) also had this to say on behavioural therapies for autism (which remain the preferred psychological treatment today):

> While both greater and lesser degrees of success in carrying out this type of treatment have been claimed, the data from most of the studies indicate that any positive response to treatment is limited to the period of time during which the treatment is maintained and does not generalize readily beyond the specific experimental conditions unless the treated child has already shown greater promise before the beginning of treatment...behaviour modification is by no means a treatment for the child's autism but is merely a way of reducing temporarily the amount of undesirable behaviours. (Ornitz, 1973: 39)

Some 32 years later Scott and Baldwin (2005) echo Ornitz's conclusion and state: 'It may be fair to say that none of the comprehensive early intervention programmes for children with autism meets the highest empirical research standards accepted within the fields of psychology or educational research' Scott and Baldwin (2005: 187). None of the interventions studied are specific to autism and could just as easily be applied to the field of learning difficulties in general. What successes are associated with the interventions seem to be situation-specific, do not generalise and are more to do with general behaviours than those that 'define' autism.

The most well-known behavioural approach is that by Ivar Lovaas as outlined in his 1981 book *Teaching Developmentally Disabled Children: The Me Book* (Lovaas *et al.*, 1981). The now-controversial approach involves intensive 'training' of young children with a diagnosis of autism, with between 30 to 40 hours a week of therapy usually beginning before a child reaches the age of three and a half years. This therapy consists of four to six hours per day of 1:1 training, five to seven days a week for two years. A typical session lasts about two to three hours. Specific instructional tasks last two to five minutes, followed by short breaks of one to two minutes. At the end of each instructional hour, a child is typically given a 15–20-minute break for snacks, 'free play' and other unstructured activities. The Lovaas method is based on operant conditioning. For example, in the 'match to sample' teaching the child has to match one object with an identical object. The teacher places a cup on a table in front of the child then hands the child a second identical cup and instructs the child to 'put with the same'. If the child responds correctly by placing the cup with its match, the child is reinforced by the teacher. Reinforcement can include food, praise, a hug, or a combination of these. If the child does not respond to the prompt he is physically assisted to make the response and then is reinforced. The physical prompt is removed (faded) over a series of trials until the child responds consistently to the verbal command. Upon mastery of this task, a second pair of objects (e.g., two spoons) is introduced into the situation. The child is then requested to match objects in the presence of a second item on the table, thus beginning to learn to discriminate between the two sets of objects. Matching training continues until the child learns to discriminate among the many potential features of objects (e.g., colour, size, shape). Teaching follows in this step-wise manner across 12 different 'programmes', such as receptive and expressive language, non-verbal imitation, social language, play and self-help skills. The therapy starts with intensive teaching at the individual level before expanding treatment into group environments that are more typical of school experiences. Lovaas has claimed that this early treatment reduces the likelihood the child will require separate educational programmes once in school.

Several aspects of this approach have emerged as controversial, both in the method of delivery and in the outcomes documented in the Lovaas study. The main controversy over the application of intensive behavioural therapy lies in the use of aversive techniques to reduce maladaptive behaviours. *The Me Book* notes that punishment may be used to establish control both to open a window of opportunity for teaching a child alternative behaviours and as a means to exaggerate correct from incorrect responses. These 'negative consequences' take the form of verbal feedback, for example a loud 'No', through to other more physical ones such as a spank or a slap. With regards outcome, Lovaas has made bold claims – backed up by a study of 19 children – that his methods result in significant improvements that in some children can result in recovery (a cure) from autism (Lovaas, 1987, 1993). However, questions remain about the methodology (such as the lack of complete randomisation, the lack of appropriate comparison intervention for control group and differences in levels of functioning in the group before the study started) and the lack of replication of Lovaas's findings. In addition it seems reasonable to question how specific this method is to 'autism' (as opposed to, for example, learning difficulties in general, which should also respond to such intensive 'treatment') and, indeed, how valid it is to 'diagnose' young people, so early in their development, with 'autism'. Given the dangers of inappropriate early diagnosis, the lack of replication, the lack of specificity, the ethically and culturally questionable nature of the 'treatment' and its impractical and expensive nature, like all other treatments that have claimed to be specific for autism, it has failed to establish itself as a definitive treatment.

Reviewing the psychological treatment literature, it soon becomes apparent that each 'treatment' relies on very small studies, usually single-case controlled studies (where the same person is evaluated before and after receiving a specific intervention), with the studies usually conducted by those who have a strong allegiance to the method under study. The same can be said of educational and dietary interventions. For example, the evidence in support of the Treatment and Education of Autistic and Communication Handicapped Children (TEACCH) (a popular programme where the child follows structured learning activities within the school environment that are designed to build on their strengths, with concurrent training of parents) relies on only two small non-randomised controlled trials (Ozonoff and Cathcart, 1998; Panerai *et al.*, 2002), that did not compare like with like. For example, the latter study (Panerai *et al.*, 2002) had a total of 16 subjects, with the control group being selected from subjects with a diagnosis of autism attending a regular school with support teachers and the group receiving TEACCH coming from a specialist treatment institute. Furthermore, it is hard to see why such an intensive programme shouldn't be beneficial for any child with LD/school problems and until the impact of such programmes on those with significant learning difficulties, but without autism (if there are any such individuals left that is), is assessed, no conclusion can be reached about its specificity for 'treating' autistic children.

It is fair to say that the lack of diagnostic specificity of psychological treatments is not an issue that is unique to autism. An important question that has been debated for decades is whether there are any particular advantages for particular techniques with particular diagnoses, as opposed to the common factors with different psychotherapies being more important (in other words, psychotherapy in general being effective for psychiatric disorders in general with little advantage for one particular approach/method over another). This is sometimes referred to as the debate between the 'medical model' of psychotherapy (where specific techniques are viewed as having specific vital 'ingredients' that treat specific diagnostic problems) and the 'contextual model' of psychotherapy (the 'common' factors to all psychotherapies being more important than the specific techniques).

The evidence is now so overwhelming that the debate is pretty much settled. The contextual model explains the research findings much better than the medical model. With common psychiatric problems, all recognised formal psychotherapies are effective to roughly the same degree, no matter what the psychiatric problem is, and this holds with children and adolescents too (Wampold, 2001). Furthermore, decades of increasingly sophisticated research into treatment outcome for psychiatric disorders has found little to support: a) the ability of psychiatric diagnosis in either selecting the course or predicting the outcome of therapy; b) the superiority of any specific therapeutic approach over any other for any particular psychiatric problem; and c) the superiority of pharmacological (medication) over psychotherapeutic treatment for emotional complaints. What is consistently found is that psychotherapy is generally effective, that the most important factors are those inherent to the patient involving his or her resources (such as levels of motivation, socio-economic status, social support and complexity of the problems), and the quality of the relationship between patient and therapist as rated by the patient (Duncan *et al.*, 2004). Current approaches in most psychiatric services, including child and adolescent mental health services, haven't yet caught up with what the research findings are saying and tend to emphasise process 'standardisation' through following 'how to do it' technical approaches to psychiatric problems, with diagnostic-specific treatment plans. However, specific technique is a factor shown to have as much as seven times less influence on outcome than the 'common' (to all psychotherapeutic approaches) factor of the quality of the therapeutic alliance as rated by the client (Wampold, 2001).

WHAT ARE WE TREATING ANYWAY?

Before deciding on what 'treatment' to administer we should first be making a critical enquiry into what the objective of that treatment is. What is it that we wish to change in the person diagnosed with autism? In an overview of early intensive interventions, Scott and Baldwin (2005) identify the following target behaviours for treatment of children with autism to achieve:

- Compliance to adult requests.
- Turn-taking.

- Listening to directions.
- Sitting quietly during activities.
- Volunteering.
- Raising one's hand to solicit attention.
- Walking in line.
- Picking up toys after use.
- Communication of needs/wants.
- Waiting quietly.
- Reciprocating greetings.
- Participating in circle games.
- Initiating play activities with peers with or without adult prompts.

For young children (five and under) this is a very culture-specific list, reflecting more the value system of white middle-class Western society, where compliant but autonomous (some might say 'adultified') children, who don't require too much active intervention from teachers in particular, are the desirable state, rather than a list of behaviours that is universally recognised as developmentally normal, appropriate or even desirable at such a young age.

If we were to try and draw up a similar list of culturally specific desirable behaviours for, for example, traditional North African young children; then it may look like this (extrapolated from Gregg, 2005):

1. Show modesty and politeness to elders.
2. Demonstrate loyalty to family and to the 'home'.
3. Show interest and preoccupation with food.
4. Demonstrate obedience to parents and elder kin.
5. Show frequent 'whining' and attention-seeking behaviour.
6. Boys to demonstrate active and aggressive sibling rivalry.
7. Boys to play with older children.
8. Girls to help with household chores, including looking after younger siblings.
9. To demonstrate fear, particularly of supernatural entities and certain creatures such as scorpions and snakes.

As one can readily appreciate by contrasting the above two lists, each culture has its own set of specific expectations and therefore, by implication, its own specific values and standards as to what it deems requires some sort of corrective action/treatment. If a boy in a traditional North African family is not demonstrating sibling rivalry, then parents and others in the extended family may try to provoke this by shaming the young child or comparing them negatively with their brother or another relative. This is regarded as developmentally desirable in order that the son grows into a man who does not have blunted or passive emotions and is not easily provoked. In the West, of course, sibling rivalry is largely viewed negatively and its presence may lead to attempts to intervene to diminish or eradicate it.

III
AUTISM
POLITICS AND SOCIETY

9
GENDER

In the next three chapters we turn our attention to social and political processes surrounding autism and posit these as providing the best explanation for why a concept with such little scientific support has nonetheless become so popular. It is out of these socio-political processes that the current autism epidemic was born.

In 1966 the ratio of males to females deemed suitable for a diagnosis of autism, was about two to one (Lotter, 1966a). It is now thought to be more in the region of between four and ten to one. Such a gender distribution is very similar to that found in the rest of child psychiatry (with 'disorders' such as attention deficit hyperactivity disorder (ADHD) and conduct disorder). Such a gender distribution that seems to sweep across the entirety of psychiatric disorders found in the school years (particularly primary school years) implies either that boys are biologically weaker or 'disabled' in some way or that (more probably) we have come to be more troubled by boys' than girls' behaviour. What is likely to be involved is a complex interplay between: shifting ideas of masculinity and femininity, the role and position of men and women in society and the relentless progression of the project of 'individualism'. This chapter seeks to explore this relationship further.

It is, indeed, remarkable to reflect on how gender is an issue that confronts practising child mental health clinicians routinely. Yet so little is written on this subject in the mainstream child and adolescent mental health (particularly medical or psychiatric) literature. The statistics provide a stark illustration of the gender split with which child psychiatry is riddled. The bread and butter of Western child psychiatric practice are boys whose behaviour is not conforming to (often female) adult expectations. As a result diagnoses, such as ADHD, conduct disorder and now autistic spectrum disorders (ASD), that are based largely on others' assessment of the child, are handed out to boys three to four times more often than girls, with (largely ineffective and sometimes dangerous) psychotropic medication to 'treat' these children being even more disproportionately prescribed for boys (Timimi, 2005, 2007a). The fact that by the time people reach their 20s psychiatric diagnosis assignment by gender has reversed itself in terms of prevalence, with women twice as likely as men to get a psychiatric diagnosis (particularly eating disorders, anxiety and depression), raises interesting and important questions about the relationship between gender and psychiatric nosology. What happened to all those boys with psychiatric disorders once they became adults? Where did all these mentally 'ill' women come from and why had they not been picked up or badly affected during their childhoods? Why are doctors apparently more preoccupied with behaviour and its problems in children, but mood and its problems in adults? And so on.

That much of mainstream psychiatry seems more preoccupied with (the thus far fruitless) searching for biological markers to support current nosology than asking such basic questions about it suggests that its institutions can't see the proverbial wood for the trees. Without reflecting on this and attempting to make sense of this statistic with reference to different theoretical possibilities, we simply carry on building castles on sand. If diagnoses like ASD and ADHD are telling us more about the state of gender relations in late capitalist societies than about biological processes in children's brains, then clearly a better understanding of the former may be of greater importance to how we intervene than illuminating the biological processes that contribute to greater impulsivity or social awkwardness in boys than girls. Of course, these are not mutually exclusive phenomena; the hope would be that both can be better understood – however, in terms of priority we have got things upside down. The focus on biology has produced little new knowledge that is specific enough to be clinically useful. None of these boy disorders are associated with any physical or, for that matter, psychological markers (for further discussion on this see Timimi, 2002, 2005; Timimi and Maitra, 2006, and Chapters 4 and 5), nor has any biological causation theory found an adequate explanation for the gender disparity, yet the boy-centric psychiatric nosology has simply avoided debating this issue. Instead, we have witnessed the growth of forms of practice (such as heavy use of psychoactive medication) based on narrow, often bio-deterministic, thinking.

GENDER, BEHAVIOUR AND THE DEVELOPMENT OF CHILD PSYCHIATRIC NOSOLOGY

Feminist critiques of DSM as being gender bias against women have been around for quite a long time. Kaplan's (1983) paper was perhaps the first and has certainly been the most widely cited critique since the appearance of DSM-III (APA, 1980). Kaplan suggested in her paper that 'a healthy woman automatically earns the diagnosis of Histrionic Personality Disorder' (Kaplan, 1983: 789), due in large part to the codification of a gender-biased criteria constructed by a DSM-III task force comprised largely of males. Since then, a variety of studies have confirmed her theory. Little attention, however, has been given the problem of gender bias in children resulting in the disproportionate attribution of psychiatric diagnoses to boys, nor, for that matter, has much attention been directed towards what would appear the 'archetypal' psychiatric unit – mothers and their sons.

As mentioned earlier, it is a curious fact that psychiatric disorders of childhood and adolescence are diagnosed much more often in boys than girls. In a systematic review of gender differences in classification rates in the DSM-IV, Hartung and Widiger (1998) concluded that

> of the 21 disorders usually first diagnosed in infancy, childhood, or adolescence for which sex ratios are provided, 17 are said to be more common in boys than girls, 1 is said to be equally common in both sexes (feeding disorder), and only 3 are said to be more common in girls than boys. (Hartung and Widiger, 1998: 263)

Two of the three disorders which are more often given to girls are Rett's disorder and selective mutism, both of which are very rare conditions. Thus the gender-specific nature of DSM-IV childhood psychiatric disorders is clear.

Early attempts at developing nosology for childhood mental health problems set in place the building blocks for a gendered framework into which we categorise children's problems. In the famous Isle of Wight study (Rutter *et al.*, 1970a, 1970b) all eight- to 11-year-old children on that little island in the south of England were screened for 'psychiatric disorder'. Two main groupings of emotional/internalising and conduct/externalising emerged from this and accounted for 96 per cent of those deemed to have a disorder. These findings contributed towards subsequent classification of child and adolescent disorders in ICD (International Classification of Diseases) and DSM (*Diagnostic and*

Statistical Manual of Mental Disorders) and popular screening questionnaires such as the child behaviour checklist (Achenbach and Edelbrock, 1978). This early split of 'conduct disorders' and 'emotional disorders' set the scene for a dualistic approach of 'externalising' (which in gender terms became boys and their behaviour) and 'internalising' (which by adolescence is setting the scene for girls and their emotions). Subsequent elaborations and refinements of this system created a more sophisticated system of subdivisions and new categories based on this externalising/internalising split. Thus, now popular more recent diagnoses, such as ASD, ADHD and oppositional defiant disorder (ODD), continue a theme of a gendered focus on the problems of boys and their behaviour.

One outcome of this ideological approach to understanding children and their mental health has been the exponential growth in the use of psychoactive medication ostensibly aimed (in gender terms) at exerting greater social control on boys' behaviour (Timimi, 2005, 2007a, 2008a). This dramatic change in child psychiatric practice has occurred (until recently) almost without the public noticing or realising the slim scientific basis behind this, despite the profound implications this holds, not only for those children diagnosed and medicated, but also for our cultural beliefs and practices around childhood and child-rearing more generally.

In one of the author's (ST) earlier books, *Pathological Child Psychiatry and the Medicalization of Childhood* (Timimi, 2002), he reported on a search he carried out on all published articles in two leading child and adolescent psychiatric journals, the *Journal of the American Academy of Child and Adolescent Psychiatry* and the *Journal of Child Psychology and Psychiatry*, between 1996 and 2001, looking for papers that discussed the cross-cultural validity of the current nosologies used for categorising child and adolescent mental health problems. Out of a total of 1,600 articles he found only one that specifically attempted to discuss this. Although we haven't done a similar search for gender, we expect to find a similar level of ignoring (ignorance) on this issue.

GENDER AND BIOLOGY

One of the interesting things about gender is that of all the usual social categories we refer to (such as class, ethnicity, race, sexual orientation, etc.) gender is the one where there is an obvious biological difference (anatomically, hormonally, developmentally). This provides an interesting opportunity not only to look at the impact of biology on behaviour but also of socio-political factors on the construction of that difference. Knowing that there are significant biological differences does not eliminate the importance of the cultural and political factors that come into play in both interpreting the significance of these differences and the degree to which we can also culturally construct differences between men and women; instead, it should help us reach out beyond reductionist or dualistic accounts that attempt to establish what is 'nature' and what is 'nurture'. The reductionist approaches that either deny biology or deny social factors have proved fruitless, possibly damaging, and definitely boring. Thus, at the macro level we can see that the lives of men and women and the types of roles that they occupy vary enormously globally, a variation that could not be accounted for by differences of gender biology alone and we also see many similarities across cultures and across time in the discourses around what it means to be a man and what it means to be a women, similarities that cannot be accounted for by social construction of gender alone (Timimi, 2009).

While our social construction of gender in terms of our beliefs, values and practices around masculinity and femininity are important and highly relevant, much of the literature on the subject has avoided an engagement with biology, leading to somewhat polarised discourses, one focusing on the biological differences between men and women, the other on the social construction of masculinity and femininity. The task, however, is not to avoid biology but to radicalise it. If there are important features of gender differences that are biologically based then apparently enlightened approaches to changing our cultural attitudes to boys and girls and men and women and their roles may well fall short of their aims if they come to be experienced as, for example, attempts to feminise men or masculinise women in biologically incongruent ways. Of course, such a task involves continual risk of drifting away from what the evidence says towards making leaps of faith involving conclusions and implications that are beyond empirical data. This can then be used to justify sexist beliefs and practices that lead to gradual erosion of hard-won equal rights. However, the converse is that a denial of any innate, biological differences between men and women can also lead to hurt, disappointment, alienation and an inability to meet expectations.

So how do we reach a better integration of biology and its social construction? In his book, *The Essential Difference: The Truth About the Male and Female Brain*, Baron-Cohen (2003) argues from a biological perspective that men's and women's brains function differently. Focusing largely on cognitive processes, he characterises men's brains as being geared towards 'systematising' (needing to understand 'systems', organised conditions, mechanics, technology, thus driven by a need to know 'how things work') and women's towards 'empathising' (power to quickly assess others' emotional states, more readily identify feelings in others, respond appropriately when sympathy is required and 'reach out' empathically when dealing with people). While we must remain concerned about the degree to which such a generalisation could become dogma and remain able to appreciate that such biological differences should not be viewed as deterministic, we can use such findings to at least posit that there are some primarily biological gender differences, thatshould be taken into account (but not allowed to limit our imagination).

Others, such as Cromby (2008) building on Merleau-Ponty's work, approach the problem of how biology affects our construction of self by focusing on the somatic nature of feeling states, which he views as more fundamental than cognitive processes. He highlights the indivisible nature of the biological body and the environment of 'meaning' it exists in, seeing this as creating a whole or 'gestalt' that cannot be understood by dividing it into its constituent parts. What this approach suggests is that our 'default' relationship to our feelings is derived from the continuous embodied engagements we have with the social and material world. Our 'automatic' felt or sensed orientation to the world tends to provide the unquestioned (and frequently unnoticed) ground from which we assess and respond to it and this automatic somatic feeling state happens before we start the cognitive processing of ascribing thoughts to it. In contemporary psychology these 'pre-reflective' stances are typically called 'beliefs' or 'schema', a terminology that moves them into the ambit of cognitive psychology and allows them to be misunderstood as primarily informational in character.

According to Cromby's reading of the evidence, however, what psychology calls a 'belief' is more properly understood as a socially derived feeling state, allied to a matrix of meanings and social practices. The beliefs that cognitive psychology typically presumes to be 'nodes' or decision-points within informational flows are fundamentally feeling states, and they frequently evade accurate reflection and concise articulation precisely because of their largely non-representational, pre-reflective, somatic character. It is this internal feeling state that is linked with the social milieu of meaning that generates our values and behaviours. Such an approach avoids the dualism of separating biology and environment, while acknowledging each has an importance if we are to understand human experience. In terms of gender, then, such an approach highlights the fact that because there are biological differences (anatomical, hormonal, etc.) between men and women, these pre-reflective somatic feeling states will contain some corresponding differences, which, when they are given meaning by the subject experiencing them, will then derive meanings based on the social discourses and personal experiences/memories, available to that person.

Getting from these general theories into more specific ones is difficult as the current evidence base is simply unable to disentangle some core questions such as how different boys' and girls' brains are and how adaptable they are to different sets of expectations. Indeed, within the confines of the current knowledge base, how useful is it to search for answers to these types of questions within the (rather masculine) linear framework that seeks to place causality (often in concrete terms, such as percentages) for the outcomes in terms of masculinity and femininity to either biology or nurture? While there is no easy, simple answer to these questions, there are alternative models that may provide useful, alternative frames through which to interpret the evidence. For example, Cromby's interactive model discussed above, that sees the interaction between nature and the broadest sense of nurture (to include not just experiences within individual families, but the broad, socio-political context in which families get their information about how to bring up boys and girls, and other institutions important in people's lives) as the 'unit' of investigation. These nature/nurture complexes (or gestalts) are something we can more reliably comment on as opposed to the rather pointless exercise of deciding what proportion nature or nurture has contributed to any presentation.

Our current ideas in the West about gender differences has interesting parallel in the recent history of Western constructions of how to deal with questions of cultural difference in our increasingly multicultural societies. In the post '9/11' world, the topics of assimilation, integration and multiculturalism have re-emerged with gusto, as concerns have grown about the danger to our society that some ethnic minority groups (particularly Muslims) pose. Undercurrents of anxiety and hostility interweave as old colonial arguments emerge in a new form, persuading us that we have shown too much tolerance to migrants and should make greater efforts to force migrants to assimilate into Western value systems. In the previous two to three decades of the 20th century, policies of assimilation had gradually given way to those of 'multiculturalism', as it became apparent that many communities had not 'assimilated' as had been hoped, but instead had learnt to defend and discover value in their own cultural legacy. Increasing racial tension, coupled with the visible social and economic deprivation of many minority communities, contributed to a growing appreciation of how racism had kept many non-whites out of positions of power and influence. Eventually this led to the gradual abandonment of monoculturalism, with new policies aimed at integration rather than assimilation, in which it was more accepted that minority groups would keep their cultural identities. The move towards integration and multiculturalism did not resolve many of the issues surrounding how we adapt to the era of globalisation and the multicultural character of modern societies. As the spectre of the 'enemy within' was reawakened by 9/11 and 7/7, so a return to more assimilation-orientated policies returned, with a re-emergence in the UK of a version of the old Thatcherite Norman Tebbit's famous 'cricket' test (based on the fact that your loyalty is reflected in what cricket team you support), with tests on knowledge of the UK being given to immigrants before they are allowed to settle in the country.

In the realm of gender our education and child-rearing efforts have increasingly moved towards an 'assimilationist' model, where the needs and wants of boys and girls are perceived to be similar and any differences between them minimised. To the 'assimilationist', the eventual goals of rearing and educating children are the same regardless of the child's sex. This means that boys should be taught in the same way as girls, and that boys will learn and be interested in the same things as girls because they develop in similar ways and will eventually occupy the same societal roles. Although there are competing discourses (such as those around lads' culture, *Men are from Mars* and a new feminism that aims to rehabilitate the importance of motherhood), they have as yet had little impact on the practices of institutions that deal with children, such as schools.

This essentially 'biology-blind' approach with regards gender, while it has brought many benefits (particularly for girls), has also produced drawbacks (particularly for boys). An important one is the increasing medicalisation (often side by side with criminalisation) of boys' behaviour, as it is boys who are increasingly unable to fulfil the cultural expectations of an essentially non-gendered childhood and, thus, it is boys' behaviours that are increasingly perceived to fall out with the norm, often with a co-existent belief that this is caused by biological abnormalities. There are, of course, many other interesting and complex interactions between male and female, masculinity and femininity at various levels of cultural organisation, which are also rendered invisible by a cultural approach that seeks to minimise differences between men and women.

As the development of child psychiatric classification had gender embedded centrally from the start when externalising (conduct) and internalising (emotion) became the building blocks for diagnostic systems, the medicalising of behaviour always had the potential for 'the problem with boys' to become a medical one. What is of interest from a sociological perspective is why we have become so focused on boyhood. From a therapeutic perspective such a cleavage of diagnostic (and hence therapeutic) practice means that, as well as perpetuating attention onto boys (now that education in the post-equal rights era shifted this from educational attainment), we continue to concentrate on that which marks them out as a problem and arguably perpetuate masculine stereotypes by shifting attention away from boys' emotional well being and towards their behaviour.

WHAT IS IT ABOUT WESTERN PATRIARCHY?

One of the dynamics at play is that related to patriarchy. The majority of societies around the globe remain patriarchal, but the behaviour of boys as a societal and medical concern is relatively recent and largely confined to the West (Timimi, 2005, 2007a, 2008a).

In some cultures boys are more highly prized than girls for a variety of reasons. Boys then grow up in a more privileged position and often with a view of themselves that reflects the preferential treatment they have received. Parents report few experiences of what we, in the West, would consider rebellious or aggressive behaviour towards them. In some cultures there is great concern about emergent female sexuality and these cultures develop a set of practices which are aimed at controlling any propensity to sexual behaviour by the female adolescent, with the main concern being young women's behaviour at this time, young men being spared the brunt of socio-cultural pressures to conform. Such culturally institutionalised sexism that favours boys is evident in many cultures around the world and will obviously have an impact on the way boys and men view themselves (Timimi, 2005). But before we in the West get smug about Western culture being more advanced and liberated in its sexual politics, I would argue that Western culture is more covertly driven by masculine (macho) ideals that are providing an even worse image of what it is to be a man than that of many more overtly patriarchal cultures. After all cross-cultural research finds considerable differences in prevalence rates for psychiatric disorder, with children, particularly boys, in politically stable developing countries appearing to have considerably lower rates of behavioural disorders than in Western societies (Cederbald, 1988; Pillai *et al.*, 2008).

Models of masculinity

Let us unpick these themes a little. Models of 'what it means to be a man' are present in all cultures, starting at different ages. In most cultures there is a differentiation between expectations for boys and girls from early childhood, often from birth (thus boys get blue clothes, girls pink, etc.). In many Western cultures (unlike most other cultures), as we have argued above, boys then enter institutions (particularly schools) that have non-gendered expectations with regards most things (such as behaviour, style of learning, teaching methods, etc.). However, within the 'playground' and peer group subcultures the gendered discourses continue.

We also live in an era of modernist Western culture, where the discourse about children has become one that can be characterised by polarised anxieties about the risks they face and the risks they pose (Timimi, 2005). These anxieties have a strong gender bias, with girls being viewed as 'at risk' and boys as posing risk (through unruly, violent and impulsive behaviours). This moral panic about boys has attracted much debate in the media and among academics, with three models of viewing and understanding the nature of the changes facing boys, and how we respond to these, emerging.

The first model, often referred to as the 'boys will be boys' perspective, starts from an assumption that boys and girls are biologically different. In this view boys are 'programmed' (e.g., via the effects of testosterone on the developing brain) to excel at visio-spatial tasks but not at verbal-emotive skills. Furthermore, boys, as evolutionary 'hunters', are more easily distractible (scanning the environment), impulsive risk takers and more active and aggressive. As our societies have changed, these 'natural' states have become pathologised and viewed as threatening. In addition, instead of having healthy role models to help boys channel these traits in healthy directions, the increase in fatherless homes and a feminised education system that is more geared to the learning style of girls mean these tendencies are all too often acted out in destructive ways (see, e.g., Gurian, 1999, 2001; Sommers, 2000).

The second model is known as the 'boy code' model. This model emphasises the dominant cultural beliefs about what it means to be a 'man' and how this affects growing boys' socialisation. The dominant cultural belief in the West remains that of men being encouraged to show stoicism, physical strength and aggression, and bravado, while discouraging any overt displays of affection and/or distress. With such a 'code', boys learn that they should not appear sad or afraid, but instead should be able to 'tough it out'. Similarly any display of warmth, tenderness and empathy should be suppressed (at least publicly), leading to feelings of shame surrounding boys' emotional life, with anger as the only emotion which is allowed in 'public'. As boys grow up, this code leads them to suppress their emotional life (with all the attendant consequences on their emotional well being) until eventually they become 'disconnected' from this inner experience. Boys' emotional life then stays buried deep behind superficial social masks, apart from occasional eruptions (sometimes extreme) in the only acceptable emotion – anger – often accompanied by violence and cruelty (see, e.g., Kindlon and Thompson, 2000; Pollack, 1998).

The third model posits a more complex interaction between culturally constructed models of masculinity. In this 'multiple masculinities' model, it is argued that an increasing number of culturally constructed models of 'what it means to be a man' are available; however, they always, to some degree, exist relative to the dominant model. The dominant model (i.e., the hegemonic model of masculinity) remains that which is outlined above in the 'boy code' (revolving around bodily abilities, non-display of emotions, control, aggression, etc.). This is the model associated with the 'patriarchal dividend' (i.e., associated with men being in a more powerful and influential position than women). Having other available models causes great anxiety, as a defined role or 'way of being' becomes diffuse and ambiguous, as well as threatening men's position of privilege. Thus, while men may depart from this hegemonic masculinity and take up other identities (from 'bookish' to 'geek' right over to 'gay'), such a contravention carries risks. Boys who stray from the hegemonic model frequently become targets for bullying, teasing and exclusion by their male peers (see, e.g., Connell, 2000, 2002; Kimmel, 2004).

Thus far in this chapter we have proposed that there are biological differences between boys and girls and men and women and that these biological differences interact with political and cultural expectations to create 'gendered' webs of meaning and systems of practice. We have reflected on how the most important institutions for children (educational) have adopted an 'assimilationist' model of gender, meaning that in these institutions there are similar expectations for boys and girls (thus minimising the biological differences between the genders). However, this assimilationist model sits next to other models of 'what it means to be a man' that often are uncomfortably detached from the institutional ones and create peer group subcultures among boys based on a kind of 'competitive socialisation'; different models are available, but these models all sit in reference to, or in the shadow of, the hegemonic (dominant) model.

These models of gender, then, interact with the broader cultural value system; attention must be paid to the impact of promoting an 'individualistic' orientation in our concept of self, with particular focus on the characteristics of that self.

Narcissism, neo-liberalism and gender

One of the dominant themes used by advocates of neo-liberal free market economy ideology is that of 'freedom', a core issue at the economic level. Companies must be as free from regulation as possible, to concentrate on competing with others, with maximizing of profits the most visible sign of success. There is little to gain from social responsibility (unless it increases your 'market share'). At the emotional level, we understand this appeal to freedom as ridding us of the restrictions imposed by authority (such as parents, communities and governments) (Richards, 1989). By implication this value system is built around the idea of looking after the wants of the individual – narcissism. Taking this a step further, once the individual is freed from the authority they can (in fantasy at least) pursue their own individual self-gratifying desires, without the impingements, infringements and limitations that other people represent. The effect of this on society is to atomise the individual and insulate their private spaces to the degree where obligations to others and harmony with the wider community become obstacles rather than objectives. In this 'look after number one' value system, other individuals are there to be competed against as they too chase after their personal desires. This post-Second World War shift to a more individualistic identity was recognised, as early as the mid-1950s, by commentators who first spoke about how the new 'fun based morality' (Wolfenstein, 1955) was privileging fun over responsibility; having fun was becoming obligatory (the emerging cultural message being that you should be ashamed if you weren't having fun). With the increase in new possibilities for excitement being presented, experiencing intense excitement was becoming more difficult, thus creating a constant pressure to push back the boundaries of acceptable and desirable experiences, and lifestyles, opening the doors, among other things, to subcultures comfortable with drinking to excess, violence, sexual promiscuity and drug taking.

This value system finally reached its zenith when economic globalisation became dominated by neo-liberal monetarist policies. In the post-credit crunch era we are now acutely aware of the impact the value system has had on global politics, economies and ultimately billions of ordinary people's lives. It is easy to look retrospectively and reappraise our opinions; however, many of us have been warning about the potential impact, at the psychological level, of the narcissistic value system that allows personal and individualistic greed to be the dominant driving force in an economy (e.g., Timimi, 2005; Cohen and Timimi, 2008): others become objects to be used and manipulated wherever possible for personal goals, and mistrust invades social exchanges as the better you are at manipulating others the more financial (and other narcissistic) rewards you will get. Such a value system, which ultimately seeks to eradicate or at least minimise social conscience as a regulator of behaviour, cannot be sustained without our moral conscience beginning to feel guilty (Richards, 1989). Thus, it is no coincidence that those who are the most vociferous advocates of free market ideology tend also to advocate the most aggressive and punitive forms of social control. Whereas some of these guilt-induced policy proposals are aimed at restraining unfettered competitiveness, greed and self-seeking to an extent, the most fanatical believers in the ability of market ideology to solve its own problems tend to find scapegoats for this anxiety. In other words, instead of facing up to the suffering the encouragement of narcissism brings to the world, our leaders need to convince us that our problems are due to other evils (like fundamentalist Islam, asylum seekers, homosexuals, single parents and bad genes). As a result, another hallmark of Western culture's immature psychological avoidance of taking responsibility for its beliefs and practices is the so-called 'blame culture', which fills the media and contemporary discourse more generally. We are, to coin a well-worn phrase, 'tough on crime/mental health', but getting nowhere with the 'causes of crime/poor mental health'. We build more prisons and employ more psychiatrists – a sure sign that, despite best intentions, our approach to 'causes' is at best naive, at worst a part of the problem.

In any culture, children and then adults come to acquire their subjective selves through incorporation of values, beliefs and practices that sustain the desired social relationships of that culture (Althusser, 1969). People, Althusser argues, can only know themselves through the mediation of ideological institutions. So how do the ideologies of modern capitalism influence the way children and their parents see themselves, their roles and subsequently the way they behave?

The problems and lack of trust associated with this narcissistic value system, mentioned above, lead to increasing dependence on professionals for advice, thereby reinforcing the idea and status of the 'expert'. As Amin points out (1988), Western capitalist ideology has necessarily led to the domination of market values, which penetrates all aspects of social life and subjects them to its logic. This philosophy pushes to the limit of absurdity an opposition between humankind and nature. The goal of finding an ecological harmony with nature disappears as nature itself, including human nature, comes to be viewed as a thing to be similarly manipulated for selfish ends.

Children are introduced into this value system by virtue of living within its institutions and being exposed daily to its discourse (most notably through the media). Through this they are socialised into a system that embraces a capitalist idea of freedom through promoting individualism and competitiveness and an expectation of renouncing dependence and showing independence from an early age. As Kovel (2002) has pointed out, such a system grew out of men's power and has a strong masculine character in its metaphors and organisation. Late capitalist/neo-liberal societies are inherently masculine in character. The recent economic crisis in the financial sector illustrated the depths to which aggressively neo-liberal market-orientated societies encourage extreme risk taking for short-term 'selfish' gain, with little thought about the potential long-term impact of such an approach (i.e., with little sense of conscience that a more socially responsible and nurturing attitude would entail).

This essentially narcissistic value system has led to a 'masculinisation' of culture. Major worldviews are usually reflections of the interests and experiences of the most powerful social groups (Foucault, 1977; Connell, 1995). In gender terms this is undoubtedly man. Men in the West are the main beneficiaries of the contemporary world order that has delivered great wealth to them and when this is coupled with increasing levels of inequality, then women and children, particularly poor women and children, bear the brunt of this massive social injustice. Across the developing world the gap between the rich and poor has continued to widen (see, e.g., http://news.bbc.co.uk/1/hi/business/6901147.stm and http://www.sciencedaily.com/releases/2007/08/070807171936.htm, accessed 25 February 2009). The gap between the richest and poorest countries of the world has also continued to increase. In 2003, out of the developing world's 4.8 billion people, 1.2 billion were living on $1 a day or less and another 2.8 billion on between $1 and $2. In addition, the richest fifth of the world's population received 85 per cent of the total world income, while poorest fifth received just 1.4 per cent of the global income (Infoplease, 2000–7). Western history of empire, conquest and – in its most nakedly and violently masculine form – fascism was made by men. Classical Western philosophy of reason and science through oppositions with the natural world and emotions led to Western science and technology becoming culturally masculinised and dominated by 'masculine' metaphors, particularly in comparison with Eastern philosophies and guiding metaphors (Seidler, 1989).

As discussed above, in the West hegemonic masculinity emphasises physical strength, adventurousness, emotional neutrality, certainty, control, assertiveness, self-reliance, individuality, competitiveness, skills, public knowledge, discipline, reason, objectivity and rationality (Connell, 1995; Kenway and Fitzclarence, 1997). These attributes then become important aspects of growing boys' developing gender identities. With a narrowing of the emotional range allowed of our masculine heroes and a distancing from displays of tenderness, compassion and dependence being culturally prescribed for boys, it is no surprise that many boys grow up feeling isolated, misunderstood and with fathers with whom they wish they had closer relationships (Frosh *et al.*, 2002).

This also has a resonance with Nancy Chodorow's (1978) ideas on the difference between boys' and girls' psycho-developmental identifications (Abell and Dauphin, 2009). Chodorow (1978) argued that gendered patterns of parenting cause a scenario that reproduces itself in the human psyche. When both young boys and girls are cared for primarily by female adults, children are placed in positions that result in a different journey for each gender. The girl may gain both her most substantial sense of gender identity and her social role from her mother, since her primary love object in childhood has been her same-sex parent. The boy, on the other hand, must somehow sever his primary identification with his female caretaker if he is to achieve gender identity as a male. How to become a man in a more feminised space of childhood in an aggressively masculine society becomes the problem for many boys.

As boys move out of the feminine identifications, so they increasingly identify with the narcissistic system of winners and losers, having been thrown into a capitalistic version of survival of the fittest where compassion and concern for social harmony contradicts the basic goal of the value system. Instead of asking ourselves painful questions about the role we may be playing in producing this unhappiness and this dog-eat-dog social system (played out through a variety vehicles such as ownership of brand names, belittling peers, physical prowess and so on), we can view our children's difficulties as being the result of biological diseases that require medical treatment (we can blame their genes). Although some superficial similarities (such as childhood being more of a female-dominated domain) with a number of non-Western cultures are apparent, a crucial difference is that in many non-Western cultures the wider cultural milieu is dominated by less narcissistic value systems, with notions such as common and familial duty, responsibility and a more spiritual cosmology providing a backdrop to a more protective (for the emotional well being of children) set of cultural discourses and practices.

These social dynamics also get projected directly onto children. Children come to be viewed as both victims (through adults using and manipulating them for their own gratification) and potentially 'evil' scapegoats (as if it is these nasty, spoilt, poorly disciplined children's bad behaviour that is causing so many of our social problems). This reflects an ambivalence that exists towards children in the West. With adults busily pursuing the goals of self-realisation and self-expression (these being the polite middle-class versions of self-gratification), having consciously or unconsciously absorbed the free market ethic, children, when they come along, will, to some degree, 'get in the way'. A human being, who is so utterly dependent on others, will cause a rupture in the value system goal of narcissism that individuals who have grown up in this society will hold to a greater or lesser degree. Children cannot be welcomed into the world in an ordinary and seamless way. They will make the dominant goals of modern life more difficult. They will, to some degree, be a burden, and boys will bear the brunt of this.

As growing boys absorb these masculine values, the absence of responsibility and the pursuit of self-gratification are then often bragged about in the adolescent playground (where boys compete to drink the most pints and sleep with the most women, etc.). The impact this masculine value system has on family and community life is profound. The system seems to have been designed for men. Men can follow the central premise of this value system to its logical conclusion: having brought children into the world, responsibility for child-rearing and for maintaining family life usually falls on the mother. If the going gets too tough then many fathers in the West choose to leave the family in order to chase freedom and self-gratification, their sense of duty, responsibility and personal attachment disappearing with them. Guilt is often dealt with by displacing this through blaming the child's mother (e.g., she tried to control me, wouldn't let me have my freedom) or their child (e.g., he has chosen not to see me). The price boys are paying for this is incalculable. Not only are boys denied secure, stable and nurturing homes to engender the sense of loyalty that comes through belonging, but, in addition, they are given a model of masculinity to aspire towards that devalues notions of responsibility, duty, love and emotionally intimate relationships based on mutual dependency.

The process of having a child can also be viewed through the prism of a narcissistic consumer value system. Thus, the desire to have a child can be seen as linked to a perceived need, many feeling that they are only 'complete' (like a Hollywood- or Disney-fantasised ideal life) once they have had a child; from this perpective, Western adults have children for their own emotional gratification (Stephens, 1995). This causes a cultural shift in relation to gender, with girls becoming more highly prized for this purpose than boys, as girls are more likely to reciprocate and provide these emotional 'presents' to their parents (predominantly mothers, of course, with whom they can have a closer mutual identification). For some boys these dynamics leave them in a lonely place, where they feel unwelcome, unvalued and caught in cycles of progressive alienation, negative attention-seeking behaviour, jealousy and guilt, often with few male role models to turn to for help to find a healthy way out of their situation. With increasing mutually dependent relationships with the one person they can still rely on (their mother), this in turn affects these boys' self-perception as they fail to live up to the 'hegemonic' masculine ideal.

The institutions that work with children and parents reflect various aspects of this masculinised freedom/guilt dynamic. Schools in the United Kingdom have been colonised by free market managerial style, with the encouragement of greater competitiveness between schools and with each school's success being measured by the exam grades of their pupils, published in national league tables. As well as their lesser contribution to performance league tables, boys in general absorb the larger proportion of resources for additional support and special needs. You have to be pretty thick-skinned to survive as a loser in this system without it affecting your view of yourself and your behaviour in some way. Particular groups end up at particular risk. Thus, many black and ethnic minority pupils in Western schools, feeling like humiliated outsiders, turn to a macho subculture that shows defiance towards the authority of the system that is hurting them, but also embraces a culturally congruent solution that is 'hyper-masculine' (Mac An Ghaill, 1994; Sewell, 1995). For many working-class boys the change in educational demands that has shifted the expectation for qualifications upward (reflecting the decline in manufacturing and a rise in demand for a more skilled labour force) has made experience of educational failure even more problematic (Frosh *et al.*, 2002).

Within a value system that promotes freedom to pursue your wishes/instincts a number of common escape routes are available to those who feel like they are the losers/failures/rejects of this culture. If you perceive yourself to be a failure within the school system then there are other ways to rebuild your sense of self-worth and personal power such as a hyper-masculine subculture of cruelty that encourages you to seek gratification through alternative routes, including bullying, theft, drugs, alcohol and virtual- and real-world violence. This is often done through gangs (which operate like mini capitalist cultures where those who can be the most self-serving are to be most admired), which provide alternative 'families' to belong to. These dynamics start in school, where it has been found that those students who are most likely to develop an anti-school value system that includes asserting their masculinity through physical strength are boys who are failing academically (Mac An Ghaill, 1994). Other escape routes operate in the mushrooming of technology and toys (such as computer games and internet chat rooms), that provide the lonely youngster with hours of hypnotically absorbing activities, enabling them to pass the time without needing to interact (face-to-face) with others.

Although this system may be a good training ground for many of the future participants in the capitalist, market economy, where it is desirable for individuals to be competitive, self-seeking and able to use relationships for the purpose of manipulating others to serve their own needs, this leaves the problem of how to deal with the failures that this system inevitably produces. This is where the increasing tendency to medicalise behavioural problems becomes appealing for parents worried about their boys 'failing', schools worried about league tables and legislation forbidding them acting out their hostility to the defiant youngster and governments eager for easy 'technical' solutions to the problem of deviance. Of course, boys are not the only victims of this culture, nor is there only one stereotypical way in which they are affected; many young women struggle with body image, eating disorders and absorbing the 'fun morality' ethic (leading to increasing problems with alcohol, drug misuse and violence among them) – indeed, young men also are increasingly aware of fashion, image, body grooming and so on.

Feminisation within a masculine culture

As we have just argued, free market capitalism can be seen as the most complete and organised example of a political, social and economic system based on the values of masculinity that the world has ever seen. Its social and psychological values are based on aggressive competitiveness, putting the needs of the individual above those of social responsibility, an emphasis on control (rather than harmony), the use of rational (scientific) analysis and the constant pushing of boundaries. Such a system produces gross inequalities (both within and between nations) and has reduced the status and importance of nurture – and therefore the esteem attached to the role of mother. As more and more women are brought into the workplace – an economic necessity to increase the workforce needed to service the market economy's demand for continuous growth – new forms of selfhood need to be developed in order for such a shift in women's social role to be sustainable psychologically. As a result, the role of professional/career woman now has more esteem attached to it than that of motherhood, which has increasingly lost its status as a culturally valued role within an individualistic society. This movement out of the family sphere and into the public sphere has not been matched by a corresponding reverse movement of men out of the public sphere into more family and nurturing roles (quite the contrary, in fact).

At the same time as there has been a movement of adults out of the family there has been a movement towards childcare becoming a professional (mainly female) activity. Thus, what appears to be happening in the psychological space of childhood is an increasing feminisation of some aspects, particularly educational ones, and a professionalisation of the task of raising children. There is now a body of literature that supports the notion that educational methods currently used in most Western schools (such as continuous assessment and socially orientated work sheets) are favoured more by girls than boys (Burman, 2005). This is then mirrored in national exam results where girls are now consistently achieving higher grades than boys even in some traditionally 'male' subjects like maths and science. Boys also dominate the special needs provision, where they are marked out as having disproportionately high (again in the region of four to one) problems with poor reading and poor behaviour. With schools under market economy political pressure to compete in national league tables, and boys coming to represent a school's biggest liability, it is hardly surprising that boys have come to be the 'failed' gender, provoking anxiety in their (primarily female) carers and teachers (Timimi, 2005).

The feminisation of certain aspects of the masculine capitalist culture we live in has also had an impact on the working environments our education is preparing us for. Ideas such as cultivating 'emotional intelligence' in management and working relations started to become more popular in the 1990s (Gordo-Lopez and Burman, 2004). Far from an enlightened move towards a nurturing and caring society, this is part of developing 'better' ways to motivate the workforce and manipulate the consumer. Thus, modern Western culture demands more convoluted and complicated forms of socialising (in an image-obsessed age) than in the past (or in many other cultures), in the context of the diminishing size of families (resulting in more intense emotional contact between members of these smaller units, and less opportunity for contact with a wider range of people).

The 1980s and early 1990s were, of course, a time of considerable economic, and cultural, change. The manufacturing sectors declined and the service industries grew. Strong, embedded communities, such as those around the coalmines withered and died. Communities of men who used their bodies in hard manual labour and then socialised together disappeared. The idea of solidarity and the working man's camaraderie forming around the trade union and principles of social justice was replaced by the individualising of problems in the form of workplace 'stress' that required counselling. This new world demanded strong 'people skills' in the workforce and the changing roles for men in the workplace meant that there was now a greater political and personal demand for men to have enhanced social competence that they didn't previously need.

In relation to autism, this leads to an interesting paradox. One of the core features of the diagnosis implies a lack of empathy. However, in this context, improving the 'emotional intelligence' of the workforce is for the purpose of using 'empathy' to successfully exploit and manipulate your customers and workforce into doing what you wish for your own personal gain. It seems strange that people who find it difficult to understand emotional nuances but who can be compassionate are pathologised, yet those who can use an understanding of others' emotional state to manipulate them for selfish ends are rewarded. This is what 'empathy' means in aggressively neo-liberal market economies. If you can use empathy to successfully manipulate people's emotions, so that they become convinced they need the product or service you are selling, without thought for the potential negative impact it has on people's lives, then that sort of lack of empathy – labelled as psychopathic in lower social classes – doesn't feature on the psychiatric radar. For years this is precisely what has been happening in banking and many other businesses, with legislation, economic regulation and the value system underpinning this, effectively encouraging such narcissistic and psychopathic behaviour. This illustrates the extent to which what we come to view as desirable or undesirable, normal or pathological, is culturally constructed, and that, in the absence of demonstrable organic lesions, understanding diagnoses such as autism requires a thorough engagement with the political, economic and social conditions in which it develops.

GENDER AND AUTISM: A SUMMARY

In this chapter we have explored some of the emerging dynamics shaping gender relations in so-called 'late capitalist' societies.

First, we noted how the gender distribution for those diagnosed with autism has changed over time, becoming a more obviously 'boy' disorder. We noted that feminist critiques of psychiatric categories as being gender-biased against women have been around for quite along time; in contrast, however, little attention has been given to the problem of gender bias in children, where there is a disproportionate attribution of psychiatric diagnoses to boys. We noted how early attempts at developing a nosology for childhood mental health problems set in place the building blocks for a gendered framework into which we categorise children's problems. We then discussed gender and biology in light of the fact that, of all the usual social categories we refer to (such as class, ethnicity, race, sexual orientation, etc.), gender is the one where there is an obvious biological difference (anatomically, hormonally, developmentally, etc.).

In relation to biology we suggested it was futile trying to arrive at an empirical measure of the relative contribution of 'nature' and 'nurture' and instead we should use theoretical models that view nature/nurture complexes (or gestalts) as something we can more reliably comment on and investigate (including empirically). However, we did also conclude that there must be a biological contribution to gender differences that cannot be resolved by cultural and political ideologies that ignore this. We then concluded that this is precisely what current educational methods do, as in the post-feminism era our educational and child-rearing models have increasingly moved towards an 'assimilationist' model, where the needs and wants of boys and girls are perceived to be similar and any differences between them minimised, with the assumption underlying this being that girls and boys learn in the same way and are interested in the same things, because they develop in similar ways and will eventually occupy the same societal roles. We then discussed how these dynamics may have emerged in our modern Western societies, noting that the behaviour of boys as a societal and medical concern is relatively recent and largely confined to the West.

We discussed what models of 'masculinity' exist in Western culture, comparing those in peer group subcultures with those in non-gendered institutional arenas. We then explored one aspect of the value system that dominates and the impact this has on children, men, women and their families – that of narcissism. We concluded that this narcissistic 'masculinisation' of culture has destabilised the family environment and that children face a potentially (emotionally) hostile environment in the West, inevitably seen – to some extent – as a burden, and that boys often bear the brunt of this. The narcissistic value system is necessary to properly pursue a neo-liberal free market economy. Such a system not only produces gross inequalities (both within and between nations), but has also reduced the status and importance of nurture, and therefore the esteem attached to the role of mother. As a result the role of professional/career woman now has higher status than the role of motherhood, causing a movement of adults (mothers joining fathers) out of the sphere of the family. This seems to be leading, in the psychological space of childhood, to an increasing feminisation in some areas, particularly education, and a professionalisation of the task of raising children.

Taking this feminisation forward into the dominant competitive, narcissistic, masculine culture led to ideas such as cultivating 'emotional intelligence' in management and working relations becoming more popular in the 1990s, as a way of developing 'better' ways to motivate the workforce and manipulate the consumer. Thus, modern Western culture demands more convoluted and complicated forms of socialising than in the past or in many other modern cultures. These new demands for strong 'people skills' in the workforce contrast with 'traditional' male labour that revolved around solidarity in a community of men doing jobs that didn't require strong empathising skills. These changing roles mean that there is greater political and personal demand for men to have enhanced social competence. Finally, we noted the paradox that being able to use 'empathy' to manipulate others is desirable, while being compassionate and responsible, but lacking the above 'social skills' to express this in society's terms, is more likely to be labelled as disordered – as being autistic.

10

CULTURE AND SOCIALISATION

In the early chapters of this book we examined the science behind the development of the concept of autism and its spectrum and found this wanting. The circumstances that created the possibility of diagnosing a child as autistic are ultimately less rooted in the biology of those diagnosed than they are in the cultural practices and economy of the time. As we discussed in Chapter 3, prior to the advent of mass schooling the standards for classifying individuals as disordered were much less nuanced, the standards of normality much broader and the mechanisms for social and individual surveillance that we take for granted today simply did not exist. This change in the way we think about and therefore classify certain behaviours in children underwent a marked acceleration towards the end the last century resulting in what some call 'an epidemic' of autism by the beginning of this millennium.

A distinct medical/psychiatric disease called autism could not have emerged until standards of normality had been formalised and narrowed and standards of paediatric screening extended to a child's earliest years so that children with ASD could be 'identified'. This is not to say that there haven't been people throughout history who have displayed the symptoms we now group and define as autism, but to remind the reader that calling this autism is simply a 'trick' of classification, as opposed to being the result of new 'scientific' knowledge.

As educational and psychological authorities were developed during the last century to meet the changing demands for social adjustment, the boundaries between normality and pathology were problematised. Psychologists, psychiatrists and paediatricians have thus become increasingly involved in 'discovering' apparent manifestations of a vast range of disorders among the children they surveyed. These developments in the way we think about childhood and its problems interact with the rapid political, economic and social changes seen in the last few decades in the West, some of the hallmarks of which are: the movement into smaller family and social networks, decreasing amounts of time that parents spend with their children, aggressive consumerism praying on children's desire for stimulation, greater involvement of professionals in child-rearing activities (and advice on child-rearing), and a sense of panic about boys' development (Timimi, 2005).

Interacting with the changing nature of gender relations and gender politics (see Chapter 9), the scene was set for the recent autism epidemic. In this chapter we continue our exploration of the social dynamics that have contributed to both the emergence of the behaviours we label as being autistic and this culture's categorisation of them as being a sign of a 'disorder'. We start by completing what we began in the previous chapter, namely the examination of political and social processes that have led to the emergence of the autism epidemic, and we finish with a critical look at the emergence of a counter discourse – that of the 'autistic rights' movement. In between, we look at the relationship between human variation and patterns of social behaviour.

SCIENCE, SOCIETY AND THE GROWING CONCERN WITH SOCIAL AND EMOTIONAL COMPETENCE

An uncritical view of the 'practice' of science might presuppose that the history of reason and scientific thought are progressive and not dependent upon being located in human endeavours. There is a tacit assumption that scientific reasoning has divorced itself from religion and politics. Historically it would appear that religion and science was by no means antithetical and that the birth of science was not a robust infant whose prognosis was guaranteed. Like Christianity itself, the 'success' of science has depended upon political forces. Science as a cultural and political 'force' became associated with knowledge and the success of technology. Discussions about whether we should do something were replaced by those about whether we can. In the field of mental health and psychology more generally, the argument that science, technology and administration would become inextricably fused was one of the contentions of the Marxist-inspired Frankfurt School of thought.

The view that ideas are inextricably linked with economic and political structures is a view that is often associated Karl Marx. While Marx and Marxism are deemed to be dead inasmuch as the inevitable victory of the proletariat now appears naive and utopian and because of its association with vicious totalitarian regimes, Marxist analysis of the problems with the economic structures of capitalism and its inability to produce justice and equity for human kind have recently received renewed interest following the collapse of the global financial world.

Marx believed that there was a ruling class that had access to privileges of wealth and power denied to other parts of the population. We are aware that a tiny proportion of the population own a disproportionate amount of wealth. It is also true that the gap between rich and poor is wider than at any time than in the past 100 years and has continued to grow (see Chapter 9). In the past the rich sought to buttress their position by means of religion, using it both as an argument for legitimising their position and to give the 'masses' something to quell their anger. Science-as-ideology can be used in a similar way. This appears to be the view of Marx, writing with Engels, in their statement, that:

> The ideas of the ruling class are in every epoch the ruling ideas, i.e. the class which is the ruling material force of society, is at the same time its ruling intellectual force. The class which has the means of material production at its disposal has control at the same time over the means of mental production, so that thereby, generally speaking, the ideas of those who lack the means of mental production are subject to it. (Marx and Engels, 1845: 64)

For Marx, ideas are related to, if not determined by, the means of production. Any analysis of human existence must look at the circumstances under which people struggle to make their living. The circumstances under which people make their living affect their capacity for a whole variety of things, including concepts of self, purpose and self-realisation. Material structures under capitalism are rarely characterised by naked force, as they are under feudal or totalitarian systems; instead, democracies ostensibly rule by willing consent. From a Marxist perspective the ideas behind, in particular, Western democracies, masquerade as appeals to universality when in reality they serve a particular class interest. Under modern democracies the ruling class cannot govern by overtly maintaining ideas that serve their own interests; instead, they have to articulate ideas that purport to serve the common, thus suggesting that the beliefs, practices and values that support and maintain the interests of the ruling classes are universal and, to a large degree, indispensable.

However, this apparently 'benign' style of ruling has increasingly given way to more draconian methodologies. With the demise of 'welfarism' in the 1980s and the growth of a more aggressively competitive neo-liberalism, some modern Western governments have developed some features of totalitarian regimes, though this is done through methodologies involving the policing of interiority (such as the self) rather than more obvious techniques involving imprisonment and torture of political enemies (though we are discovering that this more overt approach has featured in Western democracies too in recent years). These cultural dynamics do, of course, shift and change; alienated classes found other systems developing to replace employment as a source of legitimate income – thus spending on welfare has risen again as the numbers claiming disability benefits (in particular for mental health problems) have increased markedly in the UK in the last decade.

One of the facets of the modern state is the manufacture and dissemination of fear. While the IRA or Al-Qaeda have, or may have had, the capacity to inflict real 'terror', the state uses such threats to initiate systems of surveillance, discipline and control. At the more micro level, the paedophile is a real social danger, but focusing on this individualised form of danger has the capacity to divert attention away from state activities that are arguably causing more diffuse harm at a larger scale (such as child poverty, supporting advertising to children, businesses that produce ever-more adultified fashion for children, a culture that encourages unstable home circumstances and so on).

As discussed in Chapter 9, an economic system that requires a narcissistic value system that allows personal and individualistic greed to be the dominant driving force cannot sustain itself without our moral conscience beginning to feel guilty, leading, consequently, to aggressive and punitive forms of social control (Richards, 1989). State and media apparatuses are thus governed by the identification and dissemination of moral and social panics: Muslims, teenage mothers, junkies, teenagers, hoodies, chavs, loonies and loners are just some of the targets, as the government and a 'sensationalist', market-driven media whips up a series of populist frenzies to massage mass fear. The scrutiny and surveillance of childhood that we currently undertake in Northern Europe, Australasia and North America has to be understood in this context. Bad children can be seen as risk and sad children as a poor investment.

This book suggests that psychiatry and psychology can easily become political tools, as they have in the past – not just in totalitarian societies but also in democratic ones. The needs of a service-based economy are different to those of a primarily manufacturing one. In a service economy, poor socialisation skills (of the superficial variety that we discuss below under 'Socialisation rituals and emotional intelligence') in the workforce are perceived as putting the economy at a disadvantage. The need to inculcate early 'social skills' and 'emotional intelligence' thus becomes a concern and site of action for the ruling classes. Under New Labour in the UK a whole variety of policies and initiatives aimed at developing such skills are apparent, from Sure Start early parenting programmes, through increasing nursery provision with new learning targets for pre-school children, up to 'citizenship' and social skills classes in schools. The state can no longer trust parents to deliver such teaching and skills to their children – in any case, the parents are needed in the workplace; thus (as we discussed in Chapter 9) child-rearing becomes a task that is increasingly the remit of a veritable army of professionals acting on behalf of the state.

Foucault (1977) also recognised the importance of power in shaping our attitudes and beliefs, but located the dynamics for these in more subtle processes, not necessarily tied to economic needs, but more closely tied to a set of power relations that are 'local' and reside within the structures and purposes of particular groupings. He observes that:

> At the heart of all disciplinary systems functions a small penal mechanism. It enjoys a kind of judicial privilege with its own laws, its specific offences, in particular forms of judgement...they defined and repressed a mass of behaviour that the relative indifference of the great systems of punishment had allowed to escape. (Foucault, 1977: 178)

Thus, although few schools in present Western society resemble the more rigid authoritarian schools of 19th-century Europe, mechanisms for disciplining children have not disappeared, they have simply taken on a subtler form. In the practice of diagnosing and medicating a child with ADHD, for example, we see surveillance and identification followed by an attempt to intervene to correct and 'discipline' children who refuse to accommodate to certain expectations of teachers. While the school may be engaged in a process of producing future citizens and thus has an interest in making, creating and enforcing assumptions about the citizenship potential of the child, acknowledgement of the individuality of each child becomes superficial semantics as definitions derived from cultural assumptions about what a 'normal' child should be take precedence. Teachers then become part of imposing a different form of discipline to render a child 'docile' and obedient enough for a teacher to carry out their job, without breaking the law on children's welfare and rights (i.e., without beating the child).

Kirschner (2006) has summarised this tension that modern liberal democratic societies often have between acceptance of difference (pluralism) on the one hand and imposing homogeneity on the other:

> All societies seek to ensure their legitimacy. That is, they need to ensure that people are willing to submit to the governing authority and to the rule of law. In premodern societies, much of this was accomplished through the threat of punishment – through forms of coercion and constraint that were external to the individual person's will. But in modern liberal democratic societies, legitimacy is ensured by subjugating individuals from within – by inciting individuals to scan themselves (as well as others) for possible signs of deviance, thereby motivating them to try to maintain or re-establish their 'normality'. Such a dynamic...ensures that subjects will not only act in accord with the social order, but will also experience themselves as endorsing it. It is a process by which 'others' are identified both within and outside the self...Such others serve to more sharply delineate the character and boundaries of the positive, 'normal' self. These others are then marginalized and excluded, or rehabilitated and cured, so that the self comes to experience itself and to be perceived as more closely harmonized with the normal order. (Kirschner, 2006: 5)

The process is therefore both a social and an individual (psychological) process. The child is 'acted' upon by the relatively powerful adults around them, who in effect create the discourse of problems associated with the child. The child, in turn, internalises the discourse and may, in fact, become an endorser of this view (Cohen and Morley, 2009).

Some of the ideas of the influential German thinker Max Weber are also helpful here. Weber believed modern societies (referring primarily to European and North American) were characterised as operating in an increasingly rationalised manner – for example, using quantification and evaluation as a method for understanding the world. He observed, further, that these values penetrated all levels of society, thus indicating that economic features can permeate other spheres. Much of this can be achieved through the mechanism of bureaucratisation, which is a form of administrative rationality (Poggi, 2005). We can see the phenomena of administration tied to a quantitative quasi-behaviourism in the 'target' culture, which the New Labour government in the UK became obsessed with. Targets, and the attainment of those targets, became a central plank of reforms in many public services such as health, social services and education. In order to monitor these targets, a high level of administration and bureaucracy is required. This emphasis on targets has echoes of totalitarian-style systems, involving little discussion within government or with the public about potential drawbacks of a target culture in such domains (which are based primarily on negotiating the space of human relationships as opposed to 'producing' a commodity). The over-riding focus is the 'means' to attain them.

Measurements of childhood progress makes reference to 'normal' stages of development, with systems of surveillance in place to pick up those who are deemed to have failed to attain them and who are then subject various interventions (see Chapter 4). What 'works' in these interventions is largely handed over to 'experts', as long as such experts do not challenge the prevailing ideology of the culturally constructed universalised standards. The idea of professional or expert care then becomes itself a commodity that is subject to targets and a variety of administrative bureaucratisation. Professionals may have 'quotas' for how many have been diagnosed with what, according to what standardised normal percentage is expected; if 1 per cent of school-aged children are expected to have an ASD, but one area has only 0.1 per cent and the next has 10 per cent, then the former is 'under-diagnosing', the latter 'over-diagnosing', even though the 1 per cent is based on a largely arbitrary quantification of a subjective set of criteria.

As the modern state becomes increasingly monolithic, having successfully commodified a large variety of phenomena, from objects to subjects, and having successfully individualised goals and ambitions under a narcissistic value system, opportunities for dissent, challenge and a genuinely different approach to organising society become fewer. As a result, despite the spectacular failure (yet again) of current dominant capitalist ideology to produce economic stability, justice, equity, peaceful international relations, sustainable development and elimination global poverty, etc., even though we are in the midst of a catastrophic global economic collapse, no alternative discourse or political party supporting an alternative to global capitalism has found the socio-political space to emerge.

The emergence of the service economy has seen the harnessing and manipulation of human desires and sexuality, especially through advertising, to encourage increased demand for a whole variety of products (which in turn stimulates economic growth). The service economy is dependent upon selling – including selling one's self. In such a framework, what place is there for truth or the inability to manipulate one's facial expression and body language to sell one's produce? In such a society the inability to do this 'properly' (i.e., to be savvy enough to emotionally manipulate the consumer into buying your product) renders the person 'unproductive' and thus problematic to the smooth running of such an economic system. The adoption of autism as a label of choice for those professionals faced with such alienated 'freaks', 'geeks' and rejects of today's society provides a way of turning this problem from a human one, generated in large part by the socio-political system in which people are trying to survive, into a technical problem for the 'expert' (with the help of the state that appoints him/her) to turn into a commodity that can be quantified, manipulated and potentially exploited.

Having articulated a variety of theoretical perspectives to help us understand a little bit about how cultural and political forces act to shape our conceptions of childhood and personality and their problems, and the relation this has to the dominant economic system, we think that it is not mere coincidence that the explosion in medicalising childhood behaviours, including the dramatic expansion of autism, began in the 1980s and really took off in the UK following a 'New Labour' government coming into power. Parton (2006) delineates the way that various UK governments since the Second World War have had to deal with the possibility of making interventions to the family unit. By the late 1970s radical changes in patterns of employment were starting to take place: 'New jobs in Britain required either higher level of skill and training or were lower paid, part time and in the service industries and usually for female workers' (Parton, 2006: 51). A process of downsizing and deregulation led to the emergence of youth, particularly male youth, as problematic. This contributed to emerging identities and cultural phenomena characterised by ontological insecurity and moral panics. The UK governments of Margaret Thatcher and John Major, being fundamentally laissez-faire and orientated towards non-interference and the lifting of any restrictions on markets, faced philosophical dilemmas with regards how to deal with the emerging disquiet and anti-social trends.

New Labour, however, was not so constrained by such ideological baggage. Following well-known tragedies in the UK, such as those of Victoria Climbie and Jamie Bulger, coverage of paedophile scares and child abuse, as well as media-whipped concerns about 'out of control' youth involved in drug abuse, stabbings, happy slapping and so on meant that childhood was coming to be viewed as at risk and a risk. Jamie Bulger's case involved the death, in 1993, of a two-year-old boy who was abducted from a Merseyside shopping centre by two ten-year-old boys who took him to a railway line, beat him and left him for dead. Victoria Climbie died in February 2000 in London, aged eight. To escape poverty, her parents (from the Ivory Coast) entrusted her to her great aunt who brought her to Europe. However, Victoria was tortured to death by that great aunt and her boyfriend, despite police, doctors and social workers all having had contact with her while she was being abused. These cases became symbolic of a powerful and public discourse: in gendered terms, the development of boys was seen as needing greater intervention as they potentially posed a danger to society, while girls (particularly ethnic minority girls) were seen as being in danger of abuse, thus requiring greater protection by the state from their parents.

For New Labour childhood is not only a risk but also an investment. Parton quotes Tony Blair to the effect that, 'if the knowledge economy is an aim, then work, skill and above all investing in children become essential aims of welfare ...' (Parton, 2006: 95). From its inception New Labour has produced a wealth of policies directed at children, some positive, at least in their aims (such as the intention to eliminate child poverty, on which the government has sadly not delivered), others (such as Sure Start and Every Child Matters), whether wittingly or unwittingly, have problematic assumptions at their core.

Sure Start, for example, is an initiative designed for parents with children under the age of four. The aim of Sure Start was to work with disadvantaged parents and their children to promote the physical, intellectual, social and emotional development of children. Criticisms of Sure Start have revolved mostly around the programme's expense and practicality rather than its basic ideological premise. Sure Start places a heavy emphasis on the social and emotional development of the child, particularly the child's early relationship with parents/caregivers (see http://www.surestart.gov.uk/surestartservices/healthrelated/socialandemotional/ accessed 3 March 2009). On the Sure Start website there is an interesting document called 'What Works in Promoting Children's Mental Health: The Evidence and the Implications for Sure Start Settings' by Zarrina Kurtz. Kurtz articulates a view that has the laudable aims of promoting good mental health and through this preventing mental health problems developing in children as they grow up. This is seen as a vital function of Sure Start. Prevention is described as occurring on a four-step continuum:

- Universal public health promotion.
- Targeted intervention for specific groups (for example, teenage mothers).
- Selective intervention at an early stage in the onset of an identified problem.
- Treatment for established disorders, with the aim of reducing their severity, duration or recurrence and the development of complications.

Surveillance of very young children from poor families is thus part of the reason for establishing Sure Start. Given the poor evidence base (part of which we have outlined in this book in relation to ASD) for supporting the idea that early diagnosis and treatment of psychiatric disorders improves outcome and the possibility of, instead, scripting a child's future self-definition of disability, this seems an ill thought-out and risky strategy.

Needless to say, Sure Start facilities are most typically found in disadvantaged areas. Their function is to keep an eye on poor parents and their children, as they cannot be trusted to draw on their own cultural heritage and communities to find sufficient wisdom and understanding to bring their children up properly. Echoing discourse on childhood being a risk and at risk (symbolised by the Jamie Bulger and Victoria Climbie cases respectively), Sure Start sets the starting point for intervening to prevent such occurrences very early in a child's life – a poor child's life, that is. Within Sure Start, a child 'learning' social and emotional competence seems to be more important than anything else.

We believe that there is a connection between this growing emphasis in government policy on developing social and emotional 'competence' in the young for both economic and social reasons and the explosion of rates of ASD diagnosis. We need more socially and emotionally savvy individuals to keep our service-orientated economy competitive and we need to develop early social and emotional competence in the young of our society to stop the perceived slide of children down the path of socially disruptive and dangerous antisocial behaviour. We can no longer trust poor parents to bring up their children 'properly' so we must create policies, institutions and train large numbers of professionals to scrutinise them and their children and intervene early when we pick up problems. By turning this into a technical activity mediated by 'experts', the state reassures the population of its positive, welfare-orientated ideals. The lack of evidence for such initiatives producing better outcomes for either children or their parents seems to matter little.

An evidence-based approach, however, suggests that we cannot separate mental well being from social inequality. A recent World Health Organization (2009) report concluded:

> It is abundantly clear that the chronic stress of struggling with material disadvantage is intensified to a very considerable degree by doing so in more unequal societies. An extensive body of research confirms the relationship between inequality and poorer outcomes, a relationship which is evident at every position on the social hierarchy and is not confined to developed nations. The emotional and cognitive effects of high levels of social status differentiation are profound and far reaching: greater inequality heightens status competition and status insecurity across all income groups and among both adults and children. It is the distribution of economic and social resources that explains health and other outcomes in the vast majority of studies. (WHO, 2009: III)

Ingleby (1985) makes the claim that as groups of children become the new dangerous classes then governments perceive that the socialisation process for children can no longer be trusted to families but has to be taken over by the state and its agencies. According to Ingleby, there is 'a growing army of professionals operating in the psychological sphere' (Ingleby, 1985: 79), professionals who are essentially acting on behalf of the state to maintain power over and through the parent, by educating the parent about the professional's worldview, ultimately aiming to produce ways of living and thinking consistent with the dominant social order. Professionals themselves are duped into thinking that the ends are benevolent and the means of achieving them are rational.

The interventions of the current British government in the affairs of the family bear some comparison with pre-First World War British welfare provision. From the late 19th century onwards, as children were removed from the workplace, the sphere of education became a sphere of enclosure, discipline and regimentation (see Chapter 3). Measures of a child's capability, at first envisaged as a beneficial intervention, became instead a tool for marginalisation and exclusion (Rose, 1985). While the emphasis in those early years of mass state-supported education, was on intelligence testing (the economy required semi-skilled labour in particular), in the current political and economic climate this has been replaced by social and emotional 'competence', as the state's interest in fitness to work in a modern service economy and attempts to placate fears about the risks associated with un-socialised children, takes precedence. Hendrick (2003) recognises that, since 1974, educability has been conceptualised in social and moral terms. As we have argued, initiatives such as Sure Start, apart from making availability for work easier for mothers, is concerned with the inculcation of social and emotional competence in children. With women in work and children as young as three months and upwards in the nursery, the state has become *in loco parentis*. Parents are needed in the workplace and, in any case, have failed to socialise their children properly, so the state has taken it upon itself to do just that.

From pre-school, through PHSE to citizenship, teaching has become about fitness – fitting in and fit for work, that is, skilled in face-to-face interaction. One of the 'gurus' of New Labour, Anthony Giddens, has apparently stated that the main function of education is 'social and emotional competences' (cited in Hendrick, 2003). Today, those who are not 'fit' for this type of society are considered sick – no fault of their own or their parents for 'tis in their genes. Genetic determinism married to evolutionary psychology has provided an ideology that has given a modern slant on the 'great chain of being'. With autism we have witnessed more and more individuals who do not have a learning disability, but are failing to 'fit in' to our brave new world, being assigned a diagnosis of autism.

Since embracing neo-liberalism and New Labour's extension of this into the social sphere, we have witnessed a growing populism which has resulted in new attempts to reconfigure British society with new inclusion and exclusion criteria. While these are linked to 'welfare' promotion and passed to 'experts', a positive gloss and the appearance of benign intentions are easy to achieve; however, we must remain concerned that processes such as the medicalisation of social problems have, and can again, cause immense suffering despite the good intentions of those administering the process (see Chapter 11).

Much of the work on defining who does and doesn't fit in is done by individuals themselves. In a capitalist, market-driven economy, mass consumption is vital to maintenance of the system and therefore becomes an important part of our self and consciousness. In Western society even personal relations and the self become objects of consumption (Broughton, 1986): like the stereotypical consumer wife comparing the whiteness of her sheets with those of her neighbours, the subjects of consumer societies constantly compare their own inadequacies with those of others. This practice of self-examination causes a cult of self-awareness, affecting the way we see personal growth; there is pressure, every day, to seek to make oneself a better product – new, improved, best and brightest yet. This internal monitoring can become as draconian as the secret police; if you find yourself inadequate in some way you will keep consuming to remedy whatever shortfall you have discovered and so keep the economy moving and fit in – if you don't, you risk a variety of professionals becoming concerned about your 'well being'.

Reliance on consumerism also leads to a kind of growth fetish, whereby Western culture and politics are obsessed with an ideology that demands never-ending growth and expansion. Yet, despite several decades of sustained economic growth, we are no happier. Growth not only fails to make people contented; it destroys many of the things that do through weakening social cohesion (Hamilton, 2003). In response to the financial crises gripping the world economy, the same ideology keeps driving attempted solutions; we must, we are told, create conditions for growth to occur again, so we can recommence endless consumption. But there is ample evidence that current economic and fiscal strategies for growth may also be undermining family and community relationships (WHO, 2009). This means that we pursue economic growth at the cost of social and emotional recession.

The attention given to individual cases of child abusers whom society can disown as not belonging to or being (at least in part) the product of our culture masks Western governments' implementation of national and international policies that place children at risk and the extent to which our culture is abusive. Rightwing policies of the 1980s and 1990s cut health, social, welfare and education programmes as well as enforcing similar austerity measures on developing countries, policies that had a particularly adverse effect on children and families (De Mause, 1984; Kincheloe, 1998). This also had a class-specific character with the plight of poor children being viewed as self-inflicted and the more insidious problem of middle-class parents' neglect of their children often passing unnoticed (Rabin, 1994).

With the increase in the number of divorces and two working parents, fathers and mothers are around their children for less of the day. A generation of 'home aloners' are growing up; kids who, by and large, have to raise themselves. Since the late 1960s the amount of time children in the USA have with their parents has dropped, from an average of 30 hours per week to 17 hours per week by the early 1990s (Lipsky and Abrams, 1994). As kids are forced to withdraw into their own culture the free market exploits this, praying on their boredom and desire for stimulation (Kincheloe, 1998). In this environment poor children are constantly confronted with their shortcomings by media that tell them they are deficient without this or that accessory. In this unhappy isolation, post-modern Western children respond to the market's push to 'adultify' them (at the same time as the culture of self-gratification 'childifies' adults) by entering into the world of adult entertainment earlier and without adult supervision, resulting in sexual knowledge and experience of drugs and alcohol (Aronowitz and Giroux, 1991). This then becomes the new norm for many, particularly in hegemonic male subcultures (see Chapter 9). What happens to those 'home aloners' that do not wish or are unable to break into these subcultural groupings? It is not any easier for young women trying to negotiate a path into adulthood. Not only must they cope with competitive cultures that focuses on their surface identity, linking virtue and desirability to unnatural thinness, but adultifying children may also be exposing them to greater risk of sexual abuse through consumer culture's eroticisation of the young as seen in popular images (e.g., in advertising, presenting alluring little girls with make-up [Walkerdine, 1996], and beauty pageants, where they no longer look like little girls but coquettish young women who are encouraged to walk suggestively across the stage [Giroux, 1998]).

With the goal of self-fulfilment, gratification and competitive manipulation of relationships to suit the individual's own selfish ends central, and the development of deep interpersonal attachments discouraged, it is not difficult to see why so-called narcissistic disorders (such as anti-social behaviour) are on the increase (Dwivedi, 1996). As governments become aware of the problems of 'empathy' and lack of it, so interest in conditions deemed to be based on or caused by this lack grows, and support for those researchers and services that claim to be interested in early detection, prevention and treatment of this increases. However, the individualisation of these problems, such that they become the responsibility of professionals to 'treat', can act as a distraction, allowing the state to avoid taking more genuine and lasting steps to improve the well being of these individuals and society more generally:

> A focus on social justice may provide an important corrective to what has been seen as a growing over-emphasis on individual pathology.

> Mental health is produced socially: the presence or absence of mental health is above all a social indicator and therefore requires social, as well as individual solutions...A preoccupation with individual symptoms may lead to a 'disembodied psychology' which separates what goes on inside people's heads from social structure and context. The key therapeutic intervention then becomes to 'change the way you think' rather than to refer people to sources of help for key catalysts for psychological problems: debt, poor housing, violence, crime. (WHO, 2009: V)

Children are cultured into this value system by virtue of living within its institutions and being exposed daily to its discourse (most notably through television). Through this they are socialised into a system that embraces a capitalist idea of freedom through promoting individualism and competitiveness. They are expected to renounce dependence and show independence from an early age. Ultimately this is a system of winners and losers, a kind of survival of the fittest where compassion and concern for social harmony contradicts the basic goal of the value system. As this system is showing itself to be bad for children's happiness, a similar process works to try and distance us from the anxiety arising from the guilt thus produced. Instead of asking ourselves painful questions about the role we may be playing in producing this unhappiness, we can view our children's difficulties as being the result of biological diseases that require medical treatment (we can blame their genes).

DIAGNOSIS AND POWER

Thomas Szasz (1974) has described how a system that ultimately has more to do with social, economic and political developments than science, can easily be abused or distorted. Clinicians can gain both status and income by declaring a large group of individuals to be their clients. In a well-known historical analysis, Szasz (1974) traces the problem back to the French neurologist Jean-Martin Charcot, and his famous work with hysterical patients. Szasz describes how, as Charcot's knowledge and prestige increased, his interest shifted from neurological disorders to those which simulated such conditions. Such patients were then classified either as hysterics or malingerers, depending on the observer's point of view. Those labelled 'hysterics' were seen as more respectable and so became objects fit for serious study.

By promoting the concept of hysteria, Charcot greatly increased his patient population while enhancing his status as a leading expert on a new and serious medical disorder, rather than merely working with people who were 'pretending' to be ill.

Unfortunately, dubious motives for diagnostic categorisation are not limited to a quest for social respectability or increased income. Diagnosticians can align themselves with those in power by agreeing to pathologise a particular group of individuals. Foucault (1961, 1962) put forward similar arguments about diagnostic categories and social power, often with a greater emphasis on class issues. Foucault suggested that modern treatment of the insane is not primarily a matter of medical compassion, but instead represents a thinly veiled effort to bring 'deviant' individuals under the control of bourgeois morality. Whether or not one accepts all of Foucault's arguments, it seems clear that diagnostic authority, like any well-established power structure, can be abused.

A recent example came out of the Soviet Union before its demise. In Soviet psychiatry, there was a long history of studying a form of schizophrenia known in the West as 'sluggish schizophrenia'. This illness was thought by the Soviet psychiatric establishment to represent an independent diagnostic category with a particular set of symptoms, course and outcome. This diagnostic category was often applied to political or religious dissidents whose 'symptoms' (including those concerning anti-state sentiments) were deemed sufficiently 'pathological' to warrant detention and 'treatment'. It is not surprising that these symptoms of schizophrenia began to subside gradually, as the dissident/patients were held in an involuntary basis in Soviet psychiatric hospitals. Dissidents knew that in order to win their release they had to recant their expressions of protest, so that the mental health establishment could pronounce them to be cured of their disorder (Abell and Dauphin, 2009). While the notion of 'sluggish schizophrenia' may have begun its life as an honest attempt to help those struggling to make their way through life, it became a classic example of how nosology can be distorted and abused by the power structure of a society, with few of the psychiatrists involved being aware that the category now served an overtly political function (Timimi, 2002).

Since the nosology of mental health relies heavily on social and political construction, it can become a logical battleground for unresolved social conflict. Indeed, so can another rather powerless group – children. Children, in particular, come to symbolise and receive our unfulfilled wishes. In the language of psychoanalysis they receive the projections of our unconscious wishes and fantasies. How many of us who are parents have not at one time or other found ourselves imagining our child(ren) achieving something we didn't but would have liked to? On a societal scale this projection comes up routinely in 'romanticised' sentiments (e.g., politicians' speeches) where 'the future' and 'children' are continuously linked in order to tug at our heart-strings. Thus, in times of high cultural, social and political anxiety, the discourse around children and childhood being in danger becomes more prevalent, and in a culture used to medicalising such social processes, we should not be surprised that one outcome is a proliferation of childhood psychiatric diagnostic categories.

While behavioural abnormalities are certainly unlikely to affect all demographic groups equally, great disparities in diagnostic prevalence by race, age, gender, or socio-economic status should be a red flag for clinicians and researchers. It seems reasonable to ask why certain groups are diagnosed so disproportionately. While market forces can easily promote or discourage the popularity of a particular diagnostic category, as argued above, economic conditions can influence how young people are perceived. For example, Enright and colleagues (1987) analysed articles published in a prominent developmental psychology journal over the last 100 years. They concluded that psychological theories that became popular reflected the political and economic environment of the time. They found that in times of economic depression (when jobs for adults were scarce) theories of adolescence emerged that portrayed teenagers as immature, psychologically unstable and in need of prolonged participation in the educational system, while during wartime, the psychological competence of youth was emphasised and the duration of education that was recommended was more retracted.

As discussed earlier in Chapters 3 and 4, our view of childhood changes over time. When the economy needed large numbers of workers for manual tasks that required mentoring rather than extensive pedagogy, child labour was viewed as a normal state for children, and something that taught them discipline, numeracy and prepared them for the responsibilities of adulthood in an age of hierarchical relationships that were strongly class-based. We now look back with horror at the idea that children could have been sent to work down the pit or up the chimney, viewing such a life as 'robbing' children of their 'childhood'. Yet child labour was the normal expectation for children in Europe and North America about 150 years ago (not long ago at all in the scale human history).

What will future generations look back and say about childhood today? Will they wonder at the cruelty of creating these compulsory institutions that children have to attend for most of the first 18 years of life, where they have test after test, expected to confirm to increasingly narrow expectations of behaviour, etc.? At the very least it seems legitimate to speculate on how current economic forces and lifestyle choices have influenced our own view of childhood and how this may impact on the way we think about and raise today's children and how this, in turn, may impact on their actual behaviour. As parents deal with longer hours of work, commute greater distances and are generally less available and more stressed, children who were previously seen as merely fidgety or restless or who talked too much are now viewed as suffering from psychopathology. An expectation that children should want to pay attention, cooperate and demonstrate independence and 'empathy' within structured group settings has come to be viewed as a more important 'need' for our children, than would have been the case even a couple of decades ago.

SOCIALISATION RITUALS AND EMOTIONAL INTELLIGENCE

The controversial philosopher Jean Baudrillard (see Douglas, 1989) suggested that modern culture is saturated with imagery through the media, advertising, television and so on. The result of this, he argues, is that 'representation' has saturated reality to such an extent that experience often takes place at a distance from reality. We thus experience the world through a kind of filter of preconceptions and expectations that have been fabricated in advance by a culture swamped with images. For example, how can you express your love for someone without that expression recalling in some way innumerable soap operas or Hollywood films in which our idea of love is constructed and played out daily. Baudrillard refers to this process as 'simulation'. Features of contemporary life as diverse as fashion, environmental design, opinion polls, emotions, lifestyles and so on, are all twisted and shaped by the saturation of imagery to such an extent that our relationship to everyday reality is fashioned as much by virtual reality as by the physical one.

Simulation is not something that Baudrillard considers to be the opposite of truth; it is more that in Baudrillard's post-modern world there is no firm, pure reality left against which we can measure truth or falsity of any representations. For example, when we buy trainers, do we buy them for their practical function or because they possess a brand image? Furthermore, how far has the function of these trainers become primarily the brand image rather than their function as a particular sort of footwear? Some of these themes are expanded upon by the American critic Fredrick Jameson (1991) who sees contemporary culture as constructing a reality that changes our focus from depth to the surface. He sees the commercialised space created by a consumer culture as causing a kind of detachment of the object from all meaningful connections (like the trainers in the example above, whose function has arguably become detached to a large extent from that of protective footwear, to becoming that of 'image' and even a way you define self and identity) to the point where things are abstracted from their true origins and reused in meaningless and, often, trivial ways.

Such consumerism creates a heightened awareness of appearance and style. The increasing invasion of images from media and advertising creates a dream world, a virtual reality to fantasise about, as commercials sell us images of ideal lifestyles that they attach to their products. Our culture has become so consumed by this perpetual imagery that we can now literally take off one identity and slip on another as we change our clothes, make-up, shoes, etc. We are seduced into becoming so concerned with our surface identity, that we submit ourselves to long surgical procedures to change the shape and appearance of our bodies.

In the world of consumer capitalism everything becomes a potential object for exploitation and profit. Advertising aimed specifically at children complements markets in toys, foods, educational equipment, fashion, sportswear and so on. Indeed, the dominance of the idea of mental 'health' (as opposed to, say, spiritual or social well being) is a product, at least in part, of market-economy consumer capitalism. Conceptualising problems as 'health' individualises suffering (thereby absolving and mystifying the role of social factors) and creates new markets (e.g., for the pharmaceutical industry). It is within the ideology that creates such fractured, superficial identities that we discover the same superficial labelling of identities on those decreed by modern institutions as mentally ill or disordered in some way.

One of the outcomes of this current cultural milieu is a move away from understanding based on depth and a connection with physical reality and everyday functionality, towards a culture where surface factors, such as image, appearance, the short term and the immediate, has become more enduring and characteristic of current conditions. This impacts on our view of children and their behaviour (more likely to be shaped by surface signs – such as ASD and a search for short-term, immediate solutions), as well as effecting on our consciousness more deeply (including, of course, children's).

We have, in modern free –market, 'selfish capitalist' cultures, developed complex socialisation rituals in order to keep some semblance of psychological survival in an image-obsessed, surface-orientated culture. As the principles of the market have been allowed to become the guiding values, it should be no surprise that within the world of relationships a form of 'competitive socialisation' has emerged; to some extent, we have the survival of the 'smarmiest'! Smarmy people (also known as smooth operators) are those who have developed the means, through being socially perceptive, to pursue their own personal agenda, often at the expense of others. That, after all, is what a 'marketplace' rewards. Of course, in the real world people have very mixed bags of talents, using a blend of hard work and social manipulation to achieve a given end. However, recent political and economic realities have favoured this rise of social competition. Kenneth Gergen (1991) argues that the modernist, rational and firm sense of self has given way to a post-modern multiphrenia, in which we adapt our sense of self to the occasion as we engage with an ever-widening multitude of people in different locales, roles and contexts. In this 'social saturation' an individual markets him/herself in the same way as one markets a consumer product.

Many recent societal trends that began in the USA and UK have made life unbearable for anyone who fails to dance to this new beat. In less than a generation skilled jobs in the manufacturing sector have been replaced by new professions more focused on persuasion and social networking (see Chapter 9). A good carpenter or a competent mechanic can easily prove their worth to employers and customers alike; many of us would still prefer an impolite mechanic who gets the job done at an affordable price to a smooth-talking receptionist who reassures us that the repair job has been assigned to their best mechanic and subjected to rigorous quality control in order to justify an extortionate fee.

If we take a broader view of recent societal developments, such as concern over criminality, terrorism, public health, political extremism and sexual abuse of minors, it is easy to reappraise the promotion of and preoccupation with personality disorders as part of an agenda for increasing the surveillance and control of the general population, in order to introduce new methods for policing and preventing the emergence of these dangerous selves. Expansion of the ASD construct provides a new category of potentially dangerous people – those who lack empathy or social skills – and so new potential ways of categorising these individuals and dealing with them, hopefully (from a government's point of view) outside the ever-expanding criminal justice system, with the reassurance of having 'experts' who have the technical 'know-how' to sort these dangerous loners out.

THE SEARCH FOR QUICK-FIX SOLUTIONS

One of the features of modern, economically developed, consumer societies is the continuous advance of technologies and our ever-greater reliance on them. When technologies are functioning properly, they operate in the background of our attention and their efficiency, function and use are thus taken for granted. The better the technology the less we have to think about it – it is there functioning just outside our awareness and making life easier for us. Thus, in our efforts to get from A to B, we first had the bicycle, then the car, which made the journey easier and more efficient. The car then evolved to become faster, safer, smoother and more comfortable and the technology continues to evolve, so we get the automatic car, satellite navigation, lights that come on and off automatically, a climate-controlled atmosphere and so on. The attraction of technological advance has had a huge impact on our day-to-day life and, indeed, our consciousness. So attractive are these developing technologies that apparently make life easier, more efficient and streamlined, that hardly a discipline can be found that has not turned, to some extent, to technology to find new, innovative solutions.

In this respect, medicine is a good example of a profession whose core value system has shifted from a primary focus on the care ethic towards a primary focus on a more technologically orientated ethic, which revolves around efficiency, accuracy, efficacy and economy (Sadler, 2005). Thus, the focus is on the more technical aspects rather than the human aspects of the job – as in the cliché of the consultant on the ward round identifying patients through their ailment (this is a case of kidney stones, this is a case of heart failure, etc.), like objects rather than people.

This general technicalisation of life has meant that we increasingly search for simple solutions where we rely on the technical expertise of various technicians in their trade. These 'experts' bring to bear their scientific, technical knowledge and devise a simple technical solution which requires minimum thought by the user and which, when applied, will fix the problem and render it into the background as all good technologies should. In this respect it is easy to see the appeal of the notion that the interpersonal problems that life inevitably brings can be reduced to a simple underlying disorder (such as ASD) which can be fixed with a straightforward technique (preferably a pill or surgical procedure). It is also easy to see why, in such a cultural context, more time-consuming approaches such as psychotherapeutic ones that require thought, reflection, mental effort and great engagement with the subject matter have receded in their popularity.

Interestingly, the technicalisation of modern culture has not been without its critics and, indeed, an ambivalent relationship with technology has been noted. Yes, we all want to own a car and drive one so that we can go from A to B efficiently, but we are also aware that this technology contributes to global warming, so this short-term gain may lead to long-term pain. Furthermore, the existence of mass means of transport, like the car, has had a profound effect on the mobility of people, which, in turn, has led to a weakening of social support structures as families and communities venture to all corners of the earth, often leaving behind them a sense of connection and belonging. To bring it to a more personal level, it is great to have technology that allows me to wake up in the morning, lie in bed and use the remote control to turn on the television in a house which is kept nice and warm with gas central heating which comes on automatically at certain times of the day. In fact, it is so nice I could stay there all morning, but my partner pulls me out of this technological comfort zone, persuading me to put on my coat and scarf and go out for a walk in the crisp, winter morning scenery. Not only is this invigorating but it forces me to re-engage with the simple human pleasures of being with, talking to and deepening a relationship with someone of far greater importance in my life than the central heating and television.

AUTISM AND SOCIAL ALIENATION

Could some ASD symptoms emerge as a reaction to social alienation, rather than resulting from something we are calling autism? For example, ASDs have been found to be more common in immigrant children (Gillberg and Gillberg, 1996). Where a person's family background differs culturally to a significant degree from the rest of the local community, together with accompanying stress and psychosocial adversity that often accompanies such a dramatic change in people's circumstance (particularly if there isn't an already existent community that could provide support and cultural familiarity), could this not lead to autism-type symptoms (lack of social reciprocity, withdrawal, etc.)? Similarly, children and young people with a variety of 'imperfections' (lack of motor coordination, facial disfigurement, speech difficulties, etc.) could also find themselves struggling to make friends and out of necessity withdrawing into pursuing solitary interests. Changes in lifestyle may also cause changes in patterns of socialisation similar to those that are described by ASD symptoms. Thus, as has been found with ADHD (Christakis *et al.*, 2004), a positive association between the amount of television viewed in the early years and a subsequent diagnosis of autism has been documented (Waldman *et al.*, 2006). It could be therefore that early absorption in visual media could reduce interest in face-to-face socialisation and instead forge a preference for the escapism found in TV, computer games etc., particularly if home circumstances provide few other opportunities for socialisation. Are such inverse pathways not also possible (lack of opportunity for socialisation causing ASD symptoms, rather than an ASD causing lack of socialisation)?

Thus, in addition to the social construction of the meanings associated with the behaviours said to be indicative of autism, we also have a diverse set of possibilities for the potential pathways that may lead to experiencing such behaviours. For some cerebral abnormalities causing difficulties in learning and proper functioning of the body and nervous system may be all that is needed to explain their behaviours. For some, severe environmental insult (such as the deprivation experienced by many in the now infamous Romanian orphanages) is a sufficient explanation. For most, a unique set of circumstances involving the interaction of biological and psychological factors could provide an explanation. As mentioned above, minor biological differences responsible for physical traits, including hand–eye coordination and sensory processing, can have significant psychological impact, especially if experienced throughout childhood in a climate of intense social competition. A combination of subtle differentiating factors may be at stake; for example, a child may come from a culturally atypical family and, owing to mild dyspraxia, fail to integrate into the local community by failing to participate in sports and having a few minor aesthetic defects that leave him or her vulnerable to exclusion. A friendless child may then withdraw into an atomised world, sometimes centred on the addictive attractions of electronic gadgetry, making it easier than ever before in human history for the disillusioned simply to join a parallel virtual universe. The autism label is of no assistance to us if we wish to develop this more complex diagnostics. Indeed, it is a hindrance as the 'autism script' focuses on establishing early diagnosis, followed by standardised interventions. The nuances of each person's circumstances are often lost in such an approach.

The behaviour of human beings is much more adaptable and susceptible to environmental conditions than that of other animals. Consider a newborn lamb that walks within minutes of her birth and contrast this with a human child who only learns to walk after months of prolonged observation and experimentation. One of the authors (NG) observed, when he took his kids' eight-month-old Labrador for a walk in the woods, that when the dog discovered a pond she splashed around happily in the shallow end, but soon began swimming in the deep end to fetch a stick his son had thrown. Their dog had never had an opportunity to swim before. So who had taught her? Obviously this behaviour is instinctual, something that can be easily learnt by her with minimal experimentation. To swim, or at least stay afloat, all one essentially needs to do is merely to move one's arms and legs around in the water, yet millions of able-bodied adult human beings have yet to overcome their fear of deep water and feel they cannot swim or have not learnt how to swim. The point here is that human beings are in different circumstances, capable of a huge range of behaviours that are much more difficult to relate to 'instinctive' drives. While all but a tiny minority of men would never dream of raping a woman, in numerous wars invading troops, aware of their newfound power in circumstances where the value of human life is severely diminished, have raped the womenfolk of the vanquished population, only to return home as apparently normal, decent citizens. In one context, the act of rape is seen as little more than a boyish prank practised at a time and place when they (literally) get away with murder. In another context, rape is (quite rightly) the act of a brutish criminal with a 'disordered' mind.

In many cultures around the world definitions of the self and concepts of self place this in a social context. For example, the concept of *Ubuntu*, prevalent in certain parts of African culture, defines a person thus: 'a person is a person through other persons'. In such cultures you are not deemed to be able to exist as a human being in isolation. It speaks about our interconnectedness. The idea of the individual as the locus of the self is a relatively recent Western invention and such a framework creates the psychological preconditions necessary for accepting the 'atomised' social worlds that have been created. In the last few generations, we have seen huge changes in the way we interact with each other and within and without our smaller atomised family units.

A growing section of the population is culturally isolated, unable, as it were, to dance to the same beat as others and compete socially. As discussed in Chapter 9, the value system of narcissism, to a large extent, pervades and structures our moral framework and sense of self in aggressively neo-liberal societies. In the atomised world this causes, socialisation patterns are as affected as any other area of life. Thus, we have an environment of competitive socialisation, often based on surface/superficial markers of identity where there is a subtext of having to market ourselves. Playing games of continuous subtle deception is one consequence, as is a difficulty in developing trusting and enduring relationships. In autism we have encapsulated the modernist paradox of creating atomised, often isolated, social units and simultaneous anxiety about the consequences of this.

Clumsiness (dyspraxia) may result from inherited or acquired neurological traits, minor brain damage, drugs, diet or psychoactive food additives, or possibly even from a sedentary lifestyle immersed in a virtual world. Whatever causes this clumsiness, being clumsy puts boys in particular at a distinct disadvantage in the male social grouping, where in the competitive playgrounds of the young, an inability to play football or show physical prowess puts you low down the pecking hierarchy. Unable to break into and find acceptance in these dominant social groups, isolated kids then need to find interests. While it may be possible to find genetic markers for dyspraxia, this does not mean that the resulting development of divergent behavioural traits necessarily results from cerebral abnormalities rather than the psychological and social consequences of 'underperformance' in popular social pastimes.

Autism and the internet

It is probably more than just coincidence that the epidemic of autism diagnoses has taken place at the same time as the rise of the internet. Someone experiencing feelings of alienation and emotional stress may first watch a documentary on mental health or even a soap opera with a character diagnosed with an ASD and then turn to the internet to learn more. Soon they are joining mailing lists and fora to learn more from those who have already been diagnosed or work with people on the autistic spectrum. Characters with Asperger's syndrome have featured in popular British TV programmes like *Grange Hill* in 1999 and *Holby City* in 2005. A quick Web search for Asperger's will lead the casual investigator to a plethora of sites promoting the orthodox neurological disorder theory and a fair number of sites maintained by 'Aspies' (a term that those diagnosed with Asperger's have adopted as a self-description), often putting a very positive spin on mainstream autism theories. In this regard we may consider the language used in these accounts, as it would certainly have confused your average Anglophone in the 1970s.

Those who consider themselves to share some affinity with the extended autistic spectrum are encouraged to refer to their autism with the first person possessive pronoun. 'My autism' is thus viewed as an inseparable part of the author or speaker. This mirrors the language used in promotional literature for antidepressants in the USA, where actors inform the target audience of 'my depression' or 'my social anxiety'. Of course, we live in a culture where people commonly refer to numerous services provided and overseen by large corporations as 'My Space', 'My MSN' or 'My Outlook'. As you delve deeper you find the ASD scene has acquired a vocabulary of its own, with terms such as 'perseverate', 'stimming' and 'sensory overload' regularly confusing the uninitiated. However, one person's autism is seldom the same as another's. For one individual it may justify atypical personal habits, mannerisms or tastes, while for another it may explain their anxiety in the presence of strangers or an uncanny tendency to express opinions when not asked. Of course, once people get drawn into spending more time in solitary activity (surfing the net), interacting with an object (the computer) rather than a real person, then this will serve as further confirmation of their 'autistic tendencies'.

AUTISTIC RIGHTS

Even if it were to be discovered that there are genuine biological differences in the brains of the most high-functioning people labelled with an ASD then so what? What do we make of these differences? Do we view those who are different in some way to a homogeneous normal (which is increasingly narrow) with some sort of suspicion or fear or 'Mother-Teresa-like' pity? Do we notice what it is that is valuable about them (do we notice them at all)? Can we accept these differences or do we have to 'fix' all (perceived) imperfections? These questions have rightly begun to concern the growing number of people diagnosed with ASDs. As a result, while psychiatry generally considers people on the autistic spectrum to be (to a large extent) disordered, some diagnosed people prefer to consider the label in a much more positive light.

One of the main tenets of the autism rights movement is the pervasiveness and monolithic continuum of the autistic spectrum. Unlike the psychiatrists, from Bleuler to Wing, who shaped our conceptions of autism and later the autistic spectrum within the context of psychiatric and more latterly neurodevelopmental disorders, the advocacy movement does not consider the diagnosed conditions pathological, but merely different, and thus worthy of the same sort of advocacy as other persecuted groups such as women, people of colour and differing sexual orientations. While this is a welcome step forward from conflating the autistic spectrum with 'disorder' of some sort, it retains features that continue to render this position problematic.

First it assumes severely retarded autistics and eccentric professor types are somehow on the same spectrum sharing a similar biogenetic aetiology, an absurd and rather meaningless idea. Second, it equates biological differences over which people have no control, such as gender and race, with largely behavioural phenomena such as sexual preferences and social behaviours. Third, there are clear distinctions to be made between culturally mediated functionality and social acceptability of various behaviours. If a culture considers a behavioural pattern dysfunctional or anti-social, that does not mean people liable to indulge in such conduct have a clearly defined genetic deviation, whether caused by a single gene or by a complex interaction of multiple genes. The ideology of genetic determinism that considers the more benign aspects of ASD to be caused by deviant genes, applies the same logic to psychopaths and paedophiles. As some deviant behaviour is clearly anti-social, this empowers psychiatry to intervene in case of any persistent deviant behaviour that conflicts with the dominant socialisation model. One may reasonably wonder why watching *EastEnders* every day and spending over ten hours a week gambling online is not considered pathological, while checking and collecting outdated bus timetables and spending over ten hours a week exploring obscure websites about defunct programming languages is somehow a sign of a genetic disorder or difference. Both are equally dysfunctional in terms of wasting time, whereas the former activity may expose the addict to greater financial risk, the latter is in itself harmless, but rendered more pathological, because of its uncommon nature.

In its most radical form this 'autistic rights' movement has been likened (by its adherents) to campaigns by other repressed variations of the human condition, such as women, ethnic minorities, racial groups and homosexuals. However, these are very disparate groups. People classified on the spectrum have an enormous range of functional adaptation. At the milder end of the ASD spectrum, a teenager, who dedicates his spare time to learning new programming languages, may forgo many socialising opportunities, but this obsessive interest may build the foundations of a future career. By contrast, a stereotypical autistic savant may exhibit detailed knowledge of obscure subjects such as the history of London buses, but would lack the accompanying skills required to transform a special interest into career. The former's divergence from the norm may prove functionally adaptive and even socially useful in certain situations and contexts (e.g., successful athletes, by focusing less on frivolous socialising one can nurture talents that may prove useful to certain employers), while the latter is unlikely to be capable of such achievement. By lumping these disparate 'autisms' together, the call for 'equal rights' with (for example) employment discrimination, is a bit ludicrous.

If the autistic spectrum lacks scientific validity, resulting in the label being applied to a group of people that range from sufferers of severe cerebral abnormality to a wider group of people who have developed mild autistic-like traits for a variety of reasons, we should question the role of such a diagnosis. Do those who work with severely withdrawn or learning disabled 'autistics' have that much in common with articulate 'Aspies' who have set themselves a mission to make the world more autistic-friendly? Much could indeed be done to accommodate 'Aspies' both at school and at work. For example:

- Smaller class sizes make it easier for teachers to attend to the varying emotional and didactic needs of their students without isolating children with different learning patterns.
- More socially cohesive and inclusive communities, in which people do not have to earn respect by conforming to culturally defined behavioural norms and are valued simply because they belong to a community.
- Promotion of a range of more community-centred activities that may appeal to different subsets of the local community with differing natural strengths and weaknesses.
- Greater respect for individual creativity and talent rather than forcing everyone to conform by channelling their creative talents to an amorphous 'hive mentality'.

- Removal of unnecessary sensory interference such as background pop music in the workplace and relinquishing the demand to engage in 'networking'.
- Dealing effectively with bullies.
- Trying to understand the particular circumstances that have led a particular individual to become isolated and alienated. And so on.

To many it may seem paradoxical that disability rights have taken a higher profile in the same time frame as the transition from the post-Second World War welfare state and a largely industrial economy to a predominantly service-orientated, post-industrial neo-liberal economy with a widening wealth gap. While some physical and sensory impairments are obvious cases for social intervention in any compassionate society, most of the UK's 2.5 million disabled residents are not paraplegic, blind or deaf. Anything from diabetes, dyslexia, myalgic encephalitis to depression may be classified as a disability. This transforms a diverse set of illnesses, divergent learning patterns and emotional problems into neat categories of victimhood, in which the culprit is nature rather than society (Summerfield and Veale, 2008). This trend also erects an artificial barrier between the general population and the perceived victims. Within the field of mental functioning/disability, three broad groupings have had differing discourses developing around them: mental retardation/learning difficulties, character/personality disorders and emotional/mental health problems.

In relation to this, the autistic spectrum is interesting as it has spurred a variety of discourses that span all three groupings. To gain acceptance by clinicians and patients alike, we no longer talk of mental handicaps but of learning disabilities, a concept that may apply both to cognitive deficits and a lack of social acumen. While a person with severe learning difficulties may not be expected to distinguish the relative value of a £20 banknote and a 20p coin, a socially inept high-functioning autistic may not be expected to be aware of the offence caused by his eccentric behaviour. By this logic the kind of cerebral differences responsible for severe mental retardation are equated with relative degrees of street wisdom and tact, with the unacknowledged underlying assumption being that the social skills expected in certain communities and settings in modern Anglo-American societies depend on innate biological tendencies. Likewise, developments in psychiatry have blurred the boundaries between mental health/illness and personality disorders.

While autism-promotion organisations do not claim a one-to-one correlation between anti-social personality and the extended autistic spectrum, as a lack of empathy is meant to be a core feature of the spectrum, it should not surprise us that ASD is now becoming linked with various forms of criminality. As (particularly male) ASD-diagnosed individuals are meant to be less likely to form stable consensual relationships and may not be as aware of the emotional consequences of their actions, it follows that they will, for example, come to be viewed as more susceptible to the attractions of sexual liaisons with emotionally immature and vulnerable minors. This is the embedded logic of preventative psychiatric screening – to identify children exhibiting behaviours that may potentially lead to psychopathic traits and ASD is becoming a key figure in this drama.

We have become familiar with a mental health problem and psychiatric disorders being equated in the public's mind with 'dangerousness'. This popularised idea, promoted by the media, is aired when someone who has contact with a mental health service, or has been in receipt of a psychiatric diagnosis, commits a murderous outrage. This is often followed by sentiment that they have been failed by the mental health system (usually on the basis that they should have been locked up rather than allowed to mingle with the general public unsupervised). In a similar manner we wonder how much media publicity will be devoted to forms of criminality which are now increasingly being linked with disorders of 'empathy' of which ASD is a prime example. With the number of young people who have displayed unruly or anti-social behaviour in childhood increasingly being diagnosed with an ASD, more people already diagnosed are entering into the criminal justice system. Consider the 2004 trial of Lincolnshire resident and Asperger's syndrome-diagnosed teen Paul Smith:

> Nigel and Susan Smith say his Asperger's Syndrome has made him vulnerable. But the 18-year-old was the last person seen with the young ballet star at a party before she was found smothered to death on a bed. Incriminating traces of his DNA were discovered on a can of Guinness at the little girl's bedside...Smith was 17 at the time he murdered Rosie as 60 people gathered downstairs at his Uncle Ian's house in Normanton...Because of his Asperger's Syndrome, Smith lacked social skills and talked in an unemotional and stilted way throughout the trial. But despite a common perception of such sufferers being honest and trustworthy, Smith maintained from the start that he had not touched the youngster. Experts have found no link between the condition and violent crime, and traditionally

sufferers were said to be more likely to become victims than offenders. However, a lack of empathy for others and an inability to understand the consequences of their actions could lead an aggressive sufferer to lose control. (http://news.bbc.co.uk/1/hi/england/lincolnshire/3962293.stm, accessed 19 March 2009)

Despite the reassuring rhetoric from organisations like the National Autistic Society, the popular media have done much to associate in the public mind forms of criminality with 'personality' and other psychiatric disorders, including autism. A classic line, often repeated, is the inability of AS and autistic people to understand the relationship between cause and effect, that is, they are allegedly unaware of the consequences of their actions, however well-intentioned. Surely our ability to fully comprehend these connections varies enormously among a very wide cross-section of the population.

Although many have observed the slippery slope from psychiatric or behavioural genetics to eugenics (which we discuss in Chapter 11), much of the wishful thinking political left has not just been oblivious to this trend, but has actually jumped on the bandwagon, in a, presumably well-intentioned, wish to pursue various minority rights campaigns. For example, suggesting that sexual orientation is at least partly culturally mediated is a real 'no, no'. One potential consequence of such genetic determinism is that if homosexuality is supposed to be genetically determined, then presumably other forms of sexuality including criminal orientations such as paedophilia are also genetically determined. Behavioural genetics, like any other science, is not as concerned with morality, but rather with predicting behavioural outcomes from genetic markers. By pursuing this line of logic you could make logical arguments for biogenetic correlations between homosexuality and paedophilia, both of which lack a procreational motive and thus could be viewed as deviations from what 'mother nature' biologically originally intended (perhaps existing on a 'spectrum'). While it may well be the case that a complex set of genes may predispose individuals to exhibit certain behavioural patterns in given circumstances, even a cursory examination of the evidence reveals the significance of environmental factors. The widespread practice of what we now call homosexuality by 'heterosexual' men and adolescents in situations where other erotic outlets are unavailable (e.g., when hunting, at war, in prisons, or in single-sex institutions) is commonly known. It is largely down to society to determine the morality or social acceptability of these acts, but 'science' (or just an illusion of it) can be used to let the ruling classes, in a society based on a 'science-fearing' cosmology, gain greater control over individuals.

In today's cultural climate any statements challenging the new orthodoxy on disabilities may be viewed as offensive to the disabled themselves. If we challenge the scientific validity of the autistic spectrum theory, we risk being accused of denying hundreds of thousands of children, teenagers and young adults of the help and support they need and downplaying the extent of the emotional stress they (and their carers) experience. This, of course, assumes that a disability label and intrusive monitoring of behaviour benefits the diagnosed, something we have challenged throughout this book from both a theoretical and empirical position (see, for example, Chapter 8). Focusing resources on interventions with little to no proven benefit risks diverting these resources away from other forms of social intervention that may help the emotionally vulnerable. Furthermore, if one has been convinced or 'psycho-educated' about having an innate social ineptness, one may lower one's expectations in terms of personal and professional development.

Some of the idiosyncratic traits commonly associated with AS have to be understood in their cultural context, otherwise we risk making absurd demands for marginal rights based on idiosyncratic lifestyle habits without assuming our responsibilities as citizens. For instance, NG has come across a man diagnosed with AS in his mid-30s following years of unemployment and teenage crisis, who claims AS is the explanation for his choice to wear un-ironed shorts in all weather conditions, a choice which thus precludes him from most office jobs with minimum dress standards. While it would be perfectly rational to campaign for greater dress freedom, this particular man's claim may easily be viewed as an excuse to shun work and would certainly appear odd in societies with much stricter dress codes and harsher economic conditions, where the work-shy may simply opt to adapt or starve. For some, an AS diagnosis causes the individual to lower their expectations and self-esteem (e.g., 'I can't get a job because I lack people skills'), which then becomes a self-fulfilling prophecy (particularly in a country where most jobs now require excellent team-playing skills).

The autistic rights movement have not thought these implications through. Unlike them, we think that the best way to get proper rights and acceptance of the behavioural style of those who could or are diagnosed with an ASD is to abolish the label.

SUMMARY AND SOME CONCLUDING THOUGHTS

Having demonstrated how little support there is for the scientific validity or clinical utility of the diagnosis of 'autism' as it is currently conceived, we then turned our attention to trying to understand why 'autism' has become such a popular diagnosis. This chapter has built on the arguments we made in Chapter 9 where we highlighted a growing cultural concern in Western societies about the 'problem with boys'. Referring to the work of Karl Marx, Michel Foucault and Max Weber, we argued that the subjective ideologies any ruling system uses, including those that relate to mental health and personality development, support the ruling classes and the values that underpin the economy. In a service economy, dependent on quick face-to-face encounters, the 'hard sell' and emotional manipulation of the population, socio-cultural conditions are created for an interest in autism and the expansion of the concept.

We then discussed how cultural conditions have been created in Western societies that increase the chances of alienation, social withdrawal and peculiar solitary interests and how these essentially socially generated problems come to be viewed as the problems of an individual biogenetic disorder (autism).

We also examined the interesting parallel growth of a protest movement, calling for 'autistic rights' and arguing that autism is a (biologically based) difference not a disorder. While broadly sympathetic to their ideals and aims, we believe the concept of autism doesn't deserve the status of disorder or difference and, instead, we highlighted the dangers of this movement staying loyal with the pseudoscience supporting the concept (dangers that we further highlight in Chapter 11) while campaigning for a different interpretation. We argued that instead the term should be abolished, as it is unlikely that the cultural shift both we and the autistic rights movement would like to see – such as destigmatisation and greater tolerance of diversity – is likely to come via the 'difference' route (see Chapter 12). Indeed, we believe the very existence of such a pseudoscientific concept and its voracious expansion is a reflection of our increasingly narcissistic cultural conformism engendering a hive mentality, to a degree that our Western liberal societies are starting to look more like the totalitarian states they have consistently criticised.

It is not unusual to claim that psychiatric and psychological mythology reflects the interests of the society. This was the basis of much of the Marxist-inspired Frankfurt School of critical psychology and the more recent post-modern analyses begun by Michel Foucault. Even in the most politically aware of the psychotherapies, family therapy, Asen (2006) shows how the political climate contributes to the emergence of particular approaches, for example, brief 'solution-focused' therapy emerged during the Reagan and Thatcher years, reflecting the developing business climate of being 'deaf' to problems and with an almost compulsive looking for alleged solutions. Others such as Moncreiff (2008a) argue that the increase in psychiatric drug prescribing coincides with neo-liberalism's need to keep the population focused on individualisation of problems to render the socio-political causes of their unhappiness invisible and to service a desire to keep expanding potential markets (in this case for psychotropic drugs). Timimi (2008b) makes a similar point with regards the labelling and prescribing of psychiatric drugs to children. Here we have expanded this argument to illustrate why the rise in autism has more to do with the dynamics of a service-orientated neo-liberal economy than scientific discoveries leading to better recognition.

11
THE NEW EUGENICS

The history of the mental health movement is replete with tragic examples of well-intentioned attempts by a 'caring' medical profession to improve the mental well being of both individuals and society – attempts that wittingly or unwittingly make things worse for those individuals and the societies they live in, sometimes appallingly worse. The history of the mental health movement is just as replete with failures to learn from these examples, such that the same mistakes keep being made. Without solid empirical support for the diagnostic categories used, if we persist in using them anyway as if they already had that solid grounding then they will always be vulnerable to medicalisation processes and to being used by a variety of actors from state down to families for social-control purposes. As long as we continue to use treatments with known risks and little efficacy, then that social control agenda is in danger of being used in a way that is harmful to both individuals and society. This is why stories of historical abuses need to be told, re-told and re-told again. As Whitaker (2002) and many others (most notably the service-user movement) passionately argues, those abuses have not disappeared and 'modern' mental healthcare is just as full of examples of inhuman, degrading and unethical practice. In this chapter we remind the reader about one of the most tragic and extreme examples of these abuses. Our recounting of the eugenic story should not be read in a concrete manner as if we are suggesting that expanding into ASDs leads to eugenic policies, but it is intended to serve as the strongest warning of the potentially unintended and negative consequences of promoting medical technology as possessing the gift for solving social and political concerns.

Use of psychiatric diagnoses to support state ideology has a long history. For example, in the USA there were the diagnostic categories used for slaves before the Civil War. At that time, physicians in states with slavery could use the terms *dysathesia aetiopica* for disobedient slaves who refused to obey their masters and *drapetomania* for slaves who had what was thought to be a pathological desire to run away, because they wanted to live as free human beings rather than as slaves (Thomas, 1974). By taking this position at that time, clinicians were merely following the logic of the predominantly racist beliefs of the government and the ruling population.

THE EUGENIC MOVEMENT

The most frightening mental health-inspired movement emerged in Western psychiatry about 100 years ago. This movement, that came to be known as the 'Eugenic' movement, illustrates the sinister outcomes that can result from medicalisation based on pseudoscience, when it is fused with the aims and values of the ruling classes. With simplistic 'survival of the fittest' philosophy driving its beliefs, we see in Eugenics how 'Darwinism' can become an ideology that promotes a 'grand narrative' of biological reductionism on human life, with tragic and dangerous consequences (like Marxism can do for social reductionism or Freudianism for psychological reductionism).

Towards the end of the 19th century and the beginning of the 20th century a belief was emerging, claimed to be based on science, that the 'mentally ill' were carriers of bad genes, and that they posed a serious threat to the future health of society. Many scientific articles, newspaper editorials and popular books were written about this at that time. In these articles and books, the mentally ill were described as a degenerate strain of humanity that bred at alarming rates and burdened the 'normal' population with the great expense of paying for their upkeep. In North America this led to a wholesale societal assault on those deemed mentally ill. They were prohibited from marrying in many states, forcibly committed to state hospitals in great numbers and many were sterilised against their will (Whitaker, 2002).

This movement first started with studies conducted by Sir Francis Galton (cousin of Charles Darwin). In 1869, Galton published a scientific work, *Hereditary Genius*, in which he concluded that it was nature, rather than nurture (genes rather than up-bringing) that made the 'superior' man. Galton studied the family trees of nearly 1,000 prominent English leaders and found that this top class came from a small, select group of people. Although this was probably stating the obvious – that in a class-conscious England, privilege led to success – to Galton his research provided proof that intelligence was inherited and that a small group of successful English families enjoyed the benefits of being born with 'superior' genes. In 1883, Galton invented the term 'eugenics', derived from the Greek word 'well-born', as a name for the science that he believed would improve human beings by giving the more intelligent and superior people and races a better chance of reproducing (Kelves, 1985).

Galton was trying to apply in a crude and simplistic way the concept, discovered by his cousin Charles Darwin, of 'natural selection' to the complexities of human society. It was to be a science devoted to dividing the human race into two classes, the eugenic (or well-born) and the cacogenic (or poorly born). The cacogenic group would be seen as having inherited bad or inferior genes and therefore, as a group, they should, at the very least, not be allowed to breed. In this new eugenic view of humankind the mentally ill were seen as among the most unfit, with insanity seen as the final stage of a progressive deterioration of a family's gene pool.

The eugenic ideology found a receptive audience in the USA, where many prominent authors and scientists began arguing that the mentally unfit should not be allowed to breed. At the turn of the last century, private funding to Harvard-educated biologist Charles Davenport began the trend into the 'scientific' study of the genetics of human inheritance with the underlying agenda of proving that eugenics was based on good science. Davenport applied a genetic model to studying complex behaviours in humans, proposing that a single gene controlled each behavioural trait. After a few years Davenport was suggesting that immigrants, the mentally ill and all sorts of societal misfits were genetically inferior and confidently writing that people could inherit genes for 'shiftlessness', thieving, prostitution and insincerity (Whitaker, 2002).

The selling of the eugenic ideals to the public began in earnest in 1921 in North America, when the American museum of natural history hosted the second international congress on eugenics, a meeting financed in a large part by the Carnegie Institution and the Rockefeller Foundation. At this conference, papers on the financial cost incurred to society by caring for 'defectives', the inheritability of insanity and other disorders, and the low birth rates of the 'elite' in America were presented. Talks were given on topics such as the Jewish problem, the dangers of Negro and white intermixture and the families of 'paupers' (the poor). At the close of the conference a national eugenics society was established, sending out a message that warned that society was seeing a 'racial deterioration' and that societal leaders needed to resist what they saw as the forthcoming complete destruction of the white race, if their message was ignored. The congress was covered in the leading national newspapers that reported on the eugenic ideals in a sympathetic manner (Chase, 1980).

At the close of this international conference Davenport, together with other prominent eugenicists, formed a committee, which led to the establishment of a national eugenics society. The American Eugenics Society (AES) focused on promoting eugenics to the American public through textbooks, pamphlets and information campaigns, aimed at building support for sterilisation laws. By the 1930s eugenic ideas had become popular among the public. Franz Kallman, Chief of research at the New York State Psychiatric Institute, claimed that even lovers of individual liberty had to agree that mankind would be much happier if societies could get rid of their 'mentally ill' individuals who were, in his belief, not biologically satisfactory (Kallman, 1938). Earnest Hooton, Harvard professor of anthropology, in his 1937 book *Apes, Men and Morons*, compared the insane to cancers in society whose genes should be considered poisonous, suggesting that the situation in America was so critical that it demanded an urgent 'surgical' operation.

From the late 19th century, American eugenicists had been arguing that the mentally ill should be prevented from having children. This propaganda began to influence state legislators in the USA from 1896, when Connecticut became the first state to prohibit the 'insane' from the right to marry. By 1914, more than 20 states had passed such laws and by 1933 all states in the USA had passed laws effectively prohibiting marriage for those deemed to be mentally ill. Yet few eugenicists believed such laws did much good, most considering this to be an inadequate response to the problem. Eugenicists were instead arguing that the insane should first be segregated in asylums and then sterilised to prevent their 'bad' genes from reproducing.

In 1907, Indiana became the first state in the USA to pass a compulsory sterilisation law. It did so in the name of science, the bill stating that hereditary research (i.e., scientific activity) had shown that genetic inheritance plays a dominant role in the transmission of crime, 'idiocy' and 'imbecility'. Over the next two decades 30 state legislatures approved sterilisation bills and repeatedly they did so based on an argument that science had proven that 'defectives' bred 'defectives'. Opponents, who included Catholics and non-English immigrant groups, argued that these laws violated constitutional safeguards against cruel and unusual punishments, leading some states to be challenged on their sterilisation laws. However, in 1927 the United States Supreme Court, by an eight to one majority, in the case of *Buck* v. *Bell*, ruled that sterilization laws were constitutional, adding that scientific evidence had shown that heredity played an important part in the transmission of 'insanity' and 'imbecility' (Chase, 1980). Soon institutions such as the California Department of Mental Hygiene began listing sterilisation as a medical 'treatment' that could be provided to 'mentally ill' patients in its state hospitals (Popenoe, 1935).

Before the existence of Hitler's death camps became common knowledge in the USA, eugenics had become a popular topic among psychiatrists and psychologists there. As in Germany, the debate had by then expanded from the wisdom of breeding better humans to include the topic of preventing, and even doing away with altogether, those who were considered genetically inferior.

Two years after the United States Supreme Court, deemed it constitutional, Denmark passed a sterilisation law. Over the next few years Norway, Sweden, Finland and Iceland did too. America's influence on Nazi Germany was particularly pronounced and it was, of course, in that country that eugenics ran its full course. In the 1920s America was the world centre of eugenic activity: between 1907 and 1940 more than 100,000 Americans were involuntarily sterilised in more than 30 states. State bureaucracies determined who would be sterilised and who could breed. This banner of building national racial superiority was picked up in England, Finland, Sweden and a dozen other countries by 1930.

In other parts of the world, such as Australia, New Zealand, USA and Canada, eugenic ideals of racial purity were linked with those of cultural assimilation. First-nation and aboriginal children were removed from their parents and sent to foster homes or children's homes in order to be brought up with white Christian beliefs and values. This cultural genocide, which led to what many indigenous peoples refer to as the 'stolen generation', continued well into recent decades. For example, these policies continued in one form or another into the 1970s in Australia, leading to catastrophic disruption of families and cultural identities and a legacy of poor physical and mental health and continuing racism and discrimination that will take many generations to begin to heal.

Much as US eugenicists had done, German eugenicists sought to develop scientific evidence that 'mental illnesses' were inherited and that these 'genetic diseases' were spreading through its population and causing deterioration in the population's gene pool. In 1925, the American Rockefeller Foundation gave $2.5 million to the psychiatric institute in Munich, which quickly became Germany's leading centre for eugenic research. The Rockefeller Foundation also gave money to the Institute for Anthropology, Human Genetics and Eugenics in Berlin, which used this money to pay for a national survey of 'degenerative traits' in the German population (Whitaker, 2002).

After Hitler came to power in 1933, Germany passed a comprehensive sterilisation bill. The German eugenicists who drew up that legislation had learnt from the US experience, which many American eugenicists noted with some pride. Many in Germany and in the USA saw the Nazi bill as morally superior to any US state law, praising Germany's sterilisation programme as an example of a desirable modern health programme. Praise for German eugenics found particular favour among American psychiatrists. For example, the American Neurological Association published an official report on eugenic sterilisation, praising Hitler's sterilisation programme (Breggin and Breggin, 1998). A year before war broke out with Germany, American psychiatrist Aaron Rosanhoff, in his textbook *Manual of Psychiatry and Mental Hygiene*, favourably compared the German to the American sterilisation programme, concluding that eugenics is a scientific rather than political exercise (Rosanhoff, 1938).

With eugenic ideology talking about the 'mentally ill' as social wastage, malignant cancerous growths and so on, it was only a short step to move from sterilisation to getting rid of such people all together. In 1935, Alexis Carrel, a Nobel Prize-winning physician at the Rockefeller Institute for Medical Research in New York, made this point in his book *Man, the Unknown*. In his book Carrel wondered why societies preserve useless and potentially harmful human beings; he suggested that society should dispose of criminals and the insane in a humane and economical manner in small euthanasia institutions supplied with 'proper gasses'.

Learning from these American ideas, Nazi Germany began killing their mentally ill with these 'proper gasses', in January 1940. Over the course of the next 18 months the Nazi's gassed more than 70,000 mental patients. Euthanasia forms were filled in on thousands of patients by hospital doctors throughout Germany and these forms were then sent to Berlin for the final life and death determination by a team of

50 psychiatrists, including ten professors of psychiatry. Unlike the subsequent mass enslavement and murder of the Jews, the killing of mental patients drew heated criticism from the public and some religious leaders and, in August 1941, Hitler withdrew his approval. However, acting without official sanction doctors continued killing on their own in local mental hospitals, a practice that spread to occupied countries such as France, where without an official order, psychiatrists killed an estimated 40,000 of their patients (Breggin and Breggin, 1998). A path that had begun 75 years earlier with Galton's study of the English ruling classes had wound its way through the corridors of American science, finally reaching its stated goal in the hands of German psychiatrists, who took the lead in developing Germany's murderous euthanasia programme.

To help us understand how doctors in general, and psychiatrists in particular, have played such a leading role in developing, first the ideology and then the technology, that led initially to the extermination of thousands of psychiatric patients and then (using the euthanasia techniques developed on mental patients) to millions of Jews, we need to examine the dynamics of medicalisation (see below, under the subheading 'The dynamics of "medicalisation"'). Human experience examined through the prism of apparent scientific objectivity lends itself perfectly to be used by the political system of the day. With the idea that bad genes possess these 'deviants', it is a short step to proposing eugenic solutions for this perceived 'medical' problem. Medical practitioners can then excuse their actions by believing that they are participating in a 'treatment' that is for the good of the future medical well being of society (a kind of public health/prevention programme). Thus, psychiatrists involved in exterminating inpatients did not merely supervise; it was often the duty of a psychiatrist to open the valve of the cylinder containing the carbon monoxide as if they were supervising a treatment (Muller-Hill, 1991). If doctors can legitimise and even carry out murders (under the guise of 'treatment') then others can more easily rationalise their own participation in this endeavour.

Following the euthanasia programme on psychiatric inpatients, the equipment used in these euthanasia centres was dismantled and then used to construct the holocaust extermination camps. Not only was the equipment that psychiatrists had helped develop used, but also psychiatrists went to the camps and conducted the first official, systematic murders of Jews. These teams diagnosed and then selected victims using the euthanasia forms and then had the inmates sent to their deaths at the psychiatric extermination centres during the early stages of the holocaust. Furthermore, historians agree that the psychiatrists were in no way forced; indeed, they often did this task without protest and often on their own initiative (Proctor, 1988).

THE DYNAMICS OF 'MEDICALISATION'

With this grizzly episode in the history of medicine and psychiatry behind us you would have thought that the eugenic ideals would be firmly confined to the pages of history. Not so, this is because the central idea that made eugenics seem desirable and then turned it into a reality is still with us – that of medicalising the social complexities of the human experience. This is where we have grave concerns about the possible unintended consequences of the autism lobby and the autistic rights movement. Doctors and other senior professionals have a huge influence and power to turn our social and cultural expectations into medical definitions of physical health. As we have argued, those who don't conform to these social and cultural expectations can then be labelled as being medically unwell or disabled. We must now ask the question – can the ideals and practices of the eugenics movement slip back into current thinking (or, indeed, are they doing so already)?

While there are obvious apparent benefits from a medical conceptualisation of mental and behavioural problems (such as alleviation of blame and passing the responsibility for finding solutions to a health professional), the process is fraught with potential dangers. Conrad (1975) suggested the following are key characteristics of medicalisation of deviance: if a problem is defined as medical it is removed from public and more ordinary forums to 'expert' ones and thus expert control over the issue; it allows the use of 'medical' treatments that would otherwise not be considered; it individualises the problem, thereby removing the need to see a societal problem; and it depoliticises the problem of deviance.

Medicalisation means that a complex array of reasons for challenging behaviour and social deviance can be 'dumbed down' into simplified medical categories that become the responsibility of medical professionals to solve; others (such as teachers) are distanced from bringing their skills and knowledge into trying to understand, deal with, and change the situation. Furthermore, as medicalisation of a particular issue gathers momentum, having been taken out of the 'folk' cultural sphere and into the 'expert' medical one, it then returns back into the cultural sphere with a new language and set of practices attached to it. Thus many groups (such as doctors, researchers, advocacy groups, health services, pharmaceutical industry and media) take up the new concepts, together with the practices now attached to them, and start popularising them such that the new medical construct gets reincorporated into everyday discourse and language (Danforth and Navarro, 2001). Thus, autism started life 50 years ago as a narrow, rare, mysterious disorder and has changed its cultural position through films such as *Rain Man*, books such as *The Curious Incident of the Dog in the Night-time*, the work of advocacy organisations such as the *National Autistic Society*, media scares such as the MMR vaccine, increasing exposure (particularly in schools) to children diagnosed with the 'new' autisms and so on, to reach its current medically developed cultural status as an escalating frequent genetic disorder, with numbers of those being diagnosed increasing so rapidly that there are often alarmist claims that we are experiencing an 'epidemic'.

The movement of such large numbers of individuals out of the more everyday categories of problems on which the accumulated cultural knowledge can be drawn, into the medical expert category for which medically constituted knowledge and practices are needed, renders a large group vulnerable to being caught up in political concerns of governments for whom (as we have outlined) a perceived deficiency in social or emotional competence is something they wish to eliminate.

THE RE-EMERGENCE OF EUGENICS

After the Second World War exposed the horrors of the extermination camps, proponents of eugenics became, not surprisingly, rather quiet. The only high-profile American scientist in the 1950s who was willing to publicly suggest that we should continue eugenics programmes was Nobel Laureate William Shockley (1910–1989), a physicist at Stanford University. After winning his Nobel Prize in Physics (not in genetics), he openly suggested people with IQs lower than 100 should submit to voluntary sterilisation (see http://en.wikipedia.org/wiki/William_ Shockley, accessed 2 April 2009). His widely publicised views gave encouragement to the quiet but ongoing eugenics programmes in the USA, which were only stopped in the 1960s with the revelation by Robert Kennedy that over 100,000 poor blacks, Native Americans and mental patients had been sterilised without their knowledge or consent, as doctors in 30 states doing the sterilisations told their unwitting patients that they were performing 'a slightly painful pelvic examination' or 'routine surgery to prevent later disease'.

The field of behavioural genetics (the linking of behaviours to particular genes in a not dissimilar way to what Davenport, discussed above, was doing at the turn of the 20th century) has been discussing with great optimism the findings of the 'Human Genome Project', suggesting that in the not too distant future we will be able to test children's genes before they are born and provide so-called gene therapy to correct any genes that are considered undesirable (Corvin and Gill, 2003). Do we not already offer abortions for children with known genetic abnormalities (we are not here taking up a pro or anti choice position)? New screening methods mean we can test for hundreds of possible genetic abnormalities or mutations that may result in the carrier being afflicted with known diseases. If we discover genes or perhaps a group of genes that contribute towards, let's say, hyperactivity, which is now defined as a medical disorder, is it beyond the realms of possibility in our current culture (let alone a more totalitarian one) that we would then start offering abortions on medical grounds for children found to be carrying these genes? And what of the children already born with those genes. If we have already medicalised this problem, to what extent would or should we go to in order to 'treat' and otherwise control these children (as children and then as adults)?

A telling example comes from the government-funded violence initiative in the USA. Back in the 1970s, Mednick and Christiansen (1977) proposed a biomedical screening programme, including screening approaches based on teacher ratings, to take place at elementary (primary) schools for early detection of future criminals. This proposal came out at a time when government agencies were indeed funding psychiatrists and neuro-surgeons who claimed that urban riots that had occurred were caused by genetic defects and brain disease in individual African Americans. Some of these doctors were advocating psychiatric brain surgery for selected rioters and even their leaders. One independent project in Mississippi was actually performing psycho-surgical operations on the brains of African American children deemed to be hyperactive and aggressive (Breggin and Breggin, 1998). Fortunately, critics at the time compared these so-called treatment programmes to measures used in Nazi Germany and many of the programmes were abandoned under pressure, or took on other guises. For a time bio-psychiatrists were then discouraged from publicising their efforts to find biological forms of control for urban violence.

Then, at the beginning of the 1990s, Dr Goodwin, who was chief scientist at the National Institute of Mental Health in the USA and one of the government's top research psychiatrists, feeling that public attitudes were more favourable again, re-publicised the idea that the violence-prone individual was suffering from a physical brain ailment that could be diagnosed and treated. Indeed, in one of his speeches Goodwin went on to compare inner-city youth to monkeys who live in the jungle and who just want to kill each other and have sex. Goodwin not only re-proposed the idea of developing screening programmes to be administered to school children to discover potential violent offenders, but in addition proposed that many might then be treated from an early age with psychiatric medication (Breggin and Breggin, 1998).

Goodwin's ideas soon found favour in government circles leading the national research council in the USA to publish the report *Understanding and Preventing Violence* (Reiss and Roth, 1993), which provided a blueprint for a national violence initiative sympathetic to Goodwin's ideas and suggesting an important role for finding biomedical causes and treating them. During the same year a review of violence research taking place at the US National Institute of Health found that violence research was very much alive in the USA with over 300 research projects, totalling $42 million, being funded in 1992 and with the bulk of the work taking place at the National Institute of Mental Health. Many projects were funded by government agencies as well as private foundations and included many prominent psychiatrists, including a professor of child psychiatry at Harvard Medical School (Felton Earls). Earls' vision, like Goodwin's, was based on 'disease' prevention, with the aim of screening and identifying individual children as potential offenders in need of preventative treatment or control. As with many in similar projects, Earls hoped the research he was involved in would link key biological and environmental factors that play a role in the development of criminal behaviour with a particular emphasis on searching for biomedical markers such as neurotransmitter problems and genetic abnormalities that can then be targeted for 'preventative' treatment (Earls, 1991).

In the well-known book *The Bell Curve* (Murray and Hernstein, 1994), the authors claim it is inherited genes not environment or upbringing that is the main determinant of how well a person does in life. Since then it has become safer and more popular for those who believe there are evolutionarily superior and inferior humans, to go public with their opinions. For example, citing race as proof of evolutionary status, Michael Levin, in his 1997 book *Why Race Matters*, uses a claim that not one of the 1,500 discoveries listed in Asimov's *Chronology of Science and Discovery* was made by a Negroid person, as part of his basis for arguing that as far as he is concerned white people are smarter than blacks.

Nobel Prize-winner and driving force behind the Human Genome Project, James Watson, clearly feels that science, in the shape of manipulating genes, should be left to get on with it and should ignore any of the moral or ethical implications:

> My view is that despite the risks, we should give serious consideration to germ-line therapy. I only hope that the many biologists who share my opinion will stand tall in the debates to come and not be intimidated by the inevitable criticism. Some of us already know the pain of being tarred with the brush once reserved for eugenicists. But that is ultimately a small price to pay to redress genetic injustice. If such work be called eugenics, then I am a eugenicist. (Watson, 2003: 401)

In his book *DNA: The Secret of Life*, Watson (2003) ignores any discussion about what makes one person somehow more valuable or important than another and is eager that we start exploring how biotechnology could eliminate 'mental illness', 'violence' and 'learning difficulties'. All the same fundamental philosophical mistakes, that inspired the original eugenicists to try and biologically engineer a society free of genetic 'misfits', that led eventually to such unimaginable human tragedy, are made. Watson's main criticism of the eugenics movement seems to be that that they were poor scientists:

> There is no legitimate rationale for modern genetics to avoid certain questions simply because they were of interest to the discredited eugenics movement. The critical difference is this: Davenport and his like simply had no scientific tools with which to uncover the genetic basis for any behavioural trait they studied. Their science was not equipped to reveal any material realities that would have confirmed or refuted their speculations. (Watson, 2003: 365)

As we move to find increasing numbers of the population as behaviourally, socially or emotionally 'unfit' in some way, some physicians have now come forward to suggest that such people should be encouraged not to have children, lest their 'genetic weaknesses' or lower evolutionary status be passed on to future generations. One such voice is Dr David Comings. The theory of his book, *The Gene*

Bomb (1996), is that people with 'undesirable behaviour' (in which he includes autism) tend to have less education and to produce children at an earlier age (interpreted as a sign of a neurological weakness resulting in impulsivity, of course) than well-educated persons, and therefore have more children. This produces a surplus of 'undesirable' people, carrying 'undesirable' genes, among our population. This, he suggests is the main reason for the rates of autism in the population increasing.

The revival of the impulse to medicalise social issues has led to a revival of interest in dangerous and brain-damaging so-called treatments, with children increasingly seen as a primary target for such 'preventative' interventions. Methods such as electroconvulsive therapy and using high doses of toxic, often unlicensed psychotropic drugs normally used in adults with severe and chronic 'mental illness' are increasingly advocated for 'treating' young children with a variety of problems, including aggression. Influenced by drug company lobbying, a recent development has been the adoption by the US government of the longed-for ideal of many biological psychiatrists – that is to develop a mental health screening programme for all school children. 'Teen screen' is the scheme developed by the pharmaceutical industry and pushed forward by the Bush administration to screen the US public school population for psychiatric disorders (see http://www.teenscreen.org, accessed 2 April 2009).

Although at this stage 'Teen Screen' and other screening programmes are meant to be voluntary, there are already examples of the screen being used without parent's knowledge or consent. Critics are claiming that if a teenager doesn't like doing maths assignments, 'Teen Screen' may determine that the child has a psychiatric illness called 'developmental-arithmetic disorder'. 'Oppositional-defiant disorder' could be diagnosed if the teenager argues with their parents, and, if anybody is critical of the above two disorders, they may be suffering from 'noncompliance-with-treatment disorder'!

Underpinning the eugenic movement was the view that all manner of socially undesirable traits (including mental ill health) was the product of faulty genes and that to improve the health of society these faulty genes needed eliminating. One of the main factors that made the eugenic philosophy acceptable for such a long period was the fact that respected members of the public (doctors) were arguing that a whole array of social and psychological problems were the result of individuals having genetic disorders. Successfully medicalising such issues opened the door to the use of medical 'remedies' (such as sterilisation) to deal with these perceived societal ills, and eventually to the gas chambers of Nazi Germany.

The extended autism construct has become inadvertently linked to various societal structures of control. Technological developments, the globalisation of corporatism and the expansion of mass consumerism have contributed to a fragmentation and disempowerment of the working classes. As many critics have pointed out (particularly postmodernists such as Foucault and Baudrillard), traditional Marxist analysis, with its focus on more distinct class structures and a centrality of pure economics, is no longer sufficient to understand this multiplicity and fragmentation away from group solidarity and ideological visions and towards individualist (often hedonistic) consumerism. With an addiction to the principles of never-ending growth and the pursuit of the profit margin through promotion of crass consumerism as the god that provides meaning, we have witnessed the mass 'dumbing down' of consciousness, ever widening social inequality and the emergence of new 'under-classes' that can be easily manipulated and pitted against each other (see Chapters 9 and 10). With the undermining of solidarity within previously cohesive geographic and working communities and the spread of globalised information technologies, new virtual communities have sprung up based around special interests and professional identities. These smaller, geographically disparate movements are easier to control and currently pose little threat to the survival of the dominant regimes. The more the mass of humanity can be divided into different groups and categories, the easier it is to keep them under control and under surveillance.

Neo-liberals may genuinely believe globalisation and technocracy will bring prosperity, peace and democracy to the masses of the world's population. While it is obvious that such a model of development is unsustainable, fraught with contradictions and will, in our opinion, inevitability by marked by repeated crises of the sort we have just been witnessing in the banking sector, for the time being 'undesirables' and creating new fragmented classes of 'undesirables' serve as useful tools for the manipulation of the masses. However, there is likely to come a time in the future when the economic structures of neo-liberalism are so fragile that a more dramatic collapse than the current one will occur. At such a time the impetus to do something more radical than fragmenting and dividing social groups may become a lot more powerful. Even in relatively stable times these impulses do not disappear. Let us not forget the recent war crimes committed by the very same powers that proclaim that they stand up for freedom and democracy worldwide (such as in Iraq, Lebanon and Gaza). As we have shown, the science (bearing in mind Watson's claim that better science will make eugenic ideals achievable) behind autism is no better than it was 20, 50 or 100 years ago – only the illusion and belief in it.

Looking at autism through a more cultural framework reveals how many aspects of the construct is culture-specific. For example, the Japanese are very wary about establishing eye contact with relative strangers or seniors. Similarly, in LeVine *et al.*'s (1994) study of the Gusii tribe in Kenya, it was observed that according to their traditions mothers must make a conscious effort not to make eye contact with their children as they believe it can cause 'over-stimulation' particularly in the early years of the child's life. In many ancient cultures, reading and writing, even where they existed, were not favoured as much by the wise as (the apparently autistic by today's standards) rote memorisation, which, for sacred religious reasons, could not deviate from the original by as much as even one word. In societies that value such things it is not hard to imagine that a person lacking ability in many other respects might be considered special and even holy for possessing such a unique ability. Indeed, many autistic characteristics are not at all dissimilar to devoted religious lifestyles – for example, seeking solitude, vows of silence, non-materialistic values, lack of personal relationships, daily following of rituals and so on.

Perhaps the increasing problem of epidemic numbers of children in the West receiving diagnoses of autism is a symptom not of something 'wrong' that we should try to cure in the individual, but that it has become a barometer pointing to something wrong in the culture/society that invented this. In this respect we could do worse than learning from our apparently less 'developed' but more tolerant neighbours in the poorer south of the world (Timimi, 2005).

12
Conclusion

Three disparate people have come together to write this book. Two of us (NG and BM) have been diagnosed as having an autistic spectrum disorder and the third (ST), despite being a professional whose work revolves around an ability to empathically understand and communicate with others, is, according to the Autism-spectrum Quotient (AQ) questionnaire filled in about him by his wife (see Chapter 2), borderline autistic (of course, it could be that he is autistic and is just bad at his job and in denial about his lack of ability to empathise and communicate effectively with young people and their families). When we first started on this journey together, while we shared some scepticism about the validity of the expanded notion of autism and were thus seeking to write critically about this, we didn't predict our final destination on this journey.

We have been stunned at the extent of the absence of any real science that supports either the narrow or the broad construct, shocked at the ease with which academics and professionals alike have accepted the validity of the diagnosis and alarmed at the potential implications of large numbers being diagnosed with autism and the accompanying never-ending claims of some so-called 'experts' that we are still under-diagnosing the condition. Our journey led us into a parallel universe where we felt like we were spinning back in time to the days of the phrenologists, where all manner of mumbo-jumbo and ethically dubious activities are portrayed as science and only opinions and evidence that supports their ideas is accepted. The autism lobby has become so powerful that we have grave anxieties about the personal and professional consequences of publishing this book. However, our conclusion is the only logical, scientific and ethical one that we have felt able to support, once a more open-minded reading of the literature is allowed for – one that considers and takes seriously the possibility that there is no such thing in the real, natural world (as opposed to the socially constructed, cultural world) as autism.

So the conclusion of our studies is that *there is no such thing as autism and the label should be abolished.*

Although one of the authors (ST) is well known for previously writing from a critical perspective about other childhood psychiatric diagnoses, our conclusions go much further with regards autism. Whereas it is possible to see some uses and some utilitarian and pragmatic value for diagnoses such as ADHD (even if it does, like autism, lack biological validity), such as as a basis for research, communication and developing therapeutic approaches that deal with symptom management, it is hard to see any scientific, clinical or even research value for the construct of autism.

So how did we come to such a conclusion? Let us remind the reader of where this journey has taken us. We started by contextualising the process of studying children by referring to the way our ideas about what constitutes a 'normal' child have changed through history and how our ideas about what constitutes 'normal' child development rely on a relationship between cultural beliefs in the broader community and those in the community of people who are studying child development. In the early chapters we also introduced the reader to the thinking and work of some of the most influential academics and researchers in the autism field. Thus, our starting point was to pose questions about the validity of anyone's claim that they know what makes a child behaviourally abnormal or what makes their social and emotional development abnormal. Our ideas about what makes any childhood, child development, child-rearing, or the types of adult they are expected to become 'abnormal' have been and continue to be dependent more on cultural, political and economic circumstances than on any major scientific breakthroughs.

In the subsequent chapters we then examined the specific literature on childhood autism with a focus on the scientific evidence base that supports the concept. Entering this field and examining this literature with a critical eye, our inescapable conclusion was that our ideas about what autism is have been subject to the changing whims of influential academics and researchers. It appears to us that these 'experts'' theoretical constructs have been accepted before any rigorous scientific backing was forthcoming. Thus, when we examined the biological evidence, methodological problems were endemic, such as poor definitions of 'caseness' leading to difficult to compare studies, problems with confounding variables (such as IQ) and no consistent findings of any characteristic brain abnormality or identifiable genes. From a scientific perspective we pointed out that proper science starts with the null hypothesis (in this case that there is no characteristic biological abnormality that defines autism) and, until such time as proper evidence is forthcoming which proves that the null hypothesis cannot be true, the null hypothesis has to stand. The null hypothesis has remained stubbornly resistant to being disproven. Thus, no genes or characteristic neurological abnormalities have been found for autism. While we cannot discount the possibility that these may be found in the future, as far as the null hypothesis is concerned, until evidence to disprove it is forthcoming we must start by assuming that, from a robust scientific point of view, there is no such thing as autism in the natural biological world.

We reflected on the enormous heterogeneity of presentations that are being described as being part of the autistic spectrum and the large number of potential other psychiatric categories that these descriptions could fit into as well as the categories of behaviour currently thought of as normal/acceptable in mainstream culture (such as being fanatical about football with displays of emotion largely limited to reactions to events happening on the pitch) that could also accommodate current definitions of an ASD. Partly because of this heterogeneity, there are no unique outcomes and no unique treatments for autism.

So, we had discovered no unique or characteristic biological processes, no unique symptoms, no unique outcomes and no unique treatments. Now we began to wonder what the clinical points were, let alone the scientific ones, of diagnosis. We began to get seriously concerned. Examining the literature on screening questionnaires and diagnostic instruments turned this concern into alarm. The diagnostic instruments are based on 'face validity', in other words the behaviours being described were arrived at by subjective opinions about what sort of behaviours should be classified as 'autistic'. At no point was there any physical or psychological marker supporting these subjective ideas. As these screening and diagnostic questionnaires became popular, the potential numbers of people that could be diagnosed were increasing, the age at which to begin surveillance for possible autism was getting simultaneously lower (as low as 18 months) and higher (autism had now become an increasingly common lifelong disorder, often diagnosed for the first time in adulthood). In our opinion ethically concerning research was taking place, with whole populations being screened and previously undiagnosed cases being diagnosed as a result. Autism screening questionnaires were now appearing in popular newspapers and magazines, creating new waves of interest and potential autism recruits. The idea of putting whole population screening instruments right at the start of a child's life, and for something that is as lacking a supporting evidence base and clinical utility as autism, our fear now was that through this construct we were witnessing, whether wittingly or (more likely) unwittingly, the development of whole population surveillance rarely seen outside of totalitarian regimes.

Having concluded that the concept of autism has little scientific or clinical utility, but several dangers, we then had to ask the question: why do we have an apparent epidemic of autism with ever-increasing numbers being diagnosed each year?

Those who believe autism to be a genetically inherited, neurodevelopmental disorder put the main reason as under recognition of the disorder in the past (and, of course, in the majority of the non-Western world). Thus, according to this depoliticised perspective there have always been children who are 'suffering' with this neurodevelopmental disorder, but it is only as a result of recent scientific advances that we have discovered this to be a medical condition that affects many more individuals than we previously realised.

However, for us, this reductionist stance is difficult to maintain in the absence of good scientific evidence to support it. There are, of course, two other possibilities that could explain the dramatic increase in the diagnosis of autism and its spectrum in the West. The first is that there has been a real increase in autistic-type behaviours in children, leading to greater public scrutiny and concern about such behaviours which, in turn, has resulted in a greater professional effort to understand and alleviate these behavioural problems. If there has been a real increase in these behaviours, then understanding the causes of this would require us to turn our attention to changes in contextual factors within Western culture (where this epidemic of autism appears to be occurring) such as environmental, social, economic and political ones. Such an increase cannot be the result of genetics as, of course, genes do not change on such a large scale in a couple of generations.

The second possibility is that there has not been a real increase in autistic type behaviours among young people but there has been a change in the way we think about, classify and deal with behaviour – in other words our perceptions and the meanings we ascribe to behaviours, particularly those to do with social skills and empathy. A move from thinking about certain aspects of social behaviour as 'typically male' and therefore within the normal, expected realms for boys and men, to thinking about these behaviours as symptoms of a medical disorder would be an example of this. An examination of changes in the way we think about and classify behaviours also means an examination of contexts such as the social, cultural and political that shape our broad cultural discourses.

Both possible reasons for the increase in the diagnosis of autism (i.e., a real increase in these behaviours and a change in the meaning we ascribe to these behaviours) require an examination of contexts. Indeed the third, and probably most likely, possibility that explains the increase in diagnosis is an interaction between the aforementioned two reasons. In other words, it could be that changes in our cultural/environmental contexts are causing increases in autistic-type behaviours and these, in turn, are increasing our cultural concern about these behaviours and our perception of and the meaning we give to these behaviours, which, in turn, is changing the way we deal with these behaviours, such as increasing our surveillance and setting up services that categorise and attempt to intervene in these behaviours, which in turn increases the perception that this group is 'abnormal', further marginalising those who present with such behaviours and so on.

To try and shed some further light on this issue of the relationship between growing numbers being diagnosed with autism and changes in our culture, we first examined the nature of gender dynamics in late capitalist society, given that one of the obvious characteristics of those diagnosed with autism is that they are boys about whom mainly females in a caring role become concerned. Thus, we needed to examine what it means to be a child, what the expectations and hopes are for children in such societies, what the expected adult roles that people 'grow into' are and how this relates to gender. We looked at how changes in the economy and politics of Western neo-liberal societies altered the underlying value system and the types of concerns and preoccupations these changes engendered. We also examined how these changes may have effects on actual behaviour. We highlighted a number of features, such as the culture of narcissism, the move from an industrial to a service-based economy and the increasing perceived need for an ever-larger number of professionals to be involved in the task of rearing and educating children, as important contributing factors for the types of changes in our beliefs, values and practices that have led to a designation of the behaviours considered part of the autism spectrum as being pathological.

We also brought forth some evidence and conjecture that suggests that the type of societies that modern Western capitalism has constructed have created conditions where autistic-type behaviours are more common. Reasons for this include the individualisation of the effects of social inequality on people's emotional well being, the competitive nature of early peer relationships, the increased availability of solitary pursuits (such as computer games and the internet) and the demise of the extended family structure, all of which change early socialisation patterns and can contribute to a social withdrawal into individualistic pursuits, following non-acceptance into, or non-availability of, a larger group.

Finally, we discussed the eugenic movement, a movement that was welcomed and highly influential in Western societies of the first half of the last century. Drawing parallels with the increasing tendency towards genetic determinism that we are witnessing today, of which autism is a prime example, we noted how broad societal acceptance of the ideals of the eugenic movement (which led in the past to mass sterilisation and eventually murder of tens of thousands of those deemed to be in some way 'mentally defective') was made possible through the process of medicalisation. Doctors in this process, were not unwitting bystanders exploited by those in power; rather, they were in the forefront of persuading policy-makers to implement eugenic solutions. The argument that some modern eugenicists have put forward to differentiate modern attempts at controlling the human gene stock from previous ones is that, when compared to the old eugenics, modern attempts are based on a better 'scientific' understanding of how genes work. As we have pointed out in this book, a 'better scientific understanding' has simply not been achieved for conditions such as autism. The same mistaken ideologies are creeping in, being led by sections of the medical community who are (falsely) claiming that conditions such as autism are primarily genetic in nature. Many services already provide genetic counselling for those with an autistic child, warning parents of the increased likelihood of a subsequent child having autism. We fear that accepting the idea that there is a condition called autism, that we know how to define it and that it is a disorder primarily to do with abnormal genes, is leading us towards the slippery slope of a flourishing of a new eugenics. As we live in cultures increasingly consumed by a fear of the 'enemy within', we are concerned that the lessons of history have not been learnt and, thus, we are worried about the extent to which the new eugenics will go in order to pursue this fantasy science fiction of 'medical engineering' to eliminate human suffering by improving the human gene stock.

WE DON'T WANT TO OFFEND ANYONE WITH THE DIAGNOSIS OR THEIR CARERS

One of the hardest things about writing this book and keeping our integrity (by remaining clear about our conclusions) is knowing that those who have found themselves going down the route of seeking a diagnosis and then receiving it have confronted difficult circumstances in their lives (either in their own right or as adults in a caring/responsible position over a child). These are difficulties, moreover, that they were desperately seeking to understand. On receiving a diagnosis of autism or one of its spectrum, many people experience a sense of relief, as it can provide new hope due to feeling that the nature of their problems has finally been 'discovered'. Having sympathetic professionals who have given you the sense of 'now we know what we're dealing with' is powerful and reassuring. An 'expert' is now available who knows the cause and can hopefully help guide you through 'special' techniques that can help manage the problems through knowledge attached to this diagnosis.

Given such a process, it is understandable why the autistic spectrum construct comes to dominate how you understand the problems being faced (and those you have faced). You may then feel that the battle is trying to persuade other 'more ignorant' people you encounter of the 'true' nature of the problem you or your children are facing. The questioning of the legitimacy of the diagnosis (as herein) may, in such circumstances, feel insulting, heartbreaking, confusing, malicious and, if you're a parent (particularly a mother), it may feel like you are being blamed (yet again). To those who recognise these emotional reactions to what we are proposing, it may seem as if we are trying to turn the clock back to the disastrous, destructive and equally unscientific days of Bettleheim's ideas about the 'refrigerator parent' causing autism.

For us, these are serious problems, ones that threaten the purpose of us writing this book. We accept that we cannot entirely eliminate such reactions, however hard we try to explain ourselves, as psychic suffering by definition is such an emotive subject. Many of those who have been personally touched by diagnoses of autism will understandably hold passionate beliefs about what it is and is not, and our proclaiming that autism is an unscientific *and* unhelpful diagnosis could feel like it is threatening their sense of self, identity and, indeed, cosmology. However, if we had found that only good comes out of this label and that there are no personal or social dangers associated with using the construct (even if it lacks scientific validity), then we would not have written this book. Both NG's and BM's personal experiences with the effects of an autism label on their lives are a testament to the lack of a universal positive consequence that is derived from it (see Chapter 2). The third author, ST's experience as a clinician, is that he has come across many children, parents and families for whom the initial euphoria after receiving the diagnosis dies away and is replaced by increasing disappointment and despondency, as the same doubts and questions creep back and many of the original problems that led to seeking help return or continue unaltered. Indeed, ST has met some young people who feel the doctor who diagnosed them ignored what they considered was their 'true' problems and instead gave them a label because they didn't know what else to do with them: some young people have refused to accept the label and actively resisted it; others have reported that having the diagnosis changed little, and little has changed as a result of diagnostic-specific interventions. All this reminded us that there are other voices out there, voices that have been thus far buried under the weight of the dominant and domineering autism lobby. Not everyone experiences positive consequences or unambiguously embraces the diagnosis. Far from it.

When we first started writing this book our intention was to critique the expanded notion of autism and argue that a return to the original Kanner-type definitions was necessary. However, we had to confront some uncomfortable questions that couldn't be avoided. Was there any scientific basis for even the narrow concept of autism? Yes, this group most obviously had associated neurological impairments, which affected their learning and daily functioning; however, were there any empirical grounds to argue for a separate way of looking at this group compared to others with moderate to severe learning difficulties? Furthermore, if this type of autism had a solid empirical base, surely it would not have been so vulnerable to being expanded in the manner that it has? As we started moving in the direction of concluding that autism per se lacks an empirical basis, we did feel troubled that parents of this group, in particular, may feel offended as it may look as if we are denying that their child is disabled.

This is something we are most certainly not trying to imply, but we are questioning the scientific validity and clinical utility of separating this group out from others with moderate to severe learning difficulties. In this respect, one of the authors (ST) is reminded of a comment a head teacher of a special school for children with moderate to severe learning difficulties once said to him: 'It's the ones who don't get the label of autism that I feel most sorry for; there are very few services for them.' In other words, autism has become a 'ticket' for specific services, creating a two-tier system for help and support among this group of obviously disabled young people.

There are a number of things that we wish the reader to be reassured about. We are **NOT** saying any of the following:

1. Autism is a condition caused by poor parenting.
2. Autism is caused by environmental factors.
3. That those who seek and receive an ASD diagnosis are not suffering and not deserving of professional support, understanding and, where appropriate, therapeutic interventions.

We **ARE** saying that unless we expose the failed science behind the construct of autism and the lack of clinical usefulness of the diagnosis, we will not be able to develop and provide the types of services that can benefit those in distress, while simultaneously protecting them and the general public from the potential long-term harms of the 'life-long incurable disability' label. Unless we have services that are more flexible (and less autistic) in the way they understand and interpret people's predicaments, we create and institutionalise processes that cause 'reification' (once a diagnostic concept becomes reified and accepted, the category can take on 'a life of its own', turning an abstract construct into a concrete reality through its use in daily life, as opposed to its existence in biological reality). Instead, as things stand we have the nonsense of those who are speechless residents of special schools having the same label as gifted and talented mainstream school children (who may be struggling to make friends), as if the diagnosis has uncovered some similar causal processes, clinical needs, outcomes and specific interventions that they require.

It is our belief, therefore, that only by stripping away and then abolishing this label can we hope to move services back towards a more human engagement with people's problems, with assessments and interventions that are more able to take account of each person or family's unique circumstances, rather than trying to force that understanding into a culturally constructed box that marks you out for life.

PATHWAYS TO AUTISM

Because there is such a diverse set of presentations and problems that are being incorporated into the rubric of an ASD, one thing we won't do in this book is tell the reader how to treat or help someone who could be diagnosed, using current standards, as having autism or one of its spectrum. What we will instead do is a brief exploration of a few of the potential paths to this label and speculate on the possible implications of working with and trying to help this diverse group.

A problem with the word 'autism' is that it means different things to different people. It may mean a severe communication and learning disorder with a markedly abnormal development that can be observed within the first 24 months of life and with no easily discernible psychosocial causes. Alternatively it may mean a multidimensional continuum of behavioural traits that we consider odd or in some way 'out of step' with mainstream society. For thousands of ASD-diagnosed people autism is just the way they view their differences from the more socially integrated or emotionally involved majority. While plenty of ASD-diagnosed adults have odd mannerisms and obsessions, few would meet or recognise the description popularised in Mark Haddon's (2004) *The Curious Incident of the Dog in the Night-time*.

ASDs are defined by behaviours and not by any characteristic biological or psychological markers. A large proportion of those deemed to have severe autistic symptoms from an early age have other medical conditions (such as epilepsy) and moderate to severe learning difficulties, pointing to an underlying neurological cause for their problems. Rather than focusing on the neurodevelopmental consequences of underlying biological processes, which may result in behavioural patterns now considered autistic, autistic spectrum theorists put these individuals' problems in the same category as behaviours exhibited by people who are able to function independently in mainstream society. These latter individuals whose behavioural deviance may be associated with largely psychosocial and contextual factors are assumed to be suffering from a neurological disorder of the same type as those with more obvious neurological damage. For others still, excessive cultural emphasis on the importance of physical perfection and dexterity in culturally significant sports and pursuits (i.e., the coolness factor) provides the backdrop to the subsequent withdrawal from the social sphere of an otherwise fit and healthy person, who is unable, due to minor physical differences (such as dyspraxia), to match his or her peer expectations. This person too can attract an ASD label.

As we move further away from the original definition of autism (that of Kanner) we start reaching into the territory of culturally defined desirable and undesirable characteristics. In the industrial era there was high demand for people with narrow, highly specialised skill sets, but with automation these skills became unnecessary for the functioning of the economy. However, skills that focus on the art of persuasion, teamwork and customer relations have become central (see Chapters 9 and 10). Many ASD-associated traits, such as obsessive attention to detail, are particularly prevalent in some Asian cultures, especially Far Eastern ones, where, as a result, broad-spectrum ASD traits are valued and not viewed with suspicion. Whether you are viewed as having valuable skills or a neurological abnormality requiring professional support and intervention will, of course, have a marked influence on a your identity and sense of self-esteem.

As we highlighted in Chapters 9 and 10, family life has changed out of all recognition in the space of just a few decades. The demands of a consumerist value system and the need for constant economic growth has fragmented families, devalued the role of the mother (without encouraging more involved fatherhood) and the space of the family has been turned into small, often isolated, emotionally intense units, with fewer opportunities for early socialisation with a variety of individuals, and with a growing distrust towards poor families shown by some Western governments (such as the UK's). The fragmentation of the traditional family has been (at least in part) driven by a society with narcissistic ideals and so more orientated to adult needs. Thus, if adults wish to pursue a career, change partners, have one-night stands with strangers leading to unexpected pregnancy etc., they should be allowed to do so. Many of the emotionally insecure children that such an environment produces can also be labelled with an ASD. Their therapeutic needs are, of course, different again.

When we started writing this book we shared a belief that autism as a diagnostic label only makes sense when severe developmental impairments are observed in the early years and lead to a variety of impairments. However, even among this, more obviously neurologically afflicted group we have come to have doubts about the validity or utility of the label. If a person's brain, due to neurological damage or dysfunction (as in those at the severe end of the spectrum who often have accompanying severe learning difficulties) is unable to assimilate the full depth of what is happening in the social world around them, then they may respond more to inner bodily cues than perceptual ones. Given the usual wide variety of accompanying impairments (such as an inability to dress, cook, read, add, etc.), it is hard to see what a broad label such as autism adds, particularly following this label's metamorphosis to include such a wide range of people. While not all cases with severe learning difficulties have autistic symptoms, it is also true that not all cases can't feed themselves, not all cases have epilepsy, not all cases show violent outbursts and so on. A diagnosis of autism adds little to the types of assessments needed to help decide the sort of help and support that the afflicted individual may find useful. At the broader end of the spectrum, pathways to problems and the types of problems being experienced are so varied that the autism label is likely to prove a positive distraction from a full appreciation and understanding of the unique characteristics of that person's situation.

THE DANGERS OF LABELLING

It is likely that, at least to some degree, the labelling of every identifiable set of behavioural traits and ascribing them to neurobiological causes is just a consequence of the approach and training of psychiatrists, that is, there is no conspiracy, it's just the way psychiatrists are trained to think. Most psychiatrists are, of course, ambitious, thoughtful and humane, trying to help people with perhaps the most difficult form of suffering (mental suffering), and genuinely believe they're doing good – and often are. However, just as in any other field of human endeavour, guild interests and a paradigmatically closed 'group think' occurs. Those in the field crawl up inside their own 'branch' on the tree of knowledge, unaware of what's happening in the rest of the tree and unable to contemplate that this particular branch may be starting to rot.

We have seen it in many recent findings where biopsychiatrists, unable to contemplate that the evidence does not support their paradigms, close ranks, plead for giving psychiatry a 'special' status when it comes to evaluating the evidence and plough on with non-evidence-based practice regardless (although they often call it evidence-based) (see, for example, Parker [2009], who mounts a feeble argument that the convincing evidence for a lack of efficacy for antidepressants over placebo is due to poor methodology in the studies, while ignoring the weight of evidence from many decades of studies). Of course, some of the problems go beyond group think and involve profits and greed, with unholy alliances between psychiatrists and the drug industry, a particular problem in psychiatry more generally and child psychiatry in particular (Timimi, 2008a). For most psychiatrists and psychologists (and service users) these are issues that are of little interest as they are simply too concerned with sorting out their own lives or solving the individual problems of patients to worry too much about the bigger picture. Undoubtedly, most people diagnosed with an ASD have had some very harrowing personal experiences and so the nuances of whether there is scientific credibility behind a diagnosis will understandably matter less than the sense of hope generated by an impression that a professional (who diagnoses the ASD) has understood and worked out what's 'wrong' with them. However, submitting to this process is not without dangers.

Culturally intrinsic in the West is the idea of external expertise that has a higher hierarchical status than the person's own knowledge, none more so than the doctor. In the world of mental health, the psychiatrist remains hierarchically privileged, with their knowledge often being viewed as more expert than other professionals, although some psychiatrists have become anxious at what they perceive as a worrying decline in the power and status of psychiatrists (e.g., Craddock *et al.*, 2008). In adult psychiatry there is some evidence that other voices are being taken into account, particularly with the growing strength of the user movement in recent years. Although these alternative voices have yet to make a serious impact on clinical practice at the institutional level, at least it's a beginning, whereas in child psychiatry there is more of a vacuum. It seems that child psychiatric theory and practice has years of catching up to do before the profession can claim to be taking cross-disciplinary ideas seriously. Of course, psychiatry's hierarchical status means that it's too powerful to incorporate ways of understanding that have the potential to challenge its hegemony, therefore this is unlikely to happen without it being in some way 'forced' to do so (as user movements are doing with adult psychiatry). How can those of us who can see 'the big picture' influence practice to incorporate other views and voices? First, we must challenge our own beliefs and practices sufficiently to question those assumptions and cherished ideals that we take into our clinical encounters. First, we must clarify our own values.

In this respect we are concerned about a value system that (as enshrined in the application of a traditional medical model to mental health) privileges notions of deficit and pathology and takes as its universal template, standards derived from the dominant discourses of late-capitalist societies. As Kenneth Gergen (1991) states: 'The vocabulary of human deficit has undergone enormous expansion within the present century [last century]. We have countless ways of locating faults within ourselves and others that were unavailable to even our great-grandfathers' (Gergen, 1991: 13). Or, as Thomas Szasz (1970) states, commenting on how the impact on personal identity of the practice of pathologising is most obvious in the application of psychiatric diagnoses:

> The diagnostic label imparts a defective personal identity to the patient; it will henceforth identify him to others and govern their conduct toward him, and his toward them. The psychiatric nosologist thus not only describes his patient's so-called illness, but also prescribes his future conduct. (Szasz, 1970: 203)

The ramifications of this kind of therapeutic violence have been horrifying for many persons who have experienced the debilitating and totalising effects of diagnostic labels in terms of self-blame, self-loathing and intense self-monitoring (Tomm, 1990).

'Making sense' is a social process; it is an activity that is always situated within a cultural and historical framework. Through their social interactions with adults children create accounts of their lives that become their worldview – a sort of social map of the world (Garbarino, 1993). When adults bring attention to children's failures and the ways they don't measure up to moral, educational and/or behavioural expectations, children then enter into a worldview and self-narrative of incompetence. The educational and behavioural expectations being passed on are, of course, absorbed by adults and derived from dominant cultural discourses that are born out of Western capitalist machismo. The impact these discourses have on our everyday notions of childhood, boyhood, parenthood, adulthood and mother–boy relationships in particular, are very powerful. Doctors, psychologists, therapists, teachers and parents can strengthen this discourse or struggle to try and access a value system that challenges it.

As ASD individuals allegedly lack presentational and negotiating skills, they are often excluded from representing themselves except under the guidance of professionals and activists in the growing autism lobby. A good 'Aspie' accepts not only his or her fundamental neurological difference, but also that this puts him or her at a disadvantage in mainstream society and thus that they require some form of advocacy. If ASD-diagnosed persons were able to stand up for themselves, as some internet advocacy groups would like to suggest, and form viable independent communities, the label would become meaningless with any perceived disability, stigma, or social alienation loosing its relevance. Yet such communities do not materialise perhaps because anyone diagnosed by a mental health professional has undergone a period of emotional distress and under-achievement in an important aspect of their life and, once they have the label that renders them 'disabled' in some fundamental way, they are sucked into the mental health system with its focus on monitoring, medication, advocacy and training schemes. These can become a new way of life, a new real and virtual community of the marginalised.

Messages or therapeutic biases that remain invisible to the patient are the ones with the greatest potential for harm (particularly as they tend to be given to individuals, children and families in a manner that implies that what the doctor/psychologist is saying is the only 'truth'). Striving towards a different way of viewing the behaviours that attract the label of autism challenges the notion that professional knowledge represents the 'truth', or is at least a good reflection of it, and means finding new ways of conceptualising clinical problems. Our claim that there is no politically or socially neutral, objective way of giving meaning and therefore finding a way forward with problems (that come to be labelled ASD) is not the same as saying there is no way to find solutions to problems. On the contrary, by being mindful of the nature of the socio-cultural and political discourse we can, through conversation and discussion that privileges people's existing knowledge base derived from their cultural heritage, arrive at pragmatically helpful ways forward that are not dependent on pre-existing concrete doctor/psychologist derived notions of normality, progress and good outcome. This value challenges the notion of the doctor/psychologist as the ultimate or only arbiter of the therapeutic process.

As we have outlined, history is replete with tragic examples of over-zealous medicalisation that sometimes led to abuses by doctors, as well as governments, of their powers. What does this new bout of medicalisation hold for future generations? If we insist on medicalising an increasing variety of behavioural tendencies, how far will we go in terms of giving leverage to lifelong state intervention in the lives of people, to a degree rarely seen outside totalitarian regimes? In a democracy we attempt to promote such measures through 'willing obedience', but how short is the distance to more draconian measures, particularly when living in masculine neo-liberal cultures where all sorts of aggressive acts can and have been put down to 'defending our values of liberty and democracy'? With a population being convinced that the widening social inequality gap is simply the natural order, how easy would it be to find other scapegoats and how far will our populations go in their democratic 'right' to control these scapegoats? After all, as history teaches us again and again, one generation's most cherished therapeutic ideas and practices, especially when applied to the powerless, are repudiated by the next, but not without leaving countless victims in their wake.

References

Abell, S. and Dauphin, B. (2009) 'The Perpetuation of Patriarchy: The Hidden Factor of Gender Bias in the Diagnosis and Treatment of Children'. *Clinical Child Psychology and Psychiatry* 14, 117–33.

Abell, F., Krams, M., Ashburner, J., Passingham, R., Friston, K. and Frackowiak, R. (1999) 'The Neuroanatomy of Autism: A Voxel-based Whole Brain Analysis of Structural Scans'. *Neuroreport* 10, 1647–51.

Achenbach, T.M. and Edelbrock, C.S. (1978) 'The Classification of Child Psychopathology: A Review and Analysis of Empirical Efforts'. *Psychological Bulletin* 85, 1275–301.

Allen, D. (1988) 'Autistic Spectrum Disorders: Clinical Presentation in Preschool Children'. *Journal of Child Neurology* 3 (supplement), 48–56.

Allen, D. and Rapin, I. (1992) 'Autistic Children are also Dysphasic'. In H. Naruse and E. Ornitz (eds) *Neurobiology of Infantile Autism* (Amsterdam: Excerpta Medica).

Althusser, L. (1969) *For Marx* (Harmondsworth: Penguin).

Althusser, L. (1971) *Lenin and Philosophy and Other Essays* (London: New Left).

American and Psychiatric Association (APA) (1952) *Diagnostic and Statistical Manual of Mental Disorders (DSM)* (Washington DC: APA).

American and Psychiatric Association (1966) *Diagnostic and Statistical Manual of Mental Disorders, Second Edition (DSM-II)* (Washington DC: APA).

American and Psychiatric Association (1980) *Diagnostic and Statistical Manual of Mental Disorders, Third Edition (DSM-III)* (Washington DC: APA).

American Psychiatric Association (1987) *Diagnostic and Statistical Manual of Mental Disorders, Third Edition Revised (DSM-III-R)* (Washington DC: APA).

American Psychiatric Association (1994) *Diagnostic and Statistical Manual of Mental Disorders, Fourth Edition (DSM-IV)* (Washington, DC: APA).

Amin, S. (1988) *Eurocentrism* (New York: Monthly Review Press).

Ariès, P. (1962) *Centuries of Childhood* (London: Jonathan Cape).

Aronowitz, S. and Giroux, H. (1991) *Post-modern Education: Politics, Culture and Social Criticism* (Minneapolis: University of Minnesota Press).

Asen, E. (2006) 'Systemic Perspectives: Critique and Scope'. In S. Timimi and B. Maitra (eds) *Critical Voices in Child and Adolescent Mental Health* (London: Free Association).

Asperger, H. (1944) 'Autistic Psychopathy in Childhood', trans. and annotated by U. Frith. In U. Frith (1991) *Autism and Asperger Syndrome* (Cambridge: Cambridge University Press).

Autism Research Review (2000) 'Evidence Mounts for Epidemic of Autism'. *Autism Research Review* 14, 2.

Bailey, A., Le Couteur, A., Gottesman, I., Bolton, P., Simonoff, E., Yuzda, E. and Rutter, M. (1995) 'Autism as a Strongly Genetic Disorder: Evidence from a British Twin Study'. *Psychological Medicine* 25, 63–77.

Baird, G., Cass, H. and Slonims, V. (2003) 'Diagnosis of Autism'. *British Medical Journal* 327, 488.

Baird, G., Charman, T., Cox, A., Baron-Cohen, S., Wheelwright, S. and Drew, A. (2001) 'Screening and Surveillance for Autism and Pervasive Developmental Disorders'. *Archives of Diseases in Childhood* 84, 468–75.

Baistow, K. (1995) 'From Sickly Survival to Realisation of Potential: Child Health as a Social Project'. *Children's Society* 9, 20–35.

Barinaga, M. (1992) 'The Brain Remaps its Own Contours'. *Science*, 258, 216–18.

Baron-Cohen, S. (1995). *Mindblindness: An Essay on Autism and Theory of Mind* (Cambridge, MA: MIT Press).

Baron-Cohen, S. (2003) *The Essential Difference: The Truth About the Male and Female Brain* (New York: Basic Books).

Baron-Cohen, S., Allen, J. and Gillberg, C. (1992) 'Can Autism be Detected at 18 Months?: The Needle, the Haystack and the CHAT'. *British Journal of Psychiatry* 161, 839–43.

Baron-Cohen, S., Leslie, A.M. and Frith, U. (1985) 'Does the Autistic Child have a "Theory of Mind"?'. *Cognition* 21, 37–46.

Baron-Cohen, S., Wheelwright, S., Skinner, R., Martin, J. and Clubley, E. (2001) 'The Autism-Spectrum Quotient (AQ): Evidence from Asperger Syndrome/High-Functioning Autism, Males and Females, Scientists and Mathematicians'. *Journal of Autism and Developmental Disorders* 31, 5–17.

Baron-Cohen, S., Cox, A., Baird, G., Swettenham, J., Nightingale, N., Morgan, K., Drew, A. and Charman T. (1996) 'Psychological Markers in the Detection of Autism in Infancy in a Large Population'. *The British Journal of Psychiatry* 168, 158–63.

Barker, C. (2000) *Cultural Studies: Theory and Practice* (London: Sage).

Barkley, R.A. (2001) 'The Executive Functions and Self-regulation: An Evolutionary Neuropsychological Perspective'. *Neuropsychology Review* 11, 1–29.

Batten, A., Corbett, C., Rosenblatt, M., Withers, L. and Yuille, R. (2006) *Autism and Education: The Reality for Families Today* (London: National Autistic Society).

Baumeister, A.A. and Hawkins, M.F. (2001) 'Incoherence of Neuroimaging Studies in Attention Deficit/Hyperactivity Disorder'. *Clinical Neuropharmacology* 24, 2–10.

Bayer, R. (1981) *Homosexuality and American Psychiatry: The Politics of Diagnosis* (New York: Basic Books).

Bleuler, E. (1911) Dementia Praecox oder Gruppe der Schizophrenien. In G. Aschaffenburg (ed.) *Handbuch der Psychiatrie.* Leipzig: Deuticke.

Bloom, P. and German, T. (2000) 'Two Reasons to Abandon the False-belief Task as a Test of Theory of Mind'. *Cognition* 77, 25–31.

Bolton, P., Macdonald, H., Pickles, A., Rois, P., Goode, S., Crowson, M., Bailey, A. and Rutter, M., (1994) 'A Case-Control Family History Study of Autism'. *Journal of Child Psychology and Psychiatry* 35, 877–900.

Bottomore, T. and Rubel, M. (eds) (1961) *Karl Marx: Selected Writings in Sociology and Social Philosophy* (London: Pelican).

Bouchard Jr, T.J., Lykken, T.D., McGue, M., Segal, N.L. and Tellegen, A. (1990) 'Sources of Human Psychological Differences: The Minnesota Study of Twins Reared Apart'. *Science* 250, 223–6.

Boyle, M. (1990) *Schizophrenia: A Scientific Delusion?* (London: Routledge).

Boyle, M.H. and Jadad, A.R. (1999) 'Lessons from Large Trials: The MTA Study as a Model for Evaluating the Treatment of Childhood Psychiatric Disorder'. *Canadian Journal of Psychiatry* 44, 991–8.

Bracken, P. and Thomas, P. (2001) 'Post Psychiatry: A New Direction for Mental Health'. *British Medical Journal* 322, 724–7.

Bradley, B.S. (1989) *Visions of Infancy: A Critical Introduction to Child Psychology* (Cambridge: Polity Press).

Brambilla, P., Hardan, A., di Nemi, S.U., Perez, J., Soares, J.C. and Barale, F. (2003) 'Brain Anatomy and Development in Autism: Review of Structural MRI Studies'. *Brain Research Bulletin* 61, 557–69.

Breggin, P. (2000) 'The NIMH Multimodal Study of Treatment for Attention Deficit/Hyperactivity Disorder: A Critical Analysis'. *International Journal of Risk and Safety in Medicine* 13, 15–22.

Breggin, P. and Breggin, G. (1998) *The War Against Children of Color* (Maine: Common Courage Press).

British Medical Journal (1961) ii, 889.

Broughton, J. (1986) 'The Psychology, History and Ideology of the Self'. In K. Larsen (ed.) *Dialectics and Ideology in Psychology* (Norwood, NJ: Ablex).

Buck-Morss, S. (1987) 'Piaget, Adorno and Dialectical Operations'. In J. Broughton (ed.) *Critical Theories of Psychological Development* (New York: Plenum).

Buitelaar, J.K. and Willemsen-Swinkels, S.H. (2000) 'Autism: Current Theories Regarding Its Pathogenesis and Implications for Rational Pharmacotherapy'. *Paediatric Drugs* 2, 67–81.

Burman, E. (1994) *Deconstructing Developmental Psychology* (London: Routledge).

Burman E. (2005) 'Childhood, Neo-liberalism and the Feminization of Education'. *Gender and Education* 17, 351–67.

Butler, J. (1993) *Bodies That Matter* (London: Routledge).

Carrel, A. (1935) *Man, the Unknown* (New York: Harper & Brothers).

Castellanos, F.X., Lee, P.P., Sharp, W., Jeffries, N.O., Greenstein, D.K., Clasen, L.S., Blumenthal, J.D., James, R.S., Ebens, C., Walter, J., Zijdenbos, A., Evans, A.C., Giedd, J. and Rapoport, J. (2002) 'Developmental Trajectories of Brain Volume Abnormalities in Children and Adolescents with Attention-deficit/Hyperactivity Disorder'. *Journal of the American Medical Association* 288, 1740–8.

Cederbald, M. (1988) 'Behavioural Disorders in Children from Different Cultures'. *Acta psychiatrica Scandinavia* 78, 85–92.

Charman, T. and Baird, G. (2002) 'Practitioner Review: Diagnosis of Autism Spectrum Disorder in 2 and 3 Year Old Children'. *Journal of Child Psychology and Psychiatry* 43, 289–305.

Charman, T., Baron-Cohen, S., Baird, G., Cox, A., Wheelwright, S., Swettenham, J. and Drew, A. (2001) 'Commentary: The Modified Checklist for Autism in Toddlers'. *Journal of Autism and Developmental Disorders* 31, 145–8.

Chase, A. (1980) *The Legacy of Malthus* (Illinois: University of Illinois Press).

Chodorow, N.J. (1978) *The Reproduction of Mothering* (Berkeley, CA: University of California Press).

Christakis, D.A., Zimmerman, F.J., DiGiuseppe, D.L. and McCarthy, C.A. (2004) 'Early Television Exposure and Subsequent Attentional Problems in Children'. *Pediatrics* 113, 708–13.

Clarke, A.M. and Clarke, A.D. (1965) *Mental Deficiency: The Changing Outlook* (London: Methuen).

Cody, H., Pelphrey, K. and Piven, J. (2002) 'Structural and Functional Magnetic Resonance Imaging of Autism'. *International Journal of Developmental Neuroscience* 20, 421–38.

Cohen, E. and Morley, C. (2009) 'Children, ADHD, and Citizenship'. *Journal of Medicine and Philosophy*, 1–26.

Cohen, C. and Timimi, S. (eds) (2008) *Libratory Psychiatry: Philosophy, Politics and Mental Health* (Cambridge: Cambridge University Press).

Cohen, D.J., Paul, R. and Volkmar, F. (1987) 'Issues in Classification of PDD and Associated Conditions'. In D.J. Cohen, A.M. Donnellan and R.R. Paul (eds) *Handbook of Autism and Pervasive Developmental Disorders* (New York: Wiley).

Comings, D. (1996) *The Gene Bomb* (Duarte, CA: Hope Press).

Connell, R.W. (1995) *Masculinities* (Cambridge: Polity Press).

Connell, R.W. (2000) *The Men and the Boys* (Berkeley: University of California Press).

Connell, R.W. (2002) *Gender* (Cambridge: Polity Press).

Conrad, P. (1975) 'The Discovery of Hyperkinesis: Notes on the Medicalization of Deviant Behavior'. *Social Problems* 23, 12–21.

Conrad, P. (1999) 'A Mirage of Genes'. *Sociology of Health and Illness* 21, 228–41.

Corvin, A. and Gill, M. (2003) 'Psychiatric Genetics in the Post-genome Age'. *British Journal of Psychiatry* 182, 95–6.

Courchesne, E., Karns, C.M. and Davies, H.R. (2001) 'Unusual Brain Growth Patterns in Early Life in Patients with Autistic Disorder: An MRI Study'. *Neurology* 57, 245–54.

Courchesne, E., Yeung-Courchesne, R., Press, G.A., Hesselink, J.R. and Jernigan, T.L. (1988) 'Hypoplasia of Cerebellar Vermal Lobules VI and VII in Autism'. *New England Journal of Medicine* 318, 1349–54.

Craddock, N., Antebi, D., Attenburrow, M., Bailey, A., Carson, A. *et al.* (2008) 'Wake-up Call for British Psychiatry'. *British Journal of Psychiatry* 193, 6–9.

Craig, J., Whittington, C.J., Kendall, T., Fonagy, P., Cottrell, D., Cotgrove, A. and Boddington, E. (2004) 'Selective Serotonin Reuptake Inhibitors in Childhood Depression: Systematic Review of Published Versus Unpublished Data'. *Lancet* 363, 1341–5.

Creak, M. (1951) 'Psychosis in Childhood'. *Journal of Mental Science* 97, 545–54.

Critchley, H.D., Daly, E.M. and Bullmore, E.T. (2000) 'The Functional Neuroanatomy of Social Behaviour: Changes in Cerebral Blood Flow When People with Autistic Disorder Process Facial Expressions'. *Brain* 123, 2203–12.

Cromby, J. (2008) 'Feelings, Beliefs and Being Human'. In A. Morgan (ed.) *Being Human* (Ross-on-Wye: PCCS).

Cundall, M. (2007) 'Rethinking Autism's Role in Understanding Social Cognition'. *Journal of Philosophy* 1. Available at http://www.scientificjournals.org/journals2007/articles/1002.htm, accessed 5 February 2009.

Cunningham, H. (1995) *Children and Childhood in Western Society since 1500* (London: Longman).

Danforth, S. and Navarro, V. (2001) 'Hyper Talk: Sampling the Social Construction of ADHD in Everyday Language'. *Anthropology and Education Quarterly* 32, 167–90.

Davis, S.S. and Davis, D.A. (1989) *Adolescence in a Moroccan Town* (New Brunswick, NJ: Rutgers University Press).

De Bildt, A., Sytema, S., Ketelaars, C., Kraijer, D., Mulder, E., Volmar, F. and Minderaa, R. (2004) 'Interrelationship between Autism Diagnostic Observation Schedule-Generic (ADOS-G), Autism Diagnostic Interview-Revised (ADI-R), and the Diagnostic and Statistical Manual of Mental Disorders (DSM-IV-TR) Classification in Children and Adolescents with Mental Retardation'. *Journal of Autism and Developmental Disorders* 34, 129–37.

De Mause, L. (1984) *Reagan's America* (New York: Creative Roots).

Denham, A. and Garnett, M. (2001) *Sir Keith Joseph* (Stocksfield: Acumen).

Department of Health (2007) 'Prescription Cost Analysis: England 2006. London: Department of Health'. Available at http://www.ic.nhs.uk/webfiles/publications/pca2006/PCA_2006.pdf, accessed 2 February 2009.

Dihoff, R. (1993) 'Ordinal Measurement of Autistic Behaviour: A Preliminary Report'. *Bulletin of the Psychometric Society* 31, 287–90.

DiLavore, P.C., Lord, C. and Rutter, M. (1995) 'The Pre-Linguistic Autism Diagnostic Observation Schedule'. *Journal of Autism and Developmental Disorders* 25, 355–79.

Douglas, K. (1989) *Jean Baudrillard: From Marxism to Post-modernism and Beyond* (Cambridge: Polity Press).

Duncan, B., Miller, S. and Sparks, J. (2004) *The Heroic Client* (San Francisco, CA: Jossey-Bass).

Dwivedi, K.N. (1996) 'Culture and Personality'. In K.N. Dwivedi and V.P. Varma (eds) *Meeting the Needs of Ethnic Minority Children* (London: Jessica Kingsley).

Earls, F. (1991) 'A Developmental Approach to Understanding and Controlling Violence'. In H.E. Fitzgerald, B.H. Lester and M.W. Yogman (eds) *Theory and Research in Behavioral Pediatrics* (New York: Plenum Press).

Edwards, V. (2006) 'Not a Shred of Evidence: Are Scientists Faking Data on ADHD?'. *Investigate Magazine* May 2006, 50–3.

Ehlers, S. and Gillberg, C. (1993) 'The Epidemiology of Asperger Syndrome: A Total Population Study'. *Journal of Child Psychology and Psychiatry* 34, 1327–50.

Elias, N. (1939/1978) *The Civilizing Process* (New York: Blackwell).

Emslie, G.J., Rush, A.J., Weinberg, W.A., Kowatch, R.A., Hughes, C.W., Carmody, T. and Rintelmann, J. (1997) 'A Double-blind, Randomized, Placebo-controlled Trial of Fluoxetine in Children and Adolescents with Depression'. *Archives of General Psychiatry* 54, 1031–7.

Emslie, G.J., Heiligenstein, J.H., Wagner, K.D., Hoog, S.L., Ernest, D.E., Brown, E., Nilsson, M. and Jacobson, J.G. (2002) 'Fluoxetine for Acute Treatment of Depression in Children and Adolescents: A Placebo-controlled, Randomized Clinical Trial'. *Journal of American Academy of Child and Adolescent Psychiatry* 41, 1205–15.

Enright, R.D., Levy, V.M., Harris, D. and Lapsley, D.K. (1987) 'Do Economic Conditions Influence How Theorists View Adolescents?'. *Journal of Youth and Adolescence* 16, 541–59.

Eysenck, H.J. and Eysenck, S.B.G. (1975) *Manual of the Eysenck Personality Questionnaire (Adult and Junior)* (London: Hodder & Stoughton).

Falck-Ytter, T., Gredebäck, G. and Von Hofsten, C. (2006) 'Infants Predict Other People's Action Goals'. *Nature Neuroscience* 9, 878–9.

Fein, D., Waterhouse, L., Lucci, D. and Snyder, D. (1985) 'Cognitive Subtypes in Developmentally Disabled Children: A Pilot Study'. *Journal of Autism and Developmental Disorders* 15, 77–95.

Firth, C.D. and Corcoran, R. (1996) 'Exploring "Theory of Mind" in People with Schizophrenia'. *Psychological Medicine* 26, 521–30.

Fisher, S.E. (2006) 'Tangled Webs: Tracing the Connections between Genes and Cognition'. *Cognition* 101, 270–9.

Fitzgerald, M. (2003) *Autism and Creativity: Is there a Link Between Autism in Men and Exceptional Ability?* (London: Routledge).

Fitzgerald, M. (2005) *The Genesis of Artistic Creativity: Asperger's Syndrome and the Arts* (London: Jessica Kingsley).
Fodor, J., (2001) *The Mind Doesn't Work That Way* (Cambridge, MA: MIT Press).
Folstein, S. and Rutter, M. (1977) 'Infantile Autism: A Genetic Study of 21 Twin Pairs'. *Journal of Child Psychology and Psychiatry* 18, 297–321.
Foucault, M. (1961/1965) *Madness and Civilization*, trans. R. Howard (New York: Pantheon).
Foucault, M. (1962/1987). *Mental Illness and Psychology*, trans. A. Sheridan (Berkley, CA: University of California Press).
Foucault, M. (1972) *The Archaeology of Knowledge* (New York: Pantheon).
Foucault, M. (1973) *The Birth of the Clinic* (London: Tavistock).
Foucault, M. (1977) *Discipline and Punishment* (New York: Pantheon).
Foucault, M. (1981) *The History of Sexuality: Vol. 1, An Introduction* (Harmondsworth: Pelican).
Freitag, C.M. (2007) 'The Genetics of Autistic Disorders and its Clinical Relevance: A Review of the Literature'. *Molecular Psychiatry* 12, 2–12.
Freud, S. (1922) *Beyond the Pleasure Principle* (London: The Psycho-analytical Press).
Frith, U. (ed.) (1991) *Autism and Asperger Syndrome* (Cambridge: Cambridge University Press).
Frith, U. (2004) 'Emanuel Miller Lecture: Confusions and Controversies About Asperger Syndrome'. *Journal of Child Psychology and Psychiatry* 45, 672–86.
Frosh, S., Phoenix, A. and Pattman, R. (2002) *Young Masculinities: Understanding Boys in Contemporary Society* (Basingstoke: Palgrave).
Gaffney, G.R., Kuperman, S., Tsai, L.Y., Minchin, S. and Hassaneim, K.M. (1987) 'Midsagittal Magnetic Resonance Imaging of Autism'. *British Journal of Psychiatry* 151, 831–3.
Galton, F. (1869) *Hereditary Genius*. London: Macmillan.
Garbarino, J. (1993) 'Childhood: What Do We Need to Know?'. *Childhood* 1, 3–10.
Gardner, M. (2000) 'The Brutality of Dr Bettelheim'. *Skeptical-Inquirer* 24, 12–14.
Geertz, C. (1983) *Local Knowledge* (New York: Basic).
George, S. (1999) *A Short History of Neoliberalism*. Available at www.global-policy.org/globaliz/econ/histneol.htm, accessed 2 October 2008.
Gergen, K. (1985) 'The Social Constructionist Movement in Modern Psychology'. *American Psychologist* 40, 266–75.
Gergen, K. (1991) *The Saturated Self: Dilemmas of Identity in Contemporary Life* (New York: Basic).
Ghaziuddin, M. (2005) 'A Family Study of Asperger Syndrome'. *Journal of Autism and Developmental Disorders* 35, 177–82.
Gil'adi, A. (1992) *Children Of Islam: Concepts of Childhood in Medieval Muslim Society* (Oxford: Macmillan).

Gillberg, C. (1984) 'Infantile Autism and Other Childhood Psychosis in a Swedish Urban Region: Epidemiological Aspects'. *Journal of Child Psychology and Psychiatry* 25, 35–43.

Gillberg C. (1989) 'Asperger Syndrome in 23 Swedish Children'. *Developmental Medicine and Child Neurology* 31, 520–31.

Gillberg, C (1991) 'Autism and Autistic-like Conditions: Subclasses in Disorders of Empathy'. *Journal of Child Psychology and Psychiatry* 33, 813–42

Gillberg, C. (1992) 'Subgroups in Autism: Are There Behavioural Phenotypes Typical of Underlying Medical Conditions?'. *Journal of Intellectual Disability Research* 36, 201–14.

Gillberg, C. (2002) *A Guide to Asperger Syndrome* (Cambridge: Cambridge University Press).

Gillberg, C. and Cederlund, M. (2005) 'Asperger Syndrome: Familial and Pre- and Perinatal Factors'. *Journal of Autism and Developmental Disorders* 35, 159–66.

Gillberg, I.C. and Gillberg, C. (1996) 'Autism in Immigrants: A Population-based Study from Swedish Rural and Urban Areas'. *Journal of Intellectual Disability Research* 40, 24–31.

Gillberg, C., Ehlers, S., Schaumann, H., Jakobsson, G., Dahlgren, S.O. and Lindblom, R. (1990). 'Autism Under Age 3 Years: A Clinical Study of 28 Cases Referred for Autistic Symptoms in Infancy'. *Journal of Child Psychology and Psychiatry and Allied Disciplines* 31, 921–34.

Giroux, H. (1998) 'Stealing Innocence'. In H. Jenkins (ed.) *Children's Culture Reader* (New York: New York University Press).

Goonatilake, S. (1998) *Mining Civilizational Knowledge* (Bloomington: Indiana University Press.)

Gordo-Lopez, A. and Burman, E. (2004) 'Emotional Capital and Information Technologies in the Changing Rhetoric around Children and Childhoods'. *New Directions in Child Development* 105, 63–80.

Gramsci, A. (1971) *Selections From Prison Notebooks* (London: Lawrence & Wishart).

Gregg, G.S. (2005) *The Middle East: A Cultural Psychology* (New York: Oxford University Press).

Gurian, M. (1999) *The Good Son* (New York: Tarcher-Putnam).

Gurian, M. (2001) *Boys and Girls Think Differently!* (San Francisco: Jossey-Bass).

Habermas, J. (1972) *Knowledge and Human Interests*, trans. J. Shapiro (Boston, MA: Beacon Press).

Hacking, I. (1999*)* *The Social Construction of What?* (Cambridge, MA: Harvard University Press).

Haddon, M. (2004) *The Curious Incident of the Dog in the Night-time* (London: Vintage).

Hadjikhani, N., Joseph, R.M., Snyder, J., Chabris, C.F., Clark, J., Steele, S., McGrath, L., Vangel, M., Aharon, I., Feczko, E., Harris, G.J. and

Tager-Flusberg, H. (2004) 'Activation of the Fusiform Gyrus When Individuals with Autism Spectrum Disorder View Faces'. *Neuroimage* 22, 1141–50.

Haist, F., Adamo, M., Westerfield, M., Courchesne, E. and Townsend, J. (2005) 'The Functional Neuroanatomy of Spatial Attention in Autism Spectrum Disorder'. *Developmental Neuropsychology* 27, 425–58.

Hall, S. (1996) 'Who Needs Identity?'. In S. Hall and P. Du Gay (eds) *Questions of Cultural Identity* (London: Sage).

Hamer, D., Hu, S., Magnuson, V., Hu, N. and Pattatucci, A. (1993) 'A Linkage between DNA Markers on the X Chromosome and Male Sexual Orientation'. *Science* 261, 321–7.

Hamilton, C. (2003) *Growth Fetish* (London: Pluto).

Hardlicka, M., Dudova, I., Beranova, I., Lisy, J., Belsan, T., Neuwirth, J., Komarek, V., Faladova, L., Havlovicova, M., Sedlacek, Z., Blatny, M. and Urbanek, T. (2005) 'Subtypes of Autism by Cluster Analysis Based on Structural MRI Data'. *European Child and Adolescent Psychiatry* 14, 138–44.

Harre, R. (1983) *Personal Being: A Theory for Individual Psychology* (Oxford: Blackwell).

Harre, R. (1986) 'The Step to Social Constructionism'. In M. Richards and P. Light (eds) *Children of Social Worlds* (Cambridge: Polity Press).

Harris, G. and Carey, B. (2008) 'Researchers Fail to Reveal Full Drug Pay'. Sunday *New York Times*. 8 June 2008. Available at http://www.mindfreedom.org/kb/psych-drug-corp/ny-times-biederman-harvard/grassley-v-harvard/, accessed 9 October 2008.

Hartung, C.M. and Widiger, T.A. (1998). 'Gender Differences in the Diagnosis of Mental Disorders: Conclusions and Controversies of the DSM-IV'. *Psychological Bulletin* 123, 260–78.

Hearn, K. (2004) 'Here Kiddie, Kiddie'. Available at AlterNet. http://alternet.org/drugreporter/20594, accessed 5 February 2009.

Hendrick, H. (1994) *Child Welfare England 1870–1989* (London: Routledge).

Hendrick, H. (2003) *Child Welfare: Historical Dimensions, Contemporary Debate* (Bristol: Polity Press).

Hollander, E., Anagnostou, E., Chaplin, W., Esposito, K., Haznedar, M.M., Licalzi, E., Wasserman, S., Soorya, L. and Buchsbaum, M. (2005) 'Striatal Volume on Magnetic Resonance Imaging and Repetitive Behaviors in Autism'. *Biological Psychiatry* 58, 226–32.

Hooten, E. (1937) *Apes, Men and Morons* (New York: G. Putman & Sons).

Horwitz, B., Rumsey, J.M., Grady, C.L. and Rapoport, S.I. (1988) 'The Cerebral Metabolic Landscape in Autism: Intercorrelations of Regional Glucose Utilization'. *Archives of Neurology* 45, 749–55.

Howlin, P. and Moore A. (1997) 'Diagnosis in Autism: A Survey of Over 1200 Patients in the UK'. *Autism* 1, 135–62.

Hyman, S. (2003) 'Diagnosing Disorders'. *Scientific American* 289, 96–104.

Infoplease (2000–7) *Measuring Global Poverty* (Boston: Pearson Education).

Ingleby, D. (1985) 'Professionals as Socialisers: The "Psy Complex"'. In S. Spitzer and A.T. Scull (eds) *Research in the Law, Deviance and Social Control: A Research Annual, Vol. 7* (London: JAI Press).
Inland Revenue (2005) www.statistics.gov.uk/cci/nugget.asp?id=2, accessed 25 September 2005.
Jackson, G. (2005) *Rethinking Psychiatric Drugs* (Bloomington: AuthorHouse).
Jameson, F. (1991) *Postmodernism, or the Cultural Logic of Late Capitalism* (Durham, NC: Duke University Press).
Jensen, P.S., Arnold, L.E., Swanson, J.M., Vitiello, B., Abikoff, H.B., Greenhill, L., Hechtman, L., Hinshaw, S.P., Pelham, W.E., Wells, K.C., Conners, K.C., Elliott, G.R., Epstein, J., Hoza, B., March, J.S., Molina, B.S., Newcorn, J.H., Severe, J.B., Wigal, T., Gibbons, R. and Hur, K. (2007) '3 Year Follow-up of the NIMH MTA Study'. *Journal of the American Academy of Child and Adolescent Psychiatry* 46, 988–1001.
Jones, K. (1972) *A History of the Mental Health Services* (London: RKP).
Joseph, J. (2004) *The Gene Illusion: Genetic Research in Psychiatry and Psychology Under the Microscope* (New York: Algora).
Joseph, J. (2006) *The Missing Gene: Psychiatry, Hereditary, and the Fruitless Search for Genes* (New York: Algora).
Jung, C.G. (1923/1971) *Psychological Types* (London: Routledge & Kegan Paul).
Jureidini, J., Doecke, C., Mansfield, P., Haby, M., Menkes, D. and Tonkin, A. (2004) 'Efficacy and Safety of Antidepressants for Children and Adolescents'. *British Medical Journal* 328, 879–83.
Kakar, S. (1994) *The Inner World of the Indian Child* (New Delhi: Oxford University Press).
Kakar, S. (1997) *The Inner World: A Psychoanalytic Study of Childhood and Society in India. Second Edition* (New Delhi: Oxford University Press).
Kallman, F. (1938) 'Heredity, Reproduction and Eugenic Procedure in the Field of Schizophrenia'. *Eugenic News* 23, 105.
Kanner, L. (1943) 'Autistic Disturbances of Affective Contact'. *Nervous Child* 2, 217 – 50.
Kanner, L. and Eisenberg, L. (1956) 'Early Infantile Autism 1943–1955'. *American Journal of Orthopsychiatry* 26, 556–66.
Kaplan, M. (1983) 'A Woman's View of DSM-III'. *American Psychologist* 38, 786–92.
Karmiloff-Smith, A. (1992) *Beyond Modularity: A Developmental Perspective on Cognitive Science* (Cambridge, MA: MIT Press).
Keir, G. (1952) 'A History of Child Guidance'. *British Journal of Educational Psychology* 22, 5–29.
Kelves, D.J. (1985) *In the Name of Eugenics* (California: University of California Press).
Kenway, J. and Fitzclarence, L. (1997) 'Masculinity, Violence and Schooling: Challenging "Poisonous Pedagogies"'. *Gender and Education* 9, 117–33.

Kessen, W. (1979) 'The American Child and Other Cultural Inventions'. *American Psychologist* 34, 815–20.

Kimmel, M. (2004) *The Gendered Society* (New York: Oxford University Press).

Kincheloe, J. (1998) 'The New Childhood: Home Alone as a Way of Life'. In H. Jenkins (ed.) *Children's Culture Reader* (New York: New York University Press).

Kindlon, D. and Thompson, M. (2000) *Raising Cain: Protecting the Emotional Life of Boys* (New York: Ballantine).

Kirschner, S. (2006) ' "Good Babies" or "Goodness of Fit"? Normalizing and Pluralizing Dimensions of Contemporary Temperament Discourse'. *Culture and Psychology* 12, 5.

Klin, A., Pauls, D., Schultz, R. and Volkmar, F. (2005) 'Three Diagnstic Approaches to Asperger Syndrome: Implications for Research'. *Journal of Autism and Developmental Disorders* 35, 221–34.

Kopelman, L. (1990). 'On the Evaluative Nature of Competency and Capacity Judgements'. *International Journal of Law and Psychiatry* 13, 309–29.

Koplewicz, H. (1997) *It's Nobody's Fault: New Hope and Help for Difficult Children and Their Parents* (New York: Three Rivers Press).

Kovel, J. (2002) *The Enemy of Nature: The End of Capitalism or the End of the World?* (New York: Zed).

Laing, R.D. (1960) *The Divided Self: An Existential Study in Sanity and Madness* (Harmondsworth: Penguin).

Lancet editorial (2008) 'Children and Psychiatric Drugs: Disillusion and Opportunity'. *The Lancet* 372, 1194.

Langan, M. and Schwarz, B. (eds) (1985) *Crisis in the British State, 1890–1930* (London: Hutchison University Press).

Lashley, K.S. (1950) 'In Search of the Engram'. *Symposia of the Society for Experimental Biology* 4, 553–61.

Le Couteur A, and Baird G, (2003) *National Initiative for Autism: Screening and Assessment (NIASA). National Autism Plan for Children* (London: National Autistic Society).

Le Couteur, A., Lord, C. and Rutter, M. (2003) *Autism Diagnostic Interview-Revised (ADI-R)* (Los Angeles: Western Psychological Services).

Le Couteur, A., Bailey, A., Goode, S., Pickles, A., Robertson, S., Gottesman, I. and Rutter, M. (1996) 'A Broader Phenotype of Autism: The Clinical Spectrum in Twins'. *Journal of Child Psychology and Psychiatry* 37, 785–801.

LeVine, R.A., Dixon, S., LeVine, S., Richman, A., Leiderman, P.H., Keefer, C.H. and Brazelton, T.B. (1994) *Child Care and Culture: Lessons from Africa* (Cambridge: Cambridge University Press).

Leo, J. (2006) 'The Truth about Academic Medicine: Children on Psychotropic Drugs and the Illusion of Science'. In S. Timimi and B. Maitra (eds) *Critical Voices in Child and Adolescent Mental Health* (London: Free Association Books).

Leo, J.L. and Cohen, D.A. (2003) 'Broken Brains or Flawed Studies? A Critical Review of ADHD Neuroimaging Research'. *Journal of Mind and Behavior* 24, 29–56.

Levin, M. (1997) *Why Race Matters* (Santa Barbara, CA: Praeger).

Levitt, J.G., Blanton, R., Capetillo-Cunliffe, L., Guthrie, D., Toga, A. and McCracken, J.T. (1999) 'Cerebellar Vermis Lobules VIII-X in Autism'. *Progress in Neuropsychopharmacology and Biological Psychiatry* 23, 625–33.

Lichtman, R. (1987) 'The Illusion of Maturation in an Age of Decline'. In J. Broughton (ed.) *Critical Theories of Psychological Development* (New York: Plenum).

Lipsky, D. and Abrams, A. (1994) *Late Bloomers: Coming of Age in Today's America* (New York: Times).

Locke, J. (1989) *The Clarendon Edition of the Works of John Locke (edited by J.W. Yolton and J.S. Yolton)* (Oxford: Clarendon).

Lord, C. (1995) 'Follow-up of Two-year-olds Referred for Possible Autism'. *Journal of Child Psychology and Psychiatry* 36, 1365–82.

Lord, C., Rutter, M. and Le Couteur, A. (1994) 'Autism Diagnostic Interview-Revised: A Revised Version of a Diagnostic Interview for Caregivers of Individuals with Possible Pervasive Developmental Disorders'. *Journal of Autism and Developmental Disorders* 24, 659–85.

Lord, C., Risi, S., Lambrecht, L., Cook, E.H., Leventhal, B.L., DiLavore, P.C., Pickles, A. and Rutter, M. (2000) 'The Autism Diagnostic Observation Schedule-Generic: A Standard Measure of Social and Communication Deficits Associated with the Spectrum of Autism'. *Journal of Autism and Developmental Disorders* 30, 205–23.

Lord, C., Rutter, M., Goode, S., Heemsbergen, J., Jordan, H., Mawhood, L. and Schopler, E. (1989) 'Autism Diagnostic Observation Schedule: A Standardized Observation of Communicative and Social Behaviour'. *Journal of Autism and Developmental Disorders* 19, 185–212.

Lotter, V. (1966a) 'Epidemiology of Autistic Conditions in Young Children: I. Prevalence'. *Social Psychiatry* 1, 124–37.

Lotter, V. (1966b) 'Epidemiology of Autistic Conditions in Young Children: II. Some Characteristics of the Parents and the Children'. *Social Psychiatry* 1, 163–73.

Lovaas, O.I. (1987) 'Behavioral Treatment and Normal Educational and Intellectual Functioning in Young Autistic Children'. *Journal of Consulting and Clinical Psychology* 55, 3–9.

Lovaas, O.I. (1993) 'Long-term Outcome for Children with Autism who Received Early Intensive Behavioral Treatment'. *American Journal on Mental Retardation* 97, 359–72.

Lovaas, O.I., Ackerman, A.B., Alexander, D., Firestone, P., Perkins, J. and Young, D. (1981) *Teaching Developmentally Disabled Children: The Me Book* (Austin, TX: Pro-Ed).

Mac An Ghaill, M. (1994) *The Making Of Men: Masculinities, Sexualities And Schooling* (Buckingham: Open University Press).

Madsen, K., Hviid, A., Vestergaard, M., Schendel, D., Wohlfahrt, J., Thorsen, P., Olsen, J. and Melbye, M. (2002) 'A Population-based Study of Measles, Mumps, and Rubella Vaccination and Autism'. *New England Journal of Medicine* 347, 1477–82.

Marx, K. and Engels, F. (1845/1998) *The German Ideology* (New York: Prometheus).

McAlonan, M., Daly, E., Kumari, V., Critchley, H.D., Amelsvoort, T., Suckling, J., Simmons, A., Sigmundsson, T., Greenwood, K., Russell, A., Schmitz, N., Happe, F., Howlin, P. and Murphy, D.G.M. (2002) 'Brain Anatomy and Sensorimotor Gating in Asperger's Syndrome'. *Brain* 125, 1594 – 606.

McCracken, J.T., McGough, J., Shah, B., Cronin, P. and Hong, D. (2002) 'Resperidone in Children with Autism and Serious Behavioral Problems'. *New England Journal of Medicine* 347, 314–21.

McGeer, V. (2004) 'Autistic Self-awareness'. *Philosophy, Psychiatry, & Psychology* 11, 235–51.

Medawar, C. and Hardon, A. (2004) *Medicines out of Control? Anti-depressants and the Conspiracy of Goodwill* (Amsterdam: Aksant Academic).

Mednick, S.A. and Christiansen, K.D. (1977) *Biosocial Basis of Criminal Behaviour* (New York: Gardner Press).

Moncreiff, J. (2008a) 'Neoliberalism and Biopsychiatry: A Marriage of Convenience'. In C.I. Cohen and S. Timimi (eds) *Liberatory Psychiatry: Philosophy, Politics, and Mental Health* (Cambridge: Cambridge University Press).

Moncreiff, J. (2008b) *The Myth of the Chemical Cure* (Basingstoke: Palgrave Macmillan).

Morgan, S. and Taylor, E. (2007) 'Antipsychotic Drugs in Children with Autism'. *British Medical Journal* 334, 1069–70

Morss, J.R. (1990) *The Biologising of Childhood: Developmental Psychology and the Darwinian Myth* (Hove: Lawrence Erlbaum Associates).

Morss, J.R. (1996) *Growing Critical: Alternatives to Developmental Psychology* (London and New York: Routledge).

MTA Co-operative Group (1999) 'A 14-month Randomized Clinical Trial of Treatment Strategies for Attention Deficit/Hyperactivity Disorder'. *Archives of General Psychiatry* 56, 1073–86.

MTA Co-operative Group (2004) 'National Institute of Mental Health Multimodal Treatment Study of ADHD Follow-up: 24-month Outcomes of Treatment Strategies for Attention-deficit/Hyperactivity Disorder'. *Pediatrics* 113, 754–61.

Müller, R.A., Pierce, K., Ambrose, J.B., Allen, G. and Courchesne, E. (2001) 'Atypical Patterns of Cerebral Motor Activation in Autism: A Functional Magnetic Resonance Study'. *Biological Psychiatry* 49, 665–76.

Muller-Hill, B. (1991) 'Psychiatry in the Nazi Era'. In S. Block and P. Chodoff (eds) *Psychiatric Ethics* (New York: Oxford University Press).

Murray, C. and Hernstein, R. (1994) *The Bell Curve* (New York: Free Press).

Nadesan, M. (2005) *Constructing Autism: Unravelling the 'Truth' and Understanding the Social* (London: Routledge).

National Autistic Society (2003) *National Autism Plan for Children*. Available at http://www.nas.org.uk/content/1/c4/34/54/NIASARep.pdf, accessed 8 May 2008.

National Autistic Society (2006) http://www.nas.org.uk/, accessed 10 October 2006.

National Screening Committee (2000) *Second Report of the UK National Screening Committee* (London: Department of Health). Available at http://www.nsc.nhs.uk/pdfs/secondreport.pdf, accessed 24 January 2009.

Nuffield Council on Bioethics (1998) *Mental Disorders and Genetics*. Available at http://www.nuffieldbioethics.org/go/ourwork/mentaldisorders/introduction, accessed 21 December 2008.

Ormond, G.I. and Seltzer, M.M. (2007) 'Siblings of Individuals with Autism or Down's Syndrome: Effect on Parent Lives'. *Journal of Intellectual Disability Research* 51, 682–96.

Ornitz, E.M. (1973) *Childhood Autism: A Review of the Clinical and Experimental Literature* (California: Western Journal of Medication).

Overall, J. and Campbell, M. (1988) 'Behavioural Assessment of Psychopathology in Children: Infantile Autism'. *Journal of Clinical Psychology* 44, 708–16.

Ozonoff, S. and Cathcart, K. (1998) 'Effectiveness of a Home Program Intervention for Young Children with Autism'. *Journal of Autism and Developmental Disorders* 28, 25–32.

Panerai, S., Ferrante, L. and Zingale, M. (2002) 'Benefits of the Treatment and Education of Autistic and Communication Handicapped Children (TEACCH) Programme as Compared with a Non-specific Approach'. *Journal of Intellectual Disability Research* 46, 318–27.

Parker, G. (2009) 'Antidepressants on Trial: How Valid is the Evidence?'. *British Journal of Psychiatry* 194, 1–3.

Parker, I. (1992) *Discourse Dynamics* (London: Routledge).

Parton, N. (2006) *Safeguarding Childhood: Early Intervention and Surveillance in a Late Modern Society* (Basingstoke: Palgrave Macmillan).

Piaget, J. and Inhelder, B. (1948/1967) *The Child's Conception of Space* (New York: W.W. Norton).

Pickles, A., Starr, E., Kazak, S., Bolton, P., Papanikolaou, K., Bailey, A., Goodman, R. and Rutter, M. (2000) 'Variable Expression of the Autism Broader Phenotype: Findings from Extended Pedigrees'. *Journal of Child Psychology and Psychiatry* 41, 491–502.

Pierce, K., Haist, F., Sedaghat, F. and Courchesne, E. (2004) 'The Brain Response to Personally Familiar Faces in Autism: Findings of Fusiform Activity and Beyond'. *Brain* 127, 2703–16.

Pilgrim, D. (1997) *Psychotherapy and Society* (London: Sage).

Pillai, A., Patel, V., Cardozo, P., Goodman, R., Weiss, H.A. and Andrew, G. (2008) 'Non-traditional Lifestyles and Prevalence of Mental Disorders in Adolescents in Goa, India'. *British Journal of Psychiatry* 192, 45–51.

Pisula, E. (2007) 'A Comparative Study of Stress Profiles in Mothers of Children with Autism and Those of Children with Down's Syndrome'. *Journal of Applied Research in Intellectual Disabilities* 20, 274–8.

Piven, J., Nehme, E., Simon, J., Barta, P., Pearlson, G. and Folstein, S.E. (1992) 'Magnetic Resonance Imaging in Autism: Measurement of the Cerebellum, Pons, and Fourth Ventricle'. *Biological Psychiatry* 31, 491–504.

Poggi, G. (2005) *Weber: A Short Introduction* (Oxford: Blackwell).

Pollack, W. (1998) *Real Boys* (New York: Henry Holt & Co.).

Popenoe, P. (1935) 'Public Opinion on Sterilization in California'. *Eugenic News* 20, 73.

Popper, K. (1959) *The Logic of Scientific Discovery* (New York: Basic).

Popper, K. (1963) *Conjectures and Refutations* (London: Routledge).

Premack, D.G. and Woodruff, G. (1978) 'Does the Chimpanzee have a Theory of Mind?'. *Behavioral and Brain Sciences* 1, 515–26.

Prior, M., Perry, D. and Gajzago, C. (1975) 'Kanner's Syndrome or Early Onset Psychosis: A Taxanomic Analysis of 142 Cases'. *Journal of Autism and Developmental Disorders* 5, 71–80.

Proctor, R. (1988) *Racial Hygiene: Medicine Under the Nazis* (Cambridge, MA: Harvard University Press).

Rabin, L. (1994) *Families on the Frontline: American Working Class Speaks About the Economy, Race and Ethnicity* (New York: HarperCollins).

Rafferty, M. (2005) 'Autism Problems Explained in New Research'. Available at http://www.medicalnewstoday.com/articles/32541.php, accessed 22 December 2008.

Rapin, I. (1998) 'Progress in the Neurobiology of Autism'. *CNS Spectrum* 3, 50–79.

Reiss, A. and Roth, J. (1993) *Understanding and Preventing Violence* (Washington DC: National Academy Press).

Rice, G., Anderson, C., Risch, N. and Elbers, G. (1999) 'Male Homosexuality: Absence of Linkage to Microsatellite Markers on at Xq28'. *Science* 284, 665–7.

Richards B. (1989) 'Visions of Freedom'. *Free Association* 16, 31–42.

Ring, H., Woodbury-Smith, M., Watson, P., Wheelwrigh, S. and Baron-Cohen, S. (2008) 'Clinical Heterogeneity Among People with High Functioning Autism Spectrum Conditions: Evidence Favouring a Continuous Severity Gradient'. *Behavioral and Brain Functions* 4. Open access available at http://www.behavioralandbrainfunctions.com/content/4/1/11, accessed 1 February 2009.

Ring, H.A., Baron-Cohen, S., Wheelwright, S., Williams, S.C.R., Brammer, M., Andrew, C. and Bullmore, E. (1999) 'Cerebral Correlates of Preserved Cognitive Skills in Autism: A Functional MRI Study of Embedded Figures Task performance'. *Brain* 122, 1305–15.

Ritvo, E.R., Freeman, B.J., Mason-Brothers, A., Mo, A. and Ritvo, A.M. (1985) 'Concordance for the Syndrome of Autism on 40 Pairs of Affected Twins'. *American Journal of Psychiatry* 42, 74–7.

Ritvo, E.R., Freeman, B.J., Pingree, C., Mason-Brothers, A., Jorde, L., Jenson, W.R., McMahon, W.M., Peterson, P.B., Mo, A. and Ritvo, A. (1989) 'The UCLA-University of Utah Epidemiologic Survey of Autism: Prevalence'. *American Journal of Psychiatry* 146, 194–9.

Robins, D.L., Fein, D., Barton, M.L. and Green, J.A. (2001a) 'The Modified Checklist for Autism in Toddlers: An Initial Study Investigating the Early Detection of Autism and Pervasive Developmental Disorders'. *Journal of Autism and Developmental Disorders* 31, 131–51.

Robins, D.L., Fein, D., Barton, M.L. and Green, J.A. (2001b) 'Reply to Charman *et al.*'s Commentary on the Modified Checklist for Autism in Toddlers'. *Journal of Autism and Developmental Disorders* 31, 149–51.

Rorty, R. (1989) *Contingency, Irony and Solidarity* (Cambridge: Cambridge University Press).

Rorty, R. (1991) *Objectivity, Relativism, and Truth* (Cambridge: Cambridge University Press).

Rosanoff, A. (1938) *Manual of Psychiatry and Mental Hygiene* (New York: John Wiley & Sons).

Rose, N. (1985) *The Psychological Complex: Psychology, Politics and Society in England 1869–1939* (London: Routledge & Regan Paul).

Rose, S., Lewontin, R.C. and Kamin, L.J. (1990) *Not in our Genes* (Harmondsworth: Penguin).

Rousseau, J.J. (1762/1992) *Emile*, ed. P.D. Jimack (London: Everyman Library Series).

Rutter, M. (1968) 'Concepts of Autism: A Review of Research'. *Journal of Child Psychology and Psychiatry* 9, 1–25.

Rutter, M. (ed.) (1972) 'Infantile Autism: Concepts, Characteristics and Treatment'. *Journal of Autism and Developmental Disorders* 4 (special issue).

Rutter, M. (1978a) 'Diagnosis and Definition of Childhood Autism'. *Journal of Autism and Developmental Disorders* 8, 139–61.

Rutter, M. (1978b) 'Diagnostic Validity in Child Psychiatry'. *Advances in Biological Psychiatry* 2, 2–22.

Rutter, M. (1998) 'Dyslexia: Approaches to Validation'. *Child Psychiatry and Psychiatry Review* 3, 24–5.

Rutter, M. (2000) 'Genetic Studies of Autism: From the 1970s into the Millennium'. *Journal of Abnormal Child Psychology* 28, 3–14.

Rutter, M. (2005) 'Aetiology of Autism: Findings and Questions'. *Journal of Intellectual Disability Research* 49, 231–8.

Rutter, M. (2006) *Genes and Behaviour: Nature-Nurture Interplay Explained* (Oxford: Blackwell.)

Rutter, M. and Nikapota, A. (2002) 'Culture, Ethnicity, Society and Psychopathology'. In M. Rutter and E. Taylor (eds) *Child and Adolescent Psychiatry: Fourth Edition* (Oxford: Blackwell).

Rutter, M. and Schopler, E. (1987) 'Autism and Pervasive Developmental Disorders: Concepts and Diagnostic Issues'. *Journal of Autism and Developmental Disorders* 17, 159–86.

Rutter, M. and Schopler, E. (1992) 'Classification of Pervasive Developmental Disorders: Some Concepts and Practical Considerations'. *Journal of Autism and Developmental Disorders* 22, 459–82.

Rutter, M., Graham, P. and Yule, W. (1970) *A Neuropsychiatric Study of Childhood* (London: Spastics International Medical).

Rutter, M., Tizard, J. and Whitmore, K. (1970b) *Education, Health and Behaviour* (London: Longman).

Rutter, M., Silberg, J., O'Connor, T. and Simonoff, E. (1999) 'Genetics and Child Psychiatry: II Empirical Research Findings'. *Journal of Child Psychology and Psychiatry* 40, 19–55.

Rutter, M., Anderson-Wood, L., Beckett, C., Bredenkamp, D., Castle, J., Groothues, C., Kreppner, J., Keaveney, L., Lord, C. and O'Connor, T. (1999) 'Quasi-autistic Patterns Following Severe Early Global Privation'. *Journal of Child Psychology and Psychiatry* 40, 537–49.

Sachs, W. (1992) *The Developmental Dictionary* (London: Zed).

Sadato, N., Pascual-Leone, A., Grafman, J., Ibanez, V., Deiber, M.P., Dold, G. and Hallett, M. (1996) 'Activation of the Primary Visual Cortex by Braille Reading in blind Subjects'. *Nature* 380, 526–8.

Sadler, J. (2005) *Values and Psychiatric Diagnosis* (New York: Oxford University Press).

Said, E. (1978) *Orientalism* (London: Routledge).

Said, E. (1981) *Covering Islam* (London: Routledge).

Saunders, R., Hindi, A. and Vahia, I. (2008) 'A New Psychiatry for the New World: Postcolonialism, Postmodernism, and the Integration of Premodern Thought into Psychiatry'. In C. Cohen and S. Timimi (eds) *Liberatory Psychiatry: Philosophy, Politics, and Mental Health* (Cambridge: Cambridge University Press).

Schieve, L.A., Blumberg, S.J., Rice, C., Visser, S. and Boyle, C. (2007) 'The Relationship Between Autism and Parenting Stress'. *Pediatrics* 119, S114–S121.

Scott, F., Baron-Cohen, S., Bolton, P. and Brayne, C. (2002a) 'The CAST (Childhood Asperger Syndrome Test): Preliminary Development of UK Screen for Mainstream Primary-school Children'. *Autism* 6, 9–31.

Scott, F., Baron-Cohen, S., Bolton, P. and Brayne, C. (2002b) 'Brief Report: Prevalence of Autism Spectrum Conditions in Children Aged 5-11 Years in Cambridgeshire, UK'. *Autism* 6, 231–7.

Scott, J. and Baldwin, L. (2005) 'The Challenge of Early Intensive Intervention'. In D. Zager (ed.) *Autism Spectrum Disorder: Identification, Education and Treatment* (Mahwah, NJ: Lawrence Erlbaum Associates).

Sears, L.L., Vest, C., Mohamed, S., Bailey, J., Ranson, B.J. and Piven, J. (1999) 'An MRI Study of the Basal Ganglia in Autism'. *Progress in Neuropsychopharmacology and Biological Psychiatry* 23, 613–24.

Seidler, V. (1989) *Rediscovering Masculinity: Reason, Language and Sexuality* (London: Routledge).

Sewell, T. (1995) 'A Phallic Response to Schools: Black Masculinity and Race in an Inner-city Comprehensive'. In M. Griffiths and B. Troyna (eds) *Anti-Racism, Culture and Social Justice in Education* (Stoke-on-Trent: Trentham).

Shea, S., Turgay, A., Carroll, A., Schulz, M. and Orlik, M. (2004) 'Risperidone in the Treatment of Disruptive Behavioral Symptoms in Children with Autistic and Other Pervasive Developmental Disorders'. *Pediatrics* 114, 634–41.

Shotter, J. (1974) 'The Development of Personal Powers'. In M.P.M. Richards (ed.) *The Integration of a Child into a Social World* (Cambridge: Cambridge University Press).

Silberman, S. (2001) 'The Geek Syndrome'. *Wired* 9 (December). Available at http://www.wired.com/wired/archive/9.12/aspergers.html?pg=1&topic=&topic_set=, accessed 4 February 2009.

Skelton, C. (2001) *Schooling the Boys: Masculinities and Primary Education* (Buckingham: Open University Press).

Skuse, D. (2001) 'Endophenotypes and Child Psychiatry'. *British Journal of Psychiatry* 178, 395–6.

Sommers, C.H. (2000) *The War Against Boys* (New York: Simon and Schuster).

Sowell, E.R., Thompson, P.M., Welcome, S.E., Henkenius, A.L., Toga, A.W., and Peterson, B.S. (2003) 'Cortical abnormalities in children and adolescents with attention-deficit hyperactivity disorder'. *The Lancet* 362, 1699-1707.

Spice, B. (2004) 'Autism Seen as Problem of Connections in Brains'. *Pittsburgh Post-Gazette*. Sunday, 15 August 2004. Available at http://post-gazette.com/pg/04228/361572.stm, accessed 22 December 2008.

Sprong, M., Schothorst, P., Vos, E., Hox, J. and Van Engeland, H. (2007) 'Theory of Mind in Schizophrenia: Meta-analysis'. *British Journal of Psychiatry* 191, 5–13.

Stainton-Rogers, R. and Stainton-Rogers, W. (1992) *Stories of Childhood: Shifting Agendas of Child Concern* (Hassocks: Harvester).

Starr, E., Berument, S.K., Pickles, A., Tomlins, M., Bailey, A., Papanikolaou, K. and Rutter, M. (2001) 'A Family Genetic Study of Autism Associated with Profound Mental Retardation'. *Journal of Autism and Developmental Disorders* 31, 89–96.

Steffenburg, S., Gillberg, C., Hellgren, L., Andersson, L., Gillberg, C.I., Jakobsson, G. and Bohman, M. (1989) 'A Twin Study of Autism in Denmark, Finland, Iceland, Norway and Sweden'. *Journal of Child Psychology and Psychiatry* 30, 405–16.

Stephens S. (1995) 'Children and the Politics of Culture in "Late Capitalism"'. In S. Stephens (ed.) *Children and the Politics of Culture* (Princeton: Princeton University Press).

Stone, W.L., Coonrood, E. and Opal, Y. (2000) 'Brief Report: Screening Tool for Autism in Two-Year Olds (STAT): Development and Preliminary Data'. *Journal of Autism and Developmental Disorders* 30, 607–12.

Summerfield, D. and Veale, D. (2008) 'Proposals for Massive Expansion of Psychological Therapies would be Counterproductive Across Society'. *The British Journal of Psychiatry* 192, 326–30.

Sutherland, G. (1984) *Ability, Merit and Measurement: Mental Testing and English Education* (Oxford: Clarendon Press).

Szatamari, P. (1992) 'The Validity of Autistic Spectrum Disorders: A Literature Review'. *Journal of Autism and Developmental Disorders* 22, 583–600.

Szatamari, P. (1998) 'Differential Diagnosis of Asperger Disorder'. In E. Schopler, G.B. Mesibov and L.J. Kunce (eds) *Asperger Syndrome or High-Functioning Autism?* (New York: Plenum).

Szatamari, P., Bremner, R. and Nagy, J. (1989) 'Asperger's Syndrome: A Review of Clinical Features'. *Canadian Journal of Psychiatry* 34, 554–60.

Szatamari, P., MacLean, J., Jones, M.B., Bryson, S., Zwaigenbaum, L., Bartolucci, G., Mahoney, W.J. and Tuff, L. (2000) 'The Familial Aggregation of the Lesser Variant in Biological and Nonbiological Relatives of PDD Probands: A Family History Study'. *Journal of Child Psychology and Psychiatry* 41, 579–86.

Szasz, T. (1970) *Ideology and Insanity* (New York: Doubleday-Anchor).

Szasz, T. (1974) *The Myth of Mental Illness (Revised Edition)* (New York: Harper & Row).

Tan, R. (1993) 'Racism and Similarity: Paranoid Schizoid Structures'. *British Journal of Psychotherapy* 10, 33–43.

Tantam, D. (1988) 'Lifelong Eccentricity and Social Isolation, II: Asperger's Syndrome or Schizoid Personality Disorder'. *British Journal of Psychiatry* 153, 783–91.

Thomas, A. (1974) *Racism and Psychiatry* (Springfield, IL: Carol).

Timimi, S. (1996) 'Race and Colour in Internal and External Reality'. *British Journal of Psychotherapy* 13, 183–92.

Timimi, S. (2002) *Pathological Child Psychiatry and the Medicalization of Childhood* (London: Brunner-Routledge).

Timimi, S. (2005) *Naughty Boys: Anti-Social Behaviour, ADHD, and the Role of Culture* (Basingstoke: Palgrave Macmillan).

Timimi, S. (2007a) *Misunderstanding ADHD: A Complete Guide for Parents to Alternatives to Drugs* (Milton Keynes: Authorhouse).

Timimi, S. (2007b) 'Should Young People be Given Antidepressants? No'. *British Medical Journal* 335, 751.

Timimi, S. (2008a) 'Child Psychiatry and its Relationship to the Pharmaceutical Industry: Theoretical and Practical Issues'. *Advances in Psychiatric Treatment* 14, 3–9.

Timimi, S. (2008b) 'Children's Mental Health and the Global Market: An Ecological Analysis'. In C.I. Cohen and S. Timimi (eds) *Liberatory Psychiatry: Philosophy, Politics, and Mental Health* (Cambridge: Cambridge University Press).

Timimi, S. (2009) 'Commentary On: The Perpetuation of Patriarchy: The Hidden Factor of Gender Bias in the Diagnosis and Treatment of Children'. *Clinical Child Psychology and Psychiatry* 14, 135–44.

Timimi, S. and Maitra, B. (eds) (2006) *Critical Voices in Child and Adolescent Mental Health* (London: Free Association Books).

Timimi, S. and Leo, J. (eds) (2009) *Rethinking ADHD: International Perspectives* (Basingstoke: Palgrave Macmillan).

Timimi, S., Jureidini, J. and Leo, J. (2008) 'NICE Recommendations are Not Evidence Based and Could Expose Many to Unnecessary Harm'. *British Medical Journal* 337, a2284. Available at http://www.bmj.com/cgi/eletters/337/sep24_1/a1239#202371, accessed 22 December 2008.

Toal, F., Murphy, D.G.M. and Murphy, K.C. (2005) 'Autistic-spectrum Disorders: Lessons from Neuroimaging'. *British Journal of Psychiatry* 187, 395–7.

Tomm, K. (1990) 'A Critique of DSM'. *Dulwich Center Newsletter* 3, 5–8.

Treatment for Adolescents with Depression Study Team (2004) 'Fluoxetine, Cognitive–behavioral Therapy, and their Combination for Adolescents with Depression: Treatment for Adolescents With Depression Study (TADS) Randomized Controlled Trial'. *Journal of the American Medical Association* 292, 807–20.

Treatment for Adolescents with Depression Study Team (2007) 'The Treatment for Adolescents with Depression Study (TADS): Long-term Effectiveness and Safety Outcomes'. *Archives of General Psychiatry* 64, 1132–43.

Tsai, L. (2004) 'Autistic Disorder'. In J. Weiner and M. Dulcan (eds) *Textbook of Child and Adolescent Psychiatry (3rd Edition)* (Washington DC: American Psychiatric Association Press).

Tsai, L., Tsai, M. and August, G. (1985) 'Brief Report: Implication of EEG Diagnoses in the Subclassification of Infantile Autism'. *Journal of Autism and Developmental Disorders* 15, 339–44.

Turner, K.C., Frost, L., Linsenbardt, D., McIlroy, J.R. and Müller, R. (2006) 'Atypically Diffuse Functional Connectivity Between Caudate Nuclei and Cerebral Cortex in Autism'. *Behavioral and Brain Functions* 2, 34. Available at http://www.behavioralandbrainfunctions.com/content/2/1/34, accessed 22 December 2008.

Volkmar, F. (1992) 'Childhood Disintegrative Disorder: Issues for DSM-IV'. *Journal of Autism and Developmental Disorders* 22, 625–42.

Volkmar, F.R. and Klin, A. (2001). 'Asperger's Disorder and High Functioning Autism: Same or Different?'. In L.M. Glidden (ed.) *International Review of Research in Mental Retardation (Volume 23)* (New York: Academic Press).

Waldman, M., Nicholson, S. and Adilov, N. (2006) 'Does Television Cause Autism?'. Available at http://www.johnson.cornell.edu/faculty/profiles/Waldman/AUTISM-WALDMAN-NICHOLSON-ADILOV.pdf, accessed 22 April 2009.

Walkerdine, V. (1984) 'Developmental Psychology and the Child-centred Pedagogy'. In J. Henriques, W. Holloway, C. Urwin, C. Venn and V. Walkerdine (eds) *Changing the Subject: Psychology, Social Regulation and Subjectivity* (London: Methuen).

Walkerdine, V. (1993) 'Beyond Developmentalism?'. *Theory and Psychology* 3, 451–69.

Walkerdine, V. (1996) 'Popular Culture and the Eroticization of Little Girls'. In J. Curran, D. Morley and V. Walkerdine (eds) *Cultural Studies and Communications* (London: Arnold).

Wampold, B.E. (2001) *The Great Psychotherapy Debate* (Mahwah, NJ: Lawrence Erlbaum Associates).

Wassink, T.H., Brzustowicz, L.M., Bartlett, C.W. and Szatmari, P. (2004) 'The Search for Autism Genes'. *Mental Retardation and Developmental Disabilities Research Reviews* 10, 272–83.

Watson, J. (2003) *DNA: The Secret of Life* (London: William Heinemann).

Webb, E., Morey, J., Thompsen, W., Butler, C., Barber, M. and Fraser, W.I. (2003) 'Prevalence of Autistic Spectrum Disorder in Children Attending Mainstream Schools in a Welsh Education Authority'. *Developmental Medicine and Child Neurology* 45, 377-84.

Whitaker, R. (2002) *Mad in America* (Cambridge, MA: Perseus).

Williams J. and Brayne C. (2006) 'Screening for Autism Spectrum Disorders: What is the Evidence?'. *Autism* 10, 11–35.

Williams, J., Scott, F., Allison, C., Bolton, P., Baron-Cohen, S. and Brayne, C. (2005) 'The CAST (Childhood Asperger Syndrome Test): Test Accuracy *Autism* 45, 68.

Williams, R. and Kerfoot, M. (2005) *Child and Adolescent Mental Health Services* (Oxford: Oxford University Press).

Wimmer, H. and Perner, J. (1983) 'Beliefs about Beliefs: Representation and Constraining Function of Wrong Beliefs in Young Children's Understanding of Deception'. *Cognition* 13, 103-28.

Wing, J.K. (ed.) (1966) *Early Childhood Autism: Clinical, Educational and Social Aspects* (Oxford: Pergamon Press).

Wing, L. (1981) 'Asperger's Syndrome: A Clinical Account'. *Psychological Medicine* 11, 115–29.

Wing, L (ed.) (1988) *Aspects of Autism* (London: Gaskell).

Wing, L. (1991) 'Asperger's Syndrome and Kanner's Autism'. In U. Frith (ed.) *Autism and Asperger Syndrome* (Cambridge: Cambridge University Press).

Wing, L. (1997) *The Autistic Spectrum: A Guide for Parents and Professionals* (London: Constable & Robinson).

Wing, L. (2005) 'Reflections on Opening Pandora's Box'. *Journal of Autism and Developmental Disorders* 35, 197–203.

Wing, L. and Gould, J. (1979) 'Severe Impairments of Social Interaction and Associated Abnormalities in Children: Epidemiology and Classification'. *Journal of Autism and Childhood Schizophrenia* 9, 11–29.

Wing, L., Leekam, S.R., Libby, S.J., Gould, J. and Larcombe, M. (2002) 'The Diagnostic Interview for Social and Communication Disorders: Background, Inter-rater Reliability and Clinical Use'. *Journal of Child Psychology and Psychiatry* 43, 307–25.

Wolfenstein, M. (1955) 'Fun Morality: An Analysis of Recent Child-training Literature'. In M. Mead and M. Wolfenstein (eds) *Childhood in Contemporary Cultures* (Chicago: University of Chicago Press).

Wolff, S. (1969) *Children Under Stress* (London: Allen Lane).

Wolff, S. (1995) *Loners: Life Path of Unusual Children* (London: Routledge).

Wooldridge, A. (1995) *Measuring the Mind* (Cambridge: Cambridge University Press).

World Health Organization (WHO) (1978) *Mental Disorders: Glossary and Guide to their Classification in Accordance with the Ninth Revision of the International Classification of Diseases* (Geneva: WHO).

World Health Organization (1992) *The ICD-10 Classification of Mental and Behavioural Disorders: Clinical Descriptions and Diagnostic Guidelines* (Geneva: WHO).

World Health Organization (2009) *Mental Health, Resilience and Inequalities* (Copenhagen: WHO, Europe).

INDEX

Adorno, Theodor 85
Affective disorder 119
Althusser, Louis 94–5, 224
American Eugenics Society (AES) 272
Anti-depressants 24, 31, 192–5
Anti-psychotics 24, 199–201
Anxiety 180, 181
Ariès, Philippe 46
Asperger, Hans 55–6, 58, 61, 76, 147–50, 176
Asperger's Syndrome 8, 14, 23, 25, 26, 30, 61, 77, 107, 116, 141, 143, 146–52, 166–9, 175, 177, 188, 264
Attachment disorder 176, 181
Attention Deficit Hyperactivity Disorder (ADHD) 8, 10–13, 26, 31, 39, 124–6, 130, 180–1, 187, 195–8, 211, 214, 239, 257, 286
Autism Diagnostic Interview-Revised (ADI-R) 113, 116, 155–8, 168
Autism Diagnostic Schedule-Generic (ADOS-G) 113, 116, 156–8, 166, 168
Autism Spectrum Quotient (AQ) 38–9, 159, 188, 285
Autistic rights 260–6

Baron-Cohen, Simon 67, 68–73, 163–7, 183–4, 186, 188, 215–16
Baudrillard, Jean 252–3, 282
Bettelheim, Bruno 57
Bleuler, Eugene 54–5
Broca's area 4
Butler, Judith 97

Capitalism *see* Neo-liberalism
Charcot, Jean-Martin 249–50
Carrel, Alexis 274
Checklist for Autism in Toddlers (CHAT) 163–5
Child development 49, 79–91, 100
Child labour 48, 251
Child Study Association 80
Child Study Movement 80
Childhood Asperger Syndrome Test (CAST) 166–9
Childhood Society 80
Children and Adults with ADHD (CHADD) 196
Chodorow, Nancy 225–6
Comings, David 280–1
Conduct Disorder 176, 181, 211
Consumerism *see* Neo-liberalism
Creak, Mildred 57

Darwin, Charles 270, 271
Davenport, Charles 271–2, 278
Diagnostic Interview for Social and Communication Disorders (DISCO) 158–9
Diagnostic Statistical Manual (DSM) 31, 41, 67, 122–3, 141–7, 150–1, 176, 213–14
Deficits in Attention, Motor control and Perception (DAMP) 9–12
Depression 180–1
Developmentalism 79–91
Down's Syndrome 26, 107, 116–17, 179
'Drapetomania' 123, 270
Drug Enforcement Agency (DEA) 195

323

Drug treatment 190–201
Dyslexia 5, 63
'Dysthesia aetiopica' 270
Dysthymia 31

Early Bird programme 74
Ellinder, Leif 10–11
Emotional intelligence 252–5
Epidemiology 57–60, 213–14
Erasmus, Desiderius 47
Eugenics 265, 269–83, 290
Executive function 130
Eysenck, Hans 32
Eysenck Personality Inventory 160

Famous people and autism 53, 62, 76, 153–4, 185–8
Feminisation 229–31
Fitzgerald, Michael 186
Fluoxetine 192–5
Foucault, Michel 87–9, 95–6, 224, 239, 250, 267, 282
Fragile X 14, 107
Freud, Sigmund 86–7, 270
Frith, Uta 147

Galton, Francis 270–1
Gardner, Neil 14, 16–27, 178, 258, 266, 285, 292
Geek syndrome 187–8
Geertz, Clifford 83
Gender 2, 68–73, 90, 107, 211–33
Genetics 64–6, 105–21, 136–40, 265
Gergen, Kenneth 84, 85, 254, 297–8
Gillberg, Christopher 9–12, 147, 151–2, 154, 186, 256
Goodwin, Frederick 279
Gramsci, Antonio 98

Habermas, Jürgen 6–8
Hacking, Ian 184
Haddon, Mark 294
Hamer, Dean 123
Harre, Ron 83–4
History of
  autism 53–77
  childhood 45–53

Homosexuality 122–4, 262
Hooten, Earnest 272

Immigration 66, 69–70
Ingleby, David 245
Internet 259–60

Jameson, Fredrick 253
Jung, Carl 55

Kallman, Frantz 272
Kanner, Leo 55–6, 58, 76, 144, 174, 292, 294
Karfve, Eva 10–12
Kennedy, Robert 277
Kovel, Joel 224

Laing, R.D. 37
Learning difficulties 4, 24–5, 111–14, 117–18, 148, 151, 174, 204
Lefever, Gretchen 12–13
Levin, Michael 279
Locke, John 47–8
Lotter, Victor 57–8, 76
Lovaas, Ivar 189, 202–4

Marx, Karl 92–5, 236–7, 267
Marxism 85–6, 92–5, 270, 282
Masculinity 220–2, 227–31
McCabe, Brian 14, 27–33, 178, 285, 292
Measles, Mumps, Rubella vaccine 9, 74, 277
Medicalisation 275–7, 290, 299
Mental Deficiency Act 1913 54
Merleau-Ponty, Maurice 216
Methylphenidate 10, 24, 31, 195–7
  see also Ritalin *and* Stimulants
Minimal Brain Damage (MBD) 10
Moncrieff, Joanna 190, 268
Morss, John 81, 83, 85, 86, 89

Narcissism 229–31, 248, 259, 295
National Alliance of the Mentally Ill (NAMI) 190
National Autistic Society (NAS) 59, 74, 76, 160, 161–2, 189, 265, 277
National Council on Bioethics 106–7

Index

National Institute of Clinical Excellence (NICE) 192
National Institute of Health (NIH) 279
National Institute of Mental Health (NIMH) 125, 196
National plan for autism 160
National Screening Committee (NSC) 162–3, 165
Nazi Germany 274–6, 278, 282
Neo-liberalism 50–1, 222–31, 242, 246–7, 253, 259, 263, 268, 282, 289, 290
Neuroimaging 121–36, 138–40
Neuroplasticity 121–2
New Labour 239, 241–7

Obsessive Compulsive Disorder (OCD) 180
Oppositional Defiant Disorder (ODD) 214
Ornitz, E.M. 199, 202

Patriarchy 219–20
Permissive parenting 49–50
Personality Disorder 180, 181
Pervasive Developmental Disorders (PDD) 33, 107–8, 141, 145–6, 154, 175
Pharmaceutical industry 191–2
Phenylketonuria 120
Phrenology 126–9
Piaget, Jean 86, 182
Popper, Karl 5
Post-modernism 95–7
Post-structuralism 87–8
Psychoanalysis 97–8
Psychological treatments 202–5

Risperidone 201
Ritalin 10, 24, 31
Rousseau, Jean-Jacques 47–8
Rorty, Richard 98–9
Rosanhoff, Aaron 274
Rutter, Michael 5, 60, 62–6, 105–6, 110–13, 118–20, 144–5, 152–3, 174–5, 213

Said, Edward 100–1
Schizophrenia 8, 26, 54–5, 66, 69, 119, 123, 185, 250
Schools 79–80, 90–1, 229–30, 262
Science and society 236–49
Sertraline 31
Shockley, William 277
Social alienation 256–9
Social class 69, 92–5
Social construction 83–4
Socialisation rituals 252–5
Stimulants 195–8
Sure Start 243–4
Szasz, Thomas 249, 298

Technology 255–6
Teen Screen 281
Television (effects of) 257
Theory of Mind (ToM) 67–8, 129, 182–5
Thimerosal vaccines 73–4
Timimi, Sami 3, 33–41, 97, 122, 124, 197, 198, 214, 215, 219, 220, 223, 230, 236, 250, 268, 283, 285, 286, 292, 298
Treatment and Education of Autistic and Communication Handicapped Children (TEACCH) 204

Underconnectivity 130–2

Venlafaxine 24

Walkerdine, Valerie 88
Watson, James 280
Webber, Max 240, 267
Whitaker, Robert 269, 270, 272, 274
Wing, John 58
Wing, Lorna 58–63, 144, 146–50, 155, 174, 176
Wolff, Sula 147
World Health Organization (WHO) 245, 247

Zyprexia 24